McSorley's Wonderful Saloon

ALSO BY JOSEPH MITCHELL

The Bottom of the Harbor

Joe Gould's Secret

My Ears Are Bent

Old Mr. Flood

Up in the Old Hotel

McSorley's Wonderful Saloon

Joseph Mitchell

FOREWORD BY CALVIN TRILLIN

PANTHEON BOOKS, NEW YORK

Library of Congress Cataloging-in-Publication Data
Mitchell, Joseph, 1908–1996
McSorley's wonderful saloon / Joseph Mitchell;
foreword by Calvin Trillin.
p.cm.
ISBN 0-375-42102-5
1. New York (N.Y.)—Social life and customs—Fiction. 2. Bars
(Drinking establishments)—Fiction. 3. Eccentrics and eccentricities—
Fiction. I. Title.
PS3525.I9714 M37 2001   813'.54—dc21   00-051058

www.pantheonbooks.com

Printed in the United States of America
First Edition
2 4 6 8 9 7 5 3 1

Contents

CONTENTS

Foreword

BY CALVIN TRILLIN

JOSEPH MITCHELL, who lived and worked in New York City for a good sixty-five years, was among the people I've always thought of as resident out-of-towners. By that, I don't mean simply that he clung resolutely to his ties with the place he'd come from—the soft Southern accent, the courtliness in dress and manner that called for him to change from a fedora to a straw hat every spring, the assumption that in some instances "going home" entailed taking the subway to Greenwich Village and in other instances "going home" entailed a trip to Robeson County, North Carolina. I also mean that even after he knew the city as well as anyone—even after he knew it in the grim specifics that a police reporter has to deal with in the course of business, even after he knew it as an acknowledged master of its neighborhoods—he never lost an out-of-towner's sense of wonderment.

He was hardly the sort of writer who customarily described what he'd seen as wonderful or amazing or unprecedented or stupendous. When I try to recall a superlative in his writing, as close as I get is a statement about a conversation he'd had with a man who bought littlenecks and cherrystones and chowder clams from the clammers who worked the Great South Bay, off Long Island: "I sat down on the bucket and told him that one Sunday afternoon in August, 1937, I placed third in a clam-eating tournament at a Block Island clambake, eating eighty-four cherries. I told him that I regard this as one of the few worthwhile achievements of my life." He described what he encountered in the city—the pols and the sporting types and the freaks and the Bowery characters—in calm, unadorned prose. But reading his stories you can almost picture him shaking his head in wonderment and muttering to himself "Imagine that!" or even "Wow!"

In Nova Scotia, where I live in the summer, I sometimes go beach-combing on a remote island with an artist who has an uncommon eye for found objects, and I've become accustomed to seeing her pounce on some piece of wood or shell or rock that I would have casually walked by or maybe even kicked out of my path. Joe Mitchell did the same sort of thing with New York people like Joe Gould or King Cockeye Johnny or Lady Olga, the bearded lady. It wasn't as if nobody else had run across, say, Commodore Dutch or Mazie the ticket-taker at the Venice. But Mitchell looked, and looked again, and then came back for another look, and then observed from a different angle; somehow, the sort of character readers thought they would have pegged after the first paragraph was still being revealed pages later. Someone who might have been dismissed or condescended to by a self-consciously jaded New Yorker had been brought to life by Joe Mitchell, the resident out-of-towner. Years ago, I met a man who responded to the mention of Joe Mitchell with a disdainful shrug. "Listen," he said. "I knew that guy Joe Gould Mitchell wrote about. He was just an irritating little guy who bummed drinks in the village." To most people, that was indeed who Joe Gould was. To most people, the wood washed up on the beach all looks just about the same.

Shortly before I joined the staff of *The New Yorker*, in 1963, some-one who already worked there gave me a book written by Joe Mitchell. I'm not sure that at the time I had ever heard of him. I was bowled over. His work, I thought, was a lesson in what could be accomplished within the modest form of the magazine article. That was partly because of the simplicity and clarity of his prose. What struck me as astonishing was that he was able to get the marks of writing off his pieces. The words seemed to have just appeared on the page by some process that was the reverse of those magic slate pages that children lift to make what they've written or drawn van-ish. (The comment on Mitchell's writing that sums up this quality for me was by Joseph Epstein: "He achieved in his prose what Orwell longed for in his: the transparent lucidity of a pane of glass.") Like Joe DiMaggio, Joe Mitchell made it look perfectly natural, even though nobody else could exactly do it.

I later dedicated a book to Mitchell as "the *New Yorker* writer who set the standard." He was that not just to me but to a number of non-fiction writers I knew, inside and outside *The New Yorker*. In the seventies and eighties, when most literate Americans might have had trouble placing Joseph Mitchell's name, we were part of what I suppose could have been described as a small cult readership. We'd exchange favorite passages. We'd trade stories about scouring second-hand bookstores in search of his books, all of which were out of print until 1992, when *Up in the Old Hotel* was published by Pantheon and became a best-seller.

My own greatest moment in Mitchell book-hunting came in Seattle, where, while browsing the shelves of a dealer in used and antiquarian books, I found myself staring at a copy of *My Ears Are Bent*, an early collection of pieces from *The World-Telegram*—and the single most difficult Mitchell book to put your hands on. For a moment I didn't believe what I was seeing. Then I reached for the book. It was marked $3. I took it to the cash register, along with a couple of other books I'd picked out. When the clerk got to *My Ears Are Bent*, he said, "Where did you get this book?" For no rational reason, I feared that he was going to take it away from me. I pointed to the shelf. He informed me that everything on that shelf was half-price, and he rang up $1.50. "A dollar and a half!" I always said, when relating the story to fellow cultists. "Why, I would have left the man my shoes."

The stories in *McSorley's Wonderful Saloon* make it clear that Mitchell's preference for the simple over the ornate in his prose style had a parallel in the way he viewed the world. In "Obituary of a Gin Mill," it's obvious that he liked a smelly old dive called Dick's Bar and Grill much better than he did Dick's new joint—"a big, classy place with a chromium and glass-brick front, a neon sign in four colors, a mahogany bar, a row of chromium bar stools with red-leather seats like those in the uptown cocktail lounges, a kitchen full of gleaming copper pots, a moody chef who once worked in Moneta's, a printed menu with French all over it, and seven new brands of Scotch." In "All You Can Hold for Five Bucks," it's obvious that he loved the raucous banquets people in New York used to call beefsteaks partly because of their old-fashioned quality, and that he would have loved them even more in the days when knives and forks were considered the sort of sissified trappings that no authentic devotee of beefsteaks would have been caught utilizing.

Given the sort of subjects Joe Mitchell wrote about and the simplicity of his language and his obvious aversion to airs, people were often surprised to find that he was, of all things, an intellectual—even though he was acutely aware that he had left Chapel Hill without getting a degree. In 1970 he was elected to the American Academy of Arts and Letters, a rare honor for a reporter. He was a student of James Joyce. He was, in his own way, an architectural historian. Still, when recognition that he would have considered literary came his way, Mitchell seemed pleased but a little embarrassed. "When you write a story, you're not writing it for—God forgive me—posterity," he said in a National Public Radio interview after *Up in the Old Hotel* was published. "You're writing it for a weekly magazine, hoping that some people will laugh at it. If I had sat down and said, 'I'm going to try to write literature,' do you know what a mess that would have been?"

His colleagues, even while acknowledging his interests in subjects considerably more elevated than old Irish saloons and colorful panhandlers, insisted on emphasizing that Joe Mitchell was a modest man who'd cringe at anything that seemed like the intellectual equivalent of Dick's shiny new restaurant fixtures. "He was for decades a devoted member of the James Joyce Society," Brendan Gill wrote at the time of Joe Mitchell's death, in 1996, "and would put in many a long evening abiding some scholar's highfalutin' literary nonsense in order to feel close to Shem the Penman, his lifelong mentor." During the decades when Mitchell came to the offices of *The New Yorker* every day but never turned anything in, one of the many fanciful stories heard as an explanation for his silence was that he had been writing at the same pace as everyone else until some college professor said that he was the greatest master of the English declarative sentence in America, and that this encomium had stopped him cold.

I never felt edified by the conversations about why Mitchell hadn't written anything for so long. The mystery I wanted to see solved about him was not why he quit turning anything in but how he'd managed to create what he did write. That mystery couldn't have been solved by a set of instructions, of course. A scholar of magic once told me that by spending enough time in enough libraries you could learn how magicians did just about any trick, but that didn't mean you could do it. In the seventies, while I was on a book tour in San Francisco, a newspaper reporter asked me if there were any writers I particularly admired. I said something to the effect of being willing to trade pretty much everything I'd written for a paragraph or two of one of my favorite Joseph Mitchell pieces. In cold print, the quotation looked more flowery than I'd intended, not to speak of pretentious—the sort of praise that might have embarrassed Mitchell. The San Francisco interview was reprinted in an internal *New Yorker* newsletter, and eventually Mitchell showed up in my office, holding the newsletter in his hand.

"I wanted to thank you for the nice things you said," he told me.

"I guess I sort of got carried away," I said.

He smiled, and said, "You're not going to take it back, are you?"

"No," I said. "I'm not going to take it back."

McSorley's Wonderful Saloon

The Old House at Home

*M*cSORLEY'S OCCUPIES the ground floor of a red-brick tenement at 15 Seventh Street, just off Cooper Square, where the Bowery ends. It was opened in 1854 and is the oldest saloon in New York City. In eighty-eight years it has had four owners—an Irish immigrant, his son, a retired policeman, and his daughter—and all of them have been opposed to change. It is equipped with electricity, but the bar is stubbornly illuminated with a pair of gas lamps, which flicker fitfully and throw shadows on the low, cobwebby ceiling each time someone opens the street door. There is no cash register. Coins are dropped in soup bowls—one for nickels, one for dimes, one for quarters, and one for halves—and bills are kept in a rosewood cashbox. It is a drowsy place; the bartenders never make a needless move, the customers nurse their mugs of ale, and the three clocks on the walls have not been in agreement for many years. The clientele is motley. It includes mechanics from the many garages in the neighborhood, salesmen from the restaurant-supply houses on Cooper Square, truck-drivers from Wanamaker's, internes from Bellevue, students from Cooper Union, and clerks from the row of second-hand bookshops just north of Astor Place. The backbone of the clientele, however, is a rapidly thinning group of crusty old men, predominantly Irish, who have been drinking there since they were youths and now have a proprietary feeling about the place. Some of them have tiny pensions, and are alone in the world; they sleep in Bowery hotels and spend practically all their waking hours in McSorley's. A few of these veterans clearly remember John

3

McSorley, the founder, who died in 1910 at the age of eighty-seven. They refer to him as Old John, and they like to sit in rickety armchairs around the big belly stove which heats the place, gnaw on the stems of their pipes, and talk about him.

Old John was quirky. He was normally affable but was subject to spells of unaccountable surliness during which he would refuse to answer when spoken to. He went bald in early manhood and began wearing scraggly, patriarchal sideburns before he was forty. Many photographs of him are in existence, and it is obvious that he had a lot of unassumed dignity. He patterned his saloon after a public house he had known in his hometown in Ireland—Omagh, in County Tyrone—and originally called it the Old House at Home; around 1908 the signboard blew down, and when he ordered a new one he changed the name to McSorley's Old Ale House. That is still the official name; customers never have called it anything but McSorley's. Old John believed it impossible for men to drink with tranquillity in the presence of women; there is a fine back room in the saloon, but for many years a sign was nailed on the street door, saying, "NOTICE. NO BACK ROOM IN HERE FOR LADIES." In McSorley's entire history, in fact, the only woman customer ever willingly admitted was an addled old peddler called Mother Fresh-Roasted, who claimed her husband died from the bite of a lizard in Cuba during the Spanish-American War and who went from saloon to saloon on the lower East Side for a couple of generations hawking peanuts, which she carried in her apron. On warm days, Old John would sell her an ale, and her esteem for him was such that she embroidered him a little American flag and gave it to him one Fourth of July; he had it framed and placed it on the wall above his brass-bound ale pump, and it is still there. When other women came in, Old John would hurry forward, make a bow, and say, "Madam, I'm sorry, but we don't serve ladies." If a woman insisted, Old John would take her by the elbow, head her toward the door, and say, "Madam, please don't provoke me. Make haste and get yourself off the premises, or I'll be obliged to forget you're a lady." This technique, pretty much word for word, is still in use.

In his time, Old John catered to the Irish and German workingmen—carpenters, tanners, bricklayers, slaughter-house butchers, teamsters, and brewers—who populated the Seventh Street neighborhood, selling ale in pewter mugs at five cents a mug and putting out a free lunch inflexibly consisting of soda crackers, raw onions, and cheese; present-day customers are wont to complain that some of the cheese Old John laid out on opening night in 1854 is still there. Adjacent to the free lunch he kept a quart crock of tobacco and a rack of clay and corncob pipes—the purchase of an ale entitled a man to a smoke on the house; the rack still holds a few of the communal pipes. Old John was thrifty and was able to buy the tenement—it is five stories high and holds eight families—about ten years after he opened the saloon in it. He distrusted banks and always kept his money in a cast-iron safe; it still stands in the back room, but its doors are loose on their hinges and there is nothing in it but an accumulation of expired saloon licenses and several McSorley heirlooms, including Old John's straight razor. He lived with his family in a flat directly over the saloon and got up every morning at five and took a long walk before breakfast, no matter what the weather. He unlocked the saloon at seven, swept it out himself, and spread sawdust on the floor. Until he became too feeble to manage a racing sulky, he always kept a horse and a nanny goat in a stable around the corner on St. Mark's Place. He kept both animals in the same stall, believing, like many horse-lovers, that horses should have company at night. During the lull in the afternoon a stablehand would lead the horse around to a hitching block in front of the saloon, and Old John, wearing his bar apron, would stand on the curb and groom the animal. A customer who wanted service would tap on the window and Old John would drop his currycomb, step inside, draw an ale, and return at once to the horse. On Sundays he entered sulky races on uptown highways.

From the time he was twenty until he was fifty-five, Old John drank steadily, but throughout the last thirty-two years of his life he did not take a drop, saying, "I've had my share." Except for a few experimental months in 1905 or 1906, no spirits ever have been sold in McSorley's; Old John maintained that the man never lived who needed a stronger drink than a mug of ale warmed on the hob of a stove. He was a big eater. Customarily, just before locking up for the night, he would grill himself a three-pound T-bone, placing it on a coal shovel and holding it over a bed of oak coals in the back-room fireplace. He liked to fit a whole onion into the hollowed-out heel of a loaf of French bread and eat it as if it were an apple. He had an extraordinary appetite for onions, the stronger the better, and said that "Good ale, raw onions, and no ladies" was the motto of his saloon. About once a month during the winter he presided over an on-the-house beefsteak party in the back room, and late in life he was president of an organization of gluttons called the Honorable John McSorley Pickle, Beefsteak, Baseball Nine, and Chowder Club, which held hot-rock clambakes in a picnic grove on North Brother Island in the East River. On the walls are a number of photographs taken at outings of the club, and in most of them the members are squatting around kegs of ale; except for the president, they all have drunken, slack-mouthed grins and their eyes look dazed. Old John had a bull-frog bass and enjoyed harmonizing with a choir of drunks. His favorite songs were "Muldoon, the Solid Man," "Swim Out, You're Over Your Head," "Maggie Murphy's Home," and "Since the Soup House Moved Away." These songs were by Harrigan and Hart, who were then called "the Gilbert and Sullivan of the U.S.A." He had great respect for them and was pleased exceedingly when, in 1882, they made his saloon the scene of one of their slum comedies; it was called "McSorley's Inflation."

Although by no means a handshaker, Old John knew many prominent men. One of his closest friends was Peter Cooper, president of the North American Telegraph Company and founder of Cooper Union, which is a half-block west of the saloon. Mr. Cooper, in his declining years, spent so many afternoons in the back room philosophizing with the workingmen that he was given a chair of his own; it was equipped with an inflated rubber cushion. (The chair is still there; each April 4th for a number of years after Mr. Cooper's death, on April 4, 1883, it was draped with black cloth.) Also, like other steadfast customers, Mr. Cooper had a pewter mug on which his name had been engraved with an icepick. He gave the saloon a life-sized portrait of himself, which hangs over the mantel in the back room. It is an appropriate decoration, because, since the beginning of prohibition, McSorley's has been the official saloon of Cooper Union students. Sometimes a sentimental student will stand beneath the portrait and drink a toast to Mr. Cooper.

Old John had a remarkable passion for memorabilia. For years he saved the wishbones of Thanksgiving and Christmas turkeys and strung them on a rod connecting the pair of gas lamps over the bar; the dusty bones are invariably the first thing a new customer gets inquisitive about. Not long ago, a Johnny-come-lately annoyed one of the bartenders by remarking, "Maybe the old boy believed in voodoo." Old John decorated the partition between barroom and back room with banquet menus, autographs, starfish shells, theatre programs, political posters, and worn-down shoes taken off the hoofs of various race and brewery horses. Above the entrance to the back room he hung a shillelagh and a sign: "BE GOOD OR BEGONE." On one wall of the barroom he placed portraits of horses, steamboats, Tammany bosses, jockeys, actors, singers, and statesmen. Around 1902 he put up a heavy oak frame containing excellent portraits of Lincoln, Garfield, and McKinley, and to the frame he attached a brass title tag reading, "THEY ASSASSINATED THESE GOOD MEN THE SKULKING DOGS." On the same wall he hung framed front pages of old newspapers; one, from the London *Times* for June 22, 1815, has in its lower right-hand corner a single paragraph on the beginning of the battle of Waterloo, and another, from the New York *Herald* of April 15, 1865, has a one-column story on the shooting of Lincoln. He blanketed another wall with lithographs and steel engravings. One depicts Garfield's deathbed. Another is entitled "The Great Fight." It was between Tom Hyer and Yankee Sullivan, both bare-knuckled, at Still Pond Heights, Maryland, in 1849. It was won by Hyer in sixteen rounds, and the prize was $10,000. The judges wore top hats. The title tag on another engraving reads, "Rescue of Colonel Thomas J. Kelly and Captain Timothy Deacy by Members of the Irish Revolutionary Brotherhood from the English Government at Manchester, England, September 18, 1867." A copy of the Emancipation Proclamation is on this wall; so, inevitably, is a facsimile of Lincoln's saloon license. An engraving of Washington and his generals hangs next to an engraving of a session of the Great Parliament of Ireland. Eventually Old John covered practically every square inch of wall space between wainscot and ceiling with pictures and souvenirs. They are still in good condition, although spiders have strung webs across many of them. New customers get up on chairs and spend hours studying them.

Although Old John did not consider himself retired until just a few years before he died, he gave up day-in-and-day-out duty back of the bar around 1890 and made his son, William, head bartender. Bill McSorley was the kind of person who minds his own business vigorously. He inherited every bit of his father's surliness and not much of his affability. The father was by no means a lush, but the son carried temperance to an extreme; he drank nothing but tap water and tea, and bragged about it. He did dip a little snuff. He was so solemn that before he was thirty several customers had settled into the habit of calling him Old Bill. He worshipped his father, but no one was aware of the profundity of his worship until Old John died. After the funeral, Bill locked the saloon, went upstairs to the family flat, pulled the shutters to, and did not come out for almost a week. Finally, on a Sunday morning, gaunt and silent, he came downstairs with a hammer and a screwdriver and spent the day painstakingly securing his father's pictures and souvenirs to the walls; they had been hung hit or miss on wires, and customers had a habit of taking them down. Subsequently he commissioned a Cooper Union art teacher to make a small painting of Old John from a photograph. Bill placed it on the wall back of the bar and thereafter kept a hooded electric light burning above it, a pious custom that is still observed.

Throughout his life Bill's principal concern was to keep McSorley's exactly as it had been in his father's time. When anything had to be changed or repaired, it appeared to pain him physically. For twenty years the bar had a deepening sag. A carpenter warned him repeatedly that it was about to collapse; finally, in 1933, he told the carpenter to go ahead and prop it up. While the work was in progress he sat at a table in the back room with his head in his hands and got so upset he could not eat for several days. In the same year the smoke- and cobweb-encrusted paint on the ceiling began to flake off and float to the floor. After customers complained that they were afraid the flakes they found in their ale might strangle them to death, he grudgingly had the ceiling repainted. In 1925 he had to switch to earthenware mugs; most of the pewter ones had been stolen by souvenir hunters. In the same year a coin-box telephone, which he would never answer himself, was installed in the back room. These were about the only major changes he ever allowed. Occasionally one of the pictures his father had hung would fall off the wall and the glass would break, and he would fill in the gap. His contributions include a set of portraits of the wives of Presidents through the first Mrs. Woodrow Wilson, a poster of Barney Oldfield in a red racing car, and a poem called "The Man Behind the Bar." He knew this poem by heart and particularly liked the last verse:

When St. Peter sees him coming he will leave the gates ajar,
For he knows he's had his hell on earth, has the man behind the bar.

As a businessman, Bill was anachronous; he hated banks, cash registers, bookkeeping, and salesmen. If the saloon became crowded, he would close up early, saying, "I'm getting too confounded much trade in here." Agents for the brewery from which he bought his ale often tried to get him to open a checking account; he stubbornly continued to pay his ale bills with currency, largely silver. He would count out the money four or five times and hand it to the driver in a paper bag. Bill was an able bartender. He understood ale; he knew how to draw it and how to keep it, and his bar pipes were always clean. In warm weather he made a practice of chilling the mugs in a tub of ice; even though a customer nursed an ale a long time, the chilled earthenware mug kept it cool. Except during prohibition, the rich, wax-colored ale sold in McSorley's always has come from the Fidelio Brewery on First Avenue; the brewery was founded two years before the saloon. In 1934, Bill sold this brewery the right to call its ale McSorley's Cream Stock and gave it permission to use Old John's picture on the label; around the picture is the

9

legend "As brewed for McSorley's Old Ale House." During prohibition McSorley's ale was produced mysteriously in rows of barrels and washtubs in the cellar by a retired brewer named Barney Kelly, who would come down three times a week from his home in the Bronx. On these days the smell of malt and wet hops would be strong in the place. Kelly's product was raw and extraordinarily emphatic, and Bill made a practice of weakening it with near beer. In fact, throughout prohibition Bill referred to his ale as near beer, a euphemism which greatly amused the customers. One night a policeman who knew Bill stuck his head in the door and said, "I seen a old man up at the corner wrestling with a truck horse. I asked him what he'd been drinking and he said, 'Near beer in McSorley's.'" The prohibition ale cost fifteen cents, or two mugs for a quarter. Ale now costs a dime a mug.

Bill was big and thick-shouldered, but he did not look strong; he had a shambling walk and a haggard face and always appeared to be convalescing from something. He wore rusty-black suits and black bow ties; his shirts, however, were surprisingly fancy—they were silk, with candy stripes. He was nearsighted, the saloon was always dimly lit, and his most rigid conviction was that drink should not be sold to minors; consequently he would sometimes peer across the bar at a small-sized adult and say, "Won't sell you nothing, bud. Get along home, where you belong." Once he stared for a long time at a corner of the saloon and suddenly shouted, "Take your foot off that table!" Evidently he had been staring at a shadow; no one was sitting in the corner. Bill was tyrannical. Reading a newspaper, he would completely disregard a line of customers waiting to be served. If a man became impatient and demanded a drink, Bill would look up angrily and shout obscene remarks at him in a high, nasal voice. Such treatment did not annoy customers but made them snicker; they thought he was funny. In fact, despite Bill's bad disposition, many customers were fond of him. They had known him since they were young men together and had grown accustomed to his quirks. They even took a wry sort of pride in him, and when they said he was the gloomiest, or the stingiest, man in the Western Hemisphere there was boastfulness in their voices; the more eccentric he became, the more they respected him. Sometimes, for the benefit of a newcomer, one of these customers would show Bill off, shouting, "Hey, Bill, lend me fifty dollars!" or "Hey, Bill, there ain't no pockets in a shroud!" Such remarks usually provoked an outburst of gamy epithets. Then the customer would turn proudly to the newcomer and say, "See?" When prohibition came, Bill simply disregarded it. He ran wide open. He did not have a peephole door, nor did he pay protection, but McSorley's was never raided; the fact that it was patronized by a number of Tammany politicians and minor police officials probably gave it immunity.

Bill never had a fixed closing hour but locked up as soon as he began to feel sleepy, which was usually around ten o'clock. Just before closing he would summon everybody to the bar and buy a round. This had been his father's custom and he faithfully carried it on, even though it seemed to hurt him to do so. If the customers were slow about finishing the final drink, he would cough fretfully once or twice, then drum on the bar with both fists and say, "Now, see here, gents! I'm under no obligoddamnation to stand here all night while you hold on to them drinks." Whenever Bill completely lost his temper he would jump up and down and moan piteously. One night in the winter of 1924 a feminist from Greenwich Village put on trousers, a man's topcoat, and a cap, stuck a cigar in her mouth, and entered McSorley's. She bought an ale, drank it, removed her cap, and shook her long hair down on her shoulders. Then she called Bill a male chauvinist, yelled something about the equality of the sexes, and ran out. When Bill realized he had sold a drink to a woman, he let out a cross between a moan and a bellow and began to jump up and down. "She was a woman!" he yelled. "She was a goddamn woman!"

Bill was deaf, or pretended to be; even so, ordinary noises seemed to bother him unduly. The method he devised to keep the saloon tranquil was characteristic of him. He bought a fire-alarm gong similar to those used in schools and factories and screwed it to the seven-foot-tall icebox behind the bar. If someone started a song, or if the old men sitting around the stove began to yell at each other, he would shuffle over to the gong and give the rope a series of savage jerks. The gong is there yet and is customarily sounded at a quarter to midnight as a warning that closing time is imminent; the customers grab their ears when it goes off. Bill was consistent in his aversion to noise; he didn't even like the sound of his own voice. He was able to go for days without speaking, answering all questions with a snort or a grunt. A man who drank in McSorley's steadily for sixteen years once said that in that time Bill spoke exactly four intelligible words to him. They were "Curiosity killed the cat." The man had politely asked Bill to tell him the history of a pair of rusty convict shackles on the wall. He learned later that a customer who had fought in the Civil War had brought them back from a Confederate prison in Andersonville, Georgia, and had given them to Old John as a souvenir.

Bill would sometimes take an inexplicable liking to a customer. Around 1911 a number of painters began hanging out in McSorley's. Among them were John Sloan, George Luks, Glenn O. Coleman, and Stuart Davis. They were all good painters, they didn't put on airs, and the workingmen in the saloon accepted them as equals. One night, Hippolyte Havel, the anarchist, came in with the painters. Havel was a long-haired, myopic, gentle-mannered Czech whose speeches often got him in trouble with the police. Even Bill was curious about him. "What's that crazy-looking fellow do for a living?" he asked one of the painters. Playing safe, the painter said Havel was a politician, more or less. Havel liked the place and became a steady customer. Most nights after making a fiery speech in Union Square, he would hurry down to McSorley's. To the amazement of the old-timers, a strong friendship grew up between him and Bill, who was a Tammany Democrat and an utter reactionary; no one was ever able to figure out the basis of the friendship. Bill called the anarchist Hippo and would let him have credit up to two dollars; other customers were not allowed to charge so much as a nickel cigar. Bill had an extremely vague idea about Havel's politics. Charles Francis Murphy, the Tammany boss, occasionally dropped in, and once Bill told Havel he was going to speak a good word to the boss for him. "Maybe he'll put you in line for something," Bill said. The anarchist, who thought no man was as foul as a Tammany boss, smiled and thanked him. A police captain once took it upon himself to warn Bill against Havel. "You better keep your eyes on that long-haired nut," he said. "Why?" asked Bill. The question annoyed the police captain. "Hell fire, man," he said, "Havel's an anarchist! He's in favor of blowing up every bank in the country." "So am I," said Bill. Bill's friendship for Havel was extraordinary in every way. As a rule, he reserved his kindness for cats. He owned as many as eighteen at once and they had the run of the saloon. He fed them on bull livers put through a sausage grinder and they became enormous. When it came time to feed them, he would leave the bar, no matter how brisk business was, and bang on the bottom of a tin pan; the fat cats would come loping up, like leopards, from all corners of the saloon.

Bill had been married but was childless, and he used to say, "When I go, this place goes with me." In March, 1936, however, he changed his mind—why, no one knows—and, to the surprise of the veteran customers, sold both saloon and tenement to Daniel O'Connell, an old policeman, who, since 1900, had spent most of his leisure at a table in the back room. O'Connell retired from the Department two days before he purchased the saloon. He was the kind of man of whom people say, "If he can't speak a good word about you, he won't speak a bad one." He was almost as proud of the saloon's traditions as Bill and willingly promised he would make no changes; that was one of the conditions of the sale. Almost from the day Bill sold out, his health began to fail. He took a room in the house of a relative in Queens. Sometimes, in the afternoon, if the weather was good, he would shuffle into the bar, a sallow, disenchanted old man, and sit in the Peter Cooper chair with his knotty hands limp in his lap. For hours he would sit and stare at the painting of Old John. The customers were sure he was getting ready to die, but when he came in they would say, "You looking chipper today, Billy boy," or something like that. He seemed grateful for such remarks. He rarely spoke, but once he turned to a man he had known for forty years and said, "Times have changed, McNally." "You said it, Bill," McNally replied. Then, as if afraid he had been sentimental, Bill coughed, spat, and said, irrelevantly, "The bread you get these days, it ain't fit to feed a dog." On the night of September 21, 1938, barely thirty-one months after he quit drawing ale, he died in his sleep. As close as his friends could figure it, his age was seventy-six.

The retired policeman made a gentle saloonkeeper. Unlike Bill, he would never throw a quarrelsome drunk into the street but would try to sober him up with coffee or soup. "If a man gets crazy on stuff I sold him, I can't kick him out," he said one day. "That would be evading my responsibility." He was proprietor for less than four years. He died in December, 1939, and left the property to a daughter, Mrs. Dorothy O'Connell Kirwan. A young woman with respect for tradition, Mrs. Kirwan has chosen to remain in the background. At first customers feared that she would renovate the place, but they now realize that this fear was groundless. "I know exactly how my father felt about McSorley's," Mrs. Kirwan said, "and so long as I am owner, no changes will be made. I won't even change the rule against women customers." She herself visits the saloon only on Sunday nights after hours. Even so, early in her ownership, she made a mistake in judgment that brought about a crisis in McSorley's. She had a hard time getting over this mistake, but she now looks back on it as a blessing in disguise and regards the crisis as a kind of inevitable demarcation between McSorley's past under Old John and Old Bill and her father and McSorley's present under her. She enjoys telling about this.

"For some months after my father's death," she says, "I let things drift in McSorley's. I left everything in the hands of my father's two old bartenders, the day bartender and the night bartender, but the responsibility was too much for them and things gradually got out of hand, and I saw I had to find a manager—someone to look after the books and pay the bills and just generally take charge. And the more I thought about it the more I thought that the exact right person for the job was an uncle of mine named Joe Hnida. Well, I grew up in an Irish family that has lived in one of the old Irish neighborhoods on the west side of Greenwich Village for generations, in among the bohemians and the erratical personalities, and I thought I knew quite a lot about human behavior, but I soon found out that

I didn't. Joe Hnida is a Czech, and he's an uncle of mine by marriage—he's my father's sister's husband. He worked for a limousine service that specializes in weddings and funerals; he was the supervisor of the drivers. Joe's a kind, decent, hardworking, trustworthy man, and I spoke to him and asked him if he would care to take over the management of McSorley's. He thought it over and decided he would. Well, Joe started out in McSorley's on a Monday morning and by the end of the week I was getting telephone calls from some of the real old-timers among the customers, all of them old friends of my father's, complaining about him. What I hadn't taken into account is that Joe is a man of few words, a very few— he just doesn't have any small talk. In addition, he's unusually self-sufficient. And also in addition, and I think he himself would agree, if he has any sense of humor at all it's a Czech sense of humor— it certainly isn't an Irish sense of humor. Anyway, it seemed that some of the old men who sit in those chairs along the wall in McSorley's all day long and do a lot of talking and arguing back and forth among themselves would try to start conversations with Joe and Joe just wouldn't participate. As one of them told me, 'He'll go so far as to say "Good morning" or "How do you do?" and he'll answer you yes or no, but that's about the full extent and sum total of what he has to say. He won't even comment on the weather.' 'If he's behind the bar,' another one told me, 'he'll draw an ale for a customer and take his money and give him his change, and that's the end of it. He just will not speak a single unnecessary word.' A few of the old men developed a liking for Joe, but they were ones who never had much to say themselves. And before long, little by little, most of the old men convinced themselves that Joe considered them to be just a bunch of old bores and windbags and they also convinced themselves that he looked down on them, and to get back at him they began to mock him behind his back and call him 'that stuck-up Czechoslovakian hearse-driver.' When the old men telephoned me I tried to explain Joe to them and stand up for him and smooth things over. 'After all,' I said, 'Bill McSorley didn't exactly knock himself out talking. According to my father, there were days you couldn't get a word out of him.' But that didn't do any good. Bill McSorley was different—he owned the place and he had earned the right to do as he pleased, and he might not necessarily care if you lived or died but he didn't give you the impression that he looked down on you. This new man comes in here out of nowhere and he won't even be polite. It went on and on like that. Weeks went by and months went by and things didn't get any better. And then one day the oldest of the bartenders, a man I completely trust, telephoned me and said that just about the worst that could happen had happened. 'It's completely ridiculous, Dot,' he said, 'but the old men have discovered that Joe doesn't like ale. He's done his best to hide this, but it somehow slipped out, and they began right away picking on him about it, whereupon he got his back up and told them that he not only doesn't like the taste of ale, he doesn't like the smell of it. In fact, he said that the smell of it sometimes gives him a headache. Well, as I said, it sounds ridiculous, but the old men are acting as if they have found out something about Joe that is shocking beyond belief. And I know them—they're not going to let this die down. And furthermore, to add to everything else, a number of them have suddenly become very sensitive and touchy— the situation in general has brought back to the surface differences between them that they thought they had buried and forgotten long ago, and they have stopped speaking to each other, only sometimes they can't exactly remember why they stopped speaking, and they go around avoiding each other and at the same time looking puzzled. It's a mess.' I saw I had to do something. It was up to me. Now, it so happens that my husband, Harry Kirwan, grew up in an old, old town in Ireland named Ballyragget, down in Kilkenny. Bally- ragget is a market town that is noted for its old public houses. Harry's mother died when he was a child and he lived with his grandmother. And quite early in his schooldays he started working for an old public house called Staunton's. On his way to school, he would stop off and sweep the place out, and after school he would stop off for the rest of the afternoon and wash glasses and fill the coal box and run errands and generally make himself useful. Harry has a studious nature; he's always read a lot. He wanted very much to be a professor in Ireland, but he couldn't afford the education. So when he was around nineteen he came to the United States and got a job in a manufacturing chemist company in the Bronx, and by the time we got married—which as a matter of fact was less than a year before the death of my father—he had worked himself up to where he was head bookkeeper. And so, anyway, when Harry came home that night, I said to him, 'Sit down, Harry. I've got something very serious I have to discuss with you.' I filled him in on the situation in McSorley's, and then I said to him, 'Harry, I know how much you love your job, and I hate to ask this, but do you think you could possibly find it in your heart to give it up and take over the management of McSorley's?' 'Well, Dot,' he said, and I remember every word he said that night, 'first of all, I don't love my job, I pretend to, but I hate it. And second of all, Dot, why in the name of God did it take so long for this thought to occur to you? You've heard me talk a lot about Staunton's back in Ballyragget, and most of the customers in there were hard-to-get-along-with old men, and I got along with them. I not only got along with them, I enjoyed getting along with them. I enjoyed observing them and I enjoyed listening to them. They were like actors in a play, only the play was real. There were Falstaffs among them—that is, they were just windy old drunks from the back alleys of Ballyragget, but they were Falstaffs to me. And there were Ancient Pistols among them. And there was an old man with a broken-hearted-looking face who used to come in and sit in a chair in the corner with a Guinness at his elbow and stare straight ahead for hours at a time and occasionally mumble a few words to himself, and every time he came in I would say to myself, "King Lear." There were good old souls among those men, and there were leeches among them, leeches and lepers and Judases, and I imagine the cast of characters down in McSorley's is about the same. In other words, Dot,' he said, 'in answer to your question, yes, I'm willing to take a chance and go down to McSorley's and see if I can handle it.' The changeover didn't take long. Early next morning I went to Joe Hnida's apartment and had a heart-to-heart talk with him and begged him to forgive me for getting him into all of this, which he did, and he went back to the limousine service. And the very same day Harry gave notice up in the Bronx.

And two Mondays later, he started in at McSorley's. I remember that day so well. I was worried half sick that I might've made another big mistake, so in the middle of the afternoon I telephoned McSorley's and asked to speak to Harry. 'Everything's O.K., Dot,' he said. 'I'm amazed at how much I'm enjoying this. I feel like I'm back home again—back home in Ballyragget, back home in Staunton's.' And when he got home that night and opened the door, the first thing he said was, 'I think I have finally found my right and proper place in the world.' "

Like Old John and Old Bill and like his father-in-law and his wife, Harry Kirwan is strongly opposed to change, and since he took over he has made only one change and that was a fiscal one and long overdue. He gave raises to the old bartenders, Eddie Mullins and Joe Martoccio, and he gave a raise to Mike Boiko, the cook, who is an old Ukrainian, and he gave a raise to Tommy Kelly, who broke down and cried when Harry told him about it. Tommy Kelly is perhaps the most important member of the staff of McSorley's, but his duties are so indefinite that the old men call him Kelly the Floorwalker. When business is brisk, he acts as the potboy—he carries mugs of ale from the bar to the tables, hooking his fingers through the handles of the mugs and carrying two in each hand. He is sometimes the fill-in bartender. He makes an occasional trip to the butcher or the grocery store for Mike. He answers the coin-box telephone. In the winter he keeps the fire going in the stove. When he shows up, around 8:30 A.M., he is just a sad-eyed little man with a hangover, but by noon lukewarm ale has given him a certain stateliness; by six he is in such a good humor that he stands near the door and shakes hands with incoming customers just as if he were the proprietor. Some strangers think he is the proprietor and speak to him as Mr. McSorley. Kelly says that he had a long succession of odd jobs before he wound up in McSorley's. "And when I say odd," he says, "I mean odd." Once, for a brief period, he took a job as night clerk and night watchman in a large funeral parlor in Brooklyn, quitting because a corpse spoke to him. "I sat up front in the office all night," he says, "and I used to keep a pocket-sized bottle of gin in my coat hanging up in the locker in the back room, and I would go back there every little while and take a sip—not a real swallow, just a sip, just enough to keep me going through the night—and to get back there I had to pass through the parlor, the room where the coffins and the corpses were kept, and on this particular night I had to go past an open coffin that had a corpse in it, a man all laid out and fixed up and ready for the funeral in the morning, and I must've already gone past him a half a dozen times, passing and repassing, and this time, as I was going past him, he spoke to me, and quite distinctly too. 'Take off your hat,' he said, 'and put out that cigar and pour out that gin and turn off that damn radio.'"

To a devoted McSorley customer, most other New York City saloons are tense and disquieting. It is possible to relax in McSorley's. For one thing, it is dark and gloomy, and repose comes easy in a gloomy place. Also, the barely audible heartbeatlike ticking of the old clocks is soothing. Also, there is a thick, musty smell that acts as a balm to jerky nerves; it is really a rich compound of the smells of pine sawdust, tap drippings, pipe tobacco, coal smoke, and onions. A Bellevue intern once remarked that for some mental states the smell in McSorley's would be a lot more beneficial than psychoanalysis or sedative pills or prayer.

At midday McSorley's is crowded. The afternoon is quiet. At six it fills up with men who work in the neighborhood. Most nights there are a few curiosity-seekers in the place. If they behave themselves and don't ask too many questions, they are tolerated. The majority of them have learned about the saloon through John Sloan's paintings. Between 1912 and 1930, Sloan did five paintings, filled with detail, of the saloon—"McSorley's Bar," which shows Bill presiding majestically over the tap and which hangs in the Detroit Institute of Arts; "McSorley's Back Room," a painting of an old workingman sitting at the window at dusk with his hands in his lap, his pewter mug on the table; "McSorley's at Home," which shows a group of argumentative old-timers around the stove; "McSorley's Cats," in which Bill is preparing to feed his drove of cats; and "McSorley's, Saturday Night," which was painted during prohibition and shows Bill passing out mugs to a crowd of rollicking

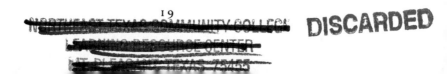

customers. Every time one of these appears in an exhibition or in a newspaper or magazine, there is a rush of strangers to the saloon. "McSorley's Bar" was reproduced in Thomas Craven's "A Treasury of Art Masterpieces," which came out in 1939, and it caused hundreds to go and look the place over. There is no doubt that McSorley's been painted more often than any other saloon in the country. Louis Bouché did a painting, "McSorley's," which is owned by the University of Nebraska. A painting, "Morning in McSorley's Bar," by a ship's purser named Ben Rosen won first prize in an exhibition of art by merchant seamen in February, 1943. Reginald Marsh has done several sketches of it. In 1939 there was a retrospective exhibition of Sloan's work in Wanamaker's art department, and a number of McSorley patrons attended it in a body. One asked a clerk for the price of "McSorley's Cats." "Three thousand dollars," he was told. He believed the clerk was kidding him and is still indignant. Kelly likes the Sloan paintings but prefers a golden, corpulent nude which Old John hung in the back room many years ago, right beside Peter Cooper's portrait. To a stranger, attracted to the saloon by a Sloan painting, Kelly will say, "Hey, Mac, if you want to see some real art, go look at the naked lady in the back room." The nude is stretched out on a couch and is playing with a parrot; the painting is a copy, probably done by a Cooper Union student, of Gustave Courbet's "La Femme au Perroquet." Kelly always translates this for strangers. "It's French," he says learnedly. "It means 'Duh Goil and duh Polly.' "

McSorley's bar is short, accommodating approximately ten elbows, and is shored up with iron pipes. It is to the right as you enter. To the left is a row of armchairs with their stiff backs against the wainscoting. The chairs are rickety; when a fat man is sitting in one, it squeaks like new shoes every time he takes a breath. The customers believe in sitting down; if there are vacant chairs, no one ever stands at the bar. Down the middle of the room is a row of battered tables. Their tops are always sticky with spilled ale. In the centre of the room stands the belly stove, which has an isinglass door and is exactly like the stoves in Elevated stations. All winter Kelly keeps it red hot. "Warmer you get, drunker you get," he says. Some customers prefer mulled ale. They keep their mugs on the hob until the ale gets as hot as coffee. A sluggish cat named Minnie sleeps in a scuttle beside the stove. The floor boards are warped, and here and there a hole has been patched with a flattened-out soup can. The back room looks out on a blind tenement court. In this room are three big, round dining-room tables. The kitchen is in one corner of the room; Mike keeps a folding boudoir screen around the gas range, and pots, pans, and paper bags of groceries are stored on the mantelpiece. While he peels potatoes, he sits with early customers at a table out front, holding a dishpan in his lap and talking as he peels. The fare in McSorley's is plain, cheap and well cooked. Mike's specialties are goulash, frankfurters, and sauerkraut, and hamburgers blanketed with fried onions. He scribbles his menu in chalk on a slate which hangs in the bar-room and consistently misspells four dishes out of five. There is no waiter. During the lunch hour, if Mike is too busy to wait on the customers, they grab plates and help themselves out of the pots on the range.

The saloon opens at eight. Mike gives the floor a lick and a promise and throws on clean sawdust. He replenishes the free-lunch platters with cheese and onions and fills a bowl with cold, hard-boiled eggs, five cents each. Kelly shows up. The ale truck makes its delivery. Then, in the middle of the morning, the old men begin shuffling in. Kelly calls them "the steadies." The majority are retired laborers and small businessmen. They prefer McSorley's to their homes. A few live in the neighborhood, but many come from a distance. One, a retired operator of a chain of Bowery flophouses, comes in from Sheepshead Bay practically every day. On the day of his retirement, this man said, "If my savings hold out, I'll never draw another sober breath." He says he drinks in order to forget the misery he saw in his flophouses; he undoubtedly saw a lot of it, because he often drinks twenty-five mugs a day, and McSorley's ale is by no means weak. Kelly brings the old men their drinks. To save him a trip, they usually order two mugs at a time. Most of them are quiet and dignified; a few are eccentrics. Some years ago one had to leap out of the path of a speeding automobile on Third Avenue; he is still furious. He mutters to himself constantly. Once, asked what he was muttering about, he said, "Going to buy a shotgun and stand on Third Avenue and shoot at automobiles." "Are you going to aim at the tires?" he was asked. "Why, hell no!" he said. "At the drivers. Figure I could kill four or five before they arrested me. Might kill more if I could reload fast enough."

Only a few of the old men have enough interest in the present to read newspapers. These patrons sit up front, to get the light that comes through the grimy street windows. When they grow tired of reading, they stare for hours into the street. There is always something worth looking at on Seventh Street. It is one of those East Side streets completely under the domination of kids. While playing stickball, they keep great packing-box fires going in the gutter; sometimes they roast mickies in the gutter fires. In McSorley's the free-lunch platters are kept at the end of the bar nearer the street door, and several times every afternoon kids sidle in, snatch handfuls of cheese and slices of onion, and dash out, slamming the door. This never fails to amuse the old men.

The stove overheats the place and some of the old men are able to sleep in their chairs for long periods. Occasionally one will snore, and Kelly will rouse him, saying, "You making enough racket to wake the dead." Once Kelly got interested in a sleeper and clocked him. Two hours and forty minutes after the man dozed off, Kelly became uneasy—"Maybe he died," he said—and shook him awake. "How long did I sleep?" the man asked. "Since the parade," Kelly said. The man rubbed his eyes and asked, "Which parade?" "The Paddy's Day parade, two weeks ago," Kelly said scornfully. "Jeez!" the man said. Then he yawned and went back to sleep. Kelly makes jokes about the constancy of the old men. "Hey, Eddie," he said one morning, "old man Ryan must be dead!" "Why?" Mullins asked. "Well," Kelly said, "he ain't been in all week." In summer they sit in the back room, which is as cool as a cellar. In winter they grab the chairs nearest the stove and sit in them, as motionless as barnacles, until around six, when they yawn, stretch, and start for home, insulated with ale against the dreadful loneliness of the old. "God be wit' yez," Kelly says as they go out the door.

(1940)

Mazie

A BOSSY, YELLOW-HAIRED BLONDE named Mazie P. Gordon is a celebrity on the Bowery. In the nickel-a-drink saloons and in the all-night restaurants which specialize in pig snouts and cabbage at a dime a platter, she is known by her first name. She makes a round of these establishments practically every night, and drunken bums sometimes come up behind her, slap her on the back, and call her sweetheart. This never annoys her. She has a wry but genuine fondness for bums and is undoubtedly acquainted with more of them than any other person in the city. Each day she gives them between five and fifteen dollars in small change, which is a lot of money on the Bowery. "In my time I been as free with my dimes as old John D. himself," she says. Mazie has presided for twenty-one years over the ticket cage of the Venice Theatre, at 209 Park Row, a few doors west of Chatham Square, where the Bowery begins.

The Venice is a small, seedy moving-picture theatre, which opens at 8 A.M. and closes at midnight. It is a dime house. For this sum a customer sees two features, a newsreel, a cartoon, a short, and a serial episode. The Venice is not a "scratch house." In fact, it is highly esteemed by its customers, because its seats get a scrubbing at least once a week. Mazie brags that it is as sanitary as the Paramount. "Nobody ever got loused up in the Venice," she says. On the Bowery, cheap movies rank just below cheap alcohol as an escape, and most bums are movie fans. In the clientele of the Venice they are numerous. The Venice is also frequented by people from the tenement neighborhoods in the vicinity of Chatham Square, such as Chinatown, the Little Italy on lower Mulberry Street, and the Spanish section on Cherry Street. Two-thirds of its customers are males. Children and most women sit in a reserved section under the eyes of a matron. Once, in an elegant mood, Mazie boasted that she never admits intoxicated persons. "When do you consider a person intoxicated?" she was asked. Mazie snickered. "When he has to get down on all fours and crawl," she said. In any case, there are drunks in practically every Venice audience. When the liquor in them dies down they become fretful and mumble to themselves, and during romantic pictures they make loud, crazy, derogatory remarks to the actors on the screen, but by and large they are not as troublesome as a class of bums Mazie calls "the stiffs." These are the most listless of bums. They are blank-eyed and slow-moving, and they have no strong desire for anything but sleep. Some are able to doze while leaning against a wall, even in freezing weather. Many stiffs habitually go into the Venice early in the day and slumber in their seats until they are driven out at midnight. "Some days I don't know which this is, a movie-pitcher theatre or a flophouse," Mazie once remarked. "Other day I told the manager pitchers with shooting in them are bad for business. They wake up the customers."

Most Bowery movie houses employ bouncers. At the Venice, Mazie is the bouncer. She tells intimates that she feels fighting is unladylike but that she considers it her duty to throw at least one customer out of the theatre every day. "If I didn't put my foot down, the customers would take the place," she says. "I don't get any fun out of fighting. I always lose my temper. When I start swinging, I taste blood, and I can't stop. Sometimes I get beside myself. Also, a lot of the bums are so weak they don't fight back, and that makes me feel like a heel." Mazie is small, but she is wiry and fearless, and she has a frightening voice. Her ticket cage is in the shadow of the tracks of the City Hall spur of the Third Avenue elevated line, and two decades of talking above the screeching of the trains have left her with a rasping bass, with which she can dominate men twice her size. Now and then, in the Venice, a stiff throws his head back and begins to snore so blatantly that he can be heard all over the place, especially during tense moments in the picture. When this happens, or when one of the drunks gets into a bellowing mood, the women and children in the reserved section stamp on the floor and chant, "Mazie! Mazie! We want Mazie!" The instant this chant goes up, the matron hastens out to the lobby and raps on the side window of Mazie's cage. Mazie locks the cash drawer, grabs a bludgeon she keeps around, made of a couple of copies of *True Romances* rolled up tightly and held together by rubber bands, and strides into the theatre. As she goes down the aisle, peering this way and that, women and children jump to their feet, point fingers in the direction of the offender, and cry, "There he is, Mazie! There he is!" Mazie gives the man a resounding whack on the head with her bludgeon and keeps on whacking him until he seems willing to behave. Between blows, she threatens him with worse punishment. Her threats are fierce and not altogether coherent. "Outa here on a stretcher!" she yells. "Knock your eyeballs out! Big baboon! Every tooth in your head! Bone in your body!" The women and children enjoy this, particularly if Mazie gets the wrong man, as she sometimes does. In action, Mazie is an alarming sight. Her face becomes flushed, her hair flies every which way, and her slip begins to show. If a man defends himself or is otherwise contrary, she harries him out of his seat and drives him from the theatre. As he scampers up the aisle, with Mazie right behind him, whacking away, the women and children applaud.

Mazie's animosity toward a stiff or a drunk usually lasts until she has driven him out to the sidewalk. Then, almost invariably, she becomes contrite and apologetic. "Look, buddy, I'm sorry," she said one afternoon recently to a drunk she had chased out because he had been screaming "Sissy! Sissy!" at George Raft during the showing of a prison picture called "Each Dawn I Die." "If you didn't see the whole show," she continued, "you can go back in." "Hell, Mazie," said the drunk, "I seen it three times." "Here, then," she said, handing him a dime. "Go get yourself a drink." Although the drunk's ears were still red from Mazie's blows, he grinned. "You got a heart of gold, Mazie," he said. "You my sweetheart." "O.K., buddy," Mazie said, stepping back into the cage. "You quit acting like a god-damn jackass and I'll be your sweetheart."

The Venice is a family enterprise. It is owned by Mazie and two sisters—Rosie, the widow of a horse-race gambler, and Jeanie, an acrobatic dancer. Mazie's sisters let her run things to suit herself. She is profoundly uninterested in moving pictures and is seldom able to sit through one. "They make me sick," she says. Consequently, she employs a manager and leaves the selection and ordering of films entirely up to him. For a theatre of its class, the Venice is prosperous, and Mazie could afford to hire a ticket girl and take things easy, but she enjoys the job and will not relinquish it, as her sisters often urge her to do. From her cage she has a good view of Chatham Square, which is the favorite promenade of Bowery drunks and eccentrics. "The things I see, by God, you wouldn't believe it," she says proudly. When she catches sight of a person she knows among the passers-by, she sticks her face up to the round hole in the front window of her cage and shouts a greeting. Sometimes she discusses exceedingly personal matters with people out on the sidewalk. "Hey there, Squatty," she yelled one afternoon to a dreamy-eyed little man, "I thought you was in Bellevue." "I was, Mazie," the man said. "They turned me loose yesterday." "Where'd they put you this time—the drunk ward or the nut ward?" "I was in with the drunks this time." "How'd they treat you?" "They didn't do me no harm, I guess." "You get drunk last night, Squatty?" "Sure did." "Guess you had to celebrate." "Sure did." "Well, take care yourself, Squatty." "Thanks, Mazie. You do the same."

Sitting majestically in her cage like a raffish queen, Mazie is one of the few pleasant sights of the Bowery. She is a short, bosomy woman in her middle forties. Some people believe she has a blurry resemblance to Mae West. Her hair is the color of sulphur. Her face is dead white, and she wears a smudge of rouge the size of a silver dollar on each cheek. Her eyes are sleepy and droopy-lidded. On duty, she often wears a green celluloid eyeshade. She almost always has a cigarette hanging from a corner of her mouth, and this makes her look haughty. Like a movie croupier, she can smoke a cigarette down to the end and not take it from her mouth once, even while talking. She has a deep cigarette cough; she smokes three and a half packs a day and says tobacco is murdering her. On her right hand she wears four diamond rings. She likes vigorous colors, and her dresses are spectacular; they come from shops on Division Street. The glass-topped Bowery and Chinatown rubberneck wagons often park in front of the Venice, and now and then a band of sightseers stand on the sidewalk and stare at Mazie. She despises sightseers and says they give the Bowery a black eye. Sometimes she thumbs her nose at them. Actually, however, she does not mind being stared at. "People walk past here just to give me the eye," she once said. "I got a public of my own, just like a god-damn movie-pitcher star."

Mazie is a talkative woman, and on most subjects she is remarkably frank, but she rarely says anything about her private life, and some people on the Bowery consider her a mystery woman. A man who had been stopping by to chat with her several times a week for years suddenly realized recently that he did not know whether she was Miss or Mrs. Gordon. "You ever been married, Mazie?" he asked. "That's for me to know, you to find out," she said sharply. A moment later she added, "I'll ask you this. Do I look and act like a girl that never had a date?" People around Chatham Square believe, among other things, that she was a belly dancer in the Hurtig & Seamon burlesque houses when she was a young woman, which isn't true. They claim, with not much relevance, that she gives her spare money to bums because she was once disappointed in a love affair. Furthermore, they believe she was born in Chinatown. Actually, she is a native of Boston, a fact which gives her a lot of satisfaction. Every winter she takes a week off and spends it in Boston, just walking around. She believes the people of Boston are superior to the people elsewhere. One night a blind-drunk bum stumbled into an "L" pillar in front of the Venice, skinning his nose, and she rushed out and dragged him into her lobby. Then she went into a nearby saloon and yelled, "Gimme some hot water and a clean rag!" "You want to take a bath, Mazie?" asked the bartender. This remark enraged her. "Don't you talk like that to me, you yellow-bellied jerk," she said. "I come from Boston, and I'm a lady."

Mazie says her real name is Mazie Phillips, but she will not tell anything about her parents. Her intimates say that around 1903, when she was a schoolgirl in Boston, her older sister, Rosie, came to New York and married Louis Gordon, an East Side gambler and promoter. They established a home on Grand Street, and a few years later Mazie and her younger sister, Jeanie, came to live with them. The family of Belle Baker, the vaudeville singer, lived nearby on Chrystie Street. Irving Becker, Belle's brother, now the manager of a road company of "Tobacco Road," once had a job loading rifles in a shooting gallery Gordon operated at Grand Street and the Bowery. "We and the Gordons were great friends," Becker said recently. "Louie Gordon was as fine a gambler as the East Side ever produced. He was a big, stately gentleman and he gave to the poor, and the bankroll he carried a billy goat couldn't swallow it. He hung around race tracks, but he would gamble on anything. He made a lot of money on horses and invested it in Coney Island. He and his brother, Leo, helped back the original Luna Park, which opened in 1903. He was one of those silent gamblers. He never said nothing about himself. He gave everybody a fair shake, and he didn't have a thing to hide, but he just never said nothing about himself. All the Gordons were that way."

In 1914, Gordon opened a moving-picture theatre in a building he owned on Park Row, naming it the Venice, after an Italian restaurant in Coney Island whose spaghetti he liked. After operating it four years, he found that it kept him away from the tracks and he gave it to Rosie, who had been working in the ticket cage. The next year he sold his Bowery shooting gallery, in which, for several months, Mazie had been running a candy-and-root-beer concession. Rosie did not like selling tickets, so Mazie took her job. Around this time, Mazie began calling herself Mazie Gordon. She will not explain why she took her brother-in-law's name. "That's my business," she says. The Gordons left Grand Street in the early twenties, moving to a house on Surf Avenue in Coney. Mazie continued to live with them. Louis was away much of the time, following the horses. Mazie says that once, after a good season in Saratoga, he gave her a Stutz which, with accessories, cost $5,000. She used to ride down to Coney in the Stutz every night after work; one of the ushers at the Venice was her chauffeur. In October, 1932, Louis fell dead of a heart attack at the Empire City race track. Mazie and her sisters left Coney Island a few years later and returned to the East Side, eventually taking an apartment together in Knickerbocker Village, four blocks from the Venice. They live quietly. Rosie, a taciturn, sad-eyed woman, looks after property left by her husband. Besides her interest in the Venice, this property includes a number of lots along the boardwalk in Coney and an ancient red-brick tenement at 9 James Street, a block from the Venice. This tenement has sixteen cold-water flats, all occupied by unmarried Chinese men. Jeanie, a handsome young woman, boasts that she has gone to the West Coast and back ten times while working in vaudeville as an acrobatic dancer. Now and then she spells Mazie in the cage at the Venice.

Mazie's hours would kill most women. She works seven days a week, seldom taking a day off, and is usually on duty from 9:30 A.M. until 11 P.M. Her cage is not much more spacious than a telephone booth, but she long ago learned how to make herself comfortable in it. She sits on two thick pillows in a swivel chair and wears bedroom slippers. In summer she keeps an electric fan, aimed upward, on the floor, replacing it in winter with an electric heater. When the weather is especially cold she brings her dog, Fluffy, an old, wheezy Pomeranian bitch, to the theatre. She lets Fluffy sleep in her lap, and this keeps both of them warm. Mazie makes change as automatically as she breathes, and she finds time for many domestic chores while on duty. She mends clothes, puts red polish on her fingernails, reads a little, and occasionally spends half an hour or so cleaning her diamonds with a scrap of chamois skin. On rainy days she sends out for her meals, eating them right in the cage. She uses the marble change counter for a table. Once, hunched over a plate of roast-beef hash, she looked up and said to a visitor, "I do light housekeeping in here." When she gets thirsty she sends an usher across the street to the King Kong Bar & Grill for a cardboard container of beer. She used to keep a bottle of Canadian whiskey, which she calls "smoke," hidden in her cash drawer, but since an appendix operation in 1939 she has limited herself to celery tonic and beer.

There are two cluttered shelves on one wall of her cage. On the bottom shelf are a glass jar of "jawbreakers," a kind of hard candy which she passes out to children, a clamshell that serves as an ashtray, a hind leg of a rabbit, a stack of paper towels, and a box of soap. When a bum with an exceptionally grimy face steps up to buy a ticket, Mazie places a couple of paper towels and a cake of soap before him and says, "Look, buddy, I'll make a bargain with you. If you'll take this and go in the gents' room and wash your face, I'll let you in free." Few bums are offended by this offer; most of them accept willingly. Occasionally she gives one fifteen cents and sends him to a barber college on Chatham Square for a shave and a haircut. If she is in a good humor, Mazie will admit a bum free without much argument. However, she says she can tell a bum by the look in his eyes, and ordinary citizens who have heard of her generosity and try to get passed in outrage her. "If you haven't got any money," she tells such people, "go steal a watch."

On Mazie's top shelf is a pile of paper-backed books, which includes "Old Gipsy Nan's Fortune Teller and Dream Book," "Prince Ali Five Star Dream Book," and "Madame Fu Futtam's Spiritual Magical Dream Book." Mazie is deeply interested in dreams, although at times she seems a little ashamed of it. "A dream just means you et something that didn't agree with you," she sometimes says, rather defiantly. Nevertheless, she makes a practice of remembering them and spends hours hunting through her books for satisfactory interpretations. Also on her top shelf are a rosary, some back numbers of a religious periodical called the *Messenger of the Sacred Heart,* and a worn copy of "Spiritual Reflections for Sisters," by the Reverend Charles J. Mullaly, S. J., which she borrowed from an Italian nun, one of the Daughters of Mary Help of Christians, who conduct a school in Chinatown. Lately Mazie has been reading a page of this book every day. She says that she understands hardly any of it but that reading it makes her feel good. Mazie is not a Catholic; she is Jewish, but she has been entranced by Roman Catholicism for many years. One of her oldest friends in the neighborhood is Monsignor William E. Cashin, rector of St. Andrew's, the little church back of the Municipal Building. She frequently shows up for the Night Workers' Mass, which is said every Sunday at 2:30 A.M. in St. Andrew's by Monsignor Cashin. She sits in a middle pew with her head bowed. Surrounded by policemen, firemen, scrubwomen, telephone girls, nurses, printers, and similar night workers who regularly attend the mass, she feels at home. On the way out she always slips a dollar bill into the poor box. Now and then she calls on the Monsignor and has a long talk with him, and whenever he takes a walk on the Bowery he pauses at her cage and passes the time of day.

Mazie also knows two mothers superior quite well. The rosary she keeps in her cage is a present from the Sisters of Our Lady of Christian Doctrine, who run Madonna House, a settlement on Cherry Street. Sister Margaret, the superior there, has known Mazie for years and has made an attempt to understand her. "On the Bowery it's probably an asset to have a reputation for toughness," Sister Margaret once told a friend, "and I'm afraid Mazie tries to give people the worst possible impression of herself, just for self-protection. She isn't really tough. At heart, she's good and kind. We can always count on her for help. A few weeks ago there was a fire in an Italian tenement near here. One of the families in it had a new baby. It was late at night and we didn't know exactly how to help them. Two of the sisters went to Mazie, and she came right down and found the family a new flat and gave the mother some money." Mazie's favorite saint is St. John Bosco. There is a statue of him in a niche in the steeple of the weatherbeaten Church of the Transfiguration in Chinatown. At night the saint can be clearly seen by the light of the galaxy of neon signs on the chop-suey joints which surround the church. When she passes through Mott Street, Mazie looks up at the saint and crosses herself. "I asked a sister once if it was O.K. for me to give myself a cross, and she told me it was," Mazie says.

Mazie became interested in Catholicism in the winter of 1920. A drug addict on Mulberry Street, a prostitute with two small daughters, came to her cage one night and asked for help. The woman said her children were starving. "I knew this babe was a junky," Mazie says, "and I followed her home just to see was she lying about her kids. She had two kids all right, and they were starving in this crummy little room. I tried to get everybody to do something—the cops, the Welfare, the so-called missions on the Bowery that the Methodists run or whatever to hell they are. But all these people said the girl was a junky. That excused them from lifting a hand. So I seen two nuns on the street, and they went up there with me. Between us, we got the woman straightened out. I liked the nuns. They seemed real human. Ever since then I been interested in the Cat'lic Church."

Mazie does not spend much time at home, so she encourages people to visit her while she is working. Her visitors stand around in the lobby at the rear door of her cage. She frequently gets so interested in a caller that she swings completely around in her swivel chair and presents her back to customers, who have to shout and rap on the window before she will turn and sell them tickets. In the morning, practically all of her visitors are bums with hangovers who come to her, scratching themselves and twitching, and ask for money with which to get their first drinks of the day. She passes out dimes regularly to about twenty-five of these men. Because of this, she is disliked by many of the hard-shell evangelists who hold hymn-singings in the gutters of the Bowery every evening. One of them, a grim, elderly woman, came to the cage not long ago and shook a finger at Mazie. "We sacrifice our nights to come down here and encourage these unfortunates to turn over a new leaf," she said. "Then you give them money and they begin using intoxicants all over again." When Mazie is faced with such a situation, she makes irrelevant or vulgar remarks until the complainant leaves. On this occasion she leaned forward and said, "Par'n me, Madam, but it sounds like your guts are growling. What you need is a beer."

Few of the men to whom Mazie gives money for eye-openers are companionable. They take her dimes with quivering fingers, mutter a word of thanks, and hurry off. Two of them, however, invariably linger a while. They have become close friends of Mazie's. One is a courtly old Irishman named Pop, and the other is an addled, sardonic little man who says he is a poet and whom Mazie calls Eddie Guest. She says she likes Pop because he is so cheerful and

Eddie Guest because he is so sad. "I come from a devout family of teetotallers," Pop once said. "They was thirteen in the family, and they called me the weakling because I got drunk on Saturday nights. Well, they're all under the sod. Woodrow Wilson was President when the last one died, and I'm still here drinking good liquor and winking at the pretty girls." "That's right, Pop," Mazie said. Pop works bus stops. He approaches people waiting on corners for a bus and asks for a nickel with which to get uptown or downtown, as the case may be. When he gets a nickel, he touches his hat and hurries off to the next bus stop. At night he sings ballads in Irish gin mills on Third Avenue. Mazie thinks he has a beautiful baritone, and every morning, in return for her dime, he favors her with two or three ballads. Her favorites—she hums them—are "Whiskey, You're the Divil," "The Garden Where the Praties Grow," "Tiddly-Aye-Aye for the One-Eyed Reilly," and "The Widow McGinnis's Pig." Sometimes Pop dances a jig on the tiled floor of the lobby. "Pop's a better show than I got inside," Mazie says on these occasions.

Eddie Guest is a gloomy, defeated, ex–Greenwich Village poet who has been around the Bowery off and on for eight or nine years. He mutters poetry to himself constantly and is taken to Bellevue for observation about once a year. He carries all his possessions in a greasy beach bag and sleeps in flophouses, never staying in one two nights in succession, because, he says, he doesn't want his enemies to know where he is. During the day he wanders in and out of various downtown branches of the Public Library. At the Venice one night he saw "The River," the moving picture in which the names of the tributaries of the Mississippi were made into a poem. When he came out, he stopped at Mazie's cage, spread his arms, and recited the names of many of the walk-up hotels on the Bowery. "The Alabama Hotel, the Comet, and the Uncle Sam House," he said, in a declamatory voice, "the Dandy, the Defender, the Niagara, the Owl, the Victoria House and the Grand Windsor Hotel, the Houston, the Mascot, the Palace, the Progress, the Palma House and the White House Hotel, the Newport, the Crystal, the Lion and the Marathon. All flophouses. All on the Bowery. Each and all my home, sweet home." For some reason, Mazie thought this was extraordinarily funny. Now, each morning, in order to get a dime, Eddie Guest is obliged to recite this chant for her. It always causes her to slap her right thigh, throw her head back, and guffaw. Both Eddie Guest and Mazie can be grimly and rather pointlessly amused by the signs over flophouse entrances and by the bills of fare lettered in white on the windows of pig-snout restaurants. When Mazie passes the Victoria House and sees its sign, "ROOMS WITH ELECTRIC LIGHTS, 30C," or when she looks at the window of the Greek's on Chatham Square, "SNOUTS WITH FRENCH FRY POTS & COFFEE, T, OR BUTTERMILK, 10C," she always snickers. Mazie has considerable respect for Eddie Guest but thinks he is kidding when he calls himself a poet. Once he read to her part of a completely unintelligible poem about civilization in the United States, on which he says he has been working for twenty years and which he calls "No Rags, No Bones, No Bottles Today." "If that's a poem," Mazie said when he had finished, "I'm the Queen of Sweden."

Mazie's afternoon visitors are far more respectable than the morning ones. The people who stopped by to talk with her between noon and 6 P.M. one Saturday included Monsignor Cashin, Fannie Hurst, two detectives from the Oak Street station, a flashily dressed young Chinese gambler whom Mazie calls Fu Manchu and who is a power in Tze Far, the Chinatown version of the numbers lottery; two nuns from Madonna House, who wanted to thank her for buying a phonograph for the girls' club at their settlement; a talkative girl from Atlanta, Georgia, called Bingo, once a hostess in a Broadway taxi-dance hall and now the common-law wife of the chef of a chop-suey restaurant on Mott Street; the bartender of a Chatham Square saloon, who asked her to interpret a dream for him; and the clerk of a flophouse, who came to tell her that a bum named Tex had hanged himself in the washroom the night before. When she was told about Tex, Mazie nodded sagely and said, as she always does when she hears about the death of someone she has known, "Well, we all got to go sooner or later. You can't live forever. When your number's up, rich or poor, you got to go." Most of the visitors on that afternoon happened to be old friends of Mazie's. Miss Hurst, for example, she has known for eleven years. She calls her Fannie and likes to tell about their first meeting.

"One night," she says, "a swell-looking dame came to my cage and said she often took walks on the Bowery and would like to meet me. She said her name was Fannie Hurst. 'Pleased to meet you, Fannie,' I said. 'My name is Mary Pickford.' It turned out she really was Fannie Hurst. At first I thought she was going to put me in a book, and I didn't go for her. Since she promised not to write no books about me, we been pals." Miss Hurst visits Mazie frequently. Each time she comes, Mazie looks at her dress, fingers the material, asks how much it cost, tells her she got gypped, and advises her to try one of the shops on Division Street. Miss Hurst does not mind this. "I admire Mazie," she said. "She is the most compassionate person I've ever known. No matter how filthy or drunk or evil-smelling a bum may be, she treats him as an equal." Until recently, Miss Hurst occasionally took friends down to meet Mazie. "I'm afraid they looked on her as just another Bowery curiosity," she says. "So I don't take people down any more. I used to invite Mazie to parties at my house. She always accepted but never came. I think she's still a little suspicious of me, although I've never written a line about her and never intend to. I simply look upon her as a friend."

From callers like Fu Manchu and Bingo, Mazie hears considerable gossip about the sleazy underworld of Chinatown. She says she never repeats such gossip, not even to her sisters. Detectives know that she has many Chinese friends and sometimes stop at her cage and ask apparently innocent questions about them; she shrugs her shoulders and says, "No spik English." In general, however, she cooperates with the police. Drunken tourists often come down to Bowery joints to see life, and when she notices them stumbling around Chatham Square she telephones the Oak Street station. "Such dopes are always getting rolled by bums," she says. "I got no sympathy for out-of-towners, but bums are the clumsiest thieves in the world. They always get caught, and it's best to get temptation out of their way." Although her language frequently shocks the Oak Street cops, they admire Mazie. Detective Kain, for instance, says that she has "the roughest tongue and the softest heart in the Third Precinct." "She knows this neighborhood like a farmer knows his farm," he says. "I believe she's got the second sight. If anything out of the way is happening anywhere along the Bowery, she senses it."

Detective Kain has for some time been trying to solve a mystery in which Mazie is involved. Mazie has a telephone in her booth, of course, and in June, 1929, a man whose voice she did not recognize began calling her daily at 5 P.M., asking for a date or making cryptic remarks, such as "They got the road closed, Mazie. They won't let nobody through." After three months he stopped calling. Then, around Christmas of the following year, he began again. He has been calling intermittently ever since. "I won't hear from him for maybe six months," Mazie says. "Then, one day around five, the phone will ring and this voice will say, 'All the clocks have stopped running' or 'Mazie, they cut down the big oak tree' or some other dopey remark. He never says more than a few words, and when I say something he hangs right up. One afternoon he gave me the shakes. He called up and said, 'Mazie, I got a nephew studying to be an undertaker and he needs somebody to practice on.' Then he hung up. A minute later he called again and said, 'You'll do! You'll do!' Somehow, I get to feeling he's across the street in a booth. The worst thing is I suspect every stranger that buys a ticket. I strike up conversations with strangers just to see if I can find one who talks like him. I think he's trying to drive me crazy." Among her friends, Mazie refers to her caller as The Man. If she has visitors around five o'clock and the telephone rings, she says, "Pick up the receiver and see what The Man has to say this time." Fannie Hurst once listened. "It was macabre," she said. Detective Kain has listened often, has warned the man, and has tried vainly to trace the calls. Mazie's number has been changed repeatedly, but that does no good.

Mazie closes her cage shortly after 11 P.M., when the final show is under way, and goes to an all-night diner near Brooklyn Bridge, where she glances through the *Daily News* while having a couple of cups of coffee and a honey bun. The only things in the *News* that she regularly reads from beginning to end are the comics, the "Voice of the People," and "The Inquiring Fotographer." She says she doesn't read political or war stories because she can't understand them and because they make her blue. "The world is all bitched up," she once said. "Always was, always will be." "Do you really believe that?" she was asked. "No," she said, after a moment of deliberation, "I guess I don't." She spends half an hour in the diner. Then, practically every night, before going home to bed, she makes a Samaritan tour of the Bowery and its environs. She carries an umbrella and a large handbag, which contains a flashlight, a number of cakes of soap of the size found in hotel bathrooms, and a supply of nickels, dimes, and quarters.

If it is a cold night, she goes first to an alley near the steps leading to the footwalk of Manhattan Bridge. Bums like to keep fires going in discarded oil drums in this alley. She distributes some change. Then she inspects Columbus Park, a block west of Chatham Square, where every winter a few bums pass out on benches and die of exposure. The police say Mazie has rescued scores of men in this park. Then, passing through Chinatown, she returns to the Bowery and heads uptown, pausing whenever she recognizes a bum and giving him enough money for a meal, a drink, or a flop. Frequently, in addition to small change, she gives a bum a cake of soap. "*Please use it, buddy*," she says pleadingly. Here and there she gets out her flashlight and peers into a doorway. She pays particular attention to the drunken or exhausted bums who sleep in doorways, on loading platforms, and on sidewalks. She always tries to arouse them and stake them to flops. In warm weather, if they don't seem disposed to stir, she leaves them where they are. "A sidewalk is about as nice as a flophouse cot in the summertime," she says. "You may get up stiff, but you won't get up crummy." In the winter, however, she badgers them until they awaken. She punches them in the ribs with her umbrella and, if necessary, gets down on her knees and slaps their faces. "When a bum is sleeping off his load, you could saw off his leg and he wouldn't notice nothing," she says. Sometimes a bum who has been awakened by Mazie tries to take a poke at her. When this happens, she assumes a spraddle-legged stance, like a fencer, and jabs the air viciously with her umbrella. "Stand back," she cries, "or I'll put your eyes out." If a man is too weak, sodden, or spiritless to get up, Mazie grabs his elbows and heaves him to his feet. Holding him erect, she guides him to the nearest flophouse and pulls and pushes him up the stairs to the lobby. She pays the clerk for the man's lodging (thirty cents is the customary price) and insists on his having at least two blankets. Then, with the help of the clerk or the bouncer, she takes off the man's shoes, unbuttons his collar, loosens his belt, and puts him to bed with his clothes on. This is usually a tumultuous process, and sometimes many of the lodgers are awakened. They stick their heads out of the doors of their cubicles. "It's Mazie!" they shout. "Hello, Mazie!" Now and then an emotional bum will walk out in his underwear and insist on shaking Mazie's hand. "God bless you, Mazie, old girl!" he will cry. Mazie does not approve of such antics. "Go back to bed, you old goat," she says. If she is acquainted with the clerk and trusts him, she leaves some change with him and asks that it be given to the bum when he wakes up. Flophouses are for-men-only establishments, and Mazie is the only female who has ever crossed the threshold of many of them.

At least a couple of times a week, Mazie finds injured men lying in the street. On these occasions she telephones Police Headquarters and asks for an ambulance from Gouverneur or Beekman Street, the hospitals which take care of most Bowery cases. She knows many of the drivers from these hospitals by name and orders them around. Police say she summons more ambulances than any other private citizen in town, and she is proud of this. "I don't over-do it," she says. "Unless a man is all stove-up and bloody, I don't put in a call, but if I had my way, the wagons would be rolling all night long. There's hardly a bum on the Bowery who don't belong in a hospital."

On her walk, Mazie usually tries to steer clear of other well-known nocturnal Bowery characters. Among these are the Widow Woman and the Crybaby. The Crybaby is an old mission bum who sits on the curb for hours with his feet in the gutter, sobbing brokenly. Once Mazie nudged him on the shoulder and asked, "What's the matter with you?" "I committed the unforgivable sin," he said. Mazie asked him what the sin consisted of, and he began a theological description of it which she didn't understand and which she interrupted after a few minutes, remarking, "Hell, Crybaby, you didn't commit no sin. You just prob'ly got the stomach ulsters." The Widow Woman is a bent, whining crone who wears a mourning veil, a Queen Mary hat, and a rusty black coat, and comes hobbling down the Bowery around midnight giving bums little slips of paper on which are scribbled such statements as "God is love" and "The fires of Hell will burn forever." Mazie is afraid of her. "She walks like a woman and she dresses like a woman, but when she talks I get the feeling that she's a man."

Most nights, before going home to bed, which is usually around two o'clock, Mazie makes brief stops in several saloons and all-night restaurants. She does not mind the reek of stale beer, greasy cabbage, and disinfectant in them. "After you been around the Bowery a few years, your nose gets all wore out," she says. She goes into these places not to eat or drink but to gossip with bartenders and countermen and to listen to the conversation of drunken bums. She has found that bums do not talk much about sex, sports, politics, or business, the normal saloon topics. She says most of them are far too undernourished to have any interest in sex. They talk, instead, about what big shots they were before they hit the Bowery. Although their stories fascinate her, Mazie is generally cynical. "To hear them tell it," she says, "all the bums on the Bowery were knocking off millions down in Wall Street when they were young, else they were senators, else they were the general manager of something real big, but, poor fellows, the most of them they wasn't ever nothing but drunks."

(1940)

Hit on the Head with a Cow

WHEN I HAVE TIME TO KILL, I sometimes go to the basement of a brownstone tenement on Fifty-ninth Street, three-quarters of a block west of Columbus Circle, and sit on a rat-gnawed Egyptian mummy and cut up touches with Charles Eugene Cassell, an old Yankee for whose bitter and disorderly mind I have great respect. Mr. Cassell has Negro, French, Portuguese, and English blood. He calls himself Captain Charley because he had charge of an ammunition barge for a brief period during the First World War and saw no reason why he shouldn't have a title. About fifteen years ago, after he got too contrary to hold down a steady job, he took out some of his savings and opened a museum—Captain Charley's Private Museum for Intelligent People—in a Harlem apartment house; some time later, after a series of robberies, he moved to the basement on Fifty-ninth Street. The Captain is a relentless and indiscriminate collector, and stored in his place are thousands of curious odds and ends he gathered during the fifty-five years he worked as a sailor or cook on navy and merchant ships, and during other years when he was a servant in clubs and hotels in Manhattan. The most valuable exhibit is a group of stuffed animals. They are moth-cut and mangy, but several times a year the Captain is able to rent them to moving picture theatres for lobby displays during the showing of jungle films. The Captain charges fifteen cents admission to his museum, but half the time he forgets to collect it. The majority of his visitors are passers-by attracted by big cardboard signs which he puts up at the head of the steps leading down to

the basement—signs such as "IF YOU CONSIDER YOURSELF INTELLI-
GENT, STEP INSIDE," "CAPTAIN CHARLEY WILL SELL A FEW ODDS AND
ENDS FROM TEN CENTS TO FIFTEEN HUNDRED DOLLARS," and "IF YOU
ARE SO DAMN SMART, WHY AIN'T YOU RICH?" A few of the visitors
are women hunting for bargains in antiques.

I like to sit in the gloomy, moldy basement and listen to the
Captain. After I have listened to him for fifteen minutes or so, I
get to thinking about something that happened to me when I was
ten years old. My father and a hired man named Alonzo were
butchering a cow in the hall of the barn in back of our house in
the small town in North Carolina that I come from, and I was
helping. We were hoisting the cow up in the air with a block and
tackle so we could skin her, and Alonzo and I had hold of the rope.
We had the cow off the ground when something went wrong with
the gear, and when I came to I was out in the barnyard running
around in circles and screeching, and my head was bloody. When
I was caught and subdued by Alonzo and stretched out on the
green grass under a pecan tree, I looked up at my father and said,
"What happened, Daddy?" My father had a faraway look in his
eyes and he said, "Son, you were hit on the head with a cow."
For at least a week after I received the blow on the head everything people said to me seemed illogical or disconnected; every
conversation I heard seemed to end unerringly and pleasantly in
confusion. That is the way I feel after I have listened to Captain
Charley for a little while. I feel as if I had been hit on the head
with a cow.

The last time I went to see him I took a notebook along, and
while he rummaged through the museum—he was searching for a
bone which he said he hacked off an Arab around 9 P.M. one full-
moon night in 1907 after the Arab had been murdered for signing
a treaty—I wrote down everything he said. He didn't pay much
attention to me while he talked; most of the time he was talking
to himself. And while he rambled along he kept plucking objects
out of the clutter on the floor of the basement. He said he wanted
to find the Arab's bone and send it to Police Commissioner Grover
A. Whalen by parcel post. "I dreamt about old Grover last night,

and I made up my mind to send him a present," he said. "In this dream old Grover was a engineer on a fast freight on the New York Central, and I was the fireman, and we was arguing over who had the right to blow the whistle. Toot! Toot! Old Grover won." (Captain Charley is a great admirer of Mr. Whalen, and I once asked him why. Mr. Whalen is noted for his sartorial daring, and it turned out that that is the reason. "I like the way old Grover dresses," Captain Charley said. "He dresses like he means it.") Before long the Captain had piled up a dusty mound of objects which included a stuffed barn owl, an old gilt picture frame, a tin lunch bucket, a stack of theatre programs and restaurant menus of the 1890's, a woman's hat with a green ostrich feather on it, a dirty beaded bag, a bashed-in pith helmet, a cigar box full of seashells, political cam- paign buttons, and Chinese coins; a big roll of yellowed newspapers around which a necktie had been knotted, a cutlass, a parasol which he said was once the property of a famous New Orleans madam named Mrs. Lilly-belle Sue-belle Russell, and the lengthy skin of a boa constrictor that killed a girl and a goat in South America at a moment when the girl was milking the goat.

"Where were you born, Captain Charley?" I asked.

"I'm born in Boston," he said. "I'm born in the Hub. I'm a bluenosed Yankee, fed on codfish and cranberries. My type of people are all dead. They broke the mold. I consider myself different from other men, on a higher plane, always been a boss, never wore overalls. Take the biggest man in the country and no matter what big deeds he did, I did twice as much. I don't smoke and I don't hang out in none of them low-down Columbus Avenue saloons. I drink in high-class places. Nothing but champagne wine and brandy, that's all I drink. High-class people invite me to their houses for dinner, just for the honor of it, send me home full of brandy. I'm very particular about my something to eat. When I got cash on hand I set a fine table, don't eat nothing but lobsters and fresh peaches and T-bone steaks. There's people that could live high on what I throw away. Use to take advantage of women, but somewhere along the line I lost my animal spirits. I can look a gangster in the eye and make him change his mind, but I can't do a thing with a woman no more. At one time I had nine big switch-tail women on my personal payroll and they all stole from me, picked me clean. Buzzards! One of these days I'm going to pack my grip and go up to Boston and die. Won't even bother to get me a cemetery lot; I'll just find me a convenient gutter and lie down in it and die. Sad, sad! Made up my mind to die in Boston because I was born there. Ashes to ashes, dust to dust. Older I get the more disgusted I get. I'm yet to find a honest man, a honest woman. I don't even believe in good deeds; once I tried to help a man out of a well and I tumbled in and broke both legs. I believe in assassination, it makes elbow room. I believe in gassing off all the old people, except me. I'm too smart to gas. I'm a taxidermist. I can mount a mosquito. I can mount a strawberry. I can mount any old fish you ever see."

At this moment a cowbell hanging from the knob on the street door began to tinkle and a middle-aged woman came in. When her eyes got used to the gloom, she peered at us and said, "May I look at the antiques?" The Captain said, "Help yourself, friend." He shambled over and collected fifteen cents admission, and then returned to his search for the Arab's bone. The woman stood stock still for a few moments and stared at the Captain. He is small, grimy, and surly. His eyes are always bleary. He wears a white, waxed mustache. He had on his customary outfit—ragged duck pants, a turtleneck sweater, a pea jacket, a captain's cap, and tennis sneakers painted with silver radiator paint. He was decorating some seashells one day with the silver paint and decided that it would look good on his sneakers.

"Look at this lunch bucket," he said. "Use to belong to Al Smith when he was in Fulton Fish Market. Never used such a common thing myself. Always had money, never broke; had the chicken pox, had the sleeping sickness, had the dropsy, had the yellow johnnies, had the walking, talking pneumonia. Didn't miss a thing in the medical line. My old man was a big man with shoulders like a mule, born on a farm in Nova Scotia, lived most of his life in Boston. He was born in a barn. When he went in a place he always left the door wide open. People would yell at him, 'Shut the door! Were you born in a barn?' and he'd say, 'That's right. How'd you guess it?' He was biggity as sin. What you call a beachcomber. He did odd jobs on the fish docks, and he fed us on fish until the bones stuck out of our ears. Comb my hair in the morning, I'd comb out a handful of bones. It got so my stomach rose and fell with the tide. Fish, fish! I was almost grown before I found out people ate anything else. Use to take me with him to the saloons when I was just a little teeniney baby. He'd set me on the bar beside his glass of whiskey. When he wasn't watching, I'd sneak me a drink of his whiskey, then I'd crawl down on the sawdust and pick a fight with the saloon cats. My old man would tuck me under his right arm like I was a bag of groceries and tote me home and throw me on the bed and I'd sleep it off. I'd grunt and snore like a full-grown man. People said I was the prettiest boy baby ever born in Boston. I was always smart. Worked all my life, never had time for baseball, never spun a top. First job I ever had, I guided a blindman beggar around the streets of Boston, a fellow named Blind Clancy, a gin drinker. I was seven years old, going on eight. He had a grip like steel. He'd hold on to my shoulder, and he had such a grip it made my shoulder ache. He was a smart blindman; he wouldn't ever let me hold the cup. We'd stumble along and he'd sing out, 'All good people please to drop a penny in the blindman's cup.' I got sick and tired of hearing that, and one day I walked off and left him right in the middle of a parade on Tremont Street. I took to knocking around the docks. At sixteen I was an A.B. on the deep sea, drawing down a man's pay. Take those old sea captains; why, I made monkeys out of them because I knew so much as- tronomy. Use to be an atheist, but I'm getting so old I'm afraid to be an atheist. Take hell and damnation. Didn't use to believe in it, but now I just don't know. It sounds so logical. I'm a Just in Case Christian. Ever so often I hunt me up a church and get right with the Holy Ghost, just in case. Still and all, I can't endure preachers. Deep down in my heart, I don't believe in pie in the sky; I believe in T-bone steak in the here and now. Look at this. Theodore Roosevelt's pith helmet. I was working in a big club full of rich old men that sat around all day in thick leather chairs dozing and grunting and scratching theirselves. And one of these rich old men said to me, 'See here, Charley, you want this helmet? It use to belong to President Roosevelt.' I sure was glad to get it. Old Theodore wore it when he was a rootin' and a tootin' around in them deep jungles. That's what I'd like, big game hunting. Bang! Bang!"

The Captain turned abruptly and scrutinized the woman visitor to make sure that she wasn't stealing anything. He believes every person who enters the museum plans to rob it. The woman pretended to be examining a stuffed crocodile, but from the perplexed look on her face I knew that she had been listening to everything the Captain said.

"The world owes me a lot," continued the Captain, "but I'll never collect. Owes me a lot of sleep. I don't get out of bed until high noon; sometimes I don't even get out of bed then. There's times I get so disgusted I just stay in bed three, four days hand running. Somebody knocks on the door, I holler out, 'Go 'way, go 'way! There's an old man in here with a severe case of the blue-green leprosy. Run for your life, whoever you are.' I just lie in bed and study over a long list of people I wish was dead. Sometimes I sit up and put a mirror in my lap and wax my mustache, wax it so sharp it's dangerous. Sometimes I sing to myself. You know that old number called 'Mother'?" The Captain threw his head back and began to sing in a quavering voice. " 'M is for the many things she gave me, O means only that she's growing old, T is for the tears she shed to save me, H is for her heart of purest gold. . . .' " His voice broke, and he snorted angrily and spat on the floor. "Oh, the hell with it. Use to run with the rowdiest women in this country until I took and married a Buffalo girl. I was up in Buffalo on political business and I seen her and I took and married her. She gave me two beautiful daughters and when they was grown I set them up in a candy store on Amsterdam Avenue, share and share alike, but they was too stuck up to wait on the customers, so I married them off to post office clerks. I didn't see no certain future in doctors or lawyers, so I married them off to post office clerks in the Bronx. Working for the government is sure and certain. If I had to do it all over again, I'd get me a good hold on the public teat and I wouldn't let loose until death do us part. Always been a leader of men, always had high-class people for my friends. Use to know O. Henry right well. Use to ask me questions about countries I had travelled in, and when I gave him an answer he'd give me a dollar. When the first bicycles came out he bought me a bicycle, bought me a suit of clothes. He was that kind of a man. Use to work for a man that ran a hotel. At 10 P.M. he'd go upstairs and leave me to run the damned hotel. I ran it, all right. Never had so much to drink before or since. I use to wash my socks in good liquor. I'm just a case of cabin boy to captain. Where in the hell is that old Arab bone? I hope the cat didn't drag it out of here. My cat's name is Steamboat Bill. I was the first man to collect stamps. If you doubt my statement, disprove it. Try to disprove me, I'll make a monkey out of you. When you think of all the things I've done, people ought to respect me more'n they do. A man don't pay me my due respect, I knock his slats in."

The woman visitor left. The cowbell on the doorknob tinkled as she shut the door.

"I bet she stole something," said the Captain, smacking a fist against a knee in a petulant, childish gesture. "They all steal something. I got a fine cat, best cat I ever had. Jumps up and pulls the electric-light cord. Jumps in bed and scratches my back. Use to have a monkey for a house pet. I got rid of him; monkeys stink. When I talk I get excited. Had so many knocks on the head in saloon fights I don't always remember. It's a nuisance when you can't remember, I be damned if it ain't. It makes you mad. Look at this here snakeskin. South American boa constrictor. You could make a woman fifty-five pairs of pretty shoes out of that snakeskin. Longest damned snakeskin in the United States. Show me any millionaire that's got a snakeskin as long as that. I'm disgusted to the full with this world. What I'd like is an expedition, a scientific expedition. I like brains. I'd kill a man for being stupid or give him credit for robbing me because that would demonstrate he had sense. Brains is what counts. I got a pension from

the Brooklyn Navy Yard and I got a pension from the Spanish-
American War, and I don't trust nobody. Don't trust the preacher,
don't trust the newspaper, don't trust the radio set, don't trust the
billboards, don't trust the pretty label on the liquor bottle where
it says eight years old; it's all big black lies. When I hear the whistle,
I don't even believe the train's coming. I got a radical nature, and
I can't help it. When I went to sea, I was always making trouble.
I was a scrapper. When I hit a port, the population scattered in-
land. In some towns, a half hour after I hit port there wouldn't
be nobody there but me. The people would take themselves a
blanket to lie on and enough groceries to last them, and they'd
hide out in the hills until I went back to sea. Once I was a
cook on a scientific expedition to the Arctic. I found a mastodon
bone and I wanted it. It was just exactly what I wanted. I was
always on the lookout for bones and historical odds and ends;
even when I was a young man with my head full of women worry
I was planning ahead for my museum. But it was a rule you had
to turn in everything you found. So a sailor said to me, 'Break it,
cook, and they'll let you keep it.' So I hefted this valuable bone
high over my head and I slammed it on the deck and it cracked all
to hell and gone. Then they let me keep it. That's a piece of it over
there in the far corner. Worth fifteen hundred dollars if it's worth
a cent."

That is a fair example of the way the Captain answers a question.
If you remember, all I asked him was "Where were you born,
Captain Charley?" After my last visit I checked up on several of the
Captain's remarks, not that it makes any difference to me if they
are true or false. First I checked up on his boast that he drinks
nothing but champagne wine and brandy. The bartender in a saloon
on Columbus Avenue around the corner from the museum said,
"Sometimes that old boy comes in here to make a phone call and
I invite him to have a beer, and he sure don't refuse." The bartender
said he once visited the museum. "Jeez," he said, "what a place! If
they really want to find Judge Crater, that's the place to look."
Later I telephoned Alfred E. Smith and asked him if he was aware
that his old tin lunch bucket was in a museum. "It couldn't be my

lunch bucket," said Mr. Smith, "because I never owned a lunch bucket. When I was working in the fish market I always went home to eat."

The Captain becomes evasive and hostile when any one tries to pin him down. Once I asked him the name of the ship of which he was captain.

"It was in 1917," he said. "War time."

"What was the name of the ship?"

"Like I said, it was war time. They called it the World War; to me, it was just a fuss, a commotion."

"What was the name of the ship?"

"Number Four."

"What kind of a ship was Number Four?"

"God damn it, sir, don't interrupt me. Haven't you got any respect for old age?"

"What kind of a ship was Number Four?"

"It was a barge. It was a munitions barge. It was towed between Wilmington and the Navy Yard in Brooklyn, and I was captain. Everybody took orders from Captain Charley. Half of Brooklyn would of blowed up one night if I hadn't cut the barge loose from the tug. The tide was throwing her around, and I took charge and cut her loose. If she'd a bumped into Brooklyn it would of been goodbye Brooklyn. Might of been a good thing. Thinned out some of them slums. I been mixed up in everything. I even been kidnapped. When my museum was situated up in Harlem a fellow and a girl I never seen before came and stood over my bed, and the fellow said, 'Are you the man that took advantage of this here girl?' And I said, 'I don't know. I might be. I'm a mean old man.' And the girl said, 'Let's slit his throat for him.' Then they kidnapped me and took me to the bank and made me draw out my account, two hundred and some odd dollars. Said they'd slit my throat if I told. I found out who the fellow was; he was a brush-boy in a barber shop four or five blocks up the street from my museum. I seen him on the street a couple of times, but I was afraid to notify the Police Department. I never said a mumbling word. I didn't care to risk it. I need my throat to swallow with. There's something about a knife that makes me shrink right up. Like that old saying my mamma use to have, 'When the big bulldog gets in trouble, puppy-dog britches fit him fine.' "

I was surprised to find out about the Captain's streak of timidity. He is small and frail-looking, but he is bellicose. He likes to push his captain's cap on the back of his head, put his fists up like a prizefighter, and give a frightful account of the way he maimed a disrespectful shipmate by throwing pepper in his eyes and striking him in the face with "the business end of a broken beer bottle." He is proud of his captain's cap. He says, "This cap takes me anywhere, right past the ticket window." The Captain seeks to give visitors the impression that he once was a great lover; tacked up in the museum is the old saloon wall-motto which states, "The happiest moments of my life were spent in the arms of another man's wife." This motto usually ends with a dash and "My mother," but the Captain chopped off the last two words. He becomes rather wistful when he tells about his conquests in Paris, among the Eskimos, and on various South Sea islands. He shakes his head, cackles, and says, "I still got the passion, but I ain't got the power. My race is run." He tells visitors that he is "seventy-seven years old, more or less." "I'm not long for this world," he likes to say. "I give myself three more years they'll have me in a box." However, there is still plenty of grit and gristle in him. The basement is so crowded he has to wrestle with exhibits to get from the museum proper back to the tiny room in which he sleeps and eats, and he shoves a massive, old-fashioned bureau or a heavy sea chest out of his way with ease a young pug might envy. He is conscious of his strength and is always threatening to let loose and knock somebody's head off. Like the museum, the room in the rear is stuffed to the ceiling with junk. He has his meals sitting on the bed. The last time I visited him there was a platter on the bed bearing the head and bones of a fish off which his cat was feeding.

Captain Charley has a good reason for his robbery phobia because the museum is frequently entered by petty burglars, a state of things for which he himself is responsible; in talking to visitors he always attributes a fabulous value to even the most worthless trinket. Naturally, some of his visitors believe him when he boasts, holding up a valueless gimcrack, "This is worth fifteen hundred and seventy-five dollars." Occasionally a visitor comes back at night, when the Captain is away, and walks right into the museum and steals a few things. I am certain these thieves are furious after they try to pawn their loot. When the Captain goes away from the museum he usually leaves it unlocked and sticks up a sign just inside the door which warns, "BEWARE OF THE ALIVE SNAKES LOOSE IN HERE." In the daytime the sign is effective, but at night, of course, it does no good. Paradoxically the Captain is proud of the frequency with which he is robbed. He laughs his high, goatlike laugh and says, "*Every*body robs Captain Charley!"

Captain Charley's most remarkable possessions are two objects which look like ironing boards wrapped with strips of brown cloth. The museum is too crowded for chairs, and I sometimes use one of these objects for a seat.

"You know what you sitting on?" the Captain asked me one day.

"No, sir," I said. "What?"

"A Egyptian mummy."

"Is that right?"

"Yes, God damn it, that's right."

"Where did you get it?"

"Got it in Egypt. My boat was tied up in Alexandria and I took a turn around Egypt. They was pulling old mummies out of the tombs by the thousands, so I took three. I took three of the middle-sized ones. I think they're he-mummies. I don't think they mummied no women. I was cook on this boat and I stood 'em up in the kitchen, in the galley. I had 'em stood up in corners. When the crew found out I had the galley full of Egyptian mummies, they became disagreeable to me. They was going to throw my mummies overboard, but that night I took and hid 'em in the lifeboats, under canvas. We was months and months getting back to the United States and it use to give me the snickers every time I thought about them three mummies hiding up in the lifeboats like stowaways. When I went to sneak my mummies ashore a queer thing happened. One of 'em was missing."

"What do you think happened to it?"

"Oh, hell, I don't know. Something real peculiar. When a man takes to meddling with Egyptian mummies fresh out of the tomb, damn near anything's apt to happen."

(1938)

Professor Sea Gull

JOE GOULD IS A BLITHE and emaciated little man who has been a notable in the cafeterias, diners, barrooms, and dumps of Greenwich Village for a quarter of a century. He sometimes brags rather wryly that he is the last of the bohemians. "All the others fell by the wayside," he says. "Some are in the grave, some are in the loony bin, and some are in the advertising business." Gould's life is by no means carefree; he is constantly tormented by what he calls "the three H's"—homelessness, hunger, and hangovers. He sleeps on benches in subway stations, on the floor in the studios of friends, and in quarter-a-night flophouses on the Bowery. Once in a while he trudges up to Harlem and goes to one of the establishments known as "Extension Heavens" that are operated by followers of Father Divine, the Negro evangelist, and gets a night's lodging for fifteen cents. He is five feet four and he hardly ever weighs more than a hundred pounds. Not long ago he told a friend that he hadn't eaten a square meal since June, 1936, when he bummed up to Cambridge and attended a banquet during a reunion of the Harvard class of 1911, of which he is a member. "I'm the foremost authority in the United States," he says, "on the subject of doing without." He tells people that he lives on "air, self-esteem, cigarette butts, cowboy coffee, fried-egg sandwiches, and ketchup." Cowboy coffee, he says, is strong coffee drunk black without sugar. "I've long since lost my taste for good coffee," he says. "I much prefer the kind that sooner or later, if you keep on drinking it, your hands will begin to shake and the whites of your eyes will turn yellow."

While having a sandwich, Gould customarily empties a bottle or two of ketchup on his plate and eats it with a spoon. The countermen in the Jefferson Diner, on Village Square, which is one of his hangouts, gather up the ketchup bottles and hide them the moment he puts his head in the door. "I don't particularly like the confounded stuff," he says, "but I make it a practice to eat all I can get. It's the only grub I know of that's free of charge."

Gould is a Yankee. His branch of the Goulds has been in New England since 1635, and he is related to many of the other early New England families, such as the Lawrences, the Clarkes, and the Storers. "There's nothing accidental about me," he once said. "I'll tell you what it took to make me what I am today. It took old Yankee blood, an overwhelming aversion to possessions, four years of Harvard, and twenty-five years of beating the living hell out of my insides with bad hooch and bad food." He says that he is out of joint with the rest of the human race because he doesn't want to own anything. "If Mr. Chrysler tried to make me a present of the Chrysler Building," he says, "I'd damn near break my neck fleeing from him. I wouldn't own it; it'd own me. Back home in Massachusetts I'd be called an old Yankee crank. Here I'm called a bohemian. It's six of one, half a dozen of the other." Gould has a twangy voice and a Harvard accent. Bartenders and countermen in the Village refer to him as the Professor, the Sea Gull, Professor Sea Gull, the Mongoose, Professor Mongoose, or the Bellevue Boy. He dresses in the castoff clothes of his friends. His overcoat, suit, shirt, and even his shoes are all invariably a size or two too large, but he wears them with a kind of forlorn rakishness. "Just look at me," he says. "The only thing that fits is the necktie." On bitter winter days he puts a layer of newspapers between his shirt and undershirt. "I'm snobbish," he says. "I only use the *Times.*" He is fond of unusual headgear—a toboggan, a beret, or a yachting cap. One summer evening he appeared at a party in a seersucker suit, a polo shirt, a scarlet cummerbund, sandals, and a yachting cap, all hand-me-downs. He uses a long black cigarette holder, and a good deal of the time he smokes butts picked up off the sidewalks.

Bohemianism has aged Gould considerably beyond his years. He has got in the habit lately of asking people he has just met to guess his age. Their guesses range between sixty-five and seventy-five; he is fifty-three. He is never hurt by this; he looks upon it as proof of his superiority. "I do more living in one year," he says, "than ordinary humans do in ten." Gould is toothless, and his lower jaw swivels from side to side when he talks. He is bald on top, but the hair at the back of his head is long and frizzly, and he has a bushy, cinnamon-colored beard. He wears a pair of spectacles that are loose and lopsided and that slip down to the end of his nose a moment after he puts them on. He doesn't always wear them on the street and without them he has the wild, unfocussed stare of an old scholar who has strained his eyes on small print. Even in the Village many people turn and look at him. He is stooped and he moves rapidly, grumbling to himself, with his head thrust forward and held to one side. Under his left arm he usually carries a bulging, greasy, brown pasteboard portfolio, and he swings his right arm aggressively. As he hurries along, he seems to be warding off an imaginary enemy. Don Freeman, the artist, a friend of his, once made a sketch of him walking. Freeman called the sketch "Joe Gould versus the Elements." Gould is as restless and footloose as an alley cat, and he takes long hikes about the city, now and then disappearing from the Village for weeks at a time and mystifying his friends; they have never been able to figure out where he goes. When he returns, always looking pleased with himself, he makes a few cryptic remarks, giggles, and then shuts up. "I went on a bird walk along the waterfront with an old countess," he said after his most recent absence. "The countess and I spent three weeks studying sea gulls."

Gould is almost never seen without his portfolio. He keeps it on his lap while he eats and in flophouses he sleeps with it under his head. It usually contains a mass of manuscripts and notes and letters and clippings and copies of obscure little magazines, a bottle of ink, a dictionary, a paper bag of cigarette butts, a paper bag of bread crumbs, and a paper bag of hard, round, dime-store candy of the type called sour balls. "I fight fatigue with sour balls," he says. The crumbs are for pigeons; like many other eccentrics, Gould is a pigeon feeder. He is devoted to a flock which makes its headquarters atop and around the statue of Garibaldi in Washington Square. These pigeons know him. When he comes up and takes a seat on the plinth of the statue, they flutter down and perch on his head and shoulders, waiting for him to bring out his bag of crumbs. He has given names to some of them. "Come here, Boss Tweed," he says. "A lady in Stewart's Cafeteria didn't finish her whole-wheat toast this morning and when she went out, bingo, I snatched it off her plate especially for you. Hello, Big Bosom. Hello, Popgut. Hello, Lady Astor. Hello, St. John the Baptist. Hello, Polly Adler. Hello, Fiorello, you old goat, how're you today?"

Although Gould strives to give the impression that he is a philosophical loafer, he has done an immense amount of work during his career as a bohemian. Every day, even when he has a bad hangover or even when he is weak and listless from hunger, he spends at least a couple of hours working on a formless, rather mysterious book that he calls "An Oral History of Our Time." He began this book twenty-six years ago, and it is nowhere near finished. His preoccupation with it seems to be principally responsible for the way he lives; a steady job of any kind, he says, would interfere with his thinking. Depending on the weather, he writes in parks, in doorways, in flophouse lobbies, in cafeterias, on benches on elevated-railroad platforms, in subway trains, and in public libraries. When he is in the proper mood, he writes until he is exhausted, and he gets into this mood at peculiar times. He says that one night he sat for six or seven hours in a booth in a Third Avenue bar and grill, listening to a beery old Hungarian woman, once a madam and once a dealer in narcotics and now a soup cook in a city hospital, tell the story of her life. Three days later, around four o'clock in the morning, on a cot in the Hotel Defender, at 300 Bowery, he was awakened by the foghorns of tugs on the East River and was unable to go back to sleep because he felt that he was in the exact mood to put the old soup cook's biography in his history. He has an abnormal memory; if he is sufficiently impressed by a conversation, he can keep it in his head, even if it is lengthy and senseless, for many days, much of it word for word. He had a bad cold, but he got up, dressed under a red exit light, and, tiptoeing so as not to disturb the men sleeping on cots all around him, went downstairs to the lobby.

He wrote in the lobby from 4:15 A.M. until noon. Then he left the Defender, drank some coffee in a Bowery diner, and walked up to the Public Library. He plugged away at a table in the genealogy room, which is one of his rainy-day hangouts and which he says he prefers to the main reading room because it is gloomier, until it closed at 6 P.M. Then he moved into the main reading room and stayed there, seldom taking his eyes off his work, until the Library locked up for the night at 10 P.M. He ate a couple of egg sandwiches and a quantity of ketchup in a Times Square cafeteria. Then, not having two bits for a flophouse and being too engrossed to go to the Village and seek shelter, he hurried into the West Side subway and rode the balance of the night, scribbling ceaselessly while the train he was aboard made three round trips between the New Lots Avenue station in Brooklyn and the Van Cortlandt Park station in the Bronx, which is one of the longest runs in the subway system. He kept his portfolio on his lap and used it as a desk. He has the endurance of the possessed. Whenever he got too sleepy to concentrate, he shook his head vigorously and then brought out his bag of sour balls and popped one in his mouth. People stared at him, and once he was interrupted by a drunk who asked him what in the name of God he was writing. Gould knows how to get rid of inquisitive drunks. He pointed at his left ear and said, "What? What's that? Deaf as a post. Can't hear a word." The drunk lost all interest in him. "Day was breaking when I left the subway," Gould says. "I was coughing and sneezing, my eyes were sore, my knees were shaky, I was as hungry as a bitch wolf, and I had exactly eight cents to my name. I didn't care. My history was longer by eleven thousand brand-new words, and at that moment I bet there wasn't a chairman of the board in all New York as happy as I."

GOULD IS HAUNTED by the fear that he will die before he has the first draft of the Oral History finished. It is already eleven times as long as the Bible. He estimates that the manuscript contains

9,000,000 words, all in longhand. It may well be the lengthiest unpublished work in existence. Gould does his writing in nickel composition books, the kind that children use in school, and the Oral History and the notes he has made for it fill two hundred and seventy of them, all of which are tattered and grimy and stained with coffee, grease, and beer. Using a fountain pen, he covers both sides of each page, leaving no margins anywhere, and his penmanship is poor; hundreds of thousands of words are legible only to him. He has never been able to interest a publisher in the Oral History. At one time or another he has lugged armfuls of it into fourteen publishing offices. "Half of them said it was obscene and outrageous and to get it out of there as quick as I could," he says, "and the others said they couldn't read my handwriting." Experiences of this nature do not dismay Gould; he keeps telling himself that it is posterity he is writing for, anyway. In his breast pocket, sealed in a dingy envelope, he always carries a will bequeathing two-thirds of the manuscript to the Harvard Library and the other third to the Smithsonian Institution. "A couple of generations after I'm dead and gone," he likes to say, "the Ph.D.'s will start lousing through my work. Just imagine their surprise. 'Why, I be damned,' they'll say, 'this fellow was the most brilliant historian of the century.' They'll give me my due. I don't claim that all of the Oral History is first class, but some of it will live as long as the English language." Gould used to keep his composition books scattered all over the Village, in the apartments and studios of friends. He kept them stuck away in closets and under beds and behind the books in bookcases. In the winter of 1942, after hearing that the Metropolitan Museum had moved its most precious paintings to a bombproof storage place somewhere out of town for the duration of the war, he became panicky. He went around and got all his books together and made them into a bale, he wrapped the bale in two layers of oilcloth, and then he entrusted it to a woman he knows who owns a duck-and-chicken farm near Huntington, Long Island. The farmhouse has a stone cellar.

Gould puts into the Oral History only things he has seen or heard. At least half of it is made up of conversations taken down verbatim or summarized; hence the title. "What people say is history," Gould says. "What we used to think was history—kings and queens, treaties, inventions, big battles, beheadings, Caesar, Napoleon, Pontius Pilate, Columbus, William Jennings Bryan—is only formal history and largely false. I'll put down the informal history of the shirt-sleeved multitude—what they had to say about their jobs, love affairs, vittles, sprees, scrapes, and sorrows—or I'll perish in the attempt." The Oral History is a great hodgepodge and kitchen midden of hearsay, a repository of jabber, an omnium-gatherum of bushwa, gab, palaver, hogwash, flapdoodle, and malarkey, the fruit, according to Gould's estimate, of more than twenty thousand conversations. In it are the hopelessly incoherent biographies of hundreds of bums, accounts of the wanderings of seamen encountered in South Street barrooms, grisly descriptions of hospital and clinic experiences ("Did you ever have a painful operation or disease?" is one of the first questions that Gould, fountain pen and composition book in hand, asks a person he has just met), summaries of innumerable Union Square and Columbus Circle harangues, testimonies given by converts at Salvation Army street meetings, and the addled opinions of scores of park-bench oracles and gin-mill savants. For a time Gould haunted the all-night greasy spoons in the vicinity of Bellevue Hospital, eavesdropping on tired internes, nurses, orderlies, ambulance drivers, embalming-school students, and morgue workers, and faithfully recording their talk. He scurries up and down Fifth Avenue during parades, feverishly taking notes. Gould writes with great candor, and the percentage of obscenity in the Oral History is high. He has a chapter called "Examples of the So-called Dirty Story of Our Time," to which he makes almost daily additions. In another chapter are many rhymes and observations which he found scribbled on the walls of subway washrooms. He believes that these scribblings are as truly historical as the strategy of General Robert E. Lee. Hundreds of thousands of words are devoted to the drunken behavior and the sexual adventures of various professional Greenwich Villagers in the twenties. There are hundreds of reports of ginny Village parties, including gossip about the guests and faithful reports of their arguments on such subjects as reincarnation, birth control, free love, psychoanalysis, Christian Science, Swedenborgianism, vegetarianism, alcoholism, and different political and art isms. "I have fully covered what might be termed the intellectual underworld of my time," Gould says. There are detailed descriptions of night life in scores of Village drinking and eating places, some of which, such as the Little Quakeress, the Original Julius, the Troubadour Tavern, the Samovar, Hubert's Cafeteria, Sam Swartz's T.N.T., and Eli Greifer's Last Outpost of Bohemia Tea Shoppe, do not exist any longer.

Gould is a night wanderer, and he has put down descriptions of dreadful things he has seen on dark New York streets—descriptions, for example, of the herds of big gray rats that come out in the hours before dawn in some neighborhoods of the lower East Side and Harlem and unconcernedly walk the sidewalks. "I sometimes believe that these rats are not rats at all," he says, "but the damned and aching souls of tenement landlords." A great deal of the Oral History is in diary form. Gould is afflicted with total recall, and now and then he picks out a period of time in the recent past— it might be a day, a week, or a month—and painstakingly writes down everything of any consequence that he did during this period. Sometimes he writes a chapter in which he monotonously and hideously curses some person or institution. Here and there are rambling essays on such subjects as the flophouse flea, spaghetti, the zipper as a sign of the decay of civilization, false teeth, insanity, the jury system, remorse, cafeteria cooking, and the emasculating effect of the typewriter on literature. "William Shakespeare didn't sit around pecking on a dirty, damned, ninety-five-dollar doohickey," he wrote, "and Joe Gould doesn't, either."

The Oral History is almost as discursive as "Tristram Shandy." In one chapter, "The Good Men Are Dying Like Flies," Gould begins a biography of a diner proprietor and horse-race gambler named Side-Bet Benny Altschuler, who stuck a rusty icepick in his hand and died of lockjaw; and skips after a few paragraphs to a story a seaman told him about seeing a group of lepers drinking and dancing and singing on a beach in Port-of-Spain, Trinidad; and goes from that to an anecdote about a demonstration held in front of a moving-picture theatre in Boston in 1915 to protest against the showing of "The Birth of a Nation," at which he kicked a policeman; and goes from that to a description of a trip he once made through the Central Islip insane asylum, in the course of which a woman pointed at him and screamed, "There he is! Thief! Thief! There's the man that picked my geraniums and stole my mamma's mule and buggy"; and goes from that to an account an old stumble-bum gave of glimpsing and feeling the blue-black flames of hell one night while sitting in a doorway on Great Jones Street and of seeing two mermaids playing in the East River just north of Fulton Fish Market later the same night; and goes from that to an explanation made by a priest of Old St. Patrick's Cathedral, which is on Mott Street, in the city's oldest Little Italy, of why so many Italian women always wear black ("They are in perpetual mourning for our Lord"); and then returns at last to Side-Bet Benny, the lockjawed diner proprietor.

Only a few of the hundreds of people who know Gould have read any of the Oral History, and most of them take it for granted that it is gibberish. Those who make the attempt usually bog down after a couple of chapters and give up. Gould says he can count on one hand or on one foot those who have read enough of it to be qualified to form an opinion. One is Horace Gregory, the poet and critic. "I look upon Gould as a sort of Samuel Pepys of the Bowery," Gregory says. "I once waded through twenty-odd composition books, and most of what I saw had the quality of a competent high-school theme, but some of it was written with the clear and wonderful veracity of a child, and here and there were flashes of hard-bitten Yankee wit. If someone took the trouble to go through it and separate the good from the rubbish, as editors did with Thomas Wolfe's millions of words, it might be discovered that Gould actually has written a masterpiece." Another is E. E. Cummings, the poet, who is a close friend of Gould's. Cummings once wrote a poem about Gould, No. 261 in his "Collected Poems," which contains the following description of the history:

> . . . *a myth is as good as a smile but little joe gould's quote oral*
> *history unquote might (publishers note) be entitled a wraith's*

*progress or mainly awash while chiefly submerged or an amoral
morality sort-of-aliveing by innumerable kind-of-deaths*

Throughout the nineteen-twenties Gould haunted the office of
the *Dial,* now dead, the most highbrow magazine of the time. Finally,
in its April, 1929, issue, the *Dial* printed one of his shorter essays,
"Civilization." In it he rambled along, jeering at the buying and
selling of stocks as "a fuddy-duddy old maid's game" and referring
to skyscrapers and steamships as "bric-a-brac" and giving his opinion
that "the auto is unnecessary." "If all the perverted ingenuity which
was put into making buzz-wagons had only gone into improving
the breed of horses," he wrote, "humanity would be better off."
This essay had a curious effect on American literature. A copy of
the *Dial* in which it appeared turned up a few months later in a
second-hand bookstore in Fresno, California, and was bought for a
dime by William Saroyan, who then was twenty and floundering
around, desperate to become a writer. He read Gould's essay and
was deeply impressed and influenced by it. "It freed me from
bothering about form," he says. Twelve years later, in the winter
of 1941, in Don Freeman's studio on Columbus Circle, Saroyan saw
some drawings Freeman had made of Gould for *Don Freeman's Newsstand,* a quarterly publication of pictures of odd New York scenes
and personalities put out by the Associated American Artists. Saroyan
became excited. He told Freeman about his indebtedness to Gould.
"Who the hell is he, anyway?" Saroyan asked. "I've been trying to
find out for years. Reading those few pages in the *Dial* was like
going in the wrong direction and running into the right guy and
then never seeing him again." Freeman told him about the Oral
History. Saroyan sat down and wrote a commentary to accompany
the drawings of Gould in *Newsstand.* "To this day," he wrote, in
part, "I have not read anything else by Joe Gould. And yet to me
he remains one of the few genuine and original American writers.
He was easy and uncluttered, and almost all other American writing
was uneasy and cluttered. It was not at home anywhere; it was
trying too hard; it was miserable; it was a little sickly; it was literary;
and it couldn't say anything simply. All other American writing was
trying to get into one form or another, and no writer except Joe

Gould seemed to have imagination enough to understand that if the worst came to the worst you didn't need to have any form at all. You didn't need to put what you had to say into a poem, an essay, a story, or a novel. All you had to do was say it." Not long after this issue of *Newsstand* came out, someone stopped Gould on Eighth Street and showed him Saroyan's endorsement of his work. Gould shrugged his shoulders. He had been on a spree and had lost his false teeth, and at the moment he was uninterested in literary matters. After thinking it over, however, he decided to call on Saroyan and ask him for help in getting some teeth. He found out somehow that Saroyan was living at the Hampshire House, on Central Park South. The doorman there followed Gould into the lobby and asked him what he wanted. Gould told him that he had come to see William Saroyan. "Do you know Mr. Saroyan?" the doorman asked. "Why, no," Gould said, "but that's all right. He's a disciple of mine." "What do you mean, disciple?" asked the doorman. "I mean," said Gould, "that he's a literary disciple of mine. I want to ask him to buy me some teeth." "Teeth?" asked the doorman. "What do you mean, teeth?" "I mean some store teeth," Gould said. "Some false teeth." "Come this way," said the doorman, gripping Gould's arm and ushering him to the street. Later Freeman arranged a meeting, and the pair spent several evenings together in bars. "Saroyan kept saying he wanted to hear all about the Oral History," Gould says, "but I never got a chance to tell him. He did all the talking. I couldn't get a word in edgewise."

AS LONG AS HE can remember, Gould has been perplexed by his own personality. There are a number of autobiographical essays in the Oral History, and he says that all of them are attempts to explain himself to himself. In one, "Why I Am Unable To Adjust Myself To Civilization, Such As It Is, or Do, Don't, Do, Don't, A Hell Of A Note," he came to the conclusion that his shyness was responsible for everything. "I am introvert and extrovert all rolled in one," he wrote, "a warring mixture of the recluse and the Sixth Avenue auctioneer. One foot says do, the other says don't. One foot says shut your mouth, the other says bellow like a bull. I am painfully shy, but try not to let people know it. They would take advantage of me." Gould keeps his shyness well hidden. It is evident only when he is cold sober. In that state he is silent, suspicious, and constrained, but a couple of beers or a single jigger of gin will untie his tongue and put a leer on his face. He is extraordinarily responsive to alcohol. "On a hot night," he says, "I can walk up and down in front of a gin mill for ten minutes, breathing real deep, and get a jag on."

Even though Gould requires only a few drinks, getting them is sometimes quite a task. Most evenings he prowls around the saloons and dives on the west side of the Village, on the lookout for curiosity-seeking tourists from whom he can cadge beers, sandwiches, and small sums of money. If he is unable to find anyone approachable in the tumultuous saloons around Sheridan Square, he goes over to Sixth Avenue and works north, hitting the Jericho Tavern, the Village Square Bar & Grill, the Belmar, Goody's, and the Rochambeau. He has a routine. He doesn't enter a place unless it is crowded. After he is in, he bustles over to the telephone booth and pretends to look up a number. While doing this, he scrutinizes the customers. If he sees a prospect, he goes over and says, "Let me introduce myself. The name is Joseph Ferdinand Gould, a graduate of Harvard, *magna cum difficultate,* class of 1911, and chairman of the board of Weal and Woe, Incorporated. In exchange for a drink, I'll recite a poem, deliver a lecture, argue a point, or take off my shoes and imitate a sea gull. I prefer gin, but beer will do." Gould is by no means a bum. He feels that the entertainment he provides is well worth whatever he is able to cadge. He doesn't fawn, and he is never grateful. If he is turned down politely, he shrugs his shoulders and leaves the place. However, if the prospect passes a remark like "Get out of here, you bum," Gould turns on him, no matter how big he is, and gives him a shrill, nasal, scurrilous tongue-lashing. He doesn't care what he says. When he loses his temper, he becomes fearless. He will drop his portfolio, put up his fists, and offer to fight men who could kill him with one halfhearted blow. If he doesn't find an audience on the trip up Sixth, he turns west on

Eleventh and heads for the Village Vanguard, in a cellar on Seventh Avenue South. The Vanguard was once a sleazy rendezvous for arty people, but currently it is a thriving night club. Gould and the proprietor, a man named Max Gordon, have known each other for many years and are on fairly good terms much of the time. Gould always hits the Vanguard last. He is sure of it, and he keeps it in reserve. Since it became prosperous, the place annoys him. He goes down the stairs and says, "Hello, Max, you dirty capitalist. I want a bite to eat and a beer. If I don't get it, I'll walk right out on the dance floor and throw a fit." "Go argue with the cook," Gordon tells him. Gould goes into the kitchen, eats whatever the cook gives him, drinks a couple of beers, fills a bag with bread crumbs, and departs.

Despite his shyness, Gould has a great fondness for parties. There are many people in the Village who give big parties fairly often. Among them are a rich and idiosyncratic old doctor, a rich old spinster, a famous stage designer, a famous theatrical couple, and numbers of painters and sculptors and writers and editors and publishers. As often as not, when Gould finds out that any of these people are giving a party, he goes, and as often as not he is allowed to stay. Usually he keeps to himself for a while, uneasily smoking one cigarette after another and stiff as a board with tenseness. Sooner or later, however, impelled by a drink or two and by the desperation of the ill at ease, he begins to throw his weight around. He picks out the prettiest woman in the room, goes over, bows, and kisses her hand. He tells discreditable stories about himself. He becomes exuberant; suddenly, for no reason at all, he cackles with pleasure and jumps up and clicks his heels together. Presently he shouts, "All in favor of a one-man floor show, please say 'Aye'!" If he gets the slightest encouragement, he strips to the waist and does a hand-clapping, foot-stamping dance which he says he learned on a Chippewa reservation in North Dakota and which he calls the Joseph Ferdinand Gould Stomp. While dancing, he chants an old Salvation Army song, "There Are Flies on Me, There Are Flies on You, but There Are No Flies on Jesus." Then he imitates a sea gull. He pulls off his shoes and socks and takes awkward, headlong skips about the room, flapping his arms and letting out a piercing caw with every skip. As a child he had several pet gulls, and he still spends many Sundays on the end of a fishing pier at Sheepshead Bay observing gulls; he claims he has such a thorough understanding of their cawing that he can translate poetry into it. "I have translated a number of Henry Wadsworth Longfellow's poems into sea gull," he says.

Inevitably, at every party Gould goes to, he gets up on a chair or a table and delivers some lectures. These lectures are extracts from chapters of the Oral History. They are brief, but he gives them lengthy titles, such as "Drunk as a Skunk, or How I Measured the Heads of Fifteen Hundred Indians in Zero Weather" and "The Dread Tomato Habit, or Watch Out! Watch Out! Down with Dr. Gallup!" He is skeptical about statistics. In the latter lecture, using statistics he claims he found in financial sections in newspapers, he proves that "the eating of tomatoes by railroad engineers was responsible for fifty-three per cent of the train wrecks in the United States during the last seven years." When Gould arrives at a party, people who have never seen him before usually take one look at him and edge away. Before the evening is over, however, a few of them almost always develop a kind of puzzled respect for him; they get him in a corner, ask him questions, and try to determine what is wrong with him. Gould enjoys this. "When you came over and kissed my hand," a young woman told him one night, "I said to myself, 'What a nice old gentleman.' A minute later I looked around and you were bouncing up and down with your shirt off, imitating a wild Indian. I was shocked. Why do you have to be such an exhibitionist?" "Madam," Gould said, "it is the duty of the bohemian to make a spectacle of himself. If my informality leads you to believe that I'm a rum-dumb, or that I belong in Bellevue, hold fast to that belief, hold fast, hold fast, and show your ignorance."

GOULD IS A NATIVE of Norwood, Massachusetts, a suburb of Boston. He comes from a family of physicians. His grandfather, Joseph Ferdinand Gould, for whom he was named, taught in the

Harvard Medical School and had a practice in Boston. His father, Clarke Storer Gould, was a general practitioner in Norwood. He served as a captain in the Army Medical Corps and died of blood poisoning in a camp in Ohio during the First World War. The family was well-to-do until Gould was about grown, when his father invested unwisely in the stock of an Alaska land company. Gould says he went to Harvard only because it was a family custom. "I did not want to go," he wrote in one of his autobiographical essays. "It had been my plan to stay home and sit in a rocking chair on the back porch and brood." He says that he was an undistinguished student. Some of his classmates were Conrad Aiken, the poet; Howard Lindsay, the playwright and actor; Gluyas Williams, the cartoonist; and Richard F. Whitney, former president of the New York Stock Exchange. His best friends were three foreign students—a Chinese, a Siamese, and an Albanian.

Gould's mother had always taken it for granted that he would become a physician, but after getting his A.B. he told her he was through with formal education. She asked him what he intended to do. "I intend to stroll and ponder," he said. He passed most of the next three years strolling and pondering on the ranch of an uncle in Canada. In 1913, in an Albanian restaurant in Boston named the Scanderbeg, whose coffee he liked, he became acquainted with Theofan S. Noli, an archimandrite of the Albanian Orthodox Church, who interested him in Balkan politics. In February, 1914, Gould startled his family by announcing that he planned to devote the rest of his life to collecting funds to free Albania. He founded an organization in Boston called the Friends of Albanian Independence, enrolled a score or so of dues-paying members, and began telegraphing and calling on bewildered newspaper editors in Boston and New York City, trying to persuade them to print. long treatises on Albanian affairs written by Noli. After about eight months of this, Gould was sitting in the Scanderbeg one night, drinking coffee and listening to a group of Albanian factory workers argue in their native tongue about Balkan politics, when he suddenly came to the conclusion that he was about to have a nervous breakdown. "I began to twitch uncontrollably and see double," he says. From that night on his interest in Albania slackened.

After another period of strolling and pondering, Gould took up eugenics. He has forgotten exactly how this came about. In any case, he spent the summer of 1915 as a student in eugenical field work at the Eugenics Record Office at Cold Spring Harbor, Long Island. This organization, endowed by the Carnegie Institution, was engaged at that time in making studies of families of hereditary defectives, paupers, and town nuisances in several highly inbred communities. Such people were too prosaic for Gould; he decided to specialize in Indians. That winter he went out to North Dakota and measured the heads of a thousand Chippewas on the Turtle Mountain Reservation and of five hundred Mandans on the Fort Berthold Reservation. Nowadays, when Gould is asked why he took these measurements, he changes the subject, saying, "The whole matter is a deep scientific secret." He was happy in North Dakota. "It was the most rewarding period of my life," he says. "I'm a good horseman, if I do say so myself, and I like to dance and whoop, and the Indians seemed to enjoy having me around. I was afraid they'd think I was batty when I asked for permission to measure their noggins, but they didn't mind. It seemed to amuse them. Indians are the only true aristocrats I've ever known. They ought to run the country, and we ought to be put on the reservations." After seven months of reservation life, Gould ran out of money. He returned to Massachusetts and tried vainly to get funds for another head-measuring expedition. "At this juncture in my life," he says, "I decided to engage in literary work." He came to New York City and got a job as assistant Police Headquarters reporter for the *Evening Mail*. One morning in the summer of 1917, after he had been a reporter for about a year, he was basking in the sun on the back steps of Headquarters, trying to overcome a hangover, when the idea for the Oral History blossomed in his mind. He promptly quit his job and began writing. "Since that fateful morning," he once said, in a moment of exaltation, "the Oral History has been my rope and my scaffold, my bed and my board, my wife and my floozy, my wound and the salt on it, my whiskey and my aspirin, and my rock and my salvation. It is the only thing that matters a damn to me. All else is dross."

GOULD SAYS THAT HE RARELY has more than a dollar at any one time, and that he doesn't particularly care. "As a rule," he says, "I despise money." However, there is a widely held belief in the Village that he is rich and that he receives an income from inherited property in New England. "Only an old millionaire could afford to go around as shabby as you," a bartender told him recently. "You're one of those fellows that die in doorways and when the cops search them their pockets are just busting with bankbooks. If you wanted to, I bet you could step over to the West Side Savings Bank right this minute and draw out twenty thousand dollars." After the death of his mother in 1939, Gould did come into some money. Close friends of his say that it was less than a thousand dollars and that he spent it in less than a month, wildly buying drinks all over the Village for people he had never seen before. "He seemed miserable with money in his pockets," Gordon, the proprietor of the Vanguard, says. "When it was all gone, it seemed to take a load off his mind." While Gould was spending his inheritance, he did one thing that satisfied him deeply. He bought a big, shiny radio and took it out on Sixth Avenue and kicked it to pieces. He has never cared for the radio. "Five minutes of the idiot's babble that comes out of those machines," he says, "would turn the stomach of a goat."

During the twenties and the early thirties Gould occasionally interrupted his work on the Oral History to pose for classes at the Art Students' League and to do book-reviewing for newspapers and magazines. He says there were periods when he lived comfortably on the money he earned this way. Burton Rascoe, literary editor of the old *Tribune,* gave him a lot of work. In an entry in "A Bookman's Daybook," which is a diary of happenings in the New York literary world in the twenties, Rascoe told of an experience with Gould. "I once gave him a small book about the American Indians to review," Rascoe wrote, "and he brought me back enough manuscript to fill three complete editions of the Sunday *Tribune.* I especially honor him because, unlike most reviewers, he has never dogged me with inquiries as to why I never run it. He had his say, which was considerable, about the book, the author, and the subject, and there for him the matter ended." Gould says that he quit book-reviewing because he felt that it was beneath his dignity to compete with machines. "The Sunday *Times* and the Sunday *Herald Tribune* have machines that review books," he says. "You put a book in one of those machines and jerk down a couple of levers and a review drops out." In recent years Gould has got along on less than five dolllars in actual money a week. He has a number of friends—Malcolm Cowley, the writer and editor; Aaron Siskind, the documentary photographer; Cummings, the poet; and Gordon, the night-club proprietor, are a few—who give him small sums of money regularly. No matter what they think of the Oral History, all these people have great respect for Gould's pertinacity.

GOULD HAS A POOR OPINION of most of the writers and poets and painters and sculptors in the Village, and doesn't mind saying so. Because of his outspokenness he has never been allowed to join any of the art, writing, cultural, or ism organizations. He has been trying for ten years to join the Raven Poetry Circle, which puts on the poetry exhibition in Washington Square each summer and is the most powerful organization of its kind in the Village, but he has been blackballed every time. The head of the Ravens is a retired New York Telephone Company employee named Francis Lambert McCrudden. For many years Mr. McCrudden was a collector of coins from coin telephones for the telephone company. He is a self-educated man and very idealistic. His favorite theme is the dignity of labor, and his major work is an autobiographical poem called "The Nickel Snatcher." "We let Mr. Gould attend our readings, and I wish we could let him join, but we simply can't," Mr. McCrudden once said. "He isn't serious about poetry. We serve wine at our readings, and that is the only reason he attends. He sometimes insists on reading foolish poems of his own, and it gets on your nerves. At our Religious Poetry Night he demanded permission to recite a poem he had written entitled 'My Religion.' I told him to go ahead, and this is what he recited:

> *'In winter I'm a Buddhist,*
> *And in summer I'm a nudist.'*

And at our Nature Poetry Night he begged to recite a poem of his entitled 'The Sea Gull.' I gave him permission, and he jumped out of his chair and began to wave his arms and leap about and scream, 'Scree-eek! Scree-eek! Scree-eek!' It was upsetting. We are serious poets and we don't approve of that sort of behavior." In the summer of 1942 Gould picketed the Raven exhibition, which was held on the fence of a tennis court on Washington Square South. In one hand he carried his portfolio and in the other he held a placard on which he had printed: "JOSEPH FERDINAND GOULD, HOT-SHOT POET FROM POETVILLE, A REFUGEE FROM THE RAVENS. POETS OF THE WORLD, IGNITE! YOU HAVE NOTHING TO LOSE BUT YOUR BRAINS!" Now and then, as he strutted back and forth, he would take a leap and then a skip and say to passers-by, "Would you like to hear what Joe Gould thinks of the world and all that's in it? Scree-eek! Scree-eek! Scree-eek!"

(1942)

A Spism and a Spasm

A GARRULOUS OLD SOUTHERNER, the Reverend Mr. James Jefferson Davis Hall, is the greatest and the most frightening street preacher in the city. He is an Episcopal priest in good standing, but he hasn't had a church since 1904. "The gutter is my pulpit," he says, "and the roaring traffic is my pipe organ. Halleluiah!" He has preached in the streets and squares of Manhattan for twenty years. Before coming here, he had been, successively, a rector in several cotton-gin towns in Alabama, a convict-camp chaplain, and the superintendent of a nickel-a-meal, dime-a-flop mission for down-and-outs in Philadelphia. Hall used to preach in Wall Street at noon, in Madison Square or Union Square in the afternoon, and in Columbus Circle at night, but for the last seven years he has concentrated on the theatrical district, an area which he once described as "the belly and the black heart of that Great Whore of Babylon and mother of abominations, the city of New York." He has a little band of disciples, the majority of whom are elderly spinsters or widows, and they sometimes refer to him as the Bishop of Times Square.

Every fair evening, after a dinner which customarily consists of an onion, a bulb of garlic, and a head of cabbage, all raw, he leaves his flat in a tenement on Forty-fifth Street, just east of Ninth Avenue, and walks around for three or four hours, shouting at people and threatening them with the delirium tremens, the electric chair, potter's field, and the blue and bubbly flames of hell. As a rule, he goes forth alone, carrying a couple of oilcloth banners, a batch of newspaper clippings about women suicides neatly pasted on pieces of cardboard, and a pocketful of tracts of his own composition. He has written and published scores of tracts; among them are "Seven Communists the Night Before DEATH," "A Conversation Between a Whiskey Flask and a Cigarette," and "The Cry of the Meat-eaters is 'MORE HOSPITALS!' " Hall is especially outraged by drunken women, and he edges up to every one he sees and hands her a suicide clipping. "It's a souvenir of the Great White Way, sister," he told one woman not long ago, "a souvenir and a warning. Nay, nay! Don't throw it down. Put it in your purse and read it the first thing in the morning. Are you an actress? I bet you're an actress! You're riding on the hell-bound train, sister, right up with the engineer. Next stop, the padded cell! Next stop, the Bellevue morgue!" He despises the theatre and has an idea that most of the drunken women he encounters are actresses; the very word "actress," when he says it, sounds sinister.

Hall has a frantic voice. When lifted, particularly in a dimmed-out street, it is extraordinarily disquieting. "I can speak on any old subject, just about, and make my audience uneasy," he once said. "A street preacher's job is to frighten people—shake them up, put the everlasting fear of God into them, and I reckon my voice is my best asset." He developed a quality of hysteria in it years ago in Alabama by going deep into a cypress swamp for an hour or so a day and screaming warnings of one kind or another at an imaginary crowd. "Look out! Look out!" he would scream. "Here comes a mad dog running loose! Fire! Fire! The barn's on fire!" "After a while," he says, "I got so good I scared myself."

His appearance is also an asset. He is tall and bony, with sunken cheeks, haunted eyes, a pale face, and a grim, cackling laugh. He is a bachelor. He likes to be asked his age. "I'm seventy-nine," he says. "No aches or pains, no pills or powders, no doctors or drugstores." His hair is white and unkempt, and he has a mustache and a goatee, both badly trimmed; he brags that he hasn't put foot in a barber shop in twenty-some-odd years. He owns a set of barber's tools which he ordered from Sears Roebuck, and once a month he and a colleague, an old colporteur from Staten Island, get together and cut each other's hair. He disapproves of barber shops because he thinks they charge too much and because of what he calls "the shame and the disgrace of the manicure woman." "I won't be seen in a place," he says, "that has a pretty woman a-sitting in there for the pure and simple purpose of holding hands with any man that'll pay the price. No good can come of that."

Hall is fully as opinionated on a number of other subjects. For example, he is opposed to the use of coffins (he calls them "boxes" or "bone boxes"), and sometimes he puzzles a street audience by denouncing "the funeral-parlor trust." He thinks that people should be buried in winding sheets, as in Biblical times. Fifteen years ago he got the directors of the Elmwood Cemetery, in Birmingham, Alabama, in which he owns a plot, to sign a document permitting him, when the time comes, to be put away in this manner. "I'm not a reactionary," he says. "I wouldn't be against the coffin custom if they were made out of old packing cases and sold for two or three dollars. That would be all right. If coffins just *have* to be used, they should be stacked on top of each other, a whole family in one grave. Think of the saving in space! Otherwise, in a few more generations the U.S.A. will be one vast and widespread cemetery." Hall is also opposed to soda fountains. "First the sody fountain," he says. "Then comes the saloon. Ice water, milk shakes, ginger ale, beer, hot toddies, straight whiskey, the D.T.'s—those are the steps the drinker takes." He is a confident prohibitionist. He is convinced that, one way or another, liquor will be illegal within five years. He corresponds with other street preachers all over the country, and recently, to one of them, he wrote, "My dear brother in Christ: I am so sure of Prohibition I have quit fretting about it. I have a good, bedrock reason that if the Whiskey Trust knew about it they would be quite agitated. This is it. For years upon years every time I brought up the subject of Prohibition on the streets of New York the people would snicker and snort. Well, they do not snicker any more. Nay, nay. Quite the contrary. They look serious, and some nod their heads. Even the liquor-head sots, they know it's coming. They feel it in their bones. Over a year ago Dr. Gallup said that thirty-six per cent of the people were ripe and ready to vote for it. Facts and figures. And the per cent is rising, rising, rising, like water in a tub. Five more years, I estimate, and we'll put King Whiskey in the tomb, R.I.P. And the first grand rascal that D-double-dares to open up a speak-easy—why, the good Christians will descend on him and pull him apart."

Other institutions Hall disapproves of are laundries and cleaning and pressing establishments. "This is a democratic country," he says, "and no able-bodied man should have the right to call on some other man to scrub his duds. If people in general, even the highly educated, even Nicholas Murray Butler, had to bend over a washtub once a week, it would give them some sense of proportion; it would keep them from getting biggity." Hall does his own washing and ironing, and now and then he takes a flatiron and puts some crooked creases in his trousers. He is shabbily dressed. He buys his suits in a Ninth Avenue rummage store. He paid $7.15 for his last one, and a hat he has worn for almost three years cost thirty-five cents. "It's still as good as new," he says. He wears a clerical collar, a clerical shirt, and a gold cross. The cross was given to him by a group of converted highwaymen, safe-crackers, and cop-killers in Flattop, an Alabama convict camp, where he was once a chaplain. He keeps a celluloid badge with only a red question mark on it pinned to his left lapel. When asked what it signifies, he narrows his eyelids and says, "Friend, every step you take, Death walks right in behind you. No matter how fat and sassy you may be, you're living every second on the lip of the grave. The question is, 'Are you ready for the shroud and the box, are you ready for the Judgment Day?' "

HALL USUALLY BEGINS AN EVENING'S WORK by delivering brief harangues—he calls them "halleluiah hypodermics"—in the doorways of a dozen or so Eighth Avenue saloons. He never goes inside a saloon and he never tries to take up a collection; he just stands in the doorway and shouts. Bartenders are used to him. They address him as "Dad," "Reverend," or "Shadrach." One evening recently he stopped first at the Dublin Restaurant, a saloon just above Forty-second Street. He stuck his head in, cleared his throat, and cried out, "Distilled damnation and liquid death, that's what you're a-swilling and a-guzzling!" Many of the people along the bar abruptly turned around. While they stared, he unrolled one of his oilcloth banners. Lettered on it in red was this message: "PUT DOWN THAT GLASS AND GO. THE SALOON IS THE GATE TO HELL. DREADFUL ARE THE MORNINGS OF A DRUNKARD. PREPARE TO MEET THY GOD." (Hall is a good amateur sign-painter, and he makes his own banners.) Holding up the banner, Hall shouted, "Brothers! Sisters! That's not the brass rail you're resting your feet upon. Nay, nay! That's the third rail! Whiskey and beer! Wrack and ruin! Death and destruction! The cup that stings, the frolic, the midnight brawl, the strait jacket! Hark to the destiny of the whiskey drinker: forsaken by his friends, his furniture seized, his wife broken-hearted, his babies starving, his liver a sieve, his mind a tangle, his nerves a snarl, not a shoe to his foot. Don't you people ever sleep? Go home! Go to bed! Are you ready for the Judgment Day? You may be taken suddenly. On your way home, rooting and tooting, drunk and disorderly, *you may be taken!* You, sister, a-sitting there in that booth with a cigarette in one hand and a glass of distilled damnation in the other, a sorry sight, are *you* ready?" Hall was interrupted by one of the bartenders, who walked up to the front end of the bar and said, "O.K., Dad, break it up. That's enough racket for one night." "Why, howdy-do, young man, howdy-do," Hall said. "Haven't seen you in quite some time. Have you been on the day shift? Be sure your sins will find you out. I'll go, but I'll be back." "Yes, indeed," said the bartender sadly, "I'm sure you will."

Holding his banner aloft, Hall proceeded up the avenue. In an hour and a half, after making stops at O'Donnell's, Kieran & Dineen's, Larry's, the Eagle Bar, Gilhuly's, Pete Moran's, the Ranch Bar, Morahan's, McGreevy's, Mickey Walker's, and the Ringside, he reached Fiftieth Street, which is about as far uptown as he ever goes. En route he passed out a couple of dozen tracts. He came across one reeling woman and tried to make her take a suicide clipping, but she flung it down and said, "Get out of here, you old wolf. Go to hell, you old wolf." "You'll have to excuse me, sister," Hall told her. "I'm not going your way."

On Fiftieth Street, Hall headed east. Reaching the northeast corner of Broadway and Fiftieth, where most nights horse-race gamblers congregate along the curb to argue over the racing charts in the early edition of the *Mirror,* he got out his second banner and unrolled it. It said, "GAMBLERS ARE THIEVES AND WILL STEAL. SATAN AND THE GAMBLER WALK HAND IN HAND. SMOKING WILL KILL YOU. WHERE WILL YOU SPEND ETERNITY?" Displaying both banners, he stood for about ten minutes in front of the Paddock Bar & Grill, a hangout of racing people, staring upward with a soulful expression on his face, not saying a word. Then, as is his custom, he started south on Broadway, a banner upheld in each hand, walking slowly and preaching, most of the time at the top of his voice.

To stay in one spot on Broadway and preach requires a Police Department permit; by keeping in motion, Hall gets along without one. He walks close to the building line, so that his banners can be read by the lights in the show windows. Even in the busiest blocks, he is seldom caught in a crowd; flustered by his voice, people give him plenty of room. He rarely plans a street sermon but depends upon whatever comes into his head. Occasionally he sings a snatch of a hymn or quotes a verse of Scripture, usually a chilly one from Job, the Revelation, or the Lamentations. Like Father Divine, he makes up words. Also like Divine, he frequently pairs words of similar meanings—"hoot and howl," "shudder and shake," "masses and multitudes," "swill and swig." He deeply accents the first syllable in many words; "disturbed and perturbed," for example, becomes "*dee*sturbed and *pee*turbed."

He is profoundly discursive. This particular evening, in the course of one block, the block between Fiftieth and Forty-ninth, he made the following remarks: "A lost city, hungry for destruction, aching for destruction, the entire population in a fuss and a fret, a twit and a twitter, a squit and a squat, a hip and a hop, a snig and a snaggle, a spism and a spasm, a sweat and a swivet. Can't wait for night to fall, can't wait for day to break. Even the church bells sound jangly in New York City; they ring them too fast. And the women! Into *every*thing! Free livers! They've gone hog-proud and hog-wild. Wearing britches, wearing uniforms, straining their joints for generations to come with high-heel shoes. They're turning into Indians. Their mouths smeared and smiddled and smoodled with paint, *and* their cheeks, *and* their fingernails. And what color do they pick? Old Scratch's favorite. The mark of the beast, that's what it is. And they've taken to painting their toenails! Why don't they get a bucket of paint and turn it over on themselves, top to bottom, like a whooping red Indian, and be done with it? Save time and trouble. Oh, my! Tell you what I saw last Sunday! I visited St. Bartholomew's, and there was an old sister in the pew in front of me with her hair dyed *blue,* and I mean *blue!* Call the doctor!

"My name is Daddy Hall, and I love you one and all. An old-time preacher, believes *every*thing in the Bible, including the crosses on the t's, the dots on the i's. I'm just a stranger here; heaven's my home. Don't claim to be a highly educated man, but I can still read Latin; used to read Greek. If put to the test, I can recite Shakespeare. No degrees but D.D.—Divine Dynamiter; S.S.—Shining Saint; M.A.—Mightily Altered. If your troubles are more than you can bear, give me a ring—Circle 6-6483, the sanctified telephone number. I'll preach you a sermon on the telephone. I pray for you, and I warn you, but all you care for is gluttony, whiskey, movie shows, Reno divorces, cocaine dope, silk underwear, birth control, and stocks and bonds. That, and the almighty dollar; you can't get enough. Like a fine old lady said to me, 'The people this day and time, if the government was to let them back a ten-ton truck up to the front door of the U.S. Mint and haul off a bogging-down load from the million-dollar-bill department, that wouldn't by no means satisfy them.' That it wouldn't! Nay, nay! They'd be back next morning bright and early a-scratching on the door like a dog, a-begging and a-pleading for just one more load. The root of all evil. And what kind of music do you hear now days? 'Praise the Lord and Pass the Ammunition,' that's what you hear. They play it in the saloons, and they dance to it! Blasphemous music, that's what it is, blasphemous and brimstony! It's taking the Lord's name in vain. That big, stout, fool-faced man over yonder at the curb is a-laughing at me. He thinks I'm funny. Let him laugh! As the crackling of thorns under a pot, so is the laughter of fools. He probably thinks he's highly educated. The big professors these days, the highly educated, they don't believe in sin. Oh, no! It's just your glands. Glands, indeed! Glib, glab, gloody-doody! Just wait until those glandy professors hit the fiery pit, the bottomless, shoreless pond of roaring fire; they'll wish they'd kept off the subject of sin.

"The people have strayed, and God is put out and provoked, and He has plunged us into war as a test and a trial, a punishment. It's time for the locusts and the plague of boils. Famine! Food rationing! Why, it's all foretold. 'The tongue of the sucking child cleaveth to the roof of his mouth for thirst. The young children ask for bread, and no man breaketh it unto them. They that did feed delicately are desolate in the street.' People eat too much, anyway. We need a famine or two. Personally, I'm a dead-set vegetarian. There's nothing so fine in the eating line as a good green vegetable—root, stalk, and leaf. The pictures stuck up in front of these theatres along here are a scarlet shame and a purple disgrace. Grown women with their stomachs showing. Why, their very navels are showing. It's a vexation to the men. It puts thoughts of a certain nature in their minds. Sodom and Gomorrah, that's what it is. 'Rock of ages, cleft for me; let me hide myself in Thee.' My name is Daddy Hall, and I love you one and all. If suicide is on your mind, give me a ring. I'll tell you what to do. Write it down—Circle 6-6483. Look at that poor brother. He's certainly under the influence; he's trying to walk on both sides of the street at once. I reckon he was bit by the brewer's dog. He looks like he had quite a tilt and a tussle with the brewer's big hungry dog. At this hour of the night, all over town, the people are pouring it in—rivers of highballs, rivers of cocktails, whole train-loads of distilled damnation; they're just about washing their faces in it, the boozy, bedaddled old buzzards.

"A pickpocket I converted here the other day told me they have a school out in Chicago, a pocket-picking school, and the beginning rule they teach is 'No stimulants!' Have to keep their heads clear. Why, friends, you set a bucket of beer in front of a pig and he'll grunt and walk away. Highballs! Cocktails! Winston Churchill! I read in *Life* where it said he drinks a quart of champagne a day and nobody knows how much Scotch whiskey in between. Thinks nothing of it! Just like a Christian man drinks buttermilk. A pig won't touch it, nor a pickpocket, but Mr. Churchill, he'll get right down and wallow in it. A fine example for the soldier boys! Oh, yes! Oh, yes! The city of New York is just about ready for a great religious upswelling. It's a bud, getting bigger by the minute. Pretty soon now it's going to bust wide open and blossom. People are slapping the dust off their Bibles, and regretting their misdeeds, and getting ready for the wrath to come. Back before Pearl Harbor there wasn't much use passing out tracts on the street. People would throw them down and trample on them. Now they fold them up and put them in their pockets. That they do. It's coming! It's on the way! My name is Daddy Hall, and I love you one and all. . . ."

Hall kept this up, even while crossing streets, all the way down to Broadway and Forty-second. There, hoarse but happy, he rolled up his banners and called it a night. "I warned them," he said to a policeman. "I put the fear of God into them. Now I'm going home, and I'm going to eat me a big Bermuda onion and drink me a glass of pure, God-given water. And I'm going to bed. And during the night, if there's a doomsday rumbling in the earth and a flicker of fire in the sky, I'll be ready."

HALL HAS A SOUND REASON for believing in the imminence of a religious upswelling in the city. Off and on, ever since he came here, he has been in the habit, in the course of his street sermons, of announcing his telephone number and inviting people in trouble to call him. "I'll comfort you," he says. "I'll preach you an old-time sermon on the telephone." For seventeen years there was no response. Finally, one morning in December, 1939, a stranger called. He was worried about his daughter. She was sixteen; she had gone out with a sailor without permission, she had drunk some beer, and so on. He asked Hall to pray for her soul. Hall did, then and there. Later in the day the man's wife called and put the wayward daughter on the telephone. Hall gave her such a rampant description of hell that she began to sob and dropped the receiver. The wife picked it up and said, as well as Hall can remember, "Why, Reverend, you made her cry! Why, she's crying like her little heart will break. Thank you! Oh, thank you so much! I'm *so* grateful." "Don't mention it, sister," Hall told her. "If you have friends or neighbors with trouble on their mind, tell them to phone me. Pass the word around." The woman said she certainly would. Next day Hall got four calls from strangers, all wanting a telephone sermon. The third day, according to his records, he got seven. The fourth day he got sixteen. "All of a sudden, among the humble and the heavy-hearted," Hall says, "the fame of Daddy Hall began to spread like wildfire. One told another. Something like a chain letter. Wheels within wheels." One of his converts, a scrubwoman, got so interested that she commenced leaving anonymous notes—"There is a message for you at Circle 6-6483"—on desks in the office building in which she worked at night. She got other scrubwomen to do the same. When the recipient of one of these notes called, Hall would begin, "Yes, siree-bob, friend, I do have a message for you. Are you prepared to die? Are you ready for the shroud and the box, are you ready for the Judgment Day?" Then, if the caller did not snort and hang up, Hall would preach a brief, violent sermon.

Day by day, the number of calls increased. In a couple of years, Hall was getting around seventy-five a day. He was overjoyed. From 6 A.M. until 7 P.M., he sat beside his telephone, going out to preach in the streets only at night. "Things went along real smooth," he says, "until the Monday after Pearl Harbor. That day I preached until my jaw got stiff. There wasn't a moment's letup. The instant I put the receiver down and caught my breath, the phone rang again. I preached I think it was eighty-three sermons in a row, some over five minutes long, and then my head began to swim. I took the receiver off the hook and went in and flopped down on the bed, all wore out." Presently an investigator from the telephone company knocked on the door, aroused him, and told him that scores of people had complained that they got only a busy signal when they dialled his number. Hall sighed, went to his telephone, and started in again. In the morning he summoned to his apartment six of his disciples, all elderly women who make a practice of handing out his tracts and all lay preachers; they agreed to come to his rescue and take turns on the telephone.

Nowadays, Hall seldom preaches on the telephone more than a couple of dozen times a day; he saves his energy for his saloon harangues and his nightly journey down Broadway. His disciples, who model their sermons on his, handle most of the calls. In return, he gives them carfare, an occasional grassy meal, and his blessing. The most zealous is an Englishwoman named Frances Woodcock. She comes in from Queens each day and preaches from around 8:30 until 11:55 in the morning. Then she hastens around the corner to the Gospel Tabernacle, a Fundamentalist, nondenominational mission on Eighth Avenue, in whose work Hall is a believer, and plays the organ at the noon meeting. Frequently she returns in the afternoon. The sole male helper is Joseph Serafin, an elocutionary Rumanian, who is renting agent for an Eighth Avenue loft building owned by the Tabernacle. He drops in whenever he has an hour or two to spare. Calls are answered constantly from 6 A.M. until midnight, when the receiver is removed. Hall says that more than a hundred and fifty thousand sermons have been preached over his telephone since December, 1939. He estimates that around one-fourth of the callers are curiosity seekers, practical jokers, or the victims of practical jokers. Many of these victims are under the impression that horse-race bets are taken at Circle 6-6483. One practical joker spoke double-talk. After listening to him for a few moments, Hall exclaimed, "Speak out, man, speak out! What *are* you, anyhow, a Mohammedan?" Finally he summoned Serafin, who was in the adjoining room, eating a head of cabbage. "Come here, Serafin," Hall said. "I think I've got a poor Mohammedan brother on the wire. He seems to be in sore distress." Serafin, who is more worldly, listened for a moment or two and then explained double-talk to Hall. "I fixed that brother," Hall says, cackling. "I interrupted him and shouted at him in Latin until he got mad and told me to go to you know where."

Hall quizzes his callers, and has come to the conclusion that the majority are repentant backsliders. "They *had* the old-time religion," he says, "but somewhere along the line they lost it. The war makes them ache to find it again. 'Turn over a new leaf,' I tell them. 'Repent. Pray. Read your Bible. Find an old-time church and go to it. Don't go to one of those Fifth Avenue churches that all they have is weddings.' The most of them are hungry to confess. Oh, my! Some confess to sins I never even heard of before. I hear things I wouldn't discuss with *any*body, not even another preacher. Some call from saloons; while I'm exhorting I can hear the racket from one of those monstrous nickel phonographs a-coming over the wire. Some are lonely, some have sons fighting across the water, some have consciences that hurt and hurt, some are unwed girls that got in a family way after heeding a rascal's promise, some are booze-fighters, some are studying suicide. Oh, I get *more* people now days that are studying suicide."

Some of Hall's more desperate callers insist on conferring with him face to face, and most mornings there are a few sitting in his living room, waiting to be admitted to his study. Hall lives in a cold-water tenement at 360 West Forty-fifth Street, paying $30 a month for five small rooms. He has been there for twelve years. He has one of those rear flats whose entrance is through the kitchen and whose windows overlook a blind court with a single, sooty ailanthus tree in it. His telephone has nine feet of cord; in winter it is kept on a stand near the coal range in the kitchen and in summer it is moved to a desk adjacent to a window in the living room. The telephone costs him only $3.54 a month; since he is a clergyman, he gets a reduction of twenty-five per cent below the basic rate. Hall's study is cluttered. In it are an enamelled iron bed, a radio, a bureau, a couple of straight-back chairs, three tables, and a pigeonhole cabinet which holds bales of tracts. Leaning against the wall in one corner are three collapsible cots. Hall is acquainted with scores of itinerant colporteurs and evangelists, and when they are in New York they sleep in his flat. Sometimes he has so many guests that there are not enough cots to go around and he has to spread pallets on the floor. There is a typewriter on one table, and a great rat's-nest of correspondence and manuscripts. Hall is editor of a tiny monthly magazine, the *Church Militant,* which sells for a quarter a year and has thirteen hundred subscribers. The policy of this paper is extraordinary—it favors prohibition, savings banks, osteopathy, and women preachers; it opposes church suppers, vaccination, bingo, and aspirin tablets.

Under the iron bed is a pile of newspapers, mostly tabloids. Hall rarely buys a newspaper; these were picked up by his disciples off subway seats. He says that when the pile gets large enough to bother with he goes through it and clips out stories proving that the wages of sin is death, such as stories about women suicides and electrocutions at Sing Sing; he has two bureau drawers full of clippings. One wall is covered with snapshots of Hall converts. On another wall are two oilcloth signs. One says, "LOST: A HUMAN SOUL OF UNTOLD VALUE. ANYONE BRINGING SAME TO CHRIST WILL BE RICHLY REWARDED." The other says, "CIGARETTE SMOKERS WILL PLEASE CRAWL INTO THE STOVE AND OPEN THE BACK DRAFT." Hall is an enemy of tobacco. "My daddy was murdered by the tobacco trust," he says. "He was a cigar smoker and he dropped dead long before his time." Hall occasionally marries couples in his study, most of whom came to know him by way of the telephone. The study is cleaned for weddings, but not often otherwise. A disciple once pointed at one of the windowsills, on which grit and dust was half an inch thick, and said, "That's a mess if ever I saw one. Why don't you dust it off?" "I don't dust off windowsills," Hall said indignantly. "I dust off human souls."

HALL'S OUTLOOK ON LIFE IS A PRODUCT of the grayness of the Reconstruction period in the South. He was born in 1864, during the winter of the fourth year of the Civil War, in Greenville, Alabama, a small county seat. His family has been in the South since pre-Revolutionary days. His father's forebears came from Scotland, his mother's from Holland. The family, once affluent, was impoverished by the war, in which Hall's father, Dr. James Woodward Hall, served as a Confederate Army physician. "I had a real stony childhood," Hall says. "I was one of eleven children, and there was never enough to go around, duds or vittles. I didn't wear shoes until I was eighteen, except Sundays and cold spells. I went through the fifth grade, living on grits and greens, and then I had to stay home and plow cotton. I plowed with an ox. There weren't any mules in that country when I was a young un; the Yankees had shot them all to entertain themselves. We had a hard, hard time." Hall was tutored at night by his mother, who had what he calls "a rock-bottom Latin and Shakespeare education." When he was twenty, he quit the cotton fields and became a schoolteacher.

In Anniston, Alabama, in 1888, he had his first memorable encounter with sin. "I was teaching in a boys' school and rooming and boarding at a hotel, the finest in town," he says. "Some show people by the name of Graw's Dixieland Grand Opera Company came to Anniston and put up at my hotel. I had never been to the theatre and I took a foolish notion to go. I don't know what possessed me to do so. I'm not what you'd call narrow, but oh, my! I was shocked! And that night, back in the hotel, those strutty show women were up and about until fully 2 A.M., a-giggling and a-carrying on. I suspect they drank. I looked out my door and saw one a-tiptoeing down the hall in her nightshift. Her hair was down. It was long, yellow hair, more gold than yellow. I believe until this day that she was on her way to some man's room. I still pray for her; I *do* hope she reformed. Next morning I got on my knees and asked God to forgive me for going to the theatre, and I asked Him to make me a preacher, so I could go forth and fight such wickedness." Hall says that he has never been in a theatre again. He takes great pride in this. Recently, on the Forty-second Street crosstown trolley, he heard one woman say to another, "I haven't been to the theatre in months." Hall leaned across the aisle and said, "Sister, *I* haven't been to the theatre since 1888."

In 1892, when Hall was twenty-eight, he took his school-teaching savings and entered the Protestant Episcopal Seminary in Alexandria, Virginia. Four years later he became an Episcopal priest. He started out with churches in two Alabama small towns, Troy and Union Springs, which are forty miles apart. "I preached one Sunday here," he says, "and the next Sunday yonder." He received $50 a month. In 1904 he was appointed Episcopal chaplain for Pratt City and Flattop, two convict camps on the outskirts of Birmingham, at a salary of $1,000 a year, which is the most he has ever made. Flattop was a Siberia; only the worst criminals were sent there, to work in a coal mine. Hall prepared men for the scaffold, and he has since used his experiences to illustrate many a grisly sermon. He says he converted hundreds. "The best time to convert a convict," he says, "is directly after there's been a hanging. One Good Friday I walked to the scaffold with three train-robbing brothers, and each time the trap was sprung there came forth a certain sound. Ka-chug, *crack!* Ka-chug, *crack!* Ka-chug, *crack!* I went straight from the hanging yard to the cell occupied by Tom Fay, a new convict. Tom was a real boa constrictor; he was the crown prince of the Miller Duncan gang of highwaymen, and he was feared by the whole of Alabama. I described this certain sound to Tom, and I chatted with him on the subject of hell. Lo and behold! Not only did I convert him, but a few months later he became a preacher himself."

Hall's work with convicts got to be well known among evangelists all over the country, and in 1908 he was invited to Philadelphia to take charge of Galilee Mission, on Vine Street. Galilee is a meeting hall and dormitory, supported by Episcopalians, for down-and-outs. It is patterned after the rescue missions on the Bowery. The job paid only $900 a year, but Hall took it. "The main thing I learned at Galilee," he says, "is that the scourges of mankind are adultery, drink, drugs, and doubt. Every night of the year we held a three-hour meeting and the derelicts you might call them stood up, one by one, and testified. They came from every walk of life, even the ministry, but there was a sameness about their confessions—adultery, drink, drugs, or doubt, night after night. Among the derelicts I ran into were sixty-one of the reverend clergy, all sots. I'll say this for the preacher sot. When he hits the bottle, he doesn't do any jackleg, halfway job. He puts his mind to it. He *works* at it. An awful, awful thing to see!" After twelve years as superintendent of Galilee, Hall resigned and became a street preacher. He wandered for four years, seldom staying in one city longer than a couple of weeks. "One night in Los Angeles in 1923," he says, "I decided that I was about ready to unpack my grip and stay a while somewhere, and I asked myself a question. 'Brother Hall,' I said to myself, 'which city is the most wicked city, pluperfect and parboiled, you've ever been in?' Without a bit of hesitation the answer came forth, 'New York, N.Y.' Consequently, I got on a train and came here and took root. If you're determined to fight the devil, you might as well get right up in the front-line trenches."

HALL DIFFERS FROM OTHER STREET PREACHERS in that he never takes up a collection. If he is offered money on the street, he accepts it, but this happens infrequently. "When it comes to religion," he says, "the common run of New York people aren't stingy; they just don't believe in giving anything away." His preaching has been subsidized, ever since he came here, by a succession of old, wealthy, Fundamentalist ladies, most of them of Southern birth. One, for example, the widow of a real-estate man, gave him $75 a month for more than five years, asking only that he preach at noon in front of J. P. Morgan & Company as often as possible. Another, also a widow, who lived at the Plaza, used to hand him an envelope containing from one to five $10 bills every time he went to call on her. In 1930 she gave him $500 and sent him to London to attend the Lambeth Conference. "Once I dropped in on this lady and found her taking a glass of wine," Hall says. "She turned it off by saying it was doctor's orders. Except for wine, she was a good old soul." Since 1933, when Hall reached the retirement age, he has been receiving $50 a month from the Pension Fund of the Episcopal Church.

Among themselves, street preachers are a squabbly lot. Hall is atypical in that he has never fought with his colleagues on matters of doctrine or dogma. "I have preached side by side in Columbus Circle with unknown tonguers, and Jehovah's Witnesses, and Salvation Army soldiers, and Pillar of Fire women, and Father Divine angels, and Happy Am I shouters, and with brothers that had one-man theologies that they thought up for themselves," Hall says, "but I never had any back talk with any of them. Take the matter of baptism. Way I figure, you can sprinkle a man, or you can totally immerse him face forward, sideways, head first, or feet first, and it's all the same, so long as the water is pure and he doesn't drown." The one street speaker with whom Hall has fought a feud is Charles Lee Smith, president of the American Association for the Advancement of Atheism. Smith is also a Southerner. Hall refers to him as the Atheist Pope and has shouted him down in Wall Street, in Union Square, and in the Circle. "It's not so much that he's an atheist," Hall says. "I could overlook that. It's that middle name of his. He was named for Robert E. Lee. Said so himself. How a man named after that great lion-hearted Christian hero General Robert E. Lee could turn into a common, street-corner atheist is more than I can understand." Smith, on the contrary, is fond of Hall. "Next to W. C. Fields," Smith says, "I don't know any man I'd rather listen to than old James Jefferson Davis Hall. I'd pay good money any day to hear him preach his sermon on the D.T.'s. I must've heard him preach that sermon a dozen times, and I've never heard him preach it the same way twice. He digresses quite a lot, and I do enjoy his digressions. They can be really wild." This sermon, "Cases of the D.T.'s I Have Known," is Hall's masterpiece. One of the cases he takes up in the course of it is that of Bobcat Jones, an old song-and-dance man.

"Mr. Jones was a derelict, an old vaudeville actor," Hall says, "and I converted him at the Galilee Mission in 1917, but he backslid. He went on a bat that lasted for weeks, and one day he showed up, a-muttering and a-raving. He was holding his head with both hands; said he was afraid the spiders would crawl in his ears. 'Repent, Mr. Jones!' I said to him. 'Repent!' He began to duck and dodge; said that Old Scratch was throwing a spear at him. I took him up the stairs to the dormitory on the second floor, and no sooner did I get him in bed than he cried out, 'There's an old goat a-coming through the transom. It's the devil. His horns are on fire. Get back there, goat! Don't let that goat butt me!' 'Why, Mr. Jones,' I said, 'I don't see any goat. Repent, repent, and ye shall be saved.' He leaped out of bed and tied three neckties together and he cried out, 'I'm a-going to lasso Old Scratch. I'm a-going to lasso him and tie him down and kick him.' I got him back in bed, but I had a struggle doing so. There was an electric fan in the room, and next he took a notion that the fan was the devil. He picked up an alarm clock and chunked it. It hit the fan and began to ring. And Mr. Jones was a-howling all the time. Oh, my, what a racket! Then he ran over and tried to take hold of the fan, and it scraped his hand, and he leaped backwards about fifteen feet and howled out, 'Old Scratch bit me! Let me out of here!' He shot out of the door, and next thing I knew he fell head over heels down the stairs, hitting every step on the way down. As my good old grandmother a long time ago way back in Alabama would've put it, 'Ass over teakettle,' and it was perfectly all right for my grandmother to use that kind of language, nobody looked down on her for doing so, good old sanctified cow-milking butter-churning biddy-hatching bee-keeping huckleberry-picking hickory-nut-cracking pole-fishing catfish-catching rabbit-trapping snuff-dipping cotton-picking hardworking old countrywoman that she was. She was a living saint, but she was very plainspoken and she was known far and wide for some of her sayings. 'Ass over teakettle,' she used to say about almost anything that happened accidentally. 'Butt, behind, bottom and all!' she used to say. 'Gut, gallus, goozle and all!' So I stood there at the head of the stairs and looked down at Mr. Jones all sprawled out on the floor at the bottom of the stairs, and I was just so afraid that he had hurt himself severely—a broken hip at the very least. He might never walk again! Permanently crippled! Or ruptured on both sides! Ruined! Done for! But nay, nay, in a minute or two the D.T.'s took control of Mr. Jones again, and he got to his feet and began to do a skippy little dance and he sung a song called, 'Cut a Watermelon on My Grave and Let the Juice Soak Through.' " At this point in the sermon Hall slowly shakes his head, and a deeply mournful look comes on his face. "Whiskey! Whiskey! Whiskey!" he exclaims. "I don't even believe in ginger ale!"

(1943)

Lady Olga

*J*ANE BARNELL OCCASIONALLY CONSIDERS HERSELF an outcast and feels that there is something vaguely shameful about the way she makes a living. When she is in this mood, she takes no pride in the fact that she has had a longer career as a sideshow performer than any other American woman and wishes she had never left the drudgery of her grandmother's cotton farm in North Carolina. Miss Barnell is a bearded lady. Her thick, curly beard measures thirteen and a half inches, which is the longest it has ever been. When she was young and more entranced by life under canvas, she wore it differently every year; in those days there was a variety of styles in beards—she remembers the Icicle, the Indian Fighter, the Whisk Broom, and the Billy Goat—and at the beginning of a season she would ask the circus barber to trim hers in the style most popular at the moment. Since it became gray, she has worn it in the untrimmed, House of David fashion.

The business of exhibiting her beard has taken her into every state in the Union. In fact, she has undoubtedly travelled as widely in the United States as any other person, but she has always been too bored to take much notice of her surroundings and probably would not do well with a grammar-school geography quiz. "I been all over everywhere, up, down, and sideways," she says. "I've hit thousands of towns, but I don't remember much about any of them. Half the time I didn't even know what state I was in. Didn't know or care." Miss Barnell is sixty-nine years old and was first put on exhibition shortly after her fourth birthday; she claims she has been bearded since infancy. As Princess Olga, Madame Olga, or Lady Olga, she has worked in the sideshows of at least twenty-five circuses and carnivals for wages ranging between twenty and a hundred dollars a week. She has forgotten the names of some of these outfits; one circus she remembers only as "that ten-car mess on the West Coast where I and my third husband had to knock the sideshow manager on the noggin with a tent stake to get my pay." She started out with a tramp circus, or "mud show," whose rickety, louse-infested wagons were pulled by oxen, and worked her way up to Ringling Brothers and Barnum & Bailey.

She spent six years in the Ringling circus. She was with it last in 1938, when its season was cut short by a strike in Scranton, an occurrence which made her hysterical. Ringling's sideshow, the Congress of Strange People, is as highly esteemed by freaks as the Palace used to be by vaudeville actors, but she would not sign a contract for the 1939 season. It pained her to make this decision; for six consecutive seasons she had occupied the same berth in Old Ninety-six, the Ringling sleeping car for sideshow people, and had grown attached to it. "Once I heard about a man in the penitentiary who broke down and cried when he finished his term and had to leave his cell for the last time," she says. "It had got to be a home to him. That's how I felt about my berth." She turned down the 1939 contract because she had become obsessed with a notion that out on the road she would somehow be forced to join the circus union. Unions frighten her. Although she has never voted, she is a violently opinionated Republican. Also, she is a veteran reader of Hearst newspapers and believes everything she reads in them. She thinks the average union organizer carries a gun and will shoot to kill. When she sees pickets, she immediately crosses to the other side of the street. "Just as sure as I go back to Ringling's, that union will get me," she told a circus official who tried for hours to reason with her, and added, "To tell you the truth, I think that old union is a corporation, like everything else these days." She also has a fear of corporations; to her, they are as sinister as unions. Since she left, Ringling's has been without a bearded lady. Fred Smythe, manager of the Congress, offers her a contract every spring, but she always tells him that she will never again work for the Big Show. This never surprises Smythe. "Short of blasting," he says, "there's no way of getting a fool notion out of the head of a freak. I'd sure like to get her back. She's the only real, old-fashioned bearded lady left in the country. Most bearded ladies are men. Even when they're women, they look like men. Lady Olga is a woman, and she looks like a woman." Smythe says that bearded ladies are not particularly sensational but they are traditional in sideshows, like clowns in the circus itself. "People don't laugh at clowns any more but they want to see them around," he says. "Likewise, if there isn't a bearded lady in a sideshow, people feel there's something lacking."

Miss Barnell has not been on the road since leaving the Big Show but has stuck pretty close to New York City, which, as much as any other place, she considers home. In the winter she works intermittently in the basement sideshow of Hubert's Museum on West Forty-second Street. She has shown her beard in practically every dime museum in the country and likes Hubert's best of all; she has come to look upon it as her winter headquarters. Professor Le Roy Heckler, who operates the Flea Circus concession in Hubert's, is an old friend of hers. They once lived in the same farming community in Mecklenburg County, North Carolina, and she worked in circuses long ago with his father, the late Professor William Heckler, who was a sideshow strong man before he developed a method of educating fleas and established the family business. She has great respect for Le Roy; she calls him "the young Professor" and says she has known him since he was "diaper size." In the summer she divides her time between Hubert's and Professor Sam Wagner's World Circus Side Show, also a dime museum, in Coney Island. She likes Coney because she feels that salt air is good for her asthma; also, she has a high regard for the buttered roasting-ear corn that is sold in stands down there.

On the dime museum circuit she does not work steadily; she works two or three weeks in a row and then lays off for a week. "I don't want to go nuts," she says. In museums, her hours are from 11 A.M. to 11 P.M. There is an average of two shows an hour and during a show she is on the platform from five to ten minutes.

Between appearances, she is free. At Hubert's she kills most of this time dozing in a rocking chair in her dressing room. Sometimes she visits with other performers, usually with Albert-Alberta, the half-man-half-woman. Twice a week she goes into Professor Heckler's booth and watches him feed his fleas. This spectacle always amazes her, although she has seen it scores of times. The Professor rolls up one sleeve, picks the fleas out of their mother-of-pearl boxes with tweezers, and drops them, one by one, on a forearm, where they browse for fifteen minutes. While the fleas are feeding, the Professor reads a newspaper and she smokes a cigarette. They seldom say anything to each other. Taciturn herself, Miss Barnell does not care for talkative people. At least once an afternoon she wraps a scarf around her beard and goes out for coffee or a mug of root beer. She usually goes to the lunchroom in the American Bus Depot, a few doors west of Hubert's. She finds the atmosphere of a bus terminal soothing to her nerves. When showing in Coney Island, she takes brisk turns on the boardwalk between appearances.

In the past, while filling engagements in and around the city, Miss Barnell always lived in small Broadway hotels. A year or so ago she gave up hotel life. One Saturday night, after working late in Hubert's, she walked into a hotel off Times Square in which she had been living since the Ringling strike and a drunk in the lobby saw her and said, "By God, it's the bearded lady!" He followed her to the elevator, shouting, "Beaver! Beaver!" Next day she moved out and took a furnished apartment in a theatrical rooming house on Eighth Avenue, not far from the Garden. The house was recommended by a colleague, a man who eats electric-light bulbs. Among the other tenants are a magician, an old burlesque comedian, a tattooed woman, and a retired circus cook. Surrounded by such people, she feels at ease; when she meets them on the stairs they simply take her for granted and do not look startled. "If an old baboon was to walk down the hall tooting on a cornet, nobody in my house would give him a second look," she says.

Miss Barnell would like to spend the rest of her life in the city, but she knows that sooner or later she will become a stale attraction in the dime museums and will have to run an "At Liberty" notice

in *Billboard* and get a job with a circus or carnival again. She wants
to put this off as long as possible because she has grown to like
apartment life; it has given her a chance, she says, really to get
acquainted with Thomas O'Boyle, her fourth husband, and with
Edelweiss, her cat. O'Boyle is a veteran Joey, or clown, but recently
he has been employed as a talker—the sideshow term for barker—
on the box at the gate at Hubert's. He is nineteen years younger
than Miss Barnell and, unlike her, is enthralled by sideshow life. He
wears dark-blue shirts, lemon-yellow neckties, and Broadway suits.
He believes Miss Barnell is one of the great women of all time and
treats her accordingly. When she comes into a room he leaps to
his feet, and when she takes out a cigarette he hurriedly strikes a
match for her. They were married after working together during
the season of 1931 in the Johnny J. Jones Exposition, a carnival.
Both are short-wave-radio fans, and O'Boyle says that this mutual
interest is what brought them together. "Since our marriage, I and
Mr. O'Boyle have travelled with the same outfits," Miss Barnell said
recently, "but I never felt like I really knew him until we settled
in an apartment. In a sleeping car you just don't feel married. To
get to know a husband, you have to cook and wash for him." Next
to O'Boyle, Edelweiss is her chief concern. Edelweiss is a sullen,
overfed, snow-white Persian, for which she paid twenty-five dollars
when it was a kitten and which now weighs sixteen pounds. She
has nicknamed it Edie, and when she speaks to it she uses baby
talk. She owns a comfortable old canvas chair—it came out of a
circus dressing tent—and she likes to loll in this chair, hold the
cat in her lap, and sing to it. Interminably, one after the other, she
sings "Eadie Was a Lady" and "Root, Hog, or Die," an old circus
song. Cats and dogs are not permitted in the sleeping cars of most
circuses, so when she is on the road she usually has to board Edie
in a pet store. "Sometimes out in the sticks," she says, "I get so
lonesome for Edie I feel like I just can't bear it." She thinks Hubert's
is much nicer than other museums because the manager there
understands how she feels about the cat and lets her bring it with
her to work. While she is on the platform, Edie sits beside her,
purring. After cats, Miss Barnell likes horses best. She is one of

those women who cannot pass a horse standing at a curb without trying to stroke its head; she keeps a handful of wrapped cube sugar in her bag for horses. Once a month, no matter how lean the season, she sends a contribution to the A.S.P.C.A. "To an animal, if you're bearded, it don't make no difference," she says.

Miss Barnell has not only a beard but side whiskers and a droopy mustache. In a white, loose-fitting house dress, she looks like an Old Testament prophet. Her appearance is more worldly when she dresses for a party; on such occasion she uses lipstick and rouge. Monty Woolley saw her once when she was dressed for the evening and said she looked like Elsa Maxwell in a property beard. Someone repeated Woolley's remark to her and she snorted with indignation. "Mr. Woolley must not have good eyesight," she said. She is not as plump as Miss Maxwell. She is five feet five and weighs a hundred and eighty-three pounds. She does not look her age; she has few wrinkles and she walks with a firm step. Her face is round and gloomy. Her bobbed gray hair is brushed pompadour style, and on the platform she wears a Spanish comb and two side combs. Once a year she gets a permanent wave. Before going on the street, she always covers her face with a veil and wraps a Paisley scarf around her neck, hiding her beard. To keep it curly, she sleeps with her beard in a pigtail plait; on days off she does not unplait it. She wears a thick gold wedding ring. Her voice is low and feminine.

Years of listening to barkers has had an effect on her speech; she makes long words longer. To her, a monstrosity is a "monsterosity." She uses some circus slang. The men who haunt the pinball machines on the first floor of Hubert's and never spend a dime to visit the sideshow in the basement are "lot lice" to her; in circuses, this term is applied to townspeople who do not buy tickets but stand around the lot, gaping at everything and getting in the way. She uses the word "old" to express contempt. She once said, "If that old Mayor they have here can't think up anything better than that old sales tax, he ought to lay down and quit." She consistently says "taken" for "took." This is a sample of her conversation: "When I was a young'un I taken the name Princess Olga. After I first got married I changed to Madame, but when every confounded swami-woman and mitt-reader in the nation taken to calling herself Madame So-and-So, I decided Lady was more ree-fined." She has a dim but unmistakable Southern accent, and many of her habits of speech are North Carolinian. She heavily accents the first syllable in words like "hotel" and "police." She uses "one" as a contraction for "one or the other." She says, "I'm going to the movie pitchers this afternoon, or down to Coney Island, one." When she gets ready to do her kitchen shopping, she doesn't say, "I'm going up the street"; she says, "I'm going up street," or, "I'm going down street." Another heritage from her years in rural North Carolina is a liking for snuff. She and O'Boyle own an automobile, and occasionally they get it out of storage and take a long trip. While riding along with the windows lowered, they both dip snuff. "Out in the country, snuff is better than cigarettes," she says. "Of course, I'd never think of using it indoors." She smokes a pack and a half of cigarettes a day. The use of tobacco is her only bad habit. As a rule, sideshow performers are fond of the bottle, but she is a teetotaler and a believer in prohibition.

On a sideshow platform or stage, Miss Barnell is rather austere. To discourage people from getting familiar, she never smiles. She dresses conservatively, usually wearing a plain black evening gown. "I like nice clothes, but there's no use wasting money," she says. "People don't notice anything but my old beard." She despises pity and avoids looking into the eyes of the people in her audiences; like most freaks, she has cultivated a blank, unseeing stare. When people look as if they feel sorry for her, especially women, it makes her want to throw something. She does not sell photographs of herself as many sideshow performers do and does not welcome questions from spectators. She will answer specific questions about her beard as graciously as possible, but when someone becomes inquisitive about her private life—"You ever been married?" is the most frequent query—she gives the questioner an icy look or says quietly, "None of your business." Audiences seem to think that this is admirable. Now and then, after she has told off a persistent or insulting questioner, people will applaud. Miss Barnell's temper has been a blessing; it has kept her from succumbing to utter apathy, which is the occupational disease of freaks. "I don't take no back talk from nobody," she says. She guards her dignity jealously. Once she slapped an apology out of a carnival owner who had suggested that she dye her beard so he could bill her as "Olga, the Lady Bluebeard." Wisecracking professors, or talkers, annoy her; she prefers to be introduced by one who is deadly serious and able to use long medical words. Except for midgets, the majority of freaks in American sideshows are natives, but talkers hate to admit this. Consequently, at one time or another, Miss Barnell has been introduced as having been born in Budapest, Paris, Moscow, Shanghai, and Potsdam. In one carnival she was "the daughter of a Hungarian general," and in another "the half sister of a French duke." She does not have a high opinion of foreigners and is sorely vexed by such introductions. She was grateful to the late Clyde Ingalls, who was once married to Lillian Leitzel and preceded Smythe as manager of Ringling's Congress, because he never seemed to resent the fact that she was born in North Carolina. Ingalls would bow to her, turn to the audience, click his heels, and say, "It gives me the greatest pleasure at this time to introduce a little woman who comes to us from an aristocratic plantation in the Old South and who is recognized by our finest doctors, physicians, and medical men as the foremost, unquestioned, and authentic fee-male bearded lady in medical history. Ladies and gentlemen, Lay-dee Oolgah!"

Among freaks it is axiomatic that Coney Island audiences are the most inhuman, but Miss Barnell has found that a Surf Avenue dime museum on a Saturday night is peaceful compared with a moving-picture studio at any time. She talks bitterly about her experiences in Hollywood, where she has been used in a number of horror and circus pictures. Her most important role was in "Freaks," a Metro-Goldwyn-Mayer study of sideshow life filmed in 1932. It was probably the most frightening picture ever made. In it, among other things, a beautiful trapeze girl of a European circus permits a dwarf to fall in love with her in order to obtain some money he has inherited. At their wedding feast, with a fantastic group of sideshow people around the table, she gets drunk and lets slip the fact that she despises the dwarf. A few nights later, during a terrible storm when the troupe is on the road, the freaks climb into her private wagon and mutilate her, turning *her* into a freak. Miss Barnell thinks this picture was an insult to all freaks everywhere and is sorry she acted in it. When it was finished, she swore she would never again work in Hollywood.

Her self-esteem suffers least of all when she is working in circuses, where sideshow class distinctions are rigidly observed. She herself divides freaks into three classes: born freaks, made freaks, and two-timers. Born freaks are the aristocrats of the sideshow world. She, of course, is a member of this class. So are Siamese twins, pinheads, fat girls, dwarfs, midgets, giants, living skeletons, and men with skulls on which rocks can be broken. Made freaks include tattooed people, sword-swallowers, snake charmers, and glass-eaters. Normal people who obtain sideshow engagements because of past glory or notoriety are two-timers to her. Examples are reformed criminals, old movie stars, and retired athletes like Jack Johnson, the old prizefighter, and Grover Cleveland Alexander, the old ballplayer, both of whom starred for a while on the dime museum circuit. Because Johnson wears a beret and because she has heard that he sips beer through a straw, she particularly dislikes him. "To the general public, old Jack Johnson may be a freak," she says, "but to a freak, he ain't a freak." Paradoxically, she bears no animosity toward fake bearded ladies. They amuse her. She was greatly amused when Frances Murphy, the Gorilla Lady in the "Strange As It Seems" sideshow at the New York World's Fair in 1940, got into an altercation with a truck-driver and was exposed as a male. "If any man is fool enough to be a bearded lady," she says, "it's all right with me."

Some of Miss Barnell's genuine but less gifted colleagues are inclined to think that she is haughty, but she feels that a woman with a beard more than a foot long has a right to be haughty. She undoubtedly does have the most flamboyant female beard in American sideshow history. The beard of Joséphine Boisdechêne, a native of Switzerland and one of P. T. Barnum's most lucrative freaks, was only eight inches long, and she had no mustache. She did, however, have a bearded son—Albert, billed as "Esau, the Hairy Boy"—who helped make up for this shortcoming. Grace Gilbert, who came from Kalkaska, Michigan, and spent most of her professional life in Barnum & Bailey's Circus, had a lush beard, but it was only six inches long. Miss Gilbert used peroxide and was billed as "Princess Gracie, the Girl with the Golden Whiskers." Records of non-professional female beards are scarce. Margaret of Parma, Regent of the Netherlands from 1559 to 1567, had a "coarse, bushy beard." She was proud of it, believing it gave her a regal appearance, and she required court physicians to mix tonics for it. Charles XII of Sweden had a bearded female grenadier in his army, a reputedly beautiful amazon, who was captured by the Russians in the battle of Poltava in 1709 and subsequently taken to St. Petersburg and presented to the Czar, at whose court she was popular for several years. There was a Spanish nun called St. Paula the Bearded, who grew a miraculous beard, according to sacred history. She was being pursued one night by a man with evil intent when hair suddenly sprouted from her chin. She turned and confronted the man and he fled. No reliable statistics on the length of these beards have come down to us.

Most freaks are miserable in the company of non-freaks, but unless she is sunk in one of the morose spells she suffers from occasionally, Miss Barnell welcomes the opportunity to go out among ordinary people. One morning in the winter of 1940 Cole Porter went to her dressing room at Hubert's and asked her to go with him to a cocktail party Monty Woolley was giving at the Ritz-Carlton. Porter told her that Woolley was a student of beards, that he was known as The Beard by his friends, and that he had always wanted to meet a bearded lady. "I'll have to ask my old man," Miss Barnell said. O'Boyle told her to go ahead and enjoy herself. Porter offered to pay for the time she would lose at the museum. "Well, I tell you," she said, "I and you and Mr. Woolley are all in show business, and if this party is for members of the profession, I won't charge a cent." Porter said non-professionals would be present, so she set a fee of eight dollars. Late that afternoon he picked her up at her house. She had changed into a rhinestone-spangled gown. In the Ritz-Carlton elevator she took off the scarf she was wearing around her beard, astonishing the other passengers. There were more than a hundred stage and society people at the party, and Porter introduced her to most of them. Woolley, who got quite interested in her, asked her to have a drink. She hesitated and then accepted a glass of sherry, remarking that it was her first drink in nine years. "I like to see people enjoying theirselves," she said after finishing the sherry. "There's too confounded much misery in this world." She was at the party an hour and a half and said she wished she could stay longer but she had to go home and cook a duck dinner for her husband. Next day, at Hubert's, she told a colleague she had never had a nicer time. "Some of the better class of the Four Hundred were there," she said, "and when I was introduced around I recognized their names. I guess I was a curiosity to them. Some of them sure were a curiosity to me. I been around peculiar people most of my life, but I never saw no women like them before." She was able to recognize the names of the society people because she is a devoted reader of the Cholly Knickerbocker column in the *Journal & American*. She is, in fact, a student of society scandals. "The Four Hundred sure is one cutting-up set of people," she says.

Several endocrinologists have tried vainly to argue Miss Barnell into letting them examine her. She is afraid of physicians. When sick, she depends on patent medicines. "When they get their hands on a monsterosity the medical profession don't know when to stop," she says. "There's nobody so indecent and snoopy as an old doctor." Her hirsuteness is undoubtedly the result of distorted glandular activity. The abnormal functioning of one of the endocrine, or ductless, glands is most often responsible for excessive facial hair in females. Hypertrichosis and hirsutism are the medical terms for the condition. Miss Barnell once read a book called "The Human Body" and is familiar with the glandular explanation, but does not take much stock in it. She says that her parentage was Jewish, Irish, and American Indian, and she believes vaguely that this mixture of bloods is in some way to blame, although she had three beardless sisters.

Miss Barnell has to be persuaded to talk about her early life. "What's the use?" she tells people. "You won't believe me." She says that her father, George Barnell, an itinerant buggy- and wagonmaker, was a Russian Jew who had Anglicized his name. Around 1868, while wandering through the South, he visited a settlement of Catawba Indians on the Catawba River in York County, South Carolina, and fell in love with and was married to a girl who had a Catawba mother and an Irish father. They settled in Wilmington, the principal port of North Carolina, where Barnell established himself in the business of repairing drays on the docks. Miss Barnell was their second child; she was born in 1871 and named Jane, after her Indian grandmother. At birth her chin and cheeks were covered with down. Before she was two years old she had a beard. Her father was kind to her, but her mother, who was superstitious, believed she was bewitched and took her to a succession of Negro granny-women and conjure doctors. Around her fourth birthday, her father inherited some money from a relative and went up to Baltimore to see about starting a business there. While he was away a dismal little six-wagon circus came to Wilmington. It was called the Great Orient Family Circus and Menagerie, and was operated by a family of small, dark foreigners; Miss Barnell calls them "the Mohammedans." The family was composed of a mother, who was a snake charmer; two daughters, who danced; and three sons, who were jugglers and wire-walkers. The wagons were pulled by oxen, and the show stock consisted of three old lions, a few sluggish snakes, some monkeys, a cage of parrots, an educated goat, and a dancing bear. There were many tramp circuses of this type in the country at that time. On the last day of the Great Orient's stay, Mrs. Barnell sold or gave Jane to the Mohammedan mother. "I never been able to find out if Mamma got any money for me or just gave me away to get rid of me," Miss Barnell says bitterly. "She hated me, I know that. Daddy told me years later that he gave her a good beating when he got home from Baltimore and found out what had happened. He had been in Baltimore two months, and by the time he got home I and the Mohammedans were long gone. He and the sheriff of New Hanover County searched all over the better part of three states for us, but they didn't find hide or hair."

She does not remember much about her life with the Great Orient. "My entire childhood was a bad dream," she says. The

Mohammedans exhibited her in a small tent separate from the circus, and people had to pay extra to see her. On the road she slept with the Mohammedan mother in the same wagon in which the snakes were kept. Her pallet on the floor was filthy. She was homesick and cried a lot. The Mohammedans were not intentionally cruel to her. "They did the best they could, I guess," she says. "They were half starved themselves. I didn't understand their talk and their rations made me sick. They put curry in everything. After a while the old Mohammedan mother taken to feeding me on eggs and fruits." The circus wandered through the South for some months, eventually reaching a big city, which she thinks was New Orleans. There the Mohammedans sold their stock and wagons to another small circus and got passage on a boat to Europe, taking her along. In Europe, they joined a German circus. In Berlin, in the summer of 1876, after Jane had been exhibited by the German circus for four or five months, she got sick. She thinks she had typhoid fever. She was placed in a charity hospital. "I was nothing but skin and bones," she says. "The day they put me in the hospital was the last I ever saw of the Mohammedans. They thought I was due to die." She does not remember how long she was in the hospital. After she recovered she was transferred to an institution which she thinks was an orphanage. One morning her father appeared and took her away. "I disremember how Daddy located me," she says, "but I think he said the old Mohammedan mother went to the chief of police in Berlin and told who I was. I guess he somehow got in touch with the chief of police in Wilmington. That must have been the way it happened."

Barnell brought Jane back to North Carolina but did not take her home; she did not want to see her mother. Instead, he put her in the care of her Indian grandmother, who, with other Catawbas, had moved up from the settlement in South Carolina to a farming community in Mecklenburg County, near Charlotte. Jane worked on her grandmother's farm, chopping cotton, milking cows, and tending pigs. She never went to school but was taught to read and write by a Presbyterian woman who did missionary work among the Catawbas. Jane remembers stories this woman told her about

Florence Nightingale; they made her long to become a nurse. In her teens she taught herself to shave with an old razor that had belonged to her grandfather. When she was around seventeen she went to Wilmington to visit her father, and a doctor he knew got her a place as a student nurse in the old City Hospital. She worked in the hospital for perhaps a year, and she still thinks of this as the happiest period of her life. Eventually, however, something unpleasant happened which caused her to leave; what it was, she will not tell. "I just figured I could never have a normal life," she says, "so I went back to Grandma's and settled down to be a farmhand the rest of my days." Three or four years later she became acquainted with the senior Professor Heckler, who owned a farm near her grandmother's; he worked in circuses in the summer and lived on the farm in the winter. Heckler convinced her she would be happier in a sideshow than on a farm and helped her get a job with the John Robinson Circus. As well as she can remember, she got this job in the spring of 1892, when she was twenty-one. "Since that time," she says, "my beard has been my meal ticket." Until the death of her grandmother, around 1899, Miss Barnell went back to North Carolina every winter. She had three sisters and two brothers in Wilmington, and she visited them occasionally. "They all thought I was a disgrace and seeing them never gave me much enjoyment," she says. "Every family of a freak I ever heard of was the same. I've known families that lived off a freak's earnings but wouldn't be seen with him. My parents passed on long ago, and I reckon my brothers and sisters are all dead by now. I haven't seen any of them for twenty-two years. I had one sister I liked. I used to send her a present every Christmas, and sometimes she'd drop me a card. She was a nurse. She went to China twenty-some-odd years ago to work in a hospital for blind Chinese children, and that's the last I ever heard of her. I guess she's dead."

Miss Barnell was with the Robinson Circus for fourteen years. While with it, she was married to a German musician in the circus band. By him she had two children, both of whom died in infancy. Soon after the death of her second child, her husband died. "After that," she says, "I never got any more pleasure out of circus life. I had to make a living, so I kept on. It's been root, hog, or die. When I got sick of one outfit, I moved on to another. Circuses are all the same—dull as ditch water." She left Robinson's to go with the Forepaugh–Sells Brothers' Circus and Menagerie, leaving it to marry a balloon ascensionist. He was killed about a year after they were married; how, she will not say. "He was just killed," she says, shrugging her shoulders. Her third marriage also ended unhappily. "That one treated me shamefully," she says. "If he was in a bottle, I wouldn't pull out the stopper to give him air. I taken out a divorce from him the year before I and Mr. O'Boyle got married."

Miss Barnell is disposed to blame circuses for much of the unhappiness in her life. Consequently she does not share her present husband's enthusiasm for them. O'Boyle was an orphan who ran away to work with a circus, and has never become disenchanted. Every week he reads *Billboard* from cover to cover, and he keeps a great stack of back copies of the magazine in their apartment; she rarely reads it. Like most old circus men, he is garrulous about the past. He often tries to get his wife to talk about her circus experiences, but she gives him little satisfaction. O'Boyle is proud of her career. Once he begged her to give him a list of the circuses and carnivals she has worked for; he wanted to send the list to the letters-to-the-editor department of *Billboard*. She mentioned Ringling, Barnum & Bailey, Forepaugh-Sells, Hagenbeck-Wallace, the World of Mirth Carnival, the Royal American Shows, the Rubin & Cherry Exposition, and the Beckmann & Gerety Shows, and then yawned and said, "Mr. O'Boyle, please go turn on the radio." He has never been able to get the full list.

In the last year or so Miss Barnell has become a passionate housekeeper and begrudges every moment spent away from her apartment. About once a week she rearranges the furniture in her two small rooms. On a window sill she keeps two geranium plants in little red pots. On sunny afternoons during her days off she places a pillow on the sill, rests her elbows on it, and stares for hours into Eighth Avenue. People who see her in the window undoubtedly think she is a gray-bearded old man. She spends a lot of time in the kitchen, trying out recipes clipped from newspapers. O'Boyle has gained eleven pounds since they moved into the apartment. Before starting work in the kitchen, she turns on four electric fans in various corners of the apartment and opens all the windows; she does not trust gas and believes that stirring up the air is good for her asthma. While the fans are on, she keeps Edie, the cat, who is susceptible to colds, shut up in a closet. She has developed a phobia about New York City tap water; she is sure there is a strange, lethal acid in it, and boils drinking water for fifteen minutes. She even boils the water in which she gives Edie a bath. In her opinion, the consumption of unboiled water is responsible for most of the sickness in the city. On her bureau she keeps two radios, one of them a short-wave set. On her days off she turns on the short-wave radio right after she gets up and leaves it on until she goes to bed. While in the kitchen, she listens to police calls. The whirring of the fans and the clamor of the radio do not bother her in the least. The walls are thin, however, and once the burlesque comedian who lives in the next apartment rapped on the door and said, "Pardon me, Madam, but it sounds like you're murdering a mule in there, or bringing in an oil well."

Miss Barnell's attitude toward her work is by no means consistent. In an expansive mood, she will brag that she has the longest female beard in history and will give the impression that she feels superior to less spectacular women. Every so often, however, hurt by a snicker or a brutal remark made by someone in an audience, she undergoes a period of depression which may last a few hours or a week. "When I get the blues, I feel like an outcast from society," she once said. "I used to think when I got old my feelings wouldn't get hurt, but I was wrong. I got a tougher hide than I once had, but it ain't tough enough." On the road she has to keep on working, no matter how miserable she gets, but in a museum she simply knocks off and goes home. Until she feels better, she does not go out of her apartment, but passes the time listening to the police calls, playing with Edie, reading the *Journal & American,* and studying an old International Correspondence Schools course in stenography which she bought in a secondhand-bookstore in Chicago years ago. Practicing short-hand takes her mind off herself. She is aware that such a thing is hardly possible, but she daydreams about becoming a stenographer the way some women daydream about Hollywood. She says that long ago she learned there is no place in the world outside of a sideshow for a bearded lady. When she was younger she often thought of joining the Catholic Church and going into a nunnery; she had heard of sideshow women who became nuns, although she had never actually known one. A lack of religious conviction deterred her. Religion has been of little solace to her. "I used to belong to the Presbyterians, but I never did feel at home in church," she says. "Everybody eyed me, including the preacher. I rather get my sermons over the radio."

Most of Miss Barnell's colleagues are touchy about the word "freak," preferring to be called artistes or performers. Years ago, because of this, Ringling had to change the name of its sideshow from the Congress of Freaks to the Congress of Strange People. Miss Barnell would like to be considered hardboiled and claims she does not care what she is called. "No matter how nice a name was put on me," she says, "I would still have a beard." Also, she has a certain professional pride. Sometimes, sitting around with other performers in a dressing room, she will say, with a slight air of defiance, that a freak is just as good as any actor, from the Barrymores on down. "If the truth was known, we're all freaks together," she says.

(1940)

Evening with a Gifted Child

PHILIPPA DUKE SCHUYLER IS PROBABLY the best example in New York City of what psychologists call a gifted child. She is nine years old. Her mental age, according to the Clinic for Gifted Children at New York University, which tests her periodically, is sixteen. She has an I.Q. of 185. Phillipa reads Plutarch on train trips, eats steaks raw, writes poems in honor of her dolls, plays poker, and is the composer of more than sixty pieces for the piano. Most of these compositions are descriptive, with such titles as "Spanish Harlem," "Men at Work," "The Cockroach Ballet," and "At the Circus." She began composing before she was four, and has been playing the piano in public, often for money, since she was six. She has an agreement with the National Broadcasting Company by which she plays new compositions for the first time in public on a Sunday-morning broadcast called "Coast to Coast on a Bus," and she frequently plays on other radio and television programs. A Schuyler album, "Five Little Pieces," has been published. She has gone on tour several times, playing compositions by Bach, Rimsky-Korsakoff, Debussy, Schumann, and herself in Grand Rapids, Cincinnati, Indianapolis, Columbus, Youngstown, Atlantic City, Trenton, and other cities. On one tour she averaged $175 an engagement, plus all expenses. Philippa is often called a genius by admiring strangers, and her parents find this displeasing. To them, her development is explained not by genius but by diet. They believe that humans should live on uncooked meats, fruits, vegetables, and nuts, and are convinced that the food Philippa has eaten most of her life is largely responsible for her precocity. She particularly likes raw green peas, raw corn on the cob, raw yams, and raw sirloin steaks.

Philippa's father, George S. Schuyler, whom she calls by his first name, is a Negro essayist and novelist, the son of a dining-car chef on the New York Central. He writes an influential column on national and world affairs for the Pittsburgh *Courier,* a weekly Negro newspaper, and is business manager of the *Crisis,* which is the official organ of the National Association for the Advancement of Colored People. He wrote often for the *American Mercury* when H. L. Mencken edited it. Mr. Schuyler's skin is jet black. He comes from one of the oldest Negro families in New York; long before the Revolutionary War, ancestors of his in Albany began using Schuyler as a surname. Since then, Negro Schuylers have occasionally also used the Christian names of distinguished white Schuylers. Philippa is named for Philip John Schuyler, the Revolutionary general. Philippa's mother, Mrs. Josephine Schuyler, is white. She is, in fact, a golden-haired blonde. She is a member of a pioneer west Texas ranching and banking family, and speaks with a Southern accent. When she was in her teens, she ran away from home and went to California; since then she has considered herself "a rebel." Before she and Mr. Schuyler were married in 1928, she had been, successively, a Mack Sennett bathing beauty, a ballet dancer in a San Francisco opera company, a painter, a poet, and a writer for the Negro press. She met Mr. Schuyler in New York when she visited the office of a magazine of which he was an editor and to which she had contributed poems and articles. This magazine was the *Messenger,* the official organ of the Brotherhood of Sleeping Car Porters. Mrs. Schuyler acquired her dietary convictions in California years ago; her husband is a more recent convert and is not quite as dead set. Mrs. Schuyler feels that both alcohol and tobacco are utterly unnecessary; her husband, however, drinks beer and smokes cigars. Mrs. Schuyler still writes occasionally for Negro newspapers under various names, but devotes most of her time to painting and Philippa. On tour, she serves as Philippa's manager. Philippa calls her Jody. The Schuylers live in a large apartment house on Convent Avenue. This house, which is tenanted by both white and Negro families, is on a hill overlooking the western fringe of Harlem, and is several blocks from the Convent of the Sacred Heart, where Philippa is in Grade 6A.

The Schuylers recently invited me to come and hear Philippa play. I went up one evening around eight o'clock. Mrs. Schuyler met me at the door and said that Philippa was in her own room transcribing a composition called "Caprice No. 2," which she had finished just before dinner. We went into the living room, where Mr. Schuyler, in shirtsleeves, was hunched over a desk. At his elbow was a stack of clippings about Philippa from newspapers in the cities in which she had played. He was pasting these in a large scrapbook. "We have nine scrapbooks full of stuff about Philippa, one for each year," he said. "She's never seen them. In fact, so far as we know, she's never seen a clipping about herself. We're afraid it might make her self-conscious. When she gets to be a young woman, we'll bring out all her scrapbooks and say, 'Here are some things you might find interesting.' "

There were paintings, chiefly nudes, on two walls of the living room. I noticed Mrs. Schuyler's signature in the corner of one. Bookcases lined another wall, and arranged on their top shelves were a number of pieces of African sculpture. Mrs. Schuyler pointed to one, a female fetish. "George brought that back from Africa in 1931," she said. "He was down there getting material for a book. Most of these things, however, belong to Philippa. They were sent to her by people in Liberia, Nigeria, and the Ivory Coast who heard her play on the radio. They listen in on short-wave. They write to her, and she answers their letters. They know that part of her background is African, and are proud of her. Their presents to Philippa are brought here by Africans who work on ships plying between New York and various West African ports. She has a slew of medals and prizes she won in tournaments held by the New York Philharmonic, the National Guild of Piano Teachers, and similar organizations, and she keeps them in a fancy inlaid chest that was sent to her by a craftsman in Africa. Philippa is extremely proud of her Negro blood."

Mr. Schuyler looked up from the scrapbook. "She has radio fans all over the world, not only in Africa," he said. "On her last birthday she received six sable skins and a black pearl from Alaska, a scarf from Portugal, and a doll from the Virgin Islands. However, most of her presents did come from Africa."

While we were looking at an ebony elephant, Philippa came into the room. Mr. Schuyler unobtrusively closed the scrapbook and put it in a drawer of the desk. Then he introduced me to Philippa. She shook hands, not awkwardly, as most children do, but with assurance. She is slender, erect, and exquisitely boned. Her face is oval, and she has serious black eyes, black curls, and perfect teeth. Her skin is light brown. She is a beautiful child.

"Did you get through with the piece?" her mother asked her.

"Oh, yes," Philippa said. "Half an hour ago. Look, Jody, do you remember that silly little riddle book I bought at the newsstand in the station at Cincinnati and never got a chance to look at?"

"Yes, I remember."

"Well, I've just been looking through it, and some of the riddles are funny. May I ask one, please?"

Mrs. Schuyler nodded, and Philippa asked, "What has four wheels and flies?"

We were silent a minute, and then Philippa said impatiently, "Give up, please, so I can tell you."

"We give up," Mrs. Schuyler said.

"A garbage wagon," Philippa said.

Mr. Schuyler groaned, and Philippa looked at him and burst out laughing.

"Was it that bad, George?" she asked. "Wait until you hear some of the others."

"Not now, Philippa," Mrs. Schuyler said, rather hastily. "Instead, maybe you'd like to play for us in your room."

"I'd like to very much," Philippa said.

Mr. Schuyler said that he would stay in the living room and listen. Mrs. Schuyler and I followed Philippa down the hall. A large red balloon was tethered by a string to the doorknob of Philippa's room. "I like balloons," she said, spanking it into the air with the heel of her hand. "They remind me of the circus."

The Schuylers have a four-room apartment. I noticed that Philippa's room was the largest. In it there was a grand piano, a bed, an adult-size dressing table, two small chairs, and a cabinet. Mrs. Schuyler opened the doors of the cabinet. "Philippa keeps her music and dolls in here," she said. "She made this doll house. She knitted the little rug herself and sewed dresses for the dolls. She sews very well. She made me an apron the other day." On top of Philippa's piano there was a Modern Library giant edition of Plutarch, a peach kernel, a mystery novel called "The Corpse with the Floating Foot," a copy of the New York *Post* opened to the comic-strip page, a teacup half full of raw green peas, a train made of adhesive-tape spools and cardboard, a Stravinsky sonata, a pack of playing cards, a photograph of Lily Pons clipped from a magazine, and an uninflated balloon. I was standing beside the piano, examining this rather surrealistic group of objects, when Mrs. Schuyler suddenly snapped her fingers and said, "I forgot the peaches!" She started out of the room, then paused at the door and said, "It's a kind of ice cream I make. We're going to have some later on, and I forgot to put the peaches in the icebox. I'll leave you two alone for a few minutes. Philippa, don't start playing until I get back." I took one of the chairs and Philippa sat on the piano bench. Left alone with her, I felt ill at ease. I didn't know how to go about making small talk with a gifted child.

"Do you mind if I smoke in here?" I asked her.

"Of course not," Philippa said. "I'll go get you an ashtray."

When she returned, I asked her if she had been reading the Plutarch on the piano.

"Yes," she said. "I've read most of it. I got it to read on trains."

"Don't you find it rather dry?"

"Not at all. I like biography. I particularly like the sections called the comparisons. Best of all I liked Theseus and Romulus, and Solon and Poplicola. Plutarch is anything but dry. I'm very interested in the Romans. I want to get 'The Decline and Fall' next. It's in the Modern Library, too."

"What are some other books you like?"

Philippa laughed. "Lately I've been reading a Sherlock Holmes omnibus and some mystery books by Ellery Queen."

"What book do you like best of all?"

"Oh, that's almost impossible to answer. You can't just pick out one book and say you like it better than all others. I bet you can't."

"I certainly can," I said. I was not bothered any longer by the difference in our ages, and had completely got over feeling ill at ease.

"What book?"

"Mark Twain's 'Life on the Mississippi,' " I said.

"Oh, I like Mark Twain," Philippa said, clapping her hands excitedly. "I like him very much. What other writers do you like?"

"The ones I like best," I said, "are Mark Twain, Dostoevski, and James Joyce."

Philippa deliberated for a few moments.

"I guess you're right," she said. "I *can* say that there's one book I like best of all. That's the 'Arabian Nights.' George has an eight-volume set. It's an unexpurgated edition. I read it first when I was three, and at least four times since. I based my longest composition on it. I called it 'Arabian Nights Suite.' Oh, the stories in that book are absolutely wonderful!" She laughed. "Goodness!" she said. "I didn't mean to get so"—she paused and appeared to be searching for a word—"impassioned."

Mrs. Schuyler returned, and sat down.

"Look," Philippa said to me, "do you like funnies?"

"You mean comic strips?" I asked.

"Yes," she said. "Funnies."

"Of course I do," I said. "The best comic strip is 'Moon Mullins' in the *News.*"

"Oh, no, it isn't," she said. "The best funny is 'Dixie Dugan' in the *Post,* and the next best is the full-page 'Katzenjammer Kids' in the Sunday *Journal*. The *Post* has the best funnies. I like 'Dixie Dugan,' 'Superman,' 'Tarzan,' 'Abbie an' Slats,' and 'The Mountain Boys,' and they're all in the *Post*. You know, I'm almost ready to write a composition about the funnies. I'm going to call it 'The Katzenjammer Kids.' I read a lot of mystery stories, and I've already written a composition called 'Mystery Story.' "

"Philippa tries to describe places and experiences in her music,"

Mrs. Schuyler said. "We used to live in Spanish Harlem, and she put some of the things she saw and heard in that neighborhood into a composition. She wrote 'Men at Work' while the WPA was digging a sewer in front of our apartment house. She likes the playground at Sacred Heart very much, and she described it in a piece called 'In a Convent Garden.' Once she had a canary, and it died. For its funeral she wrote a sad little piece called 'Death of the Nightingale.' Philippa, you're getting fidgety. Are you ready to play for us?"

"Yes, Jody," Philippa said, getting to her feet. She turned to me, curtsied, and said, "Think about cockroaches while I'm playing this piece. It's 'The Cockroach Ballet.' This is the story: Some cockroaches are feasting on a kitchen floor. A human comes in and kills some of them. He thinks he has killed them all. But after he leaves, one little cockroach peeps out, then another, and another. They dance a sad little dance for their dead comrades. But they aren't very sad because they know that cockroaches will go on forever and ever. Unfortunately."

Mrs. Schuyler laughed. "Philippa took that piece to Mother Stevens at Sacred Heart the afternoon she wrote it," she said. "Mother Stevens is head of the music department. She asked Philippa why she didn't write about angels instead of cockroaches. 'But dear Mother,' Philippa said, 'I've never seen an angel, but I've seen many cockroaches.' "

Philippa sat down at the piano, and began playing. I thought it was a nice piece.

Next she played a composition called "Impressions of the World's Fair, 1939." In it the sound of the tractor-train horn—that wornout phrase from "The Sidewalks of New York"—was recurrent. Then she played "Men at Work." When she finished it she asked me to enumerate the noises I had recognized. I told her I thought I had recognized an air drill, the sound of trowels knocking the tar off paving blocks, and the sound of a chisel being hammered into rock. "You're very good," Philippa said, and I felt pleased. "Here's one called 'The Jolly Pig,' " she said. In the middle of it she turned to me and asked, "Hear him laughing?" I didn't, but I said I did. After that came the "Caprice" she had finished that day. Then she played some pieces by other composers. They included Rimsky-Korsakoff's "Flight of the Bumble Bee" and Johann Sebastian Bach's "Two Part Invention No. 1." After she had played for at least an hour without any sign of weariness, she said, "I'll play just one more, one I composed a long time ago, when I was four years old. It's 'The Goldfish.' A little goldfish thinks the sky is water. He tries to jump into it, only to fall upon the floor and die."

"I'll go get the ice cream," Mrs. Schuyler said as Philippa began "The Goldfish." Just as Philippa finished playing, Mrs. Schuyler returned, bringing a tray with four saucers. She called Mr. Schuyler and he came in and sat down on the bed.

"I liked your new piece, Philippa," he said. Philippa smiled proudly.

"Thanks, George," she said. "I'm going to do a little more work on it tomorrow."

"It isn't really ice cream, and you might not like it," Mrs. Schuyler said to me as she distributed the saucers. "It's just fresh peaches and cream sweetened with honey and chilled. In this house we use almost no sugar. In her entire life, Philippa has never eaten a piece of candy. Her taste hasn't been perverted by sweets. Instead, she has a passion for lemons. She eats them the way most people eat oranges, pulp and all. Don't you, Philippa?"

"Yes, Jody," Philippa said. She was eating with gusto.

"We seldom have cooked food of any kind," Mrs. Schuyler continued. "Once in a while I broil a steak very lightly, but usually we eat meat raw. We also eat raw fish that has been soaked in lemon juice. When we're travelling, Philippa and I amaze waiters. You have to argue with most waiters before they'll bring you raw meat. Then they stare at you while you eat. I guess it *is* rather unusual to see a little girl eating a raw steak. Philippa drinks a lot of milk, and she gets quite a large daily ration of cod-liver oil. About the only cooked thing she really likes is a hardboiled egg. She mashes the yolk and squeezes a lemon over it. When she goes to the movies she sometimes takes along an ear of corn. That's better than peanuts. She always fills her pockets with green peas before she goes to school. The other children at Sacred Heart used to stare at her, but now they think nothing of it."

"Jody makes me big birthday cakes," Philippa said. "They're made of ground-up cashew nuts. Once I had one that weighed twenty pounds. It was shaped like a white piano. This year it was shaped like the map of South America. The different countries were colored with berry and vegetable juices. It was a swell cake."

"We eat all kinds of nuts, just so they're raw," Mrs. Schuyler said. "Each year my father sends me all the pecans off one big tree on his ranch in Texas. Some people think we're peculiar, but the best proof that our diet theory is sensible is Philippa's health. She's extremely healthy, mentally and physically. Her teeth, for example, are absolutely perfect. She's never had even a tiny cavity."

Mr. Schuyler looked at his watch. "It's nine-thirty, Philippa," he said.

"May I ask another riddle before I go to bed?"

"Just one," her father said.

"All right. What's smaller than a flea's mouth?"

"Oh, I know that one," Mrs. Schuyler said.

"So do I," said Mr. Schuyler.

"All right, all right," Philippa said. "Wait until tomorrow. I'll ask you some you couldn't guess in fifteen years."

We said good night to Philippa. Mrs. Schuyler went into the kitchen and Mr. Schuyler and I went into the living room. I asked him how many hours a day Philippa studies. He said that during school months she gets up at seven-thirty, has a bath and breakfast, and starts practicing on the piano at eight. She practices for two hours. Then for half an hour she plays anything she likes. At ten-thirty her music supervisor arrives. The supervisor, a young piano teacher named Pauline Apanowitz, is with her an hour and a half. Shortly before one, Philippa walks to Sacred Heart, eating green peas on the way. She spends two afternoon hours a day at the convent, attending history, geography, and English classes. She misses arithmetic, spelling, and reading, which are morning classes. However, her examination grades for these subjects are always good. "There wouldn't be much point in Philippa going to a spelling class," Mr. Schuyler said. "When she was twenty-nine months old she could spell five hundred and fifty words. She has an enormous vocabulary. She likes jawbreakers. At four, she discovered the scientific word for silicosis, which is pneumonoultramicroscopicsilicovolcanoniosis, and she spelled it morning and night. It fascinated her. We certainly got tired of that word." Once a week, Mr. Schuyler said, she goes to Antonia Brico's studio for lessons in score-reading and conducting; William Harms, an assistant of Josef Hofmann, also gives her a weekly piano lesson. Most afternoons she spends an hour in the convent playground; rope-skipping is her favorite exercise. "Philippa isn't a Catholic, and we have no religious affiliations," Mr. Schuyler told me. "My parents were Catholics, however, and Philippa will become one if she so desires. Most of the other children at the convent are Irish Catholics. She gets along with them wonderfully."

Mrs. Schuyler came into the room, bringing several small books. "When Philippa was very little I kept a careful account of the stories and poems she wrote, the words she invented, the questions she asked, and such things," she said. "I wrote them down in the form of letters to her, letters for her to read when she becomes a young woman. The people at the gifted-child clinic saw the books and had the notations transcribed for their files. Perhaps you'd like to look through some of the books."

I opened one. At the top of the page was written "Three years, seven months." Beneath this was the following notation:

You are very interested to know why some people are good and some bad. "What do they do with bad people?" you ask. "If they are very bad, they put them in jail," I say. "What is a jail?" you inquire. "A jail is a building full of little rooms with barred doors." "What do they do to bad people in jail?" "They don't have nice things to eat or wear," I explain. Several days later you heard about how poor most people are in Georgia, and you asked, "The poor people in Georgia who have nothing nice to eat or wear, are they bad?" "No," I said. "They are not bad. They are unlucky. Later, I will explain more fully." That afternoon you laughed and asked, archly, "Jody, when the weather is bad, do they put it in jail?" The same day you asked if flowers get white hair when they are old. And you asked if people who sleep on cots say at night, "I am going to cot." And you asked if mothers ever say to their children, "You must go crooked to bed." Walking along the street you said, "Jody, trees stand on one leg." Yesterday you began to giggle. "There's no Mr. Lady or Mrs. Man," you said, and enjoyed the humor of the idea very much. Today you made up a poem.

> *"Pipes are steel,*
> *But bones are real."*

Tonight you sat on the floor and made up a long story. You said, "Varnetida, a little girl, and her mother, Armarnia, went to see Slowbow, a brother who lived with his father, Solom, in a big house in Channa. They met the grandmother, Branlea, and another little girl, Jolumbow, who had a kitten named Lilgay, and a dog named Cherro. They all sat down in a chilbensian room and ate dishes of wallaga and thaga . . ." and so on, as long as I would listen. If you were at a loss for a word you simply invented one with a perfectly solemn face.

I picked up another book. In it I found a poem Philippa wrote when she was five. She wrote it on Easter morning while sitting in the bathtub:

> *The sun is lifting his lid.*
> *The sun is leaving his crib.*
> *The sun is a waking baby*
> *Who will bring the Spring maybe*
> *Thump, thump, thump! out of the earth.*

I thought that this was a wonderful poem. It was followed by this notation:

Tonight a red light flashed to green while we were walking across Fifth Avenue. The automobiles were whizzing by us. Suddenly you looked up and said, "Jody, will you please name for me all the diseases in the world?"

"Philippa must be hard to deal with at times," I said.

"She is indeed," Mrs. Schuyler said. "Women often tell me, 'You mustn't push her!' Their sympathy is misplaced. If there's any pushing done, she's the one that does it."

A few minutes later, I said good night to the Schuylers. At the door I asked Mrs. Schuyler to tell me the answer to the riddle Philippa had propounded just before she went to bed; it had been on my mind ever since. "That riddle about what's smaller than a flea's mouth?" she said. "That's an old, old nursery riddle. I guess it's the only one I know. The answer is, 'What goes in it.' I'm very sorry she got hold of that riddle book. Tomorrow at breakfast she'll have the drop on us. She'll ask us two dozen, and we probably won't know a single answer."

(1940)

A Sporting Man

COMMODORE DUTCH IS A BRASSY LITTLE MAN who has made a living for the last forty years by giving an annual ball for the benefit of himself. "I haven't got a whole lot of sense," he likes to say, "but I got too much sense to work." On big showcards which he puts up in drinking places in the theatrical district, he advertises his ball, which is usually held in the spring, as "The Annual Party, Affair, Soirée & Gala Naval Ball of the Original Commodore Dutch Association." Dutch founded this organization in 1901, because he needed the name of a sponsor to print on tickets. At first he called it simply the Commodore Dutch Association, adding "original" during the depression. "It sounds more high-toned that way," he says. "It sounds like I got imitators." No meetings of the organization have ever been held, and its headquarters are wherever Dutch happens to be. He keeps all its records in his pockets. It has one active member and three hundred honorary members. Dutch is the active member. Among the honorary members are eighteen Tammany politicians, thirteen saloonkeepers, six fight managers, six night-club proprietors, four publishers of racing dope sheets, two executives of the New York Giants, the owner of a chain of barbershops, a bail bondsman, a subway contractor, the manager of a Turkish bath, and approximately one hundred and twenty-five professional gamblers. All these men occasionally give Dutch small sums of money; that is the only requirement for membership in the Original Commodore Dutch Association. Dutch refers to these sums as dues, a euphemism which makes some of his members snicker. Joe Madden, an ex-prizefighter, who keeps a West Fifty-sixth Street saloon in which sporting and society people hang out and who has been an honorary officer of the association for twenty-seven years, not long ago defined the attitude of many of the members when he introduced a friend to Dutch and remarked, "Commodore Dutch is a bum, but he's not an ordinary bum. He doesn't make touches; he collects dues. He's the fanciest bum in town." Dutch was not offended by this remark. He beamed at Madden and said, "Thanks, pal."

Dutch lets each member decide how much dues he should pay. "You're the doctor," he says. "Give me what you think is right. I'll take anything from two bits to a million dollars." Practically every time a member pays dues, Dutch hands him a Gala Naval Ball ticket. Dutch keeps a supply in his pockets and passes out hundreds every year; they take the place of receipts. On the back of them, Dutch always writes, with a flourish, "O.K. Pd. Member in Good Standing. C. Dutch (signed)." Only a few members attend the ball, and some do not believe that he actually gives it. Less than twenty-five showed up for the last one, which was held in the back room of an obscure Third Avenue saloon. Dutch's feelings were not hurt. "When my constituents show their respect for me by coming to my swaree, I am gratified," he once said, "only I don't mind admitting that the main thing I am innarested in is dues."

The Original Commodore Dutch Association has a profusion of officers and committeemen, all appointed by Dutch. Their names are printed each year on the showcards with which the ball is advertised. Some of these men dislike seeing their names in print, so their nicknames are used. On the most recent card, interspersed among such names as Herbert H. Lehman, Robert F. Wagner, and Alfred E. Smith, are nicknames like Big Yaffie, Little Yaffie, Gin Buck, Senator Gut, Eddie the Plague, Johnny Basketball, and Swiss Cheese. With the exception of Swiss Cheese, who is the retired operator of a private detective agency, all these nicknamed men are connected with horse racing. Swiss Cheese is called that for two reasons; he has a sallow, pock-marked face, and he is a passionate yodeler. He likes to get pie-eyed, then go to Salvation Army street meetings and make a nuisance of himself by yodeling hymns. At the Gala Naval Ball he is a star performer.

There are thirty-two officers of the association, and Dutch is constantly adding to the list. He holds the highest office, Founder and Standard Bearer. Just beneath him in importance is Head President. Sam H. Harris, the theatrical producer, was Head President from 1916 until his death in 1941. The office is vacant at present. "Out of respect for Mr. Sam, I'm going to wait a year or so before I appoint a successor to him," Dutch says. "He was the most ideal officer I ever had. I put the bite on him real often, and he never bellyached. A sawbuck was the least he ever slipped me. Sometimes he made it a double sawbuck." Joe Madden is Assistant Head President and Nick the Greek, the California gambler, is Second Assistant Head President. Other high offices are Admiral, Rear Admiral, Front Admiral, Captain, Auditor, Field Marshal, Judge Advocate, Floor Manager, Gangway Overseer, High Commissioner, Master of Ceremonies, and Master of Fox Hounds. The majority of the offices are held by gamblers. "I got a lot of respect for gamblers," Dutch says. "They throw money around, and I like to see people throw money around. I figure they might throw some my way."

There are four standing committees, all made up of men who have been especially generous to Dutch. The honorary members committee is the most impressive. Except for Sam Rosoff, the subway contractor; William V. Dwyer, the Tropical Park racetrack man; and Horace Stoneham, president of the Giants, it is composed of public officials and Tammany district leaders. Former Governor Lehman, who automatically gets out his wallet whenever he catches sight of Dutch, is chairman. Dutch appoints officers and committeemen without consulting them. He was once asked if the Governor had authorized the use of his name on some showcards. "He never told me I couldn't," Dutch said. People in show business predominate on the arrangements committee. The reception committee is a hodgepodge of race-track and night-life characters; Abe Attell, the old pug, who now runs a Broadway saloon called Abe's Steak & Chop House & Bar & Grill, is chairman. The floor committee is made up entirely of prizefighters and James J. Braddock is chairman.

Dutch calls the prizefighters "my adjutants." "Years ago," he says, "anybody that came to my ball with a load on and misbehaved himself, I snapped my fingers and my adjutants rushed up from all directions and piled on top of him. Nowdays, to be an adjutant, it's just honorary."

Dutch enjoys explaining the duties of his officers and committeemen. It makes him giggle. "Except to pay dues, they don't have no duties," he says. "Anybody that slips me a buck off and on, I consider him a member in good standing of the Original Commodore Dutch Association. That entitles him to come to my ball, but it don't get him no privileges. It just makes him an ipso-facto member. If he wants to rise higher, he's got to stake me. If he stakes me, I elect him to a committee. If he stakes me good, I make him a chairman. If he stakes me real good, I elect him to be an officer and confer him with a title. An officer has privileges. He can make a speech at the ball, or sing a song, which nobody can shut him up. Also, he can take part in the grand march, providing enough people show up to have a grand march; such a thing hasn't happened in years. Any officer that gets behind in his dues, I weed him out. Take Joe Madden. I made him a high officer because he slips me a sawbuck every time I hit him for dues. Well, if he was to make a practice of slipping me a deuce instead, God forbid, I would naturally figure on getting me a brand-new Assistant Head President."

Dutch is sixty-two, but he often says that he feels much older. "I feel like I am a hundred and sixty-two," he says. He is small and wizened and hungry-looking. His cheeks are sunken, and he has big ears, a jutting nose, and distrustful pale-blue eyes. He has only one tooth, an upper incisor, and when he smiles his face takes on a distinctly hobgoblin aspect. He has such an extraordinary face that he himself is sometimes taken aback by it. One night in Attell's, after he had stared at the bar mirror for a while, he suddenly clapped his hands over his eyes and groaned. "I scare meself," he said, when he had regained his composure. "I never see such an ugly fella. My ears are a coupla sizes too big for my head, and they ain't even with each other, and I'm the hatchetest damned faced human being God ever made. I wonder why He took the trouble." However, despite Dutch's unusual countenance, he usually looks quite dapper. He keeps himself as neat as possible. He often shaves twice a day, and he gets a manicure whenever he can afford it. Several times a week he ducks into a dry-cleaner's and sits in a booth while his suit is being sponged and pressed. He brags that he was a dandy in his youth. "When I was twenty-five, I had a wardrobe consisting of twenty-five suits," he says, "and most of them hadn't ever been turned." Now, for winter wear, he owns two black suits and a double-breasted imitation camel's-hair overcoat with a belt in the back. In summer he customarily wears a black jacket, a baby-blue rayon polo shirt, seersucker pants, and a stiff straw hat. He keeps a big artificial rose in his lapel; when one gets grimy, he drops into Woolworth's and buys another.

Dutch makes a show of being blithe. Actually, he worries a lot, particularly about his health, which is good. He broods about pneumonia, and wears rubbers almost every day in winter, even though they make his feet ache. He has a germ phobia; in most of the restaurants he goes to, before he will eat anything he shakes out his napkin and painstakingly polishes his knife, fork, and spoon. On the street, he walks close to buildings, keeping as far away from automobiles as possible; he claims that one good whiff of exhaust will give him a headache. "In all the world," he says, "there's nothing I hate as much as a god-damn automobile." His eyesight is poor, but he is too vain to get spectacles. Every night he spends several hours studying the *Daily Mirror*'s horse-racing charts, which are printed in small type, and he uses a magnifying glass he bought in Woolworth's. He holds the newspaper and the glass close to his face, and while he reads his lips work. This always amuses onlookers. "My God, Dutch," Attell once told him, "you look like you're trying to chew the *Daily Mirror*." When not in use, his magnifying glass dangles by its handle from a black ribbon which he wears around his neck. He is disturbed about his hair, which is growing thin. He carries a military brush in a coat pocket and gets it out when he has time on his hands, no matter where he happens to be, and gives his hair exactly one hundred strokes, counting each stroke out loud. Sometimes, standing at a bar or sitting in a restaurant, he will suddenly start brushing and counting, startling the people around him.

Although Dutch spends at least half of his waking hours in saloons, he is a teetotaler. "In my youth," he says, "I was the scourge of the gin mills, and bartenders shuddered when they seen me coming, but I reformed." He has forgotten the year he went on the wagon, but remembers, for some reason, that William Howard Taft was President at the time. When a comparative stranger offers to buy him a drink, he looks uneasy and says, "I got a bum heart. One drink and I would most likely drop dead." He gives a different explanation to his intimates. "If I was to get a skinful," he says, "I would start right in and insult everybody I know. I would make enemies, and enemies don't pay dues. Also, I look at it from a health standpoint. What happened to all the tanks I palled with years ago? We mourn our loss. Gone but not forgotten. When I think of all the dead-and-gone crap-shooters that if they had took it easy on the schnapps they would be here today, I'm glad I swore off." Dutch prefers caffeine to alcohol. He drinks from fifteen to twenty cups of black coffee a day. He frequently gets so fidgety that he begins to stutter, or has a sudden attack of the trembles, or upsets a glass of water by just reaching for it. Although he takes coffee black, he always demands cream on the side. After finishing the coffee, he drinks the cream in one gulp, although he does not like it. "I pay for it, don't I?" he says. He carries a bag of Bull Durham smoking tobacco in his breast pocket and rolls his own cigarettes. He is as expert as any cowboy. "Made butts are too dear," he says. "Also, I think they put chemicals in them. I be damned if I think they're sanitary."

Dutch has lived in furnished rooms practically all his life. At present he has a room in a house on Thirteenth Street, just west of Third. He uses it only as a place to sleep. He customarily gets to bed around 5 A.M. and sleeps until noon. He goes to the races every day a local track is open; he always turns up at the railway station early, and most days he is able to find a member who will buy him tickets for the train and the track. After the races, on the way in, he goes down the aisle of the train looking for any members who might be aboard, soliciting dues from those who have been lucky and listening sympathetically to those who haven't. Dutch himself is an extremely timid horseplayer. He makes only one small, sure-thing bet a day, but he always has a doleful answer when someone asks, "How'd *you* do, Dutch?" "Picked wrong every race," he usually answers. "Even lost my coffee money. Don't know how I'm going to eat tonight, and already my belly thinks my throat's cut. Could you slip me some dues?" Three or four nights a week, he makes a round of saloons, restaurants, cigar stores, bowling alleys, barbershops, and hotel lobbies around Broadway in which sporting people foregather. Other nights, he goes to gambling places. He has been a hanger-on in gambling circles since adolescence and keeps on good terms with every operator of any consequence in town. Gambling-house lookouts and doorkeepers pass him in without question, although he rarely risks a dollar; he just stands around and gazes wistfully at the cash on the tables. When one of his members wins a fistful, Dutch's eyes light up; he knows he can be certain of at least a couple of bucks of it. Now and then he spends an evening away from Broadway. He considers himself a staunch Tammany Democrat, and a number of downtown Tammany district leaders are members of his association. He occasionally drops into their clubhouses, and he shows up for many of their beefsteak parties and moonlight sails; he finds out about such affairs by reading a political-gossip column in the Sunday *Enquirer*. He does not eat anything at beefsteak parties; he shakes hands with the dignitaries and watches for a chance to collect some dues. He always goes to the weighing-in ceremonies before important prizefights, and most fight nights he hangs around the outer lobby of Madison Square Garden. A couple of times a month he puts in an appearance at Jimmy Kelly's night club in Greenwich Village; he and Kelly have been friends since they were in their teens. He makes a practice of attending the funerals of prominent politicians. On these occasions he usually manages to pick up a few dollars. "Some of my big-shot members like Al Smith and Governor Lehman, the best time to put the bite on them is to bunk into them at a funeral," he says.

Dutch's demeanor fluctuates between servility and arrogance. In the company of some of his members, he is meek. "I hate to bother you, pal, but I'm flat," he will say, "and I wonder could you see your way clear to pay some dues. I wouldn't ask it, only I know I can count on you." Toward others he behaves with the wary impudence of an English sparrow among city pigeons. "Either you get yourself in good standing," he will say, "or I'll excommunicate you the hell and gone right out of my association. I don't allow no deadheads, and you know it." The majority of his members probably could not explain exactly why they give him money. Some have known him since they were young men together and are genuinely fond of him. Joe Madden, the Assistant Head President, is one of these. "I'm acquainted with Dutch almost thirty years," he once said, "and if he was to croak, I'd miss him. Whatever money he gets out of me, I figure it well spent. He hands me a lot of laughs. I like to listen to him. He keeps his ears open, and he always knows who beat the dice tables last night, and what millionaire from Hollywood lost five thousand bucks and got sick to his stomach, and who's in hock to who, and what places got thrown in the street by the cops and why. He knows everything. Say a crap game has to float from one little fleabag hotel to another; if you want the new address, Dutch can tell you. A lot of so-called underworld fellows from out of town, as soon as they hit Broadway they look Dutch up, just to hear what's new. Fellows like Boo Boo Hoff, the big Philadelphia gangster that croaked a few months ago. Use to, every time Boo Boo came to town, he and Dutch would get together and cut up touches. In his time, he gave Dutch plenty of dues."

No matter how much his members may like Dutch, practically all of them look upon him as a clown. He does not mind this; he feels that it gives him an advantage over them. "I act like a screwball," he says, "but I know what I'm doing." On his nightly rounds he encourages people to ridicule him, and in places like Lindy's, Madden's, Attell's, the 18 Club, the Paddock Bar & Grill, and the Dublin Café, he is treated as an official butt. He cannot be insulted. In situations that would be painful to the average man, he always behaves with a sort of deadpan, Chaplin-like jauntiness. A stock joke is often played on him. Someone invites him to sit down and have a free meal. He promptly accepts, and then his benefactor refuses to let him order anything but a steak. Dutch's one tooth is useless and he is forced to subsist almost entirely on soups. When a free steak is placed before him, people crowd around and watch his struggle with it. "Don't give up, Dutch, old boy!" they yell. "Keep fighting!" Dutch puts on a show; trying his best to chew the steak, he grunts, groans, looks cross-eyed, and tosses his head about like a turkey gobbler. "I can't really chew it," he says, "but I certainly can gum it."

At least once a night, wherever he may happen to be, Dutch is asked to sing. "Give us a song, Dutch," someone will say, "and I'll slip you some dues." Dutch is convinced that he has a fine baritone, and between not singing and singing and being laughed at, he greatly prefers the latter. He usually sings "My Pearl Was a Bowery Girl," "The Bowery, the Bowery! I'll Never Go There Any More," or "Down in a Coal Mine," all of which were popular in his youth. Sometimes, however, if he has an especially appreciative audience, he will put his right foot forward, clasp his hands behind his back, gaze soulfully into the distance, and sing "The Last Rose of Summer." Almost invariably, while he is singing, someone creeps up from behind and gives him a hotfoot. He has undoubtedly been a hotfoot victim oftener than any other human being. He never appears to mind. "A fella that pays his dues, I don't hold it against him if he gives me a hotfoot," Dutch says. "Maybe he figures he ought to get *something* for his money."

References to Dutch frequently appear in sports and Broadway columns, especially in Damon Runyon's and Dan Parker's. Such references are seldom complimentary, but Dutch always considers them so. Recently, commenting on the attitude of civilians toward soldiers in some parts of the country, Runyon wrote, "It is said that in certain of these spots the appearance of a guy in uniform in the vicinity of a local festivity would produce about the same coolness that might be created if Commodore Dutch showed up at Mrs. Vanderbilt's party." Dutch carried a clipping of this column around until it wore out. "Did you see the swell write-up my pal Runyon gave me?" he would ask, pulling it out. When Dutch is introduced to someone, he usually makes fun of his own face. He shakes hands and says, "Pleased to meet you, pal." Then, opening his mouth as wide as possible and exhibiting his solitary tooth, he giggles and says, "Look, pal! I'm an Elk." He seems most pleased with himself when people are making jokes at his expense and laughing at him. It makes no perceptible difference to him whether their laughter is scornful or good-natured. "When a fella is laughing at me, I'm sizing him up," he once told an intimate. "I'm giving him the old psychology. To put the bite on a man, what I call collecting dues, you got to study him. You got to figure out the right moment to nail him. With some of my members, I wait until they are drunk and happy before I bring up the question of dues. With others, I wait until they pick right in a horse race or beat the tiger in a crap game. With others, I wait until they are sitting with some doll that they want to impress with their great generosity. But with each and every one of them, before I ask for dues, I wait until I got them snickering at me." Dutch has devoted considerable thought to his peculiar position in society. He is profoundly cynical and has come to the conclusion that people enjoy his company because he makes them feel superior. "The fellas on Broadway are so low themselves," he says, "it makes them feel good to have somebody around that they can look down on, and I guess I fill the bill."

Dutch says that he was born on Tompkins Square, a lower East Side neighborhood which was then known as Little Germany. He says that he has been called Dutch for as long as he can remember, but that he doesn't know whether his parents came from Germany or Holland. "I never took no interest in where they came from," he says. He makes a mystery of his childhood and will not tell his real name. He explains that his surname is a long one and hard to pronounce. "I'm the only person in the world that knows it," he says, "and I wouldn't tell it to nobody. I don't hardly remember it myself. I haven't used it since I quit school. When I was fifteen, I just wouldn't go to school no more and had to leave home, so I got a job helping on a Bowery dray wagon. The driver said to me, 'What's your name?' I told him the kids all called me Dutch, and that's what he called me. Since then I never once used my born name, not even to vote. When I die, I don't even want it on my tombstone. Some of my pals around Broadway don't realize Dutch is a nickname, and they figure I ought to have a nickname, so they call me The Tooth."

Dutch's first boss was a drayman who owned his own cart and picked up most of his jobs around the Bowery. In the morning he and Dutch hauled for a second-hand furniture store on Chatham Square and the rest of the day they were on call, working out of a stable on Great Jones Street. At that time, in 1894, the Bowery was just beginning to go to seed; it was declining as a theatrical street, but its saloons, dance halls, dime museums, gambling rooms, and brothels were still thriving. In that year, in fact, according to a police census, there were eighty-nine drinking establishments on the street, and it is only a mile long. On some of the side streets there were brothels in nearly every house; Dutch refers to them as "free-and-easies."

Dutch is excessively proud of this period of his life. "In that day and time," he says, "a good way to get yourself educated was to work on a dray. I hadn't been on a dray a year before I could point out the head madams, the head pickpockets, the head crapshooters, and all like that. Quite a few of the free-and-easies were outfitted by the furniture store we hauled for, and we were in and out of them all the time. Also, the girls were always on the move, and we handled their trunks. And we did trunk work for the classy Bowery hotels, places like the Occidental, the Worden House, and Honest John Howard's Kenmore Hotel. The Occidental was the classiest. We called it the Ox, and I got a thrill out of it even if I only went in to horse some luggage around. It's still standing, at the southwest corner of Broome and the Bowery, but it's just a ghost of bygone days. You can stay there now for three bucks a week. It gives me the awfullest feeling just to walk past it. In my time it had a beautiful barbershop and a beautiful barroom, and the ceiling of this barroom was one enormous painting of some dames giving theirselves a bath. The old Ox was a hangout for politicians, actors, gambling men, fighters, and the like of that, the sporting element. Some of the fighters that put up there to my personal knowledge were Terrible Terry McGovern that Sam Harris managed for years, the original Jack Dempsey that they called the Nonpareil, Charlie Mitchell that throwed himself away fighting in gin mills when he should of been saving his strength for the ring, Jake Kilrain, Joe Bernstein, Tom Sharkey, and Oscar Gardner that they called the Omaha Kid, only he came from Wheeling, West Virginia; names don't mean a damn thing. I knew them all, to speak to.

"Every single night, after I knocked off work, I would wash up and walk the Bowery. I wasn't a teetotaler then by no means, and I would hit four or five gin mills and listen to the personalities, what they call celebrities nowadays, only a personality was somebody, but a celebrity, who the hell is he? Like I would listen to old Silver Dollar Solomon. He was high up in a combination of white slavers, the Max Hochstim Association, that bossed over the free-and-easies, and he ran a saloon that had one thousand silver dollars stuck in the concrete floor. And drunks would bring cold chisels in and they would kneel down when they thought nobody was looking and try to pry themselves up some silver dollars, but they would just get throwed out. And I would listen to Steve Brodie that took a leap off Brooklyn Bridge, only he didn't, and a brewery set him up in a saloon because he got so much attention for himself they figured he would draw trade, and he would wear your ears out discussing Steve Brodie; that's all he knew. I never thought he was so much. All the write-ups about the Bowery I ever read, they made Brodie a hero. People that really knew him, like me, we considered him ninety-nine per cent jaw. But a personality I liked was George Washington Connors that they called Chuck. He had three girl friends and claimed all of them was his wife—one named The Truck, one named The Rummager, and one named Chinatown Nellie, only she was Irish. Chuck was a guide for slummers, and he had Nellie and an old Chinee fella lying in bunks in a fake opium den on Mott Street, and Nellie sometimes couldn't keep a straight face when Chuck brought some slummers in. She would bust out laughing, and the slummers would think it was the opium taking effect. Chuck was the squarest of all the personalities. Some nights there were more slummers around than one man could handle, and Chuck would let me guide a party. Him and I were pals. The first cigar I ever smoked, he give it to me. The first drink of champagne I ever had, it was out of a bottle he bought."

Dutch says that he quit the dray wagon in 1898, when he was nineteen, and began living by his wits. For a while he had a job steering sailors to a saloon at 295 Bowery called John McGurk's Suicide Hall, where in one year five back-room girls killed themselves by swallowing carbolic acid. He says he got the title of Commodore while working for McGurk's. "I wore a sailor cap and a pea jacket," he says, "and I knocked around South Street and gave out cards to the sailors describing the attractions at McGurk's. Sometimes I would collect a mob and take them up. One night I came in with about two dozen sailors and a fella says to McGurk, 'Who the hell,' he says, 'is that little squirt that brings all the sailor trade into here?' 'Why, that's my Commodore,' old McGurk says to him. 'That's Commodore Dutch, the Commodore of the Bowery Navy.' And that's how I got my title. I was proud of it. Back in those days all the personalities had a nickname or a title. If you was known by your real name you didn't have no standing."

Dutch's period of greatest affluence began in the spring of 1899, when Timothy D. Sullivan, the Tammany boss of the Bowery district, gave him a job. Big Tim was the most powerful and the most open-handed politician in the city. He was a member of a syndicate which controlled all the gambling houses in Manhattan, he owned saloons, race horses, and prizefighters, and he had a partnership in a chain of vaudeville and burlesque theatres. His clubrooms were at 207 Bowery, but he also kept a suite on the second floor of the Occidental, where he and other politicians played poker and he received reports from the managers of his various enterprises. One evening he summoned Dutch to the Occidental. "I had run errands for Big Tim and he knew I was O.K., and he asked me did I want a job of a confidential nature," Dutch says. "He was the silent partner in eight saloons and he was anxious to know what went on in them. He trusted his managers, still and all he didn't, and he wanted somebody neutral to circulate around in an unbeknownst way and watch conditions and listen to the talk that went on. That was right up my alley. I would wander in and out of Big Tim's various gin mills every night and enjoy myself to the full, and every afternoon I would go to the Ox and report to him what I seen and heard. Some days he wouldn't have time to hardly listen, other days he'd keep me talking two, three hours. He paid me irregular. One Saturday night it would be a hundred bucks and the next Saturday it would be a ten spot, all according to the humor he was in. Anyway, he seen to it I had plenty of coconuts."

Big Tim had a number of retainers and hangers-on whose duties were similarly vague and confidential. He rewarded some by permitting them to run balls, or "rackets," for which all the saloon-keepers and divekeepers in the Bowery district were obliged to buy so many tickets. Among them were Larry Mulligan, Big Tim's half-brother, who operated a profitable St. Patrick's Eve ball in Terrace Garden Hall, and Harry Oxford, a fixer, who ran one on Washington's Birthday Eve in Webster Hall. Chuck Connors, whose fanciful conversation amused Big Tim, was allowed to run an annual ball in Tammany Hall; it was sponsored by the Chuck Connors Association, of which Chuck was the sole member. Biff Ellison, a gunman who shepherded gangs of repeaters to the polls every Election Day, imitated Connors and formed a Biff Ellison Association, which ran three rackets a year.

On New Year's Eve of 1900, Dutch and a girl friend went on a champagne spree; he woke up owing two saloons a total of $285. He asked Big Tim for a loan. "He wouldn't give me no loan," Dutch says. "He told me that wasn't no way to do business. He says to me, 'Dutch, you have certainly behaved like a fool, but I tell you what I'll do. I'll give you a franchise to run a racket. Hire yourself a date in a hall and get some tickets printed, and I'll pass the word around.' So I told him it might look nicer to the public if I had an association behind me, like Chuck and Biff. It would look more businesslike. So he says, 'Go right ahead. If those hoodlums can be a one-man association, so the hell can you.' I had two thousand tickets printed, a buck a head, ladies free. Everybody on the Bowery knew I was professionally associated with Big Tim in some way or other—why ask too many questions?—so naturally I didn't have no trouble unloading my tickets."

Dutch's racket, the first Gala Naval Ball of the Commodore Dutch Association, was held on the night of April 30, 1901, in Everett Hall, on East Fourth Street, just off the Bowery. Big Tim, of course, was the guest of honor. With him, in a box, sat Photo Dave Altman, his bodyguard; Sarsaparilla Reilly, his valet; and Flatnose Dinny Sullivan, one of his brothers, who later became boss of Coney Island. The music was furnished by Professor Pretzel Wolf's East Side Society Orchestra. Dutch led the grand march with a red-haired Irish girl whose name he has forgotten. He wore an admiral's outfit he had purchased from a theatrical costumer; it consisted of a cocked hat, a pair of swords, and a uniform with gold-starred epaulets and a red, white, and blue belly sash. In the grand march was Connors, who had The Truck on one arm and Chinatown Nellie on the other. The Rummager was escorted by Eat-'Em-Up Jack McManus, a fighter who sometimes worked as night bouncer at McGurk's. Dutch says there were at least fifteen couples in the march, all personalities, but he has forgotten the names of the others.

"After we sashayed two times around the ballroom, bowing to the right and then to the left," he says, "I blowed on a police whistle and the fun began. I had got a cut rate on two dozen kegs of beer from a brewery that was indebted to Big Tim for a favor, and I had them resting in washtubs full of ice. The instant I let loose with my whistle, whoosh, most of the mob descended on the beer, and the way they helped theirselves it was a disgrace to the human race. I was nuts about waltzing—never got enough—and I waltzed around an hour or more, not paying much attention to anything but the music. Then I stopped to get my breath and I took a look around, and I never see so many drunks. The place was swarming with drunks. Each fella was singing at the top of his voice, or slugging somebody smaller than him, or trying to steal some other fella's girl. One fella was flat on his back and he had his mouth right under a spigot on a beer keg, and the spigot was wide open and the beer was pouring into him; it was coming out of his ears. And the girls were wrestling with the fellas and squealing. I took one look and I felt like fleeing out of there. 'Ladies and gentlemen,' I said, 'Jesus Christ!' I thought to myself, 'No good can come of this. People will die before morning, people by the dozens.' But to tell the truth, it was a most successful swaree. Nobody was killed and everybody got all the beer they could hold, and I cleared damned near fifteen hundred bucks. When I told Big Tim how much I drew, he took me off his steady payroll. He says to me, 'Let the racket be your meal ticket. Go ahead and run yourself one every year. All the joints in the district know I'm in back of you, and if any one of them refuses to take their quota of tickets, you just let me know."

For twelve years, with Big Tim's support, Dutch netted an average of $2,000 a year out of the Gala Naval Ball. He abandoned Everett Hall, which had become too small, and switched to the old Tammany Hall, on Fourteenth Street. Shortly after the 1912 ball, however, everything went to pieces. In the summer of that year Big Tim began to suffer from delusions of persecution and had to be placed in a sanitarium. In February, 1913, he was removed to a house in the Williamsbridge section of the Bronx and friends hired a staff of guards to watch him. Occasionally he would tire his guards out and escape, usually turning up hours later at the Occidental on the Bowery, where, according to Dutch, he would "just sit in the lobby and stare until they come and took him away." "I seen him one day," Dutch says, "and I went over to him and I said, 'Jesus Christ, Big Tim, old pal, ain't there something I could do for you?' He just sat and stared at me. It broke my heart." Big Tim's last escape took place on the evening of August 30, 1913. Next morning, around dawn, the body of a man who had been struck by a train was found beside the New York, New Haven & Hartford tracks just north of the Westchester freight yards. It was carried to the Bronx morgue, where it lay unidentified fourteen days. Just before it was to be removed to potter's field a policeman took a look at it and said, "It's Big Tim Sullivan, God rest his soul." Big Tim's funeral, held in old St. Patrick's Cathedral on Mott Street, was one of the largest in the city's history. "I marched in the procession," Dutch says, "and I cried every step of the way."

The decay of the Bowery as a night-life street set in after Big

Tim's funeral. The gamblers drifted up to Broadway and Dutch followed them. He found the going hard. Without political support, he was unable to sell tickets, and his 1914 ball was a flop. "With Big Tim in his grave, I was Mr. Nobody," he says. "Until then, I hadn't paid no attention to the Commodore Dutch Association; it was just a name. I seen I had to do something, so I figured to build up the association. I made honorary officers out of all the Bowery personalities that had moved uptown and for members I took in all the Broadway crowd I could get. And when you have members, naturally you collect dues. I began collecting dues in 1914 and I'm still at it. My ball don't amount to a damn any more, but without I run a ball, what would be the excuse for an association?"

After old Tammany Hall was torn down in 1928, Dutch began the practice of using the back rooms of lower Third Avenue saloons for his balls. For his most recent ball, which was a typical one, he used the Stuyvesant Grill, a neighborhood saloon on Third Avenue near Fifteenth Street. The Stuyvesant's back room has a tiny bandstand and a small dance floor, on either side of which are seven booths, the kind with trellises to which artificial grapevines are fixed. Dutch got it rent free, of course. On his showcards, he had advertised that "festivities will begin with a bang at 9 sharp." However, most guests had sense enough to go late. Dutch himself did not show up until eleven. By that time approximately fifty men and women were sitting at tables in the booths. About half were members of the association. The others were curiosity-seekers from uptown, or regular customers of the saloon who had left the bar to see what was happening in the back room and had stayed. No tickets were collected; Dutch doesn't bother any more. Drinks were brought in from the bar by a waitress; no free beer has been served at a Gala Naval Ball since 1912. Mr. and Mrs. Swiss Cheese sat at one table. Swiss Cheese, in a gay mood, was yodeling "Mexicali Rose" and his wife was urging him to shut up. At another table sat Assistant Head President Madden and eight friends, among whom were Ed and Pegeen Fitzgerald, the radio commentators, and Father A. R. Hyland, chaplain of Clinton Prison, at Dannemora. At still another table sat Fiddler Cronin, F. X. Fitzsimmons, Peanuts Pelletier, and the Iron Horse, all elderly and irritable pugs who have known Dutch since his Bowery days. Pelletier, the youngest, fought last in 1906. They always show up for Dutch's balls. Until they are drunk, they insult each other. After they are drunk, they call each other the greatest fighter that ever lived. "What you doing now, Peanuts?" Cronin asked at the last ball. Pelletier said that he had just got a job as a night watchman for a big steam laundry in the Bronx. "I bet you're one hell of a fine night watchman," Cronin said. "If some robbers was to come around, I bet you would pitch in and help them open the safe." "Listen here, Fiddler," Pelletier said, "you remember the night you fought Boxhead Tommy Hansen at the Pelican A.C.? As I remember it, you didn't last out the first round. If ever I saw a no-good, two-bit fighter, it was you." "Oh, go to hell," said Cronin.

With Dutch, when he came in, was a band he had hired, an outfit called the New York Ramblers, consisting of an elderly piano player, a banjo picker, and a girl violinist. The Ramblers, looking bored, went over to the bandstand, took their places, and promptly started playing "The Star-Spangled Banner." Everybody stood up. Dutch had a pasteboard suitbox under his arm, and after people began to sit down again he ducked into the men's room. When he reappeared, he was wearing his admiral's uniform. He lost his cocked hat and his pair of swords shortly after his first ball, but for forty years he has been lugging the moldy old uniform from one furnished room to the next; it is his most precious possession. Across the chest he had pinned four badges—"Private Detective," "Special Officer," "Sheriff," and "Sharpshooter," The guests clapped as Dutch walked jauntily across the dance floor to the bandstand. It had rained a little during the afternoon and he wore rubbers. He stepped up on the stand, held his clasped hands over his head for several moments like a prizefighter, and then took a bow. "Well, folks," he said, "we're all here for a good time, so let's all have a good time. The world-renowned New York Ramblers will play for you and I want everybody to step out and dance. That's all the speech I'm going to make. I thank you one and all."

Swiss Cheese stood up unsteadily and shouted, "Just a minute,

Dutch. Would it be all right if I entertained the crowd?" "Certainly, Cheese," said Dutch, "go ahead and yodel all you want to." "Yodel, hell," said Swiss Cheese, "I'm going to do a dance." He walked to the middle of the floor, squatted on his heels, and began a Cossack dance. After two kicks, he sat on the floor. He got to his feet, guffawing, and yelled, "Hey, Dutch, you know what I am? I'm a gentleman and a scholar." Dutch looked at him disapprovingly. "You're a very foolish man," he said. "You're going to get your blood pressure all shook up and tomorrow you'll feel awful. I wish you'd come up here and yodel." A few moments later, with Swiss Cheese yodeling happily, the Ramblers started on "My Wild Irish Rose." Several couples stepped out on the floor and began waltzing.

Dutch went over to Madden's table. "I got a party of slummers here that would like to meet you," Madden told him. Dutch was introduced. "Mr. Commodore Dutch," said one of Madden's friends, a young woman who didn't know any better, "I understand you were quite a well-known figure on the Bowery during the gay nineties." "Madam," said Dutch, giving his one-toothed grin, "I am the last of the Bowery Boys." He unbuttoned the stiff, gold-braided collar of his uniform, sat down, and put his elbows on the table. Then, interminably, while the New York Ramblers played waltzes, while Swiss Cheese yodeled, while the old pugs drank beer and insulted each other, and while one curiosity-seeker after another became disgusted with the proceedings and stalked out, Dutch talked about the Bowery in the days of Big Tim Sullivan. He talked steadily until 1 A.M. At that time the music stopped and the piano player came over and said that the New York Ramblers did not propose to play another note until they had been paid. Dutch looked gloomily at his Assistant Head President. "Joe, old pal," he said, "could you slip me a couple of sawbucks? I wouldn't ask it, only I know I can count on you."

(1941)

The Cave Dwellers

*T*HE WINTER OF 1933 WAS A PAINFUL ONE. It seems like
a hundred and thirty-three years ago, but I remember it distinctly.
That winter, the fifth winter of the depression and the winter of
repeal, I was a reporter on a newspaper whose editors believed that
nothing brightened up a front page so much as a story about human
suffering. "The man on the street is so gloomy nowadays," one of
the editors used to say, "that a story about somebody else's bad
luck cheers him up." In the three weeks preceding Christmas there
was, of course, an abundance of such stories, and for one reason
or another I was picked to handle most of them. One morning I
spent a harried half-hour in the anteroom of a magistrate's court
talking with a stony-faced woman who had stabbed her husband to
death because he took a dollar and eighty cents she had saved for
Christmas presents for their children and spent it in one of the new
repeal gin mills. "I sure fixed his wagon," she said. Then she began
to moan. That afternoon I was sent up to the big "Hoover Village"
on the Hudson at Seventy-fourth Street to ask about the plans the
people there were making for Christmas. The gaunt squatters stood
and looked at me with a look I probably never will get over; if they
had turned on me and pitched me into the river I wouldn't have
blamed them. Next day I was sent out to stand on a busy corner
with a Salvation Army woman whose job was to ring a bell and
attract attention to a kettle in the hope that passers-by would drop
money into it for the Army's Christmas Fund. "Just stand there
three or four hours," I was told, "and see what happens; there

ought to be a story in it." The bellringer was elderly and hollow-eyed and she had a head cold, which I caught.

Day in and day out, I was sent to breadlines, to relief bureaus, to evictions; each morning I called on cringing, abject humans who sat and stared as I goaded them with questions. My editors sincerely believed that such interviews would provoke people to contribute to the various Christmas funds, and they undoubtedly did, but that did not help me conquer the feeling that I had no right to knock on tenement doors and catechize men and women who were interesting only because they were miserable in some unusual way. Also, the attitude of the people I talked with was disheartening. They were without indignation. They were utterly spiritless. I am sure that few of them wanted their stories printed, but they answered my questions, questions I absolutely had to ask, because they were afraid something might happen to their relief if they didn't; all of them thought I was connected in some way with the relief administration. I began to feel that I was preying on the unfortunate. My faith in human dignity was almost gone when something happened that did a lot to restore it.

Early one bitter cold morning, only a few days before Christmas, a man telephoned the newspaper and said that the evening before, while walking his dog in Central Park, he had come upon a man and woman who said they had lived for almost a year in a cave in the park. This was one of the caves uncovered when the old lower reservoir was emptied and abandoned, an area since filled in for playgrounds. He said he had discovered the man and woman squatting in the cave beside a little fire, and had been afraid they would freeze to death during the night, so he had persuaded them to leave the Park and had put them up in a furnished room.

"I wish your newspaper would run a story about them," said the man on the telephone. "It might help them get jobs."

I went up to see the man and woman. They were living in one of a cluster of brownstone rooming houses on West Sixtieth Street, off Columbus Avenue, two blocks from the park. They were on the fourth floor. An inch and a half of snow had fallen during the night and there was a ridge of it on the window sill of their furnished room. The man said his name was James Hollinan and that he was an unemployed carpenter. He was small, wiry, and white-haired. He wore corduroy trousers and a greasy leather windbreaker. The woman was his wife. Her name was Elizabeth and she was an unemployed hotel maid. When I arrived, Mr. Hollinan was preparing to go out. He had his hat on and was getting into a tattered overcoat. I told him who I was.

"I'd like to ask a few questions," I said.

"Talk to my wife," he said. "She does all the talking."

He turned to his wife. "I'll go get some breakfast," he said.

"Get egg sandwiches and some coffee," she said, taking a few coins out of her purse and placing them, one by one, in his hand, "and we'll have seven cents left."

"O.K.," he said, and left.

I asked Mrs. Hollinan to tell me about their life in the cave. While she answered my questions she made the bed, and she appeared to get a lot of pleasure out of the task. I could understand it; it was the first bed she had made in a long time.

"Well, I tell you," she said, smacking a pillow against the iron bedstead, "we got dispossessed from a flat up in Washington Heights the middle of last December, a year ago. When we went to the relief bureau they tried to separate us. They wanted to send my husband one place and me another. So I said, 'We'll starve together.' That night we ended up in Central Park. We found the cave and hid in it. Late at night we built a fire. We been doing that almost every night for a year."

She smoothed out the counterpane until there wasn't a wrinkle in it and then rather reluctantly sat down on the bed. There was only one chair in the room.

"Of course," she continued, "some nights it got too cold and rainy. Then we'd go to a church uptown that's left open at night. We'd sleep in a pew, sitting up. Most mornings we'd part and look for work. He hardly ever found anything to do. It was worse for him. He's older than me. Couple of times a week I'd pick up a cleaning job and that would mean a few dollars, and we'd eat on that. We'd carry water to the cave and make stews."

"How did you sleep in the cave?" I asked.

"We'd take turns snoozing on a bed we made of a pile of cardboard boxes," she said. "We kept a fire going. A little fire, so the cops wouldn't run us off. The Park cops knew we were there, but so long as we didn't build up a big fire and attract attention they'd let us alone. Last summer the cave was better than a house. But lately, when it rained, we'd get rheumatism, and it was awful."

Mrs. Hollinan's dress was nearly worn out, but it was clean and neat. I wondered how she had kept so clean, living in a cave. I think she guessed what was on my mind, because she said, "We'd go to a public bath about twice a week, and I used to put my dresses and his shirts in an old lard stand in the cave and boil them." We talked for about fifteen minutes and then her husband returned. He had a cardboard container of coffee and two sandwiches in a paper bag. I knew they didn't want me around while they ate breakfast, so I said goodbye.

"I hope we get some relief this time," said Mrs. Hollinan as I went out the door, and I realized she thought I was a relief investigator. I didn't have the nerve to tell her she was mistaken.

I wasn't especially interested in Mr. and Mrs. Hollinan; compared with some of the people I had seen that winter, they were living off the fat of the land. In the story I wrote about them I mentioned the incident in which Mrs. Hollinan told her husband that when breakfast was paid for they would have seven cents left, and I gave the address of the rooming house in case someone wanted to offer Mr. Hollinan a job. I wrote the story hurriedly and it was printed on the front page of the first edition, which reached the newsstands around noon, and, unlike many stories in the first edition of an afternoon newspaper, it wasn't dropped from subsequent editions but was kept in, and on the front page, throughout the day.

Next day was my day off, but late that afternoon I dropped by the office to get my mail. My box was stuffed with letters and telegrams from people who had read the story about Mr. and Mrs. Hollinan, and attached to many of the letters were bills or checks to be turned over to them. In all, there was eighty-five dollars, and there were two telegrams, offering jobs.

I had promised my wife that I would meet her and help her with some Christmas shopping, and I telephoned her that I couldn't do so, that I had to go give eighty-five dollars to a man and woman who had spent a year in a cave. She wanted to go with me. I met her at Columbus Circle and we walked over to the rooming house. The streets were crowded with Christmas shoppers and store windows were full of holly and tinsel and red Christmas bells. The cheerful shoppers depressed me. "How can men and women be so happy," I thought, "when all over the city people are starving?"

The landlady of the rooming house met us at the door. She appeared to be in an angry mood. I told her I was the reporter who had come to see Mr. and Mrs. Hollinan the day before. She said people had been calling on them since early morning, bringing them money and food.

"They read that story you had in the paper last night," the landlady said. "They keep coming, but I haven't let anybody upstairs this afternoon. That was a lot of baloney you had in the paper. Why, those cave people are upstairs celebrating."

"I don't blame them," said my wife.

"Well, I do," said the landlady.

She wouldn't let my wife go upstairs with me.

"You'll have to wait down here, young lady," she said severely.

I went on upstairs, carrying the fistful of letters. I knocked on their door and someone shouted, "Come on in!" I opened the door. The room was in magnificent disorder. On the table were two big steamer baskets, cellophane-wrapped, with red ribbons tied to their handles. The steamer baskets looked odd in the shabby room. Also on the table were bottles of beer and gin and ginger ale and some half-eaten sandwiches. The floor was strewn with wrapping paper and boxes and cigar butts. Mrs. Hollinan was sitting on the bed with a tumbler in her hand. A cigar was sticking out of a corner of Mr. Hollinan's mouth and he was pouring himself a drink of gin. They were quite drunk, without a doubt. Mr. Hollinan looked at me, but he didn't seem to recognize me.

"Sit down and make yourself at home," he said, waving me to the bed. "Have a drink? Have a cigar?"

"It's that sneak from the newspaper," said Mrs. Hollinan. "Give him hell, Jim."

Mr. Hollinan stood up. He wasn't very steady on his feet.

"What did you mean," he said, "putting that writeup in the paper?"

"What was wrong with it?" I asked.

"You said in that writeup we only had seven cents left, you liar."

"Well, that's what your wife told me."

"I did not," said Mrs. Hollinan, indignantly. She got up and waved her tumbler, spilling gin and ginger ale all over the bed. "I told you we had *seventy* cents left," she said.

"That's right," said Mr. Hollinan. "What do you mean, putting lies about us in the paper?"

Mr. Hollinan took a square bottle of gin off the table. He got a good grip on it and started toward me, waving the bottle in the air.

"Wait a minute," I said, edging toward the door. "I brought you some money."

"I don't want your money," he said. "I got money."

"Well," I said, holding out the telegrams, "I think I have a job for you."

"I don't want your help," he said. "You put a lie about us in the paper."

"That's right, Jim," said Mrs. Hollinan, giggling. "Give him hell."

I closed the door and hurried to the stairs. Mr. Hollinan stumbled out of the room and stood at the head of the stairs, clutching for the railing with one hand. Just as I reached the landing on the second floor he threw the bottle of gin. It hit the wall above my head and broke into pieces. I was sprayed with gin and bits of wet glass. I ran on down the stairs, getting out of Mr. Hollinan's range. All the way down the stairs I could hear Mrs. Hollinan up in the room, yelling, "Give him hell, Jim!"

"Mother of God," said the landlady when I got downstairs, "what happened? What was that crash?"

"You smell like a distillery," said my wife.

I was laughing. "Mr. Hollinan threw a bottle of gin at me," I said.

"That's nothing to laugh about," said the landlady sharply. "Why don't you call an officer?"

"Let's get out of here," I said to my wife.

We went to a liquor store over on Columbus Circle. I bought a bottle of Holland gin and had it wrapped in Christmas-gift paper, and I gave the liquor-store man Mr. Hollinan's address and told him to deliver the order. My wife thought I was crazy, but I didn't mind. It was the first time I had laughed in weeks.

Early the following morning I went back to the rooming house. I had decided it was my duty to make another attempt to give the money to Mr. and Mrs. Hollinan.

"Those cave people are gone," the landlady told me. "A gentleman came here last night in a limousine, with a chauffeur. He took them away. I had a talk with him before he went upstairs, and I told him how they'd been cutting up, but he didn't care. He gave me a five-dollar bill. 'Here,' he said, 'take this for your trouble. If any mail comes for these good people, send it along to me, and I'll see they get it.' He put them in the back seat with him. He told me he was going to give Mr. Hollinan a job on his farm."

The landlady was quite angry. "They were still drunk," she said, "but that man in the limousine didn't seem to care. He was drunk, too. Drunker than they were, if you ask me. He kept slapping them on the back, first one and then the other. And when they got in the limousine they were laughing and falling all over theirselves, and that Mrs. Hollinan, that lowdown woman, she rolled down the window and thumbed her nose at me."

She had the benefactor's name and address written down and I made a note of them. It was a New Jersey address. I went back to the office and wrote letters to all the people who had sent money to Mr. and Mrs. Hollinan, returning it. I told them Mr. Hollinan had found a job and had declined their contributions.

Until perhaps a week before Christmas of the following year, I forgot about Mr. and Mrs. Hollinan. Then I recalled the experience and began to wonder about them. I wondered if the man in the limousine did give Mr. Hollinan a job and if he was getting along all right. I kept thinking about them all that week and on Christmas Eve I decided to try and get in touch with them and wish them a merry Christmas and a happy New Year. I searched through a stack of old notebooks in the bottom drawer of my desk and finally found their benefactor's name and address. I asked Information to get me his telephone number in New Jersey and I put in a call for him. He answered the telephone himself. I told him I was the reporter who wrote the story about the man and woman he had befriended last Christmas, the cave dwellers. I started to ask him if he would let Mr. Hollinan come to the telephone, but he interrupted me.

"Have you seen them lately?" he asked, irrelevantly. His voice was blurry.

"Why, no," I said. "Aren't they out there with you any longer?"

"I certainly would like to see them," he answered. "To tell you the God's truth, I was just thinking about them. I was sitting here by the fire having a few drinks and I was thinking how much I'd like to see them. I used to have a few drinks at night with old man Hollinan. He was good company, and so was the old lady. He was a funny old crock." He paused.

"What happened?" I asked.

"Well," he said, "I have a little farm out here and he took care of it for me when I was in the city. He was the caretaker, sort of. They stayed until about the end of March, and then one day the old boy and his wife just wandered off and I never saw them again."

"I wonder why they left."

"I don't know for sure," he said, "but you know what I think? I think living in that cave ruined them. It ruined them for living in a house. I think they left me because they just got tired of living in a house."

"Well," I said, "merry Christmas."

"Same to you," he said, and hung up.

(1938)

King of the Gypsies

*T*HERE ARE AT LEAST one dozen gypsy kings in the city. All are elderly, quarrelsome, and self-appointed. One of them, Johnny Nikanov, a Russian, sometimes called King Cockeye Johnny by the detectives of the Pickpocket Squad, is a friend of mine. I became acquainted with him in the fall of 1936. I was covering the Criminal Courts Building for a newspaper and spent a part of every working day in the back office of Samuel Rothberg's bail-bond establishment, diagonally across Centre Street from the Courts, where lawyers, cops, probation clerks, and the loafers of the neighborhood assembled to play pinochle. Among Rothberg's clients were practically all of the gypsy pickpockets, wallet-switch swindlers, and fortune-tellers, and King Cockeye Johnny came in now and then to get a bail bond written for one of his subjects. After transacting his business, he would always swagger into the back office and take a hand in the game. When the pinochle players saw him coming they would pretend to be alarmed. They would slap their hands over the money on the table and shout warnings at each other, such as "Stick your dough in your shoes, boys! Here comes Cockeye Johnny!" or "Make way for the king, the king of the pickpockets!" Johnny was never offended by their remarks; it seemed to give him a great deal of satisfaction to be looked upon as a thief. Whenever the gypsy reputation for thievery came up in conversation, as it frequently did, he would expand. "To a gypsy feller," he said on several occasions, with pride in his voice, "there ain't but two kinds of merchandise. Lost and unlost. Anything that ain't nailed down is lost." He professed to believe, however, that gypsies are far more honorable than *gajos,* or non-gypsies. He leaned across the table toward Rothberg one afternoon and said, "Mr. Rothberg, you never heard of a gypsy feller stealing an oil well, did you?" "I can't say I did," said Rothberg. "Well," said Johnny triumphantly, "I heard of an American feller that did. Some years back a crowd of us was coming up from Florida in a couple of Ford trucks. The womenfolks had been telling fortunes at county fairs and business had been real bad. We was awful broke. So every night we'd hit some city and siphon gas out of cars that was parked on back streets. We'd steal enough gas to run us through the next day. Nothing was safe from us. I remember draining the tank on a hearse. There was a full moon one night in Washington, D.C., and a cop caught me in the act and threw me in jail. And I got to talking to the man in the next cell and he said to me, 'There's been a lot of excitement in town over the Teapot Dome.' And I asked him what in hell was that, and he told me it was a big oil well that was stole by one of the President's right-hand men. I bet I laughed for ten minutes. You take a poor, starving gypsy feller, he'll steal a tankful of gas— there's no denying it. But you take a high-class American feller, he'll steal a whole damned oil well."

Johnny was by no means spick-and-span and was constantly scratching; this made those who sat near him at the table apprehensive. "Look here, Cockeye," a policeman said one afternoon, "you got the itch?" "No, sir, not at present," said Johnny. "I haven't had the itch in more than a month." He bummed cigarettes shamelessly, and his tongue was rarely still. Furthermore, he was the winner in almost every pinochle game he entered. However, despite all this, he was a popular figure in the back office, and he appeared to be rather proud of his popularity; at least, unlike Rothberg's other gypsy clients, he did not obviously despise *gajos.* Once he invited a few of the Criminal Courts loafers, including myself, to his home on Sheriff Street for a *patchiv,* or gypsy spree. We ate a barbecued pig, drank a punch composed of red wine, seltzer, and sliced Elberta peaches, watched the women dance, and had an exceedingly pleasant time. Since then I have often visited Johnny.

Whenever I am in the Sheriff Street neighborhood I call on him.

Johnny says that he has been a king of the gypsies off and on since he was a young man, but he has no idea how old he is. "Between forty-five and seventy-five, somewhere in there," he says with characteristic vagueness. "My hair's been white for years and years, and I got seventeen grandchildren, and I bet I'm an old, old man." Johnny is short, potbellied, and jaunty. His face is round and swarthy and sprinkled with smallpox scars. He has high cheekbones and a flattened nose. Because of a cast in his left eye, there is always an alert, skeptical expression on his face; he looks as if he does not believe a word he hears. He wears a wide-brimmed black hat and carries a copper-headed cane. Whenever he has to attend a wedding or a funeral he puts on boots, riding breeches, and a scarlet silk pajama top which buttons high around the neck and resembles a Russian blouse, but otherwise he dresses like any other American. He never owns more than one suit at a time. His current one is beetle green. Most nights he sleeps in it. As a rule Johnny is unobtrusively drunk by noon. He is a gin-drinker. He says that he never drinks less than five quarts a week. He mixes gin with Pepsi-Cola, half and half, and calls the mixture old popskull. Johnny is a highly skilled coppersmith, but he brags that he hasn't touched a tool since 1930. "I despise to work," he says. "It makes me bilious. If I had to take a steady job or be exterminated, I would beg to be exterminated."

A gypsy gets to be a king by calling himself one. There is not a king in the city who has the respect of more than fifty families, but all the kings make big, conflicting boasts about the extent of their jurisdiction. Until King Steve Kaslov was sent to a federal penitentiary in the summer of 1942 for swearing to draft boards that certain of his unmarried youths were married, he was perhaps the most powerful. Steve, whose headquarters were on Attorney Street, always claimed to be the *o boro,* or supreme ruler, of all the Russian gypsies in the United States. Actually, he was the spokesman for approximately fifty families on the lower East Side. King Frankie Mitchell, of Williamsburg, Brooklyn, who calls himself a Russian on some days and a Serbian on others, has been disputing Steve's claim to supremacy for many years. "*I* am the head of all the Russians in the United States," Frankie says. "I am also the head of all the Serbians in the same territory." Frankie is the head of about twenty families. King Tene Bimbo, of Spanish Harlem, a Serbian who has a record of a hundred and fourteen arrests, is hated by his people; detectives say that except for members of his own family there is hardly a gypsy who will go near him. He maintains, however, that he is the king of all the Russian, Serbian, and Rumanian gypsies in the United States, Canada, and Mexico.

Johnny is similarly boastful. When he is full of old popskull and talking to a *gajo,* he claims that he is the head king of all the Russian, Serbian, Rumanian, Syrian, Turkish, Bulgarian, German, and English gypsies in the whole of North America. When he is cold sober, however, and in a truthful mood he says that he is the king of exactly thirty-eight families of Russian gypsies—about two hundred and thirty men, women, and children, to all of whom he is related by blood or marriage. He refers to them as "my crowd." Officials of the Police and Welfare departments concede that Johnny has these families under his thumb, but they annoy him now and then by suggesting that he call himself spokesman rather than king. "To the Department of Welfare, I may not be no king," he recently told one of these officials, "and to the King of England, I may not be no king, but to those poor, persecuted gypsies that I run myself knock-kneed looking after their personal welfare, I am king."

Johnny does not know how many gypsies there are in the city, and neither does anyone else. Estimates range between seven and twelve thousand. Their forefathers came from every country in Europe, but the majority call themselves Russians, Serbians, or Rumanians. They are split into scores of vaguely hostile cliques, but they intermarry freely, speak practically the same dialect of Romany, the universal gypsy language, and are essentially alike. They are predominantly of the type that anthropologists call nomad gypsies; that is, unlike the Hungarian fiddler gypsies, for example, they never willingly become sedentary. They are contemptuous of the Hungarians, calling them house gypsies. In the past the nomads straggled from Maine to Mexico, spending only the winters in the city, but since the depression fewer and fewer have gone out on the road. Johnny has not been farther away than Atlantic City since 1934. At least two-thirds receive charity or relief of one sort or another. The gypsy kings are authorities on relief regulations; they know how to get their families on relief and keep them there. In the city, gypsies prefer to scatter out, but there are colonies of them on the lower East Side, on the Bowery, on the eastern fringe of Spanish Harlem, and on Varet Street in the Williamsburg neighborhood of Brooklyn. They rent the cheapest flats in the shabbiest tenements on the worst blocks. Three or four families often share one flat. They move on the spur of the moment; in the last two years one family has given seventeen addresses to the Department of Welfare. In the summer, like all slum people, they bring chairs to the sidewalks in front of their houses and sit in the sun. They nurse their babies in public. They have nothing at all to do with *gajo* neighbors. Even the kids are aloof; they play stick- and stoopball, but only with each other. The children are dirty, flea-ridden, intelligent, and beautiful; one rarely sees a homely gypsy child. They are not particularly healthy, but they have the splendid gutter hardihood of English sparrows. Practically all the adults are illiterate and only a few of the children have spent much time in public school. Johnny says he has never heard of a gypsy who went through high school. Both parents and children are opposed to education and they fight hysterically with truant officers. Not long ago one truant officer said that the very word "gypsy" made him shudder. All are able to speak slum English as well as Romany. Among themselves they use Romany exclusively. Some of the older ones are multilingual. Johnny can carry on conversations, volubly, in Russian, Rumanian, Romany, and English. They believe in child marriage; most gypsy brides and grooms are in their early teens. Brides have a price. Johnny sold his daughter, Rosie, to a Chicago gypsy in 1934 for $875. Each person has two first names, a travelling or *gajo* name, and a home or gypsy name. Johnny's home name is Lazillia. Wives use their husbands' first names; Dovie, say, becomes Dovie Steve, Annie becomes Annie Mike.

The older men are able coppersmiths and horse-traders, but their skills are anachronous. Some occasionally make a little money repairing copper stockpots for restaurants and hotels. Almost all of the younger men are good automobile mechanics. They repair their own ramshackle automobiles with odds and ends picked up in junk yards, but they are too temperamental to hold down garage jobs. A few are itinerant saloon musicians; they go from joint to joint on the lower East Side, taking up a collection after entertaining for a half-hour or so. The men pick guitars and the women learn to sing popular songs they have heard on the radio. "Amapola" is one of their favorites. The children, particularly the girls, are gifted beggars. Wearing the castoff clothes of their parents, grimy, and hungry-eyed, a pair of them will dart into a saloon, tap-dance and sing furiously for a few minutes, and then go from drunk to drunk with appealing looks and outstretched palms. When they get home, long after dark, their pockets are crammed with pretzels, potato chips, and small change.

The women are the real breadwinners. All of them are *dukkerers,* or fortune-tellers. They foretell the future by the interpretation of dreams and by the location of moles on the body, lines in the palm, and bumps on the head. This occupation is illegal in the city and they operate furtively. Each woman keeps on hand a stock of a paper-bound book called "Old Gipsy Nan's Fortune Teller and Dream Book." They buy this in bulk from Wehman Brothers, a wholesaler of cheap dream, astrology, sex-education, and joke books, at 712 Broadway, and give one to each client. Then, in case they are arrested, they are able to swear to the magistrate that they did not take money for telling a fortune, that instead they merely sold a book and taught the buyer how to use it. Practically all the *dukkerers* are thieves of one sort or another, and they give the Pickpocket Squad a lot of trouble. One member of the squad, Detective John J. Sheehan, has worked exclusively on gypsy crime for the last nine years. He has learned some Romany and has developed an admiration for gypsies. They call him Mr. Sheeny, and are quite frank with him. They invite him to weddings and he has often been asked to stand as godfather. He says that most victims of gypsy swindles are ignorant, worried, middle-aged women.

"There are thousands upon thousands of old sisters in the city so thick that any gypsy woman can con them out of their lifetime savings without half trying," Detective Sheehan says. "Women that want to know if their husbands are cheating on them, women that think they're about to die with some strange disease, superstitious old German chambermaids—the like of that. If I didn't see it every day, I wouldn't believe it." The detective says that a woman who acts and talks sensibly gets her fortune told when she visits a gypsy, and that's the end of it. "But," he says, "when one of those thick babies comes along, the *dukkerer* gets down to work. Most of them use a swindle that's old as the hills. We call it the gypsy-switch or the wallet-switch and they call it the *hokkano baro,* the big trick. First of all the gypsy convinces the victim there's something wrong with her insides; usually they say it's cancer. This may take several visits. Pretty soon the victim is so upset she'll do just about anything; when gypsies set their minds to it, they can be more scary than the stuff you'll see in the movies—Boris Karloff, the like of that. Then the gypsy says that money's what's wrong, that the money the victim has been saving for years is unclean, unholy, got the black mark on it. So the victim trots to the bank and withdraws her savings, every red cent, and gives it to the gypsy to be cleaned, or blessed. The gypsy rolls up the bills, sews them inside a little cloth bag, lights some dime-store candles, and blesses the bag with a lot of hocus-pocus. All the time the gypsy has another bag up her sleeve and this has a roll of blank paper in it. After a while she switches bags, and she sews the phony bag securely to the inside of the victim's dress over her heart, and she tells her to wear it that way seven days before opening it. At night she's supposed to put the dress with the bag on it under her pillow. That will make her well. And soon as the victim is out of sight the gypsy family packs up and moves. And a week later the victim runs howling to the police. When I arrest the gypsy, nine times out of ten the victim won't go to court to testify. Too scared. Not long ago I had a woman who had been conned out of eighteen hundred bucks, the head of a big beauty parlor, and she wouldn't go to court, not by any means. She kept saying, 'The old gypsy lady will put a curse on me and I'll die in my sleep.' "

Detective Sheehan says that now and then a man gets stung. "A gypsy girl stands in a tenement window and beckons to some man passing in the street," he says, "and the foolish fellow trots right in. He thinks he's going to have some kind of sexy adventure. The gypsy girl turns on the radio and dances around with him a few minutes, just to get his mind occupied, and while they're dancing she picks his pocket. He's so excited he doesn't know what's taking place. And then she sends him on his way. That's all that ever happens, just a dance. If he comes back looking for his money, one of the men gypsies appears and chases him off. Some of the girls are fair pickpockets, nothing to brag about. It seems to take a real one hundred per cent white man to be a good pickpocket. And all that stuff about loose, passionate gypsy girls that they have in stories is a myth. I've been hanging around gypsies nine long years and I've yet to see a real gypsy tramp. As a class, they're the straightest women in the city so far as sex is concerned. Good wives, good mothers. So far as general crookedness is concerned, they'd barbecue their grandmother for fifty cents. I guess they can't help it. I guess it's their nature."

Johnny's thirty-eight families live on Suffolk, Ridge, Pitt, Sheriff, Columbia, and Cannon streets, on the lower East Side. They usually haughtily refer to themselves as Russians, but all are American citizens, less than a dozen speak Russian, and only three families— the Nikanovs, the Sigilovs, and the Petrovs—still have Russian names. The others have long since translated their Russian names into English equivalents; among them are Smiths, Costellos, Thompsons, Mitchells, Johnsons, Stanleys, and Stevensons. Stefanovitch, for example, became Stevenson. Johnny says that his gypsies are the poorest in the United States. "If you was to turn them all upside down and give them a good shaking," he says, "you couldn't buy a quart of gin with what fell out." They are almost morbidly suspicious of American officialdom, and they send for Johnny whenever they have trouble with policemen, truant officers, relief investigators, health inspectors, clinic doctors, and landlords; he interprets and advises. They have great faith in Johnny's ability to deal shrewdly with *gajos*. Johnny is a passionate speechmaker, and he always presides at weddings, wakes, and parties. "I am the master of ceremony at everything," he says. "That's mainly what a gypsy king is for. It's a job, I tell you, because gypsies are serious about parties. You take the average gypsy, the main thing he wants out of life is a big, drunk party in his honor. Most of our parties don't amount to much. They are just *diwanos,* what we call tongue meetings. That is, we sit around and talk. I lead the talk. A *diwano* is an empty-belly affair. Other kinds are better, such as *pomanas,* where we eat and get drunk in honor of somebody that died, and *slavas,* where we eat and get drunk because somebody had a birthday, and *patchivs,* where we eat and get drunk because there don't seem to be anything better to do. Sometimes we hire a hall on Suffolk Street for big parties, but most any home will do. I guess that's one reason landlords hate the sight of us. If you want to hear some noise, you get a crowd of gypsies full of wine, you'll hear some noise."

Whenever there is a death in his crowd, Johnny goes from home to home and takes up a collection. He hires the undertaker and makes arrangements for the funeral with Father Alexander Chechila of the Church of St. Peter and St. Paul, a small, poor Russian Orthodox Catholic church on Seventh Street, between First Avenue and Avenue A. It is the mother church of all the Russian gypsies in the East and is used by those of other nationalities; in 1941 Father Alexander preached thirty gypsy funerals. "Mr. Chechila is the only preacher I ever saw that gypsies don't make him nervous," Johnny says. "You take the average church, the preacher gets beside hisself when a gypsy comes in. He's afraid the gypsy might steal the bell right out of the steeple. The most of them they won't touch a gypsy funeral. But Mr. Chechila pitches right in. He speaks the words at the church and then he climbs into one of our dirty old cars and goes along to Jersey and speaks the words at the grave. All the New York gypsies bury in a graveyard in Linden, New Jersey. It's cheap. We used to bury in Paterson, but Paterson got too dear. At a gypsy funeral everybody gets full of wine and throws their head back and wails. Sometimes it seems to get on Mr. Chechila's nerves. I guess we treat him real mean. We never go to church except for Easter and for funerals. We just ain't godly people. Here a while back he told me to make my people go to church, and I said to him, 'Mr. Chechila, please excuse me, I don't mean no disrespect, but the only kind of gypsy that needs a preacher is a corpse gypsy.'"

Johnny's gypsies bicker a lot and he often has to act as peacemaker. If a dispute is serious, he holds a Romany *kris,* or gypsy trial, in his home; each disputant and each witness is permitted to speak as fully as he wishes so long as he doesn't bore Johnny, who presides as judge. Wine is drunk at these trials and they invariably end in an oratorical carousal. "Down at the bottom of every gypsy trial is womenfolks or five dollars," Johnny says. "I never yet heard a gypsy claim another one owed him three dollars or eighteen dollars. It's always five. They five-dollar me to death." When any of Johnny's people, whether a man, woman or child, does not show up for supper, it is taken for granted that he or she is in the hands of the police. In such cases Johnny puts on his black hat, picks up his copper-headed cane, and goes over to the Police Headquarters annex for a talk with Detective Sheehan. If the missing gypsy is under arrest, Johnny finds out the nature of the charge and the name of the jail; then he trudges wearily to get a lawyer. Johnny is abler at handling such matters than any of his rivals because he can read and write; he claims that he is the only gypsy king in the United States who can read well enough to dial a number on the telephone. He says he picked up his learning, out of boredom, from a cellmate in a Michigan jail where, sometime in his youth, he spent two and a half years for stealing a horse; he has never been inside a school-room. "I can read just enough to make out the carnival news in the *Billboard* magazine, and I can handwrite just enough to fill out a money order, but that's a whole lot better than the average gypsy can do," he says. "My grandmamma had a saying that fits me to a T. 'In the country of the blind,' she used to say, 'the man that can see out of one eye is king.'"

Johnny seldom gets any money from his subjects. The position of gypsy king pays off not in money but in prestige. He is supported by his wife, Mrs. Looba Johnny Nikanov, who is one of the best *dukkerers* in the city. Looba is tall, gaunt, sad-eyed, and austere; in profile she looks exactly like the old Indian on Indian-head nickels.

She goes to sleep at sundown and seldom gets up before 10 A.M., but she is constantly yawning, stretching, and grunting. Looba smokes a pipe. She is extremely irritable. Johnny says that she rarely refers to him by name; instead, using Romany, she calls him a ratbite, a sick toad, a blue-bellied eel, a black-yolked egg, a goat, a bat, a policeman, a *gajo,* and various other loathsome things. He doesn't mind. "A gypsy woman that don't scream half the time, something is wrong with her," he says. "Screaming is their hobby." Johnny and Looba live in a red-brick tenement on Sheriff Street, between Rivington and Delancey, paying $14 a month for two small rooms and a kitchen. They have the parlor front. Like all gypsies of their generation, they sleep on the floor between two thick, goosefeather-stuffed quilts, called *perrinas.* Many younger, city-born gypsies have taken to beds, but the old ones, who spent their youths in tents, prefer the floor. "I don't feel natural in a bed," Johnny says. "I feel like a fool." During the day the *perrinas* are rolled up and stacked in a corner and Johnny uses the bedroom for his headquarters. It is a sparsely furnished room. In it are an old wooden trunk, a wicker settee with a sprung bottom, and a table, on which there is a copper candlestick and a radio. The candlestick is usually surrounded by a mound of tallow drippings. The flat is wired for electricity, of course, and Johnny owns one bulb. He rarely screws it in, however. He feels that a candle throws sufficient illumination, even for a *kris* or a *patchiv.* There are no chairs. Tacked over the door is an ikon. The walls are covered with blankets and tent carpets and with a large canvas phrenological chart—a crude drawing of a human head divided into sections—that Looba once used in fortune-telling tents. Attached to the borders of the chart are a number of photographs of race horses torn out of newspapers. A dirty blanket hangs over the door. Gypsies try to make their flats look as much like the inside of a tent as possible.

Most afternoons Johnny's room is crowded with his subjects, who squat along the walls, sitting on their heels. Johnny reclines, barefooted and serene, on the wicker settee. Lying there, half asleep, he gossips, listens to the radio, and drinks popskull or tea. He drinks a lot of tea, taking it Russian fashion, in a tumbler. Looba has the exclusive use of the parlor; she calls it her *ofisa*, or office. It looks out on Sheriff Street and she sits at the window with a lapful of sewing and beckons to passers-by who look dopey enough to her to be interested in a fortune-telling. She has a rather high opinion of human intelligence; she beckons to about two passers-by in ten. Most *dukkerers* speak of themselves as Egyptians, doubtless feeling that this identifies them with mystery. The custom had its origin in the belief, once generally held, that gypsies sprang from Egypt; anthropologists now are pretty certain that they came from northern India, leaving it for good about a thousand years ago. Looba is known professionally as Madame Johnson and she has printed cards which read, "MADAME JOHNSON. REAL EGYPTIAN FROM EGYPT. YOUR HEAD IS LIKE AN OPEN BOOK TO ME. IF YOU HAVE TROUBLES OF A LOVE OR MONEY NATURE GIVE ME A TRY." She has been arrested nine times in the last five years for wallet-switching..

Like most gypsy women, Looba is skillful with the needle. She sews all her own clothes, using extravagantly colored curtain and drapery material, some of which she shoplifts from the mill-remnants stores on First Avenue. Her costume, winter and summer, consists of a silk kerchief, a loose, low-cut blouse, and four or five skirts, the newest on the outside. The kerchief, called a *diklo*, signifies that she is married; no gypsy virgin would ever put one on. She also wears eight rings, a pair of earrings, ten copper bracelets shaped like snakes and lizards, which Johnny hammered for her years ago, and a necklace of old coins from half a dozen European countries. Clients are often inquisitive about the coin necklace, and she usually tells them that it is worth $11,300 but that she will sell it for $23 with a fortune-telling thrown in. She has never had an offer. Looba wears high-heeled shoes on the street but goes barefooted indoors. She does not spend much time in the kitchen. There is always a pot of stew on the stove and she and Johnny eat whenever they feel hungry. They may eat five meals a day, or one.

It is customary for gypsy parents to let their married children live in the same flat with them, but Johnny and Looba do not. "I may be peculiar," Johnny says, "but I like to have room enough to turn around in." They have four sons and a daughter, all married.

The sons, with their families, twenty-two persons in all, live on one floor of a ratty tenement on Cannon Street, two blocks from Johnny's house. All of them have been on and off relief since early in the depression. In 1941 each of the sons was forced by relief officials to take a job on a WPA pick-and-shovel project, and each fainted shortly after showing up for work. "Gypsy men ain't built like ordinary men," Johnny says solemnly. "They ain't fitted for shovel work. They're high-strung and they rupture easy. The relief people just can't somehow seem to understand that. It ain't that they don't want to do shovel work. Why, they would be glad to, but they got to think about their health." Igor, the oldest son, was once assigned to a downtown curb-repairing project. According to Johnny, who snickers when he tells about it, Igor began to moan as soon as he was handed a shovel; after working for about ten minutes, he mumbled, "I just can't stand it," and fainted so overwhelmingly that he frightened the foreman, who had him taken to Gouverneur Hospital in a taxicab. The daughter, Mrs. Rosie Luke Stankovitch, is, like Looba, a real Egyptian from Egypt. She is known professionally as Madame Stanley. In the winter she has an *ofisa* on Halsted Street in Chicago. In the summer she operates a mitt joint, or fortune-telling tent, for the J. B. Jericho Kentucky Wonder Exposition, a small Southern carnival. When she was a kid Johnny made her go to P. S. 4, at Rivington and Pitt, and she is fairly literate. Johnny is proud of her. He gets a postcard from her about once a month and he carries it around in his wallet and shows it to *gajo* friends. "Rosie is probably the smartest gypsy girl in the entire U.S.," he says. A recent card from Rosie was mailed in Valdosta, Georgia. It said:

DEAR PA:
    This place sure stinks. We are eating and that is about the size of it. People too smart know it all don't trust gypsies. Sure wish I could send you a M.O. but will not be able to do so at this time. Hope the Japs doesn't drop some bums on my tent. If I half to die I sure hope it don't half to be in Valdosta, Ga. Take care yourself. Kiss ma.   ROSIE

A good deal of Johnny's jauntiness deserted him after we entered the war. The last time I visited him he was deeply dejected. When I pushed aside the door blanket and stepped into his room he was alone, sitting on the edge of the settee with his elbows on his knees and his head in his hands. He lifted his head an inch or so and glanced at me, and there was an utter lack of interest in his eyes. "Hello," he said halfheartedly. He was barefoot, his eyes were bloodshot, and he needed a shave. I tore the wrapping paper off a quart of gin I had brought along as a present and he suddenly scrambled to his feet. "Gimme that," he said. He impatiently unscrewed the cap, took a couple of finger-marked glasses off the table, and slopped some gin into them. He took the gin in his glass in two gulps. He shuddered and his teeth chattered for a few moments. "First today," he said when he had his breath. "It ain't the liquor that hurts. It's the doing without that hurts. The old woman wouldn't come across with my gin money this morning and we had an awful fight. It wore me out. I been sitting here two, three hours trying to get up enough strength to go in and fight some more." He sank back on the settee, holding the bottle in one hand and the glass in the other. I went over and sat on the window sill.

"I feel sad," Johnny said, "real blue-sad."

"What seems to be the matter?" I asked.

"The same thing that seems to be the matter with the rest of the world," he said. "The war. By the time this war's over there just won't be no travelling gypsies left in the U.S. There might not be no gypsies of any kind. The most of us, we been bottled up in cities since the depression, and that there gas-rationing business put the stopper in the bottle. The families out on the highways, one by one they're going to get rid of their cars and fall back on the buses and the railroad trains. And before long the ticket agents won't be so free about selling them tickets, and when that time comes New York's going to crawl with gypsies. All the other cities where the cops are halfway decent to us, it'll be the same—cities like Philly, Baltimore, Paterson, Chicago, New Orleans, Mexico City, Los Angeles, and Frisco. When a war hits the world the most sensible thing a gypsy can do is head for the nearest slum and hole up. And hope for the best. What gets me, some of our coppersmiths could do real fine shipyard work, but they won't give them a chance. Four of the coppersmiths in my crowd were taken on by a Brooklyn Navy Yard contractor, but along about noon the foreman found out they wasn't Greek fellers, like he thought, but gypsies, and he fired them. He was afraid they'd steal the tools."

Johnny sighed and slopped some more gin into his glass. "Things have been getting worse and worse for gypsies ever since the automobile was put on the market," he said. "When I was a little knee-high boy the U.S. was gypsy heaven. Everybody was real ignorant and believed in fortune-telling. You could take their money so easy they just about gave it to you. And horses to trade. And every woman had some pots with holes in them, and if she couldn't pay you to tinker, why, a dozen fresh eggs was just as good. And our wagons was red and yellow, and we had bells on the harness, and there wasn't no motorcycle cops, and you could camp anywhere. Private property wasn't even heard of. Nowadays, if gypsies was to make a camp out in the middle of some far desert a hundred and fifty miles from nowhere, about the time they got all settled down for the night a old farmer with a shotgun would come a-running and he'd say, 'Private property. You get right off my private property or I'll shoot you dead.' The entire country is overrun with private property. Some of them farmers, I'm surprised they let the airplanes fly over their goddam private property.

"But when I was a little boy any place would do. The air would be clean, no stinking automobiles around, and we'd camp under some green shade trees near a stream of cooking water. And we'd put the horses on long halters and leave them feed theirselves. And we'd go fishing and fry the fish right off the hook. And firewood was free. And there was a violin in every family—at least a guitar—and you didn't have to get drunk to feel like dancing. And the little kids would run around strip, stark naked. And the girls and womenfolks would go down the stream a piece and take a bath, and you would hear them through the trees a-giggling and a-hollering. And the yellow gypsy dogs that we don't even have no more, they would

lie down under the wagons and scratch their fleas. These *gajo* dogs
you see in New York that the women practically nurse them, I
despise those dogs. When they bark, yah-yah, they don't even sound
mad. They sound sick. A yellow gypsy dog, even a baby one, when
he barked he sounded like a old bear. And the womenfolks would
spread out and *dukker* at all the farms for miles around, and on the
way back, after the sun went down, they would pick up a hen here
and a cabbage there, and if they come across some clothes on a
line, they would take the shirts and dresses. They never bothered
the overalls. We didn't have no use for overalls. When I think of
the whole armfuls of roasting ear corn we used to steal, and the
watermelons, and now and then a little grunty pig, why, it hurts
my heart to think of it. When I was a little boy we almost always
had enough to eat. You never saw no skinny gypsies."

Johnny was interrupted by one of his daughters-in-law, a tall,
haughty gypsy girl who came striding into the room, her heels
clicking and her head held high. She went over to Johnny's trunk,
threw the lid back, and took out a number of copies of "Old Gipsy
Nan." Johnny keeps a supply on hand and sells them to the women
in his families. "I took six," the girl said, slamming the lid shut.
She offered Johnny a five-dollar bill, and he grunted angrily. "Don't
bother me," he said. "Go get that changed and bring me sixty
cents." She strode out of the room and Johnny's eyes followed her.

"I don't mean no disrespect," he said after the girl had gone,
"but gypsy women have got it all over civilize women. They got
such a springy walk on them. No corset, no girdle, no brassy, none
of them *gajo* inventions to weight them down. When you look at
a gypsy woman you not looking at a corset, you looking at a woman.
Most *gajo* women, I bet they carry more harness than a dray horse."

Johnny kept working on the gin. Every few minutes he downed
a drink and shuddered.

"Yes, sir," he said, "years back gypsies lived high. But along about
the time I got grown up, whenever that was, the bottom fell out.
Automobiles spread and spread. No more horses to trade. Then
came aluminum and cheap kitchen pots. Aluminum was a severe
blow to gypsies, but when they took to selling pots in the five-and-

dime they should of held the gypsy funeral right then and there. Women got so they wouldn't have nothing tinkered; a pot got a hole in it, what the hell, pitch it out the window and get a brand-new one from the five-and-dime. Also, with only horses to feed, you could travel cheap. But when we took to cars we had to have gas and tire money. So we looked for big jobs. For a while we did fine. People don't generally know it, but gypsies handled some real big tinker jobs. Back in 1921, in one fall and winter, a crowd of gypsy coppersmiths I and six of my families was travelling with, old King Steve Kaslov's crowd, we did sixteen thousand dollars' worth of copper and tin work for the Arlington Mills at Lawrence, Massachusetts. Not long after we did ten thousand dollars' worth for the Waltham Bleachery and Dye Works at Waltham, Massachusetts. Bunged-up dye vats and dry cans, that kind of stuff. And Paterson, New Jersey, them big dye works out there, we handled the biggest kind of tinker jobs. We'd take the job right out of the factory and truck it to our camp in the woods. We'd leave gold coins on deposit, so the factory would trust us to bring the job back. We worked together in the woods like bees, with the old gypsy coppersmith secret that was handed down from centuries ago. We can shape a pipe sleeve so accurate it fits like a grape hull on a grape, and just use our fingers to measure by. A *gajo* coppersmith with a shopful of machinery, he can't do no better. Then came the depression, and the union fellers began to grab off all the copper work. In 1930 we handled a big job for a bleachery in Worcester, Massachusetts. After that the union fellers took everything. We was washed up."

Johnny rested his head in his hands and stared at the floor for a minute or two. "Well, we still had our gold," he said after a while. "It's hard to make people believe it nowadays, but gypsy women used to be loaded down with gold. They was our banks. In 1933 I and Looba had six thousand bucks in gold coins and she carried the most of it around sewed up in her skirts. And, compared to some gypsies, we was poor. What happened? President Roosevelt. Except he made everybody turn in their gold, I wouldn't say a word against him. Us gypsies, we had gold coins from damn near every country in the world. Some of it had been toted around for centuries.

We used to change all our money into gold. And the cops came to our camps and made us take it to the banks and turn it in. Orders from Washington, D.C. And the banks gave us paper money in exchange. What the hell good is paper money? It went like wine at a wedding. We all bought new cars—who wants a Ford? Give us a Packard. Make it two, one for Ma, one for Pa, ride in style, honk, honk! And along about that time, I don't know why, but the whole entire country turned against gypsies. Them motorcycle cops would chase us across one state line and then some more cops would chase us across another state line. Pretty soon we didn't know where the hell we was at. Whole sections of the country had to be dodged or they'd put us on the chain gang, or try to. Even the carnivals turned against us. Use to, up to the depression, every spring the carnivals and little circuses would put ads in the *Billboard* magazine, rounding up the attractions. And all of them would advertise for a gypsy mitt joint, split half and half with the carnival. And the amusement parks and beaches all up and down the Atlantic Coast would advertise for gypsies. Nowadays, you look at the carnival ads in *Billboard* and it says, 'No gypsies wanted.' Or it says, 'American palmistry only.' *Gajo* women *dukkering* for carnivals. It's sunk to that!

"So we began heading for New York, Chicago, big cities where there's slums to live in. And rent to pay. The fundamental thing a gypsy is opposed to is rent. Use to we was healthy. But now the babies get the rickets and the old folks get the itch. And colds, and t.b. And right after they're weaned the babies start eating hot dogs. And the steam heat, it's paralyzing us. It's drying us up. It takes us all summer to get over the steam heat. It makes our hair fall out. It gives us the dropsy. You take a gypsy woman, out on the road she'd have a baby every year. Let her spend a solid winter in a steam-heat room, she quits having babies. And the relief people, always wanting to know where at was you born. Now, how would a gypsy know that? You're born in a tent beside the road someplace and a week later you're in another state and there ain't nobody got time to keep track of where at you was born. Who cares? And birth certificates! Why, we never heard of birth certificates until we hit the relief. I don't have the slightest idea where I was born. All I know it was in the U.S. someplace. I'm alive, ain't I? I must of been born."

Johnny had worked himself into a frenzy. He lurched to his feet, and started to say something more to me, and then stuttered and stopped, and I could see that the gin was beginning to take hold. At this moment the tall, haughty gypsy girl returned, bringing the money for the books she had taken. She stood at his elbow and tried to give him some coins, but he disregarded her.

"And let me tell you something," he said finally, waving his hand at me with an oratorical gesture. "I just can't wait for the blowup."

"The blowup of what?" I asked.

"The blowup of the whole entire world, that's what," said Johnny. "It's going to bust wide open any day now, ask any gypsy, and I don't give a D-double-damn if it does."

"That's no way to talk," I said.

"And if it was left to me," continued Johnny, paying no attention to my remark, "I'd sure fix things up. The very first thing I'd do, I'd unlock the insane asylums all over the world and let them people out. I'd leave them run things. I'd hunt up the insanest feller of all and I'd say to him, 'Sir, you got any notion how to run the world?' And he'd say to me, 'Yes, *indeed!*' 'O.K., pal,' I'd say to him, 'take charge. You can't possibly do no worse than them that's been had charge.' And if the crazy fellers couldn't somehow straighten things out, why, I'd call on the gypsies. I'd put everything in their hands."

The gypsy girl snickered and made what I thought was a sound observation. "Uh oh!" she said.

(1942)

The Gypsy Women

*I*N THE EARLY THIRTIES, I covered Police Headquarters at night for a newspaper, and I often ate in a restaurant named the Grotta Azzurra, which is only a block over, at the southwest corner of Broome and Mulberry, and stays open until two. I still go down there every now and then. The Grotta Azzurra is a classical downtown New York South Italian restaurant: it is a family enterprise, it is in the basement of a tenement, it has marble steps, it displays in a row of bowls propped up on a table dry samples of all the kinds of *pasta* it serves, its kitchen is open to view through an arch, and it has scenes of the Bay of Naples painted on its walls. Among its specialties is striped bass cooked in clam broth with clams, mussels, shrimp, and squid, and it may be possible to find a better fish-and-shellfish dish in one of the great restaurants of the world, but I doubt it. I had a late dinner in the Grotta Azzurra one Sunday night recently, and then sat and talked for a while with two of the waiters at a table in back. We talked about the upheavals in the Police Department under Commissioner Adams; a good many police officials eat in the Grotta Azzurra, and the waiters take an interest in police affairs. I left around midnight and walked west on Broome, heading for the subway. At the northeast corner of Broome and Cleveland Place, just across Broome from Headquarters, there is an eight-story brick building that is called Police Headquarters Annex. It is a dingy old box of a building; it was originally a factory, a Loft candy factory. It houses the Narcotics Squad, the Pickpocket and Confidence Squad, the Missing Persons Bureau, the Bureau of Criminal Information, and a number of other specialized squads and bureaus. I was about halfway up the block when a middle-aged man carrying a briefcase came out of the Annex and started across the street, and as he passed under a street lamp I saw that he was a detective I used to know quite well named Daniel J. Campion. I was surprised that he should be coming out of the Annex at that hour, particularly on a Sunday night, for some months earlier I had heard in the Grotta Azzurra that he had retired from the Police Department on a pension of thirty-five hundred dollars a year and had gone to work for the Pinkertons, the big private-detective agency. He was an Acting Captain when he retired, and the commanding officer of the Pickpocket and Confidence Squad. He had been a member of this squad for over twenty-five years, and had long been considered the best authority in the United States on pickpockets, confidence-game operators, and swindlers. He was also the Department's expert on gypsies. He had become curious about gypsies when he was a young patrolman on a beat and first arrested one, and had spent a great deal of time through the years seeking them out and talking with them, not only in New York City but in cities all over the country that he visited on police business. He sought them out on his own time as well as on Department time, and he always made notes on the information that he picked up from them. He made these notes on yellow legal scratch-paper, and kept them in some file folders, on the flaps of which he had pasted detailed labels, such as "Notes in re the gypsy confidence game known as doing, making, or pulling off a *bajour* (also pronounced *bahjo, boojoo,* and *boorjo*)," "Notes in re individual techniques of Bronka, Saveta, Matrona, Lizaveta, Zorka, Looba, Kaisha, Linka, Dunya, and certain other *bajour* women in the gypsy bands that frequent New York City," and "Notes in re various different spellings of gypsy given names and family names as shown on the tombstones of gypsies in two cemeteries in New Jersey." I became acquainted with Captain Campion while I was covering Headquarters. Afterwards, during the late thirties and up through the middle forties, I used to drop into his office in the Annex whenever I was down around Headquarters and had time to spare. If he also had time to spare, he would send out for a carton of coffee and we would sit at his desk and talk, almost always about gypsies. If he was busy, he would let me take his gypsy file folders out to a table in an anteroom and go through them and read his latest notes. In recent years, I hadn't seen much of him. I called out to Captain Campion and he stopped, and I hurried up the street to him.

"I bet I know where you've been," he said as we shook hands. "Over in the Grotta Azzurra, eating striped bass."

"Yes," I said, "and if it's all right to ask, what in the world are you doing down here at this hour of the night, and a Sunday night at that? I heard you had left the Department and gone to the Pinkerton Agency."

"I was attending to some unfinished business," he said. "Six months or so before I retired, somebody over at Headquarters spoke to me about two young detectives out in precinct squads who sounded like they might be good material for Pickpocket and Confidence. I had thirty-three detectives in the squad at the time, seventeen men and sixteen women, but two of my best men were about to be transferred to Narcotics because of certain skills they had. So I looked up these two young detectives, and I was impressed by them, and I asked them would they like to work in Pickpocket and Confidence. At first, they weren't so sure, but after I explained the nature of the squad to them in some detail they came to the conclusion they would. So I put in for their transfer. Well, these things take forever. Months went by. Then I got this offer to work in the private-detective field. I hadn't intended to retire from the Department for years yet, but this offer appealed to me, and I decided to go ahead and retire. And the way things happen, the very morning of the day I was due to leave, notification came through that the transfer of these two young detectives had been approved. So I got in touch with them and told them the situation—I wouldn't be able to break them in—but I told them I would call them as soon as I got settled in my new job and would meet them and sit down with them and tell them all I possibly could about pickpockets and confidence-game operators and swindlers, give them the benefit of my experience. I felt I had a moral obligation to do so. I called them the other day and asked if they still wanted me to talk to them, and they said they did, so we agreed to meet in the squad office on Sunday night—it would be quiet then and we'd have it pretty much to ourselves. And that's what I've been doing. I talked about four hours tonight, talked and answered questions, and I hardly got started, so we decided to meet two or three more Sunday nights. And where I'm going now, I thought I'd drop in at Headquarters for a minute and say hello to the lieutenant on the main desk and find out what's new since I retired. Come on, walk me around to the back door."

We turned in to Centre Market Place, a narrow, ominous, brightly lit, block-long street that runs behind Police Headquarters.

"What about the gypsies?" I asked. "Do you still see any of them?"

"I was waiting for you to ask me that," Captain Campion said. "Sure I do. Only the night before last I drove over to Brooklyn and had a talk with an old *bajour* queen from the West Coast named Paraskiva Miller. She's a Machvanka—that is, a female member of the Machwaya tribe of Serbian gypsies—and she's seventy-five. She calls herself Madame Miller. She's been telling fortunes and pulling off *bajours* since 1898, 1899, or 1900, somewhere around there, mainly in California, and I'm pretty sure she's one of the richest gypsies in the country. According to gypsy gossip, she believes that money will be worthless before long, something she saw in a dream, and she puts her money in diamonds and keeps them sewed up in her skirts and petticoats; one of these days some gypsy from another tribe is going to strip her down to her bones. I heard about her first in San Francisco in the summer of 1945. The New York Police Department and the police departments in several other cities around the country have an arrangement by which they lend detectives to each other on certain occasions, and I was loaned to San Francisco that summer. An international conference was going on out there, the one at which the United Nations was organized, and the city was crowded, and I was supposed to watch out for criminals from the East. When I had any time to myself, I looked up the local gypsies. Paraskiva and one of her daughters were running an *ofisa* in

San Francisco then—a fortune-telling joint in a store—and I tried
several times to see her, but her daughter always came out and said
Madame Miller wasn't in, which meant she was sitting behind the
curtains and had peeped out at me and didn't like my looks. I got
word here recently that she had come East to visit one of her
granddaughters, Sabinka Uwanawich, who runs an *ofisa* on Atlantic
Avenue in Brooklyn. I know Sabinka quite well; I've arrested her I
think it's five times. So I went out to her *ofisa* the other night.
When I walked in, Sabinka began to scream insults at me, the usual
gypsy-woman insults—I was a rat, I was a stinking rat, she'd like
to pull my guts out through my ears, all that stuff—but she knew
I had left the Police Department and was curious what I wanted,
and when I told her I just wanted to ask her grandmother some
questions about gypsies on the West Coast in the old days, she
quieted down and took me in the back room. Paraskiva turned out
to be one of those stout, dark, gold-toothed, big-eyed, Hindu-looking
gypsies. She was the bouncy kind. I've seen her kind over and over
among the Serbian gypsy women; they're top-heavy—they're nine-
tenths bosom—but they hold themselves erect and they're quick
on their feet and they walk with a strut. As old and stout as she
was, she had on high-heeled shoes and lipstick and rouge. She wasn't
well. She had a cough, a persistent cough, and she said she had had
t.b. some years ago and was afraid it had come back on her, but
she talked to me an hour or more, and I got some odds and ends
of information out of her that I couldn't have got anywhere else.
She didn't tell me a whole lot, but what she told me fitted in with
what I already knew."

One side of Centre Market Place is lined with red brick tenements
whose street floors are occupied by gunsmiths, police tailors, and
police-equipment stores. An old, black, and obese cat was sitting in
the show window of one of the police-equipment stores, in the
middle of a display of cartridge belts. "She's the biggest store cat
in the neighborhood," Captain Campion said. "I've stopped and
watched her many a night on my way past here. One night I saw
her catch and eat a rat." We paused and stood in front of the show
window. While Captain Campion continued to talk, he and I

watched the cat, and the cat stared fixedly at us and slowly waved her tail.

"You remember I used to say the more I studied gypsies the less I knew about them," Captain Campion said. "Well, I've changed my tune. After all these years, I really believe I've got to the bottom of a good many gypsy matters. To tell you the truth, I found out more about some aspects of gypsy life the last few years than I did in all the years that went before. For one thing, there was an unusual amount of informing going on. During 1951, '52, and '53, the *bajour* women in three or four of the bands that hang out in the city had a run of luck pulling off *bajours* on mental cases. A high percentage of the women who go to gypsies for advice are off balance to some degree, and the gypsies would starve to death if they weren't, but what I'm talking about now are serious mental cases, advanced mental cases—women who should be in institutions or they already have been and shouldn't have been let out. As a rule, gypsies are leery of such cases. When women are that far gone, they're a good deal harder to swindle than you might think. Some of them are much more suspicious than normal people, they suspect everything and everybody, and some of them their minds are off in space and they don't retain and the gypsy can work on one of them a week and still be right where she started, and some of them are so shaky they're liable to throw a leaping, scratching, screaming hysterical fit at any moment and create a disturbance and attract the whole neighborhood into the *ofisa*. And the very best of them, when the gypsy tries to worm the facts out of them concerning do they have any money put away and they let drop they do have, it may be true and it may be a complete delusion. All the same, around 1951 the *bajour* women in the bands I'm speaking of got to be very good at handling serious mental cases and began concentrating on them. They learned how to detect which ones were safe enough to work on, and how to see things their way, and how to calm them down and reason with them and plant ideas in their minds.

"One of their victims was an Italian woman of fifty-four, a widow. She had been a widow around two years, and she and a son-in-law ran a bakery that her husband had left her, a small bakery in an

Italian neighborhood on the lower East Side. She hadn't been herself since she lost her husband—she would stay in her room for days at a time and lie in there with the bedclothes pulled up over her and refuse to speak, and about the only time she went out in the streets was to go to church. A pair of *bajour* women opened an *ofisa* in an old store in the neighborhood, and one day this Italian woman was passing by on her way to church and they stopped her and talked to her and said they could see something was bothering her, why didn't she come in and visit them, maybe they could help her. She visited them several times, and they wormed out of her that she had a total of seventeen thousand six hundred dollars in two savings banks, and then they planted the idea in her mind this money had a curse on it and that was what was making her feel bad. So she went to the banks one morning and drew it out, every cent of it, and carried it to the *ofisa* and asked the gypsies to take the curse off it. They said to leave it with them and they would work over it all night and do their best. She returned to the *ofisa* the following morning and naturally the *ofisa* was empty and the gypsies were gone, and her reaction was she went on home and didn't say a word. This was in the latter part of October. Four months went by, and then one day early in March the son-in-law was filling out her income-tax return and she was lying in bed that day refusing to speak and he got her bankbooks out of her bureau drawer to see how much interest he should report, and both books had 'CANCELLED' cut in them, perforated in them, the way savings banks do when an account is closed, and he was shocked, and he dragged her out of bed and forced her to explain to him and the rest of the family what in the name of God had happened. And when she finally did so, he took her to the police station in the neighborhood, and the detectives there sent them to the Annex to see me, and I did the usual thing—I got out the file of photographs of *bajour* women and started showing them to her. She just kind of glanced at the first one I showed her and saw it was a gypsy, and then she bent over and put her head in her hands and wouldn't look at any more. She wouldn't reply to questions or make any further response. I asked the son-in-law to step out in the hall with me, and I urged him to take her to a psychiatrist, which he said he would. And some days later he phoned me that the psychiatrist said she was suffering from involutional melancholia in an advanced state.

"Another victim was a forty-two-year-old blonde, a member of a prominent family in Brooklyn. She's had three husbands, all well-to-do, and three divorces, and she has a daughter by her first husband that the husband has the full custody of; she isn't even allowed to visit her. She has a small income of some kind, and she lives alone. She hits the bottle and she picks up men who beat her up, but what's really wrong with her, she's a schizo and she's subject to auditory hallucinations. She'll be all right for a year, a year and a half, sometimes longer, and then she'll start hearing voices and she'll wander in the streets and scream and moan and run right in front of cars, trying to get away from the voices, and she'll wind up in the psychopathic division at Kings County Hospital; it's happened over and over. She spent three or four evenings in an *ofisa* in a store on Flatbush Avenue Extension, telling her troubles to the gypsies, and the gypsies sympathized with her from the bottom of their hearts and took twelve thousand dollars from her—twelve thousand three hundred and fifty, to be exact. It was part of the settlement from one of her divorces, and for some reason of her own she had been keeping it in cash in a safe-deposit box.

"They made several touches almost as big as these, and touches amounting to a couple of thousand, a thousand, five hundred, two hundred and fifty, and the like of that were just routine. The men in these bands began driving big brand-new cars instead of used cars and drinking whiskey instead of wine, and they began throwing their weight around at gypsy parties and talking out of turn and showing entirely too much interest in the women in the other bands. The men in the other bands got sick and tired of this, and certain ones of them decided to do some informing, and instead of just getting on the phone and refusing to give their names and jabbering a minute or two and hanging up, the way gypsy informers usually do, they came right into my office and sat down and put their hats on their laps and talked and talked, and much to my surprise about twenty per cent of what they told turned out to be true. In addition to straightening me out on who did various *bajours,* they gave me a lot of incidental information on gypsy customs."

The obese cat stirred herself and jumped clumsily out of the show window and waddled into the darkness in the rear of the store. Captain Campion and I resumed our walk.

"Another good source of information on gypsy customs I had in recent years," he said, "was an investigator in the Department of Welfare named Harry Brunner. In April, 1951, the Department of Welfare put all the gypsy relief cases in the entire city into one center, the Non-Residence Welfare Center, and started weeding them out. They had had trouble with gypsy families who were using several sets of names and several addresses and getting relief from several centers at the same time, and they shouldn't have been on relief in the first place. Such as a family that owned a new Buick Roadmaster with about a thousand dollars' worth of accessories and extra equipment on it—it was practically a rolling auto-supplies store—and they were getting relief from a center in Queens and a center in the Bronx, and were also on relief over in Newark. Brunner was assigned to the Non-Residence Center, and he got in behind the gypsies. He's a big, quiet, gloomy-looking fellow from Brooklyn. He's six feet two, and he's absolutely fearless and absolutely honest. His mother taught in public schools in Brooklyn for thirty-five years. She taught ungraded children—children with psychological problems—and Brunner must've learned from her how to get along with people. In a short while, he threw dozens upon dozens of gypsy families off relief, but for some reason I've never been able to figure out, instead of hating him, the gypsies liked him and respected him. They called him Bruno, and invited him to parties and weddings and funerals. He ate gypsy goulash with them and drank gypsy tea with them, and sat up all night talking with them, and they told him things right off the bat that it took me years to learn. Gypsies ordinarily don't like it a bit when people try to find out what's the gypsy word for this, what's the gypsy word for that, but all Brunner had to do was ask; they gave him hundreds of words. I had hopes that he would become a real gypsy scholar, which is something we need in this country—when I read about

American professors studying strange tribes of people in the far corners of the earth, it burns me up; you'd think at least one of them would study a strange tribe that's right under their noses. However, he disappointed me. He was a college man—he had a B.S. in psychology from Long Island University—but he wanted to work with his hands. In August, 1952, right out of a clear sky, he quit the Department of Welfare and went down to Fort Worth, Texas—he was married to a Texas girl—and the next thing I knew, I had a postcard from him saying he had become a structural steelworker.

"Another thing I might mention that happened in recent years was an experience we had with a *bajour* woman named Pearsa. Pearsa belongs to two of the biggest gypsy families in North and South America, the Nicholases and the Demetros. Her father was George Nicholas, a Serbian gypsy, and her mother was Sabinka Demetro, a Russian gypsy, and she was born in Buenos Aires in 1907. She was brought to the United States when she was a little girl, and she was married when she was fourteen. She's married to Steve Bimbo, who's the oldest son of old man Tene Bimbo, who's the head of the Bimbo family, which is another big gypsy family. Her main stamping grounds are New York City, Baltimore, Chicago, Detroit, Buffalo, and Boston, and the record we have on her dates back to 1926 and shows thirty-two arrests in eleven cities, but that's not as bad as it sounds. There's quite a few gypsy women with a hundred or more arrests on their records. Men, too. Old man Tene Bimbo himself, he's rolled up a hundred and forty arrests for everything from murder in the first degree to stealing an automobile jack. Still and all, you can just imagine how much she's paid to lawyers and bail bondsmen. Pearsa's a red-haired gypsy, the only one I've ever seen, and she used to be extremely good-looking in a wild and woolly sort of way. She's been a big money-maker, and other *bajour* women talk about her with the greatest respect, but she's had thirteen children and her back bothers her and she's developed sinus trouble and her nerves are all shot and she and Steve fight like cats and dogs and she doesn't have much patience any more and she's begun to take chances she wouldn't've dreamed of taking when she was in better command of herself. Well, in February, 1952, with the help of the District Attorney's office, we managed to plant a certain mechanical device in an *ofisa* that Pearsa was running in a flat above a store on East Broadway, and we listened to her actual words while she worked on a victim during the final stages of a *bajour*. It was the first time we'd ever been able to use such a device on a gypsy, and it was a very educational experience. When did I see you last? It must've been around four years ago."

"It was around that," I said. "I ran into you in Grand Central and we went and had some coffee."

"I remember," Captain Campion said. "Then I've never had a chance to tell you about the devil's head. Every so often, all through the years, we'd hear from a *bajour* victim about a little devil's head that the gypsy used on her to convince her she had cancer, which only the gypsy could cure, but we couldn't seem to find one. Every time we arrested a *bajour* woman, we'd search her right down to the seams in her skirts, and every time we made a raid on gypsy premises we'd turn everything upside down, and we came across a good many queer things, but a devil's head just never showed up. Well, in the summer of 1952 we finally found one, and it was a nasty thing. It was carved out of ivory, and it was about the size of a hazelnut, and it was grinning, and it had human hair glued on it—coarse, black gypsy hair. On January 3, 1953, we found another one."

We reached the back door of Headquarters.

"What did you do with them?" I asked. "I'd like to see one."

"The District Attorney's office has the last one we found," Captain Campion said. "It'll be put in evidence when the gypsy woman who was using it's case comes up in General Sessions, if it ever does— she jumped bail, and I suspect she went to Mexico City, which is where they generally go when they jump bail. The other one belongs to me—the gypsy we took it from died before *her* case came up; she was burned to death in a tenement fire in Coney Island. I've got it home. If you'd really like to see it, I tell you what I'll do. I was going to talk to the young detectives about gypsies sooner or later, and if you want to come down to the Annex next Sunday night, I'll devote the entire session to gypsies, and you can sit in on it, and I'll bring along the devil's head."

"What time should I come?" I asked.

"Meet me in the squad office in the Annex a little after eight," Captain Campion said.

CAPTAIN CAMPION is fifty-one years old. He is blue-eyed and black-haired, and he has a calm, ruddy, observant, handsome, strong-jawed, Irish face. He is five feet ten, and he weighs around a hundred and fifty. He was born on Fifty-eighth Street between Ninth and Tenth, in Hell's Kitchen, and he grew up on Twentieth Street between Second and Third, in the old Gashouse District. He went through the second year of high school. He was an amateur fighter. He fought in four weights, beginning as a flyweight and ending as a lightweight, and he had fifty-four fights and won forty-nine. He entered the Police Department in January, 1927. It soon became apparent that he was unusually intelligent, and that he had a remarkably accurate memory for faces, names, conversations, and sequences of actions, and that he was deeply curious about human behavior, and after two years as a patrolman he was transferred to the Detective Division and assigned to the Pickpocket and Confidence Squad. He was an exceedingly hard-working detective; he made over two thousand arrests, and was cited for bravery nine times. He is serious by nature, but friendly, and he has a cheerful, youthful smile. People talk to him willingly, and he is a good listener; he is one of those who believe very little of what they hear but always look and act as if they believe every word. He is a self-taught linguist. He can speak rough-and-ready Italian, German, and Yiddish, he can speak a little Romany, the gypsy language, and he is studying Spanish. He keeps a paper-backed Spanish-self-taught manual and a Spanish-English, English-Spanish dictionary in his pockets and studies them on the subway. He is religious, and he often reflects on death. For over ten years he was a member of a committee in the Society of St. Vincent de Paul that was composed of detectives and patrolmen and that went to Welfare Island every Sunday and called on terminal patients in the City Home and the old cancer hospital and talked or listened to them, whichever they seemed to want, and brought them cigarettes and magazines and playing cards and flowers. He goes to fights and horse races. He and his wife, Gertrude Campion, live in an apartment in Flushing. They have two sons, one of whom is a graduate of Fordham and both of whom are in the Air Force.

The next Sunday night, I went down to the Annex and took the elevator to the seventh floor, where the Pickpocket and Confidence Squad is quartered. When I stepped off the elevator, I found that Captain Campion was standing in the hall, waiting for me. "We won't be able to use the squad office tonight," he said. "The ex–girl friend of a confidence man came in just now and stated she wanted to give some information concerning him, and a couple of detectives are questioning her in there. She's telling everything she knows, and enjoying it to the full, and she'll be hours, so we're going to use the private office of the commanding officer of the squad. In other words, my old office." I followed Captain Campion down the hall and into his old office. I remembered it as being about as plainly furnished as it could be, and I saw that his successor had not made any changes in it. A battered old golden-oak desk stood in the center. In back of the desk was a swivel chair and facing it were three straight chairs. On one wall was one of those maps of the city that can be rolled up and down like a shade. In one corner was a coat tree. There was one window, at which two young men were standing looking out, each with one foot resting on the sill. "These are the young detectives I told you about," Captain Campion said. "I explained to them that the text for tonight is gypsies." They came over, and Captain Campion introduced us. One was Detective Joe Kane, and he was thickset and solemn, and the other was Detective Al Gore, and he was thin and solemn. They appeared to be in their middle twenties. Captain Campion's briefcase was on the desk, and he unbuckled it and took out some file folders. "Well, gentlemen," he said, "let's be seated." He sat in the swivel chair and put on spectacles and opened one of the folders, disclosing a rat's nest of notes. The young detectives and I sat in the straight chairs.

"In Pickpocket and Confidence," Captain Campion began, peering at us over his spectacles, "you run into two breeds of gypsies, the nomad coppersmith gypsies and the Boyasch. The nomads are by far the most numerous. They're the ones we're mainly concerned with, and I'll describe them in detail, but first I want to say a few words about the Boyasch and get them out of the way. The Boyasch are what you might call Serbo-Rumanian gypsies. Serbia was the last country they lived in before they came here, and back before that they lived for many generations in Rumania. Among themselves, they usually speak Rumanian or Hrvatski, which is the Serbo-Croatian language. They claim they can't speak a word of gypsy, and I guess it is dying out among them, but I've heard some of the old ones speaking it a mile a minute. They're small and dark and strange, and if you saw some on the street you'd notice them but it probably wouldn't occur to you they were gypsies. They're cleaner and neater than the nomads, and their women don't dress gypsy style any more, although a few of the real old ones still wear gold-coin necklaces. At the same time, they're tougher-looking. I guess hard is more the word. They look hard. It's something in their eyes. They have curious cold, hard eyes, and they watch you every second, and they rarely ever smile. They look like they've thought a lot about the way life is, they and their forefathers before them, and they don't see anything funny in it. That's how they look to me, but I remember hearing one of the women detectives in the squad describing them, and the way *she* described them, she said they look like they carry knives. I don't know what Boyasch means. The nomads say it's just an old gypsy word meaning gold-washer, but I've never been able to get a satisfactory explanation out of them what a gold-washer is. The nomads and the Boyasch don't get along. The nomad women call the Boyasch women the dirty, sneaking Boyaschutza, and make contemptuous remarks about them, such as they say they'll tell fortunes for a quarter and do both palms, and the Boyaschutza call the nomad women rag-heads. In the East, the Boyasch hang out in New York City and vicinity and Philadelphia and vicinity. In the Middle West, Chicago is their headquarters. They don't travel anywhere near as much as the nomads; they sometimes stay put for years. The ones here mostly live in tenements in Williamsburg and Greenpoint, out in Brooklyn. The nomads spy on them, and a nomad informer told me recently that there are eighteen families in Brooklyn at present, and two or three in Queens and two in Harlem and six or seven more in Newark and Paterson. The principal Boyasch family names are Ivanovich, Lazarovich, Lucas, Magill, Mitchell, Morgan, Mort, Peterson, Petrovich, Stanley, and Stevens. These are typical American gypsy family names; there are nomad families with the same names.

"The Boyasch men work. Some are automobile mechanics, and some work in factories that make tents and awnings and hammocks; they used to travel with circuses and carnivals and take care of the tents. The men don't give us much trouble, it's the women. When they're young, the Boyaschutza stay home and keep house like ordinary women, but as they grow older the gypsy in them seems to grow stronger and stronger, and when they reach middle age some of them become fortune-tellers and swindlers. They don't run fortune-telling joints. Instead of sitting and waiting for victims, they go out and hunt for them. They usually work in pairs. They lug around shopping bags containing a stock of dead and dried-up specimens of a peculiar kind of plant called the resurrection plant, and they go from house to house in working-class, home-owning neighborhoods out in Brooklyn, Queens, and Staten Island, and over in Jersey, and up in the Bronx and Westchester, and ring doorbells and try to sell these plants to housewives. 'If your husband doesn't show as much interest in you as he used to,' they tell the housewives, 'buy one of these plants and sit it in a saucer of water and put it under your bed, if you and your husband sleep in the same bed, and if you don't, put it under his bed, and leave it there, and you'll soon notice a change for the better.' They're terrifying fast-talkers, and after they get inside a house and demonstrate how to sit the plant in water, they offer to tell the woman's fortune. Usually, that's as far as they go, but now and then they hit a woman who responds to their superstitious talk and who they can feel in their bones has some money hid away in the house, and they go to work on her and swindle her. They use a swindle called the *bajour,* the same as the nomad women. I'll explain this swindle, or confidence game, in a few minutes. The resurrection plant is just a means of getting the door open, and they've been using it for this purpose in and around the city for twenty years, to my knowledge. They know what they're doing—when they hold one up in front of a woman, no matter how bright she is, or suspicious, she usually takes a good look at it and starts asking questions. A couple of months before I left the Department, we apprehended a pair of Boyaschutza who were wanted for a *bajour,* and they had a hundred and sixty resurrection plants in their possession. After the case was disposed of, I took some of the plants home, and I brought one along tonight for you to see. If you stay in the Pickpocket and Confidence Squad, it won't be the last one you'll see."

Captain Campion reached into his briefcase and brought out a paper bag. He held the bag over the desk and shook it, and out dropped a dead plant whose stems and leaves were tightly curled into a dusty, mossy, lopsided ball. In size and shape, it roughly resembled a woman's clenched hand. From it hung a tuft of hairy roots.

"It's a weed that grows down in the lower parts of Texas, and over in Mexico," Captain Campion said. "It's also called Mary's hand, Our Lady's rose, and bird's-nest moss, and it belongs to the genus *Selaginella.* The reason I know, some years ago I took one out to the Brooklyn Botanic Garden and had it identified. According to the nomads, the Boyasch learned about the resurrection plant back in the days they used to travel with circuses and they have some connection down in Texas that keeps them supplied. In dry weather, the resurrection plant tightens up into a ball the same as you see here. If it gets damp, if some dew falls on it, or a little sprinkle of rain, it opens up. Even if it's dead, it opens up. This one here is as dead as a brickbat, but if you sit it in a saucer of water the roots will absorb the water and the stems will turn from gray to green and slowly uncurl and expand and stiffen up and straighten out."

"Why don't we try it?" asked Detective Kane. There was a glass ashtray on the desk and he picked it up. "I could take this out to the water cooler and run some water in it."

"I'd rather you'd wait until I get through talking," Captain Campion said. "Please don't interrupt me now."

He opened the bulkiest of his file folders. "So much for the

Boyasch," he said. "Now we come to another breed of cat." He took off his spectacles and lit a cigarette and leaned back in the swivel chair. "When people talk about gypsies," he said, "it's usually the nomad coppersmith gypsies they're talking about. The great majority of the gypsies that frequent New York City are nomads. In fact, the great majority of the gypsies in Canada, the United States, Mexico, and South America are nomads. There doesn't seem to be any way to find out when they first started coming to the United States—according to immigration statistics and census reports, there's no such thing as gypsies—but from what I've been able to piece together, I'm pretty sure the biggest migrations took place in the late seventies, the eighties, and the nineties. They came from many parts of Europe, but mostly from Russia and Serbia and the countries surrounding Serbia, and it didn't take them long to get acquainted with the country. Some bands roamed the North, some roamed the South, some roamed the Middle West, a few roamed the West, and some roamed up and down and across and all over. In the early days, in the South and Middle West, the principal occupation of the men was horse trading and horse doctoring, and coppersmith work and tinkering came second. Then the horse business gradually died out, and tinkering came first. It was about the same out West. In the North, in most of the bands, coppersmith work and tinkering always came first. And in all the bands, wherever they roamed, the women told fortunes and swindled and stole. Just about anything they saw lying around loose, if it could be eaten or worn or sold or swapped or pawned or played with, and if nobody was watching it, and if they could lift it and carry it, they'd steal it. Why I say played with, an old gypsy once told me his favorite plaything when he was a little boy was a doctor's stethoscope his mother had stolen. And while I'm on the subject, you'll never understand gypsies until you understand how they feel about stealing. It's simple: they believe they're born with the right to steal, and the reason they give, they tell the blasphemous story there was a gypsy in the crowd that followed Jesus up the hill, and on the way this gypsy did his best to steal four nails that the Roman soldiers had brought with them to nail Jesus to the Cross—two for His hands, one for His feet, and one that was extra long for His head or His heart, whichever they decided to drive it through—but the gypsy succeeded in stealing only one, and it was the one that was extra long, and when the soldiers got ready to use it and couldn't find it they suspected the gypsy and beat him bloody trying to make him tell where he had put it, but he wouldn't, and while Jesus was dying He spoke to the gypsy from the Cross and said that from then on gypsies had the right to wander the earth and steal."

"Do they really believe that?" asked Detective Kane.

"They believe it as much as they believe anything," Captain Campion said, "and they bring their children up to believe it. They like to tell it; you can't stop them; they seem to feel they're slapping you in the face with it. I must've heard it fifty times. Now, as I said, coppersmith work and tinkering always came first in most of the bands that roamed the North, and some of these bands became quite prosperous. They followed fairly regular routes through Pennsylvania, New Jersey, New York, Connecticut, Rhode Island, and Massachusetts. They'd stay a day or two in some places and a week or two in others. The men would repair and re-tin copper utensils and fixtures, mainly for hotels, restaurants, hospitals, bakeries, canneries, laundries, and cloth-dyeing factories, and the women would circulate around and tell fortunes and keep their eyes open. The men picked up jobs that ordinary American metalworkers wouldn't touch—a dye vat with so many holes eaten in it it should've been junked, a broken piece of equipment in a contagious-disease hospital, an old restaurant soup kettle so caked with grease they'd have to burn the grease off it with a blowtorch before they could mend it, jobs like that. Then the depression struck, and in a little while there weren't any jobs that American metalworkers wouldn't touch. Instead of which, no matter what the job was, they'd fight and scratch each other to get it, let alone leave it to the gypsies. By the end of 1932, in most localities, the money gypsies were able to make from tinkering wasn't enough to pay for their gasoline, and they began to leave the roads and hole up in tenements in big cities. This demoralized the men, but it didn't the women. One thing you want to keep in mind about gypsies: it would take ten of the men to make one of the women. The women talked to other women in the tenements about relief, which was just getting going then. After they learned some of the ins and outs of the relief regulations, they took off their good clothes and put on rags, and they hid their gold-coin necklaces, and they told the men to sell the automobiles or stop parking them in the neighborhood, where a relief investigator might see them and notice the licenses on them from other states and put two and two together who they belonged to. Then they went into the relief offices with their children following along behind and broke down and cried and said they were starving to death, and if that didn't impress the relief officials to the proper extent they screeched and screamed and fell on the floor and fainted and used foul and abusive language and swept papers off desks and stood in doors and wouldn't let people pass and brought everything in general to a standstill. They pretty soon got their families on relief. And after they had that attended to, they began to go shares with each other and rent stores and open fortune-telling joints—what the old ones call *ofisas* and the young ones call locations—and right from the start, even with the overhead, most of them made far more than they ever had out on the road. Any period where people are uneasy is good for fortune-tellers. The depression was good for them, and then came the war and things got even better, and then came the A-bomb and the H-bomb and the possibility the whole world may be blown out like a light any moment now, either that or you'll die of cancer from smoking cigarettes, and things got even better still, the best yet. Nowadays, in most gypsy families, I think I can safely say the women bring in ninety per cent of the money. A few of the young men in the bands around here work as parkers in parking lots—they're crazy about automobiles and they're un-usually skillful drivers. And a few have become fender-bangers—they canvass garages and get jobs now and then at cut rates ham-mering dents out of automobile bodies. And a few of the older men, once in a while the spirit moves them, or some dim memory the way things used to be, and they go out with their hammers and tongs and files and soldering irons and try to pick up jobs mending pots and pans for restaurants. But the majority of the men, young and old, they don't do anything. If it's unusually nice and sunny, they may go up to the automobile showrooms around Columbus Circle and spend the whole day lifting hoods and kicking tires and comparing prices, but they just sit around home most of the time and stare at each other and drink tea and spit on the floor and grumble. The main thing they grumble about is the women. They look down on the women, and they beat and bang them around. Of course, some of the women know how to return the compliment. A gypsy woman, the situation she's in, she's in between her husband and the police. If she becomes too cautious and lets chances go by, her husband beats her, and if she takes chances and gets arrested, then he really beats her. And as far as gratitude, if she pulls off a *bajour* running into the thousands, the way her husband feels about it, it's only what she should do, the same as she should wash the dishes, but if *he* brings in a few dollars, that's a different matter; that shows brains. I heard a gypsy talking one day whose wife promises women who come into her *ofisa* it'll cost them only fifty cents to have their fortunes told and she's so slick they hardly ever get out without paying her anywhere from a couple of dollars to fifteen or twenty, and she's made several big *bajours*; she's made at least one ten-thousand-dollar *bajour*. This gypsy was drunk, and he was bragging, but he wasn't by any means bragging about his wife, he was bragging about himself. 'When it comes to stealing,' he said, 'I believe in letting the women do it, but if I happen to feel like it, I can go into any grocery store in the United States and stand around and get in the way and ask the price of this and the price of that, and before you know it four or five cans of sardines will jump into my pockets.'

"The fundamental thing that identifies the nomad gypsies is the way the women dress. They wear head scarves, and loose, low-cut blouses, and long, full, flashy skirts. That's their basic outfit, and if one of them took it in her head to dress some other way, she'd soon regret it. The other women would call her a *kurwa,* a whore, and spit at her; I've known it to happen. That is, of course, unless she was doing it temporarily to evade the police or confuse a victim.

They buy the brightest pieces of cloth they can find for their head scarves; these scarves are what the Boyaschutza are referring to when they call the nomad women rag-heads. They take a lot of pride in their skirts. They make them themselves, and they sometimes use very expensive material, and they wear old ones underneath new ones for petticoats. When they're dressed up, nine out of ten wear Spanish shawls, or that's what they were called when I was young and they were quite the style—the kind with big red roses all over them, red or yellow, and a row of tassels on each end. There must be a factory somewhere that turns them out especially for gypsies. They generally wear cheap fur coats. They seldom wear stockings. They wear the highest-heeled shoes they can find, and I've seen them many a time knocking around the streets in broad daylight in old scuffed-up gold or silver evening slippers. When it comes to jewelry, jewelry is their be-all and end-all, the breath of life, and I've seen everything on them from dime-store junk to a stolen diamond lavaliere worth fifteen thousand dollars, but what they like best is gypsy jewelry—gold coins rigged to gold chains and worn as necklaces and bracelets and earrings. When I first started working on gypsies, the women wore quite a few foreign coins, some old, some new, and I'd see certain coins over and over, such as an Austrian four-ducat with Emperor Franz Josef's head on it that many of them used for earrings—it's a big coin but unusually thin and light. However, what I mostly saw were United States gold coins. For necklaces, they used eagles and double eagles—that is, ten- and twenty-dollar gold pieces. For bracelets and earrings, they used quarter eagles and half eagles—that is, two-fifty and five-dollar gold pieces. Then, in 1933, the government ordered everybody to exchange their domestic gold money for silver or paper, and what I think happened, I think the gypsies found some way to swap the bulk of their United States gold coins for Mexican gold coins, because ever since then that's mainly what I've seen the women wearing. They wear them and they hoard them. It isn't a bit unusual for women detectives or police matrons searching gypsy women to find dozens of Mexican gold coins sewed up in tucks running around the insides of their skirts. Every gypsy woman in the country, if she's got anything at all, she's got a few, and if she's a smart old woman who's made some big *bajours* in her time, she's liable to have a trunkful. There's no law against owning them, and the gold in them is purer even than the gold in United States gold coins, and you can pawn them anywhere or take them to a money dealer and get a good price. They come in several denominations, and the most popular among the gypsies is the fifty pesos. It's thick and heavy—it's worth sixty dollars in New York City at present—and it's just right for necklaces. I looked in on a gypsy wedding in a hall on the lower East Side one night last summer—Beethoven Hall, on East Fifth Street—and I observed a woman who was wearing three necklaces of fifty-pesos coins. She had nineteen on the top necklace, and twenty-one on the middle one, and twenty-three on the bottom one, and they overlapped on her bosom. She was a big, stout woman and she had some wine in her and it was hot in the hall and she was breathing heavily, and every time her bosom rose and fell the gold coins shifted their positions and glinted and gleamed."

CAPTAIN CAMPION got to his feet. "Before I go any further," he said, "there's something I'll just have to explain, or try to, and that's the divisions and subdivisions among these gypsies." He took a rolled-up paper from his briefcase and unrolled it and smoothed it out on the desk. It was a piece of wrapping paper about a yard long, and it was wrinkled and dog-eared and coffee-spotted, and drawn on it in ink was a chart consisting of lists of names enclosed in boxes. The boxes varied in size, and were arranged in groups, and lines linked some boxes to others. It was an untidy chart; scores of interlinear corrections had been made in the lists of names, and a number of corrections had been pasted on. In one place, a pasted-on correction had been crossed out and an arrow ran from it to a new correction, on the margin. Captain Campion studied the chart for several minutes, refreshing his memory. "This is the third one of these things I've drawn up," he remarked. "I wore out the others, correcting them and adding new information. Sometimes I wish I'd never heard the word gypsy." He sat back down.

"To continue," he said, "the nomad coppersmith gypsies are

pretty much alike in appearance, they speak the same dialect of the gypsy language, and they have the same general customs and beliefs, but during the years they've been in the United States they've gradually divided themselves into tribes. The principal tribes, and they're all represented here in the city, are the Russians, the Serbians, the Kalderash, the Argentines, the Argentinos, the Mexicans, the Machwaya, and the Greeks. Don't take some of these names at face value. As I told you, the nomads came mostly from Russia and Serbia. The Argentines are Serbians that roamed in Spain and South America before coming here. The Argentinos are also Serbians. After they left Serbia, and they'll give you twenty dates when that was, they went to Brazil and then came to the United States and then went to Argentina and then came back to the United States. The Mexicans are Russians and Serbians that go back and forth between Mexico and the United States. Their stamping grounds are Mexico City, three or four Texas cities, Philadelphia, New York City, and Boston. Like the Argentines and the Argentinos, they not only speak gypsy and English and a little Serbian and a little Russian but they also speak Spanish, and up around here, in recent years, they've specialized in skinning Puerto Ricans. The Kalderash are Russians and Serbians—in gypsy a *kalderash* is a coppersmith. The Machwaya are Serbians. They take their name from a region in West Serbia named Machva, where they roamed for generations upon generations before coming here. The Greeks are Russians who came here via Greece.

"Those are the tribes, but that's not the end of it. The tribes are subdivided into bands, or what we call bands—the gypsies call them *vitsas*. They pronounce it several ways—*vitsa, veetsa, witsa, weetsa*. In most cases, the *vitsa* is more important than the tribe. Some *vitsas* are small and compact. They consist of a few families that are closely related and that always travel together, and they generally have one leader. Other *vitsas* are big and loose and split up. Their members travel in families or in groups of families that are really *vitsas* within a *vitsa,* and about the only time the *vitsa* gathers together in anything like its full strength is when some prominent old gypsy dies and his or her family decides to hold a big funeral. The families in a *vitsa* may be scattered from Mexico City to some small town in Michigan, and it always surprises me how fast they spread the word around that So-and-So is dead and a big funeral is going to be held and when and where, but there's really nothing mysterious about it. One family knows where another family is, and gets word to it, even if they have to phone the mayor of the town or the chief of police and talk him into relaying the information, and that family knows where a couple of other families are, and gets word to them, and in a day or so, all over everywhere, everybody has been notified and everybody that can is on the way. In the big *vitsas,* there are generally several leaders, one of whom is the head leader, or king. Some *vitsas* hate other *vitsas,* and all of them are suspicious of each other; they trust each other about as much as they trust the police. If a woman in one *vitsa* pulls off a.big *bajour* and the leader of a rival *vitsa* finds out about it, he's likely to walk in and demand a cut, else he'll inform, but don't worry, sooner or later, it may take years, the leader of the woman's *vitsa* will even matters up. Also, all of them are snobbish and superior; the people in each and every *vitsa* look down on the people in all the other *vitsas.* At the same time, all of them intermarry. The way gypsy marriages are arranged, a boy's parents have to buy him a wife, and they buy him the smartest girl they can afford, no matter what *vitsa* she's in. They may buy a girl from a family in another *vitsa* in their own tribe or from a family in a *vitsa* in some other tribe. The price depends on how good a money-maker the girl promises to be. If she can probably support a family telling fortunes but obviously doesn't have the nerve and the initiative to pull off *bajours,* she'll cost only a few hundred dollars; if she's cold-blooded and sharp and greedy, and if her mother and her aunts are good *bajour* women, she'll cost from two to five thousand.

"A few *vitsas* have descriptive names, such as the Saporeschti, or the Snakes; the Cuneschti, or the Knifers; and the Foosoo Yarri, or the Bean Eaters. But the majority are named after highly respected old gypsies in the past, patriarchs and matriarchs, all of whom, the way the gypsies tell it, were twice or three times as big as ordinary people and very rich and very wise and lived to be at least a hundred.

The biggest of the *vitsas* that hang out in New York City is a Russian *vitsa*, the Frinkuleschti, and it's named after Frinka, or Frinkulo, Mikhailovich. I once asked one of the leaders of the Frinkuleschti, a skinny little fellow with stomach ulcers named Frank Ranko, what did he know about Frinka, who was he. 'All I know,' Frank said, 'he was my father's grandfather or great-grandfather, and my father told me his father told him he was the biggest gypsy in Russia. He was seven feet three, and one time when he was quite an old man, up around a hundred and ten, they put him on some scales in a hay market and he weighed four hundred and sixty.' There've been twenty-five or thirty Frinkuleschti families holed up in the city ever since the depression, and a good many others come and go. You'll always find some in Brooklyn, usually in Red Hook, the Navy Yard district, or Williamsburg, but they mostly live within twenty blocks of each other in a section of the lower East Side that's the gypsiest section in the city. This section is bounded by Houston Street, the Bowery, Canal Street, Pike Street, and the river, and families belonging to a dozen or more *vitsas* live in there. The Frinkuleschti are poor gypsies. They can't spend much on wives for their sons, and every generation they get poorer. Sometimes a family gets down to the point where they're feeding the children on bread soaked in tea. The women tell fortunes but they're no good at *bajours*; they're just too clumsy. And the men are so clumsy I've known them to get in trouble stealing canned goods in supermarkets. The next-biggest *vitsa* is the Mineschti, another Russian *vitsa*. It's named after a woman, Mina Demetro. Mina lived to be a hundred and twenty. I've never heard the exact figures on how big she was, but I've heard she had thirty children, the last one when she was sixty-five. Some say she died in the far-distant past, centuries ago, and some say she died around 1880; some say she died in Russia and some say Serbia and some say Poland; every old gypsy in the Mineschti will give you a different story. Anyway, four brothers who were direct descendants of hers left Russia with their families in the late eighties and came to the United States via Canada and spread out and multiplied. Their names were Zlatcho, Groffo, Bortchi, and Wasso, and I've arrested children of theirs, and grandchildren, and

great-grandchildren. The richest of the *vitsas* is one named the Koleschti, only the people in it don't use that name much any more.
They prefer to use their tribe name. They belong to the Machwaya
tribe, and they're very proud of it. The Machwaya are West Coast
gypsies primarily, but in recent years they've been extending their
range and showing up in Reno, Las Vegas, the big cities in Texas,
the Florida resort cities, Atlantic City, and New York City. Their
women, the Machvankas, are the best-looking gypsy women in the
country, and the sharpest. The Machwaya are big-car gypsies. They
drive Cadillacs and Packards and Lincolns. The other gypsies have
a saying that if a Machwaya had to choose between a brand-new
Ford and an old wreck of a Cadillac that you'd have trouble even
getting it to start, he'd choose the Cadillac. There's usually at least
a dozen families of them in the city. They run *ofisas* the same as the
others, and they also run gypsy tearooms—not those places where
when a woman finishes her sandwiches and tea some woman dressed
up like a gypsy comes over and stares at the leaves in the bottom
of the cup and reels off some fortune-telling talk that she thinks
sounds like gypsy talk and then she gets a tip, but ratty little second-
floor-front places on side streets in the theatrical district and along
Eighth Avenue and Sixth Avenue and Third Avenue that look like
tearooms but don't make any real pretense of being tearooms beyond
they'll bring out one cup of tea solely for the purposes of tea-leaf
reading, and when the Machvanka finishes with the tea-leaf nonsense
she really starts talking to the woman, and if the woman listens and
keeps on listening and gets involved and comes back a time or two
the Machvanka will take everything she has but her back teeth
maybe and her corset and her eyeballs.

"I don't know how many gypsies there are in the United States.
The gypsies themselves certainly don't know, although gypsy leaders
are always willing to give you a figure, the first big round figure
that pops in their minds. I've seen a wide variety of estimates, but
it was all too obvious they were based on the wildest kind of
guesswork. The fact is nobody knows, and not only that, nobody
is capable of making a good guess. I don't even know how many
there are in New York City. There may be two hundred families

in the city tonight, or there may be less; there may be six hundred, or there may be more. Some families stay here years at a time, but they move so often from borough to borough and neighborhood to neighborhood that you couldn't begin to keep up with them; a family that was up some side street in the upper Bronx last week may be down on the lower end of Staten Island this week, down in Tottenville, or it may be over in Long Island City, or then again, it may be out in Akron, Ohio. Some families spend the winter here, or part of it, and some spend the summer, or part of it, and some come in and go out several times a year, and some might show up once in five years. Even to give the loosest kind of approximate figure how many are here at any one particular time, I'd just about as soon try to estimate how many English sparrows were sitting in a certain bush in Central Park at high noon last Tuesday. Furthermore, I'm not at all sure how many *vitsas* there are in the United States, and I'll confine my remarks to the ones I'm closely acquainted with. I'm closely acquainted with twenty-three, and that's because all or most or many or some of the families that belong to them either hang out in New York City a good part of the time or show up here fairly often. I'll give you the names of these *vitsas,* and the names of their principal families. Seven are Russian *vitsas*—the Frinkuleschti, the Mineschti, the Mitteleschti, the Gooneschti, the Goneschti, the Chookooriah, and the Lydakurschti, and the names of the principal families in them are Thompson, Demetro, Ranko, Ufie, Siganoff, Vladochakowski, Vlado, Costello, Mikhailovich, Mitchell, Magill, Mittilo, Merchon, Marko, Martino, Nicholas, Stokes, Guy, Petro, and Bimbo. Some of these names are Anglicized versions of Russian, Serbian, and gypsy names—after the Mikhailovich family got to be very big and branched out, for example, one branch changed Mikhail into Mitchell and another branch changed it into Magill. A number of names, such as Nicholas and Costello, are used by families in the *vitsas* of several tribes. Also, another thing, it's hard to make a flat statement about gypsies; you have to qualify practically everything you say, and I better mention that the families in two or three of the big *vitsas,* particularly the Mineschti, don't all belong to the same tribe, or claim they don't; some families in the Mineschti claim they are Russian and some claim they are Kalderash. As I said, sometimes I wish I'd never heard the word gypsy. We'll take up the Kalderash next. Six of the twenty-three *vitsas* are Kalderash—the Risturschti, the Jaikurschti, the Macholeschti, the Wankurschti, the Gureschti, and the Yotzurschti—and the names of the principal families in them are Stevens, Stevenson, Thompson, Ristick, Johnson, Marks, Evans, Wanko, Eli, Stanley, Demetro, Urich, Costello, Ephraim, and Morgan. Three are Serbian—the Lameschti, the Tooteschti, and the Rishtoni—and their principal family names are Evans, Lee, Stevens, Uwanawich, Miller, Marino, and Marinko. Three are Mexican—the Bokurschti, the Chokurschti, and the Yonkurschti—and their principal family names are Flores, Spiro, Costello, Yonko, Steve, and John. One is Machwaya—the Koleschti—and the principal family names in it are Adams, Uwanawich, Marks, Williams, Lee, Yankovich, Stevens, Miller, and George. One is Greek—the Poopeschti. It takes its name from an old hellcat of a fortune-teller named Poopa. It's a small *vitsa,* and its principal family name is Kaslov. One is Argentine— the Cuneschti—and the names of the principal families in it are Montez, George, and Miller. One is Argentino, but it doesn't have a *vitsa* name; the families in it simply call themselves the Argentinos. Their names are Christo, Miller, Toney, and Nicholas.

"When it comes to first names, most of these gypsies have two. A man may be Joe this or John that when he's dealing with *gajos,* or non-gypsies, but when he's among his own he's Uwano or Mitya or Spirako, or some such. Likewise, a woman who may be known to the police in sixteen cities as Annie this or Rosie that, when she's home she's Repanka or Troka or Pavlena. To complicate matters, a good many have gypsy nicknames. Take a man we've often had dealings with whose *gajo* name is George Adams. I don't know his proper gypsy name, and he himself, if he was asked, he'd probably have to stop and think. He's always Bongo Nock, or Broken Nose, and if you'll look up his photograph in the gallery in the squad office—look under Male Gypsies, File 1, Tray 1—you'll see why. To further complicate matters, most of the women and many of the men have a string of aliases—*gajo* aliases and gypsy aliases.

"Now I want to give you a few details concerning the way gypsies live in the city, and then I'll describe the *bajour,* and then we'll go get some coffee. The first thing to remember, you'll almost always find gypsies living close to the street. They prefer to live in old stores, or in first-floor-front flats in tenements, or in parlor-front flats in brownstones. I've very seldom found them above the second floor. I used to think they wanted to be as close as possible to Mother Earth, but all it is, they want to be where people passing by can see them who might be interested in having their fortunes told. It's a form of advertising. More often than not, two or three families live together and operate an *ofisa* on shares. If they're prosperous, they may have the *ofisa* at one address and live at another, but in most cases they live right in the *ofisa,* back behind the curtained-off fortune-telling booths. If it's a store, they do their best to conceal this; it's illegal to live in a store. When a family or two or three families travelling together arrive in the city, they pile in with other families in their *vitsa,* if any are here, and stay with them until they can rent a place of their own, and if none are here, they ride around during the day looking at old stores with 'FOR RENT' signs on them and sleep in their cars at night. It's sometimes very hard for them to find a place; most landlords have to be tricked into renting to them. They like a location that's conspicuous but not too conspicuous; they're well aware that women don't want to be seen entering or leaving a gypsy place. What they like best is a low-rent store in a run-down block right off a busy crosstown street, such as Fourteenth or Twenty-third. I've known a Machwaya family to pay six hundred a month for a good location, but that's unusual, even for them, and the others won't pay anywhere near that. When they find a store that suits them, the man gypsy among them who looks least like a gypsy goes to the landlord or the renting agent and says he wants to open a rug store in the place, or sometimes it's a mill-remnants store or a lampshade store or a toy store. If they can come to terms, the gypsy puts down a month's rent and gets a receipt and a key. Next morning, two or three cars with trunks and bedrolls strapped on top of them park in front of the store, or maybe it's two or three station wagons, and what at first glance looks like a thousand gypsies get out and start carrying things in. They're systematic. First they bring in some folding chairs and some folding tables and some *gonyas.* A *gonya* is a pair of capacious big canvas bags joined with a strap that fits over the shoulder, and they hold a surprising amount; if a gypsy woman was determined to, she could stuff most of Macy's into one of them. The women do two-thirds of the work. They stand on the chairs and hammer nails in the walls and run wires from the nails. Then they take some curtains and draperies from the *gonyas,* yards and yards and yards of them, and hang them on the wires, dividing the store into a maze of rooms and booths. They may decorate the walls up front with some of those fake tapestries that auction joints sell on boardwalks, or they may tack up one of those pictures that they have sign painters paint for them on oilcloth—a giant human palm, or a phrenological head, or a zodiac, or a crescent and star. Next they take out a stack of moldy old paper-backed palmistry, horoscope and dream books that they've been carrying around for years, and arrange them in the front window. That's a form of camouflage. Fortune-telling is illegal in the city, and when gypsies are brought into court for it, it's their practice to screech and scream and swear to God they didn't tell the woman's fortune, far from it, they just sold her a book and showed her how to use it, if she thought she was having her fortune told she must be crazy. They work fast. They can have an *ofisa* rigged up and ready for business in an hour, and later on, if they pull off a *bajour* and have to get out in a hurry, they can unrig it down in much less time than that. They sometimes buy a couple of overstuffed chairs from a junk store and put them up front to sit on while waiting for customers, but they always leave them behind when they move on. The last things they carry in are their trunks and bedrolls—that is, if they're going to live in the *ofisa.* The bedrolls are quilts stuffed with feathers; they spread them on the floor at night and sleep between them, and in the morning they roll them up and pile them in a corner. Quite often, in one corner, they put up something, it's like a little shrine. They put a box in the corner, a box or an orange crate, and they stand a photograph on it of the last person in the family group who died.

The photograph is in a frame with a prop in back. It generally shows the person lying in state in his or her coffin. Gypsies go in for such photographs—they hire photographers to come to the funeral parlor and make them; they have them made in color, or tinted. They stand icons on both sides of the photograph—pictures of saints, Orthodox Catholic saints. And they stand a candle in front of it, usually it's a big, thick candle trimmed down at the base and fitted into the mouth of a quart milk bottle, and on certain days connected with the dead person they light the candle. For cooking facilities, if there isn't a gas stove in the place, they plug in a pair of hot plates, one for the goulash pot and one to boil water on for tea. That's the backbone of their diet—goulash and tea. That, and candy bars. They spend a good part of their time sitting around drinking tea. They make good tea, good and hot and strong, and then they spoil it. They drink it from glasses, and they not only put slices of lemon in it, they put slices of orange or apple or peach or pear in it, or most any other fruit that's in season. I've seen them take a ripe plum, one of those big purple plums, and poke holes in it with a fork until the juice was dripping out and drop it in a glass of tea. I've seen them drop strawberries in and press them against the side of the glass with the spoon until the tea was red. I've seen them put jam in their tea, spoonfuls of jam. And the amount of sugar they put in, it's a wonder they have any teeth at all, instead of which they have beautiful, strong, shiny white teeth; their teeth are far and away the healthiest things about them. If the women are making money, the men eat out quite a lot. Oh, sometimes they take the women along. They mainly eat in two kinds of places. They eat in Jewish restaurants on the lower East Side, the kind that have a sign in the window saying 'RUMANIAN BROILINGS,' and they eat in Italian restaurants, not the kind of Italian restaurants Americans know anything about but places in Italian neighborhoods, mostly in basements, called *capozzelle* places, where they specialize in sheepsheads, or *capozzelle,* that they buy in slaughterhouses for next to nothing and saw in two and broil, and various inner organs, such as lungs and tripe.

"Out on the road, for all I know, gypsies may be happy-go-lucky, rolling along, not a care in the world, the way gypsies are supposed to be, but here in the city, my experience with them, they're not happy-go-lucky. They're always complaining about the way they feel, and they've always got something; if it isn't pinkeye, it's the itch. One thing you'll always notice in the trash that gypsies leave behind anyplace they've been living is a lot of empty patent-medicine bottles. They're afraid of doctors, and they're always running to the drugstore and asking the druggist to give them something to settle their stomachs, or their nerves—they've got a pain here, a pain there, what's good for it. And one reason they understand superstitious people, they're about as superstitious as they can be themselves. They see signs everywhere, signs and warnings, especially the women. Every so often gypsy women have dreams that terrify them, the way they interpret them, and next day they keep the whole family in—nobody's allowed to go out and nobody's allowed to come in; you can knock and knock, and you can see them moving around in there, but they won't come to the door. Sometimes one of them has a premonition, and the family suddenly packs up and moves. And one thing you're always sure to find when you search a gypsy is a good-luck charm of some kind. There's an old building on the Bowery just below Canal, 42 Bowery, that's had a dozen *ofisas* in it in the last six or seven years, and they've all been run by women in the Bimbo family—some of old man Tene Bimbo's daughters and daughters-in-law and granddaughters; he's got an army of them. A pair of Bimbos will open an *ofisa* in there and run it awhile and all of a sudden they're gone, and it'll be empty a few weeks or months, and then another pair of Bimbos will turn up and take it over. They draw most of their customers from the Italian neighborhood down around here, the Mulberry Street neighborhood. They always keep a couple of cardboard signs in the window, and if you go in and they suspect you're a detective, they'll snatch them out and tear them up. One says, 'DREAM BOOKS. LADY FROM JE-RUSALEM. SPEAKS SEVEN LANGUAGES.' The other is in Italian, and it says, 'VIENI QUI CHE DIVINA LA FORTUNA,' which means 'Come here that I may tell your fortune.' There's an old Italian woman down here who peddles evil-eye charms. She has a little satchel that hangs from her neck and opens up into a tray, and at night she makes the rounds of the Grotta Azzurra and the Villa Penza and the Antica Roma and the Nuova Napoli and Angelo's and the other restaurants in the neighborhood that attract people from uptown, and goes from table to table showing the charms; people buy them for ornaments or souvenirs. One night I was standing in a doorway on Mulberry Street, working on a job that had nothing to do with gypsies. I was back in the shadows, watching the street, and I saw two women approaching each other over on the opposite side. One was the old charm woman making the rounds with her tray, and the other was one of the gypsy women from the *ofisa* on the Bowery, one of the Bimbos. Just as they were about to go past each other, the gypsy woman stopped the old charm woman and bent over and looked in her tray, and the two of them stood there several minutes with their heads close together, talking very seriously, and then the gypsy picked out a charm and paid for it, and I thought to myself, 'I've seen everything now.' "

"Taking in each other's washing," said Detective Kane.

"Either that," said Captain Campion, "or the blind leading the blind. One reason they're so superstitious, they're gypsies, it's the atmosphere they live in, and another reason, they're illiterate. They don't believe in education, and they won't send their children to school unless they're forced to. I've had them tell me that going to school is all right for *gajos,* they've been going for hundreds of years and they're used to it, but gypsies aren't used to it and the strain it puts on their minds is liable to lead to epileptic fits. I doubt if more than one out of ten of them knows how to read and write, but arithmetic is something else again; all of them seem to know enough arithmetic to take care of themselves, it's a mystery to me how they learn it.

"As far as religion, the great majority of them are Russian Orthodox or Serbian Orthodox. The Russians go to two small churches in Russian neighborhoods—St. Peter and St. Paul, which is on Seventh Street, over between First Avenue and Avenue A, and Carpatho-Russian Holy Trinity, which is on Fourth Street, over near the East River. The Serbians go to St. Sava's, which is on West

Twenty-sixth Street; it's the Serbian Orthodox cathedral. I've given up trying to understand how gypsies feel about religion. It seems to be a matter each one makes up his own rules. Some get married by a priest, and some don't. Some have their children baptized, and some don't. Very few ever go to confession. The Orthodox people bring bottles to church on the Feast of Saint John the Baptist— old medicine bottles, old whiskey bottles, old bottles of every description—and the priest fills them with holy water and the people take them home, and a good many gypsies show up that day, the most that ever do, only where the ordinary person brings one bottle, the gypsy brings two or three. A good many also show up on Easter Eve and Easter. And now and then a gypsy woman shows up and buys a candle and lights it before some particular icon. Otherwise, the bulk of them, the principal contact they have with religion is at funerals. Gypsies have the regulation Orthodox funeral services, but the heart of their funerals is at the grave. They open the coffin at the grave, even if they've already had it open at the services, and all of them crowd around it to take a last look, and then they begin to cry out in the gypsy language and moan and wail, the men and the women. The women sometimes let themselves go to such an extent it's pitiful; I've seen them run over and fall on their knees and butt their heads against tombstones, and when they stood up they'd be so dazed they'd walk around in circles and stumble into each other. And before they close the coffin for good, they drop coins in it. And after it's been lowered into the grave and the gravediggers start shovelling the dirt in, they throw coins into the grave. One of the wildest sights I've ever seen, it was in a cemetery over in New Jersey late one afternoon in February, and it was bitter cold and windy, and two gravediggers were working on one side of a gypsy grave, shovelling the dirt in, and the gypsies were crowded together on the other side, moaning and crying out, some with babies in their arms, and an old man among them was leaning over pouring wine into the grave from a gallon jug that was resting on his shoulder, cheap red wine, and one moment the wind blew some of the wine on the gravediggers and the next moment it blew some on the gypsies. After a grave has been filled, they usually spread a cloth on the ground nearby and have a funeral feast. If the family is prosperous, they'll have cold turkeys and hams and legs of lamb; if they're poor, they'll have cold cuts. And if it rains, they'll put up a tent.

"Back around 1900, gypsies started burying in Evergreen Cemetery in Elizabeth, New Jersey, and some still do, but during the thirties the Linden Cemetery in Linden, New Jersey, became more popular, and now it's used by gypsies all over the East. Evergreen is a beautiful old cemetery; it's like the deep woods, it has so many big old trees in it, and that appeals to gypsies. Linden doesn't have as many trees, but it's easier to get to; U.S. 1 passes right by it. The burial of a prominent gypsy will draw a couple of hundred cars loaded with gypsies to Linden, and the cars will have licenses on them from a dozen states. Steve Kaslov is buried over there, the old king of the Poopeschti. He's lying in a two-thousand-dollar coffin, and he's got a red granite tombstone on top of him that cost six hundred dollars, and a photograph of him covered with some kind of plastic material that you can see through is cemented to the tombstone; he's got a grin on his face. And Uwano Ufie, who was better known as Cockeye Johnny Nikanov, is buried over there. Cockeye Johnny was one of the Frinkuleschti kings, and he was quite powerful during the depression. He could read a little, and he learned the relief regulations inside out, and he was the scourge of the Welfare Department; there wasn't a regulation in the book that he couldn't get around. It was his dream to attract all the gypsies in North and South America to New York City and get them on relief, and then he'd become the supreme ruler of the whole lot of them, the Emperor of the Gypsies. He died during a heat wave in the summer of 1944; he overexerted himself carrying a heavy watermelon home to his grandchildren and had a heart attack. And Marta Evans is buried over there, who used to be the queen of the gypsies in Philadelphia. And Little Nina Marks is buried over there, the most beautiful gypsy girl I ever saw. Little Nina was an Argentino married to a Kalderash. She was one of the best of the gypsy pickpockets, and she was very good at what the gypsies call winking at a man. If a man stopped in front of her *ofisa* and stood there, peering in, she'd size him up, and if he looked as if he could be taken, she'd get up from her chair and bend over very low and rearrange the books in the show window and let the man get a good look at her and then she'd give him a wink and he'd come right in and she'd lead him into one of the booths and they'd start wrestling around and while they were wrestling she'd pick his pockets and then she'd scream rape and her husband would rush in with a knife and start slashing the air, just barely missing the man, and the man would leap out of the booth and run like a rat. She died of cancer of the breast in Memorial Hospital in 1952, when she was only twenty-seven, and she's buried on the side of a hill facing U.S. 1, under a horse-chestnut tree. And old Matrona Nicholas is over there, and Repanka Zlotkovich and Elaina Thompson and Sabinka Miller and Mary Demetro who grabbed my necktie in court one day and jerked the breath out of me and Birka Vlado who used to smoke a pipe, and dozens of other women that I spent a good part of the last twenty-five years tracking down and keeping under surveillance and apprehending and interrogating. Some of them, the first time I saw them, they were young women, young or just getting middle-aged, and they were walking around with their heads held high, wearing flashy skirts and switching their tails, and the last time I saw them, they were old and ugly and full of spite. Sometimes, on a Sunday afternoon, I drive over there and look at their graves and see if any new ones have turned up. There's women lying over there that I stood in doorways across the street from their *ofisas* many a cold night waiting and watching for the right moment to go in and nail them, and they despised me and I despised them, but I knew them very well, and I remember so many things about them, and when I look at their tombstones and read their names and dates, after all they're dead and gone, I must admit it makes me sad."

CAPTAIN CAMPION stood up again, and put the *vitsa* chart back in his briefcase. Then he sat down. "Now we come to the *bajour*," he said. "The first thing I want to impress on you is that the majority of those who visit gypsies for any purpose at all—to have their fortunes told, to seek advice, to have a dream interpreted, to ask for a good number to play in the numbers game, just to have somebody to talk to, or just blind curiosity—are women. And the great majority of those who end up as *bajour* victims are women between the ages of forty and fifty-five, a high proportion of whom are in the change of life. After you've interrogated a few of these victims, and I've interrogated hundreds, you begin to realize that they have things in common. Most of them are unhappily married or they've never been married or they're divorced or they're widows. Most of them are deeply depressed, and they either don't know why, just everything in general, or they lay it to something in their past—it might be something very complicated, or it might be something as simple as they once had an illegitimate baby and let it be adopted and never saw it again. Most of them are worried about their health—the fact is most of them are more than halfway convinced they have cancer. Most of them have a passion to talk about themselves, a passion to confess—it's probably the strain they're under, and they probably don't know they're doing it, but they talk about themselves all the time, or all the time they can get anybody to listen; they just can't stop. And most of them, they may be smart in some ways, but they're fundamentally ignorant; if it's presented to them the right way, they'll believe anything. And a good many are the kind of women who if they go out at night to walk a dog they'll unerringly head for some vacant lot or some dark corner in a park, or if they have to be out late and go home alone they'll take shortcuts through blocks that the ordinary person wouldn't go through at that hour fully armed, or if they're sitting in a barroom and it gets late and some stranger on the next bar stool offers to see them home they'll go right along.

"The second thing I want to impress on you is that gypsy women are shrewd, really shrewd, and don't make any mistake about that. When they're tiny little girls, their mothers and grandmothers and aunts start drilling the facts of life into them, and as soon as they're old enough to keep quiet and be still they're allowed to hide behind the curtains and eavesdrop while *gajo* women tell their innermost secrets; that's part of their training. By the time they're twenty, they're well acquainted with the fears that lurk around in the minds of middle-aged women, and the crazy ideas, and by the time they're middle-aged themselves they can just look at a woman and observe the expression in her eyes and the set of her mouth and the sags and wrinkles in her face and the way she holds herself and find out a good deal about her past, particularly her past in relation to men.

"The third thing I want to impress on you is that gypsy women are very skillful at making ordinary, everyday objects seem highly mysterious. The *bajour* is a flexible confidence game, and it's up to the individual gypsy's imagination how she does it. However, in recent years, in and around New York City, the majority of the women have been doing it the same way. They've been doing it with an egg, an ordinary white egg.

"Usually, when a woman enters an *ofisa* for the first time, she's apprehensive. 'Come right in, dear,' the gypsy says, and talks soothingly to her and tells her what a pretty dress she has on, so becoming, and leads her back into one of the booths. There's two chairs in there, and a little table with a candle sticking up on it about a foot and a half long and as big around as your wrist, and that's all. Every picture of a gypsy fortune-teller I've ever seen, she was gazing into a crystal ball, but I've never once seen a crystal ball in an *ofisa*. The gypsy lights the candle, and she and the woman sit facing each other, and the gypsy takes the woman's right hand and opens it and gently strokes the palm, smoothing it out, and all this time the woman is talking, telling her troubles. The gypsy concentrates on the lines in the woman's palm and doesn't appear to be listening, but she's listening; she's trying to decide if the woman is worth working on, and if the woman slows down, she asks her a question or two that encourages her to talk some more. If the gypsy decides the woman has too much sense to fall for a *bajour* and all she can hope to get out of her is the fortune-telling fee, she doesn't waste much time on her. She studies her right palm, and her left one, too, if the woman is willing to double the fee, and then she gives her the age-old fortune-telling rigamarole: a little about the past, a little about the future; she should watch this, she should be careful about that, she shouldn't make any important decisions on Tuesdays. The gypsy may go through this procedure with a long succession of women, and months may go by, and then one day she's staring at a woman's palm and the woman is talking on and on—her husband died six weeks ago last Friday and now she's all alone, there isn't a single remaining soul who cares what happens to her; sometimes she sees him in a dream, and he's sitting up in his coffin and his eyes are wide open and he's looking straight at her; she wasn't as good to him as she should've been, and her heart is broken; she hasn't slept more than a couple of hours a night since he passed away, and she doesn't see how she lives on the little she eats; she wishes she could take back some of the things she said to him, but it's too late now; he was good to her, and she didn't appreciate it; he left her everything he had, and she doesn't deserve it, she doesn't deserve a penny of it—and suddenly the gypsy knows she has a victim. She looks up from the woman's palm, and interrupts her. 'Have you noticed any unusual pains lately, dear,' she says, 'any pains you never noticed before?' or 'Come a little closer, dear,' she says, 'and let me look at that mole on your cheek.' Then she goes back to studying the woman's palm. She studies it for five minutes or so. 'Let me see your other hand, dear,' she says. She studies the left palm awhile, and then she glances from one to the other, comparing the lines, and finally she looks up and says, 'I don't want to scare you, dear—we may be able to do something about it— but I see something bad in your hand. I see something very bad.' 'What is it?' 'It's a good thing you came in here today,' the gypsy says. 'The spirits must've sent you to me.' 'What did you see in my hand?' the woman asks. 'Tell me what you saw.' 'I can't tell you now,' the gypsy says. 'There's a certain other thing I have to look into, and then I'll tell you. I want you to go home now, and on your way home I want you to buy a fresh white egg, and tonight I want you to get out the three warmest blankets you have and put them on your bed, and then I want you to get undressed and get under the blankets and lie on your back, and then I want you to take the egg and hold it on your navel with both hands clasped over it, and I want you to lie there that way until the egg feels warm, real warm, and then I want you to wrap it in a white handkerchief, and tomorrow morning I want you to bring it to me. And I don't want you to pay me anything, now or ever; in cases like yours, we work in close connection with the spirits, and we don't take money. And I want to warn you, if you say one word about this to anybody, even a priest or a minister, you'll break my power so far as you're concerned and I won't be able to help you, and you better not let that happen, dear, because the spirits must've sent you to me, they must've meant for me to help you, and if they did, I'm the only one in the world that *can* help you. I'm your only hope.'

"If the gypsy has the woman sized up right, she's back at the *ofisa* bright and early next morning, and she has the egg with her, all wrapped up in a handkerchief. They go into the booth, and the woman tries to give the egg to the gypsy; she wants to get rid of it. 'Just a moment,' the gypsy says. 'I have to use a fresh candle for this.' She steps out of the booth and goes in back to get the candle, and while she's back there she hides a tiny little object between two of the fingers of her left hand. She returns to the booth and stands the candle up and lights it. Then she takes the egg from the woman. She unwraps the egg and holds it and gives the handkerchief back to the woman and tells her to spread it on the table, which the woman does. Then the gypsy breaks the egg and empties it on the handkerchief, and while she's doing so she executes some sleight of hand and the object between her fingers drops out, and when she takes her hands away it's lying on the yolk of the egg—sometimes it's a ball of tangled hair, sometimes it's a knotted-up piece of string with some kind of stringy green matter clinging to it, and sometimes it's a hairy little devil's head."

Captain Campion dug around in his briefcase and brought out a small cardboard box that had originally contained paper clips and opened it and placed it on the desk. "Such as this," he said. In the box, on a wad of cotton, lay a devil's head carved out of ivory. It was approximately an inch and a quarter long and three-quarters of an inch wide. The devil's horns were down-turned over his forehead, his eyes were shut, his cheeks were sunken, his mouth was fixed in an agonized grin, and he had a shock of bristly black hair. "When I first saw this thing," Captain Campion said, "I was pretty sure it wasn't carved by a gypsy, and I took it uptown and showed it to a pawnbroker who's an expert on queer jewelry and bric-a-brac, and he said it's a type of ivory miniature that was quite popular in Germany during the latter part of the last century. They turn up now and then in antique stores and curiosity shops and pawnshops. When a gypsy woman buys one, she cuts off some of her own hair and glues it on the top and the back. We found this one in the possession of a Kalderash *bajour* woman named Linka Stevens. That flaky stuff sticking to the hair is dried-up egg yolk. The last time Linka used it, she took seven thousand nine hundred dollars from an old Irishwoman, a hotel maid. The old woman had worked in cheap side-street hotels in New York City for over forty years, and it was her life's savings." Captain Campion closed the box and put it back in his briefcase.

"To continue," Captain Campion said, "the gypsy and the woman stand there a few moments and look at the little object on the yolk of the egg, and then the gypsy says, 'Let's sit down, dear.' They sit down, and the gypsy says, 'It's just as I thought, dear. You've got a curse on you. You've got something growing inside you.' 'Is it a tumor?' the woman asks. 'We won't talk about what it is,' the gypsy says, but the woman interrupts her. 'Is it cancer?' she asks. 'I told you we won't talk about what it is,' the gypsy says. 'We'll talk about what we're going to do about it. You've got some money in the bank, haven't you, dear?' The woman says she has. 'That may be where the curse is coming from,' the gypsy says. 'It usually is. Back before you put that money in the bank, you or your husband or whoever put it in, some of it might've passed through the hands of a man who ruined his own child, or some of it might've passed through the hands of Antichrist, or, the way it often happens, a man might've killed himself making it. The actual same money may not be in the bank any more, but the curse is there, waiting; it's in among all that dirty, filthy, stinking money piled up down there in the vaults of the bank, waiting. And it'll jump to any money that replaces the actual same money; it'll jump to any money that you draw out. I want you to go home now and get your bankbook, and then I want you to go to the bank and draw out a small bill—a five-dollar bill will do—and then I want you to buy another white egg and a white handkerchief, and then I want you to bring the five-dollar bill and the egg and the handkerchief back here to me.

While you're gone, I'm going to burn this handkerchief and the egg I broke and that thing that's on the egg. I'm going to put them in a bucket and pour kerosene on them and burn them.'

"When the woman returns, she opens her handbag and starts to give the bill and the egg and the handkerchief to the gypsy, but the gypsy backs away. 'Oh, no,' she says. 'I don't want to touch that money.' She leads the woman into the booth. 'Now, dear,' she says, 'I want you to wrap the five-dollar bill around the egg, and then I want you to wrap the handkerchief around it, and then I want you to lay it on the floor, over in the corner.' Which the woman does. 'I'm going to leave you in here by yourself a little while,' the gypsy says. 'Just sit there and be quiet until I come back.' Fifteen minutes go by, a half hour, an hour, and then the gypsy comes back. 'You can pick up the egg now, dear,' she says. 'Spread the handkerchief on the table, and put that five-dollar bill back in your handbag and give the egg to me.' The woman does as she's told, and the gypsy bends over the table and breaks the egg and empties it on the handkerchief, and once again there's that little object lying on the yolk of the egg. 'This is no surprise to me,' the gypsy says. 'The money you have in the bank has a curse on it, just as I expected, and it's responsible for that thing that's growing inside you, and there's only one thing you can do. You've got to go to the bank and draw out that money and bring it here, and I've got to hold it in my right hand and get in connection with the spirits and ask them to throw the curse off.' The woman comes to her senses for a moment. 'What will happen if I don't?' she asks. The gypsy shrugs her shoulders. 'Look, dear,' she says, 'I'm not getting anything out of this, and it doesn't make any difference to me what you do. The spirits are using me, and I'm doing my part. If you do your part, the spirits will throw the curse off the money and that thing that's growing inside you will dissolve and disappear. If you don't do your part, the spirits won't hold me responsible for what happens to you.' 'Do you know what will happen to me?' the woman asks. 'Yes, dear,' the gypsy says, 'I know. One morning before long you'll wake up and you'll notice you have a gumboil, that's the first thing you'll notice, and by and by you'll have dozens of gumboils, and then your gums will grow soft and your teeth will come loose and drop out two or three at a time, you'll spit them out like cherry pits, and then a goiter will grow on your neck and big, hairy moles will sprout out all over you, and then your bones will start to rot and clog your blood—if you were to cut your hand around this time and rub some of the blood between your fingers, it would feel gritty—and pretty soon you won't be able to sit in a chair, let alone stand on your feet, and you'll have to go to bed for good, and then your lungs will start drying up, and then one day your heart will race a few minutes and stop and race a few more minutes and stop again and suddenly a pain will plunge through you like a flash of lightning, and that will be the end.' 'Do I have to draw out all the money?' the woman asks. 'You have to draw out every cent of it,' the gypsy says. 'And if the man at the bank asks you any questions why you're drawing it out, tell him it's a confidential matter, you're investing in some real estate. And tell him to give it to you in large denominations, such as fifties and hundreds, so it won't be such a nuisance to handle.'

"There are several ways of bringing a *bajour* to a conclusion. The two most frequently used are the sew-up and the burn-up. If the gypsy isn't quite sure how much power she has over the woman and feels she'd better work fast, she does a sew-up. When the woman returns from the bank with her money, the gypsy takes her into the booth and tells her to sit down at the table. 'Don't worry, dear,' she says. 'You're doing the right thing, and it'll all be over in a few minutes.' Then she gets a needle and thread and a piece of coarse white cloth cut into the shape of paper money, only a little wider and a little longer. She tells the woman to lay the stack of bills flat on the cloth, and then she tells her to fold them over once, both the cloth and the bills, with the cloth on the outside, which the woman does, and then the gypsy sews up the three open sides of the cloth, enclosing the bills in a snug little bag. That's the basic meaning of the word 'bajour'—a little bag of money. The gypsies claim it's an old gypsy word, but I had a Serbian Orthodox priest tell me it's really a Serbian word, 'bozur,' that the gypsies borrowed and changed; 'bozur' means a beautiful flower, and it can be extended to mean anything unusually beautiful. The gypsy clutches the bag in her right hand and gets down on her knees on the floor. 'Kneel down beside me, dear,' she tells the woman, 'and hold my left hand and close your eyes. While I'm talking to the spirits, I want you to pray in your own way. I want you to pray that I get the right answer.' The woman joins the gypsy on the floor, and then the gypsy begins to jibber-jabber in the gypsy language. She talks, and then she chants, and then she talks, and then she chants, and it sounds as if she's begging and beseeching. The gypsy has two slit pockets in the right side of her skirt. One pocket is empty. While she's jibber-jabbering, she slips the money bag into this pocket. In the other pocket, she has an assortment of bags similar to the money bag, only they're phonies; they vary in thickness, and all they contain are pieces of crackly bond paper cut to paper-money size. She feels around in this pocket and picks out a phony bag that corresponds in thickness to the money bag, and she takes it out and holds on to it. She continues to talk to the spirits for a few minutes, and then she suddenly lets out a cry of joy and rises to her feet and pulls the woman up with her. 'Now, dear,' she says, 'I'll have to ask you to undo your dress, or take it off, so I can get at your underclothes.' The woman does as she's told, and the gypsy sews the phony bag to the woman's slip or whatever kind of underclothes she has on. 'Now, dear,' she says, 'I want you to go straight home and lie down, and as it begins to grow dark the curse will begin to leave you. It won't leave you all at once. It'll leave you gradually, and at midnight it'll be gone entirely. It'll take longer for the curse to leave the money. I want you to wear this slip with the bag on it every day for the next seven days, and I want you to sleep with it under your pillow. On the eighth day, the money will be clean, and you can take it out of the bag and put it back in the bank. Only I want to warn you, if you open the bag beforehand, or if you say one word about this matter to anybody, if you even hint at it, the money will turn to plain white paper and the curse will jump back on you.'

"That's the sew-up, and it's the easiest way. However, if the gypsy feels she has the woman completely in her power, she does it differently; she does a burn-up. It's more trouble, but it makes a deeper impression on the woman, and in the long run it's safer— it's very hard for us to get a conviction on a burn-up. In most cases, the victim won't go near the police unless some relative finds out what's happened and forces her to, and that's usually weeks later, and then, if we knock ourselves out and succeed in apprehending the gypsy, half the time the victim will back down at the last minute and refuse to go into court and testify. A burn-up takes longer than a sew-up. 'Look, dear,' the gypsy says when the woman returns from the bank, 'I've got to hold that money while I'm talking to the spirits, and there's always a danger the curse will jump from the money to me, and I don't want to touch it with my naked hand. I'm going to give you this handkerchief, and I want you to take that stack of bills and roll it up and lay it in the middle of the handkerchief, and then I want you to pull the corners of the hand-kerchief together and tie them in two good strong knots.' The woman starts to do this, but the gypsy isn't overlooking anything. 'Just a moment, dear,' she says. 'Open your handbag and get that five-dollar bill that you wrapped around the egg, and put it in the handkerchief, too.' The woman does as she's told. When she's finished, the gypsy clutches the knotted-up handkerchief in her right hand, and gets down on her knees. She chants awhile in gypsy, and then she goes into a kind of self-induced fit. I've heard dozens of victims describe this fit. The gypsy whimpers and moans. She grinds her teeth. She beats her forehead on the floor. She tears her blouse to rags. She scratches her face until it bleeds, and it's real blood; I've arrested gypsy women several days after a burn-up and I've seen the scratches. She throws her head back and rolls her eyes and shudders and gargles, as if she's choking. One moment she's walking on her hands and knees and quivering all over, and the next moment she's flat on the floor, thrashing around. And while she's thrashing around, she slips the handkerchief with the money in it into one of the slit pockets in her skirt, and she takes another knotted-up handkerchief from the other pocket. It's a phony, of course; it contains some more of those pieces of paper cut to paper-money size. Presently, she wears herself out, and lies face forward on the floor, gasping. Then she gets up, and she's dusty and dirty and sweaty, and her blouse is hanging down in rags, and her eyes are wild, and her face is all scratched and bloody. She totters over to her chair and sits down. 'I've got good news, dear,' she says, 'and I've got bad news. The spirits will draw the curse off you, but first you'll have to destroy the money. You'll have to burn it up.' This horrifies the woman, but the gypsy is ready for her. She reminds her about that thing that's growing inside her, and goes on from that to gumboils and big, hairy moles and rotting bones, and all the rest of it, and this time she uses her imagination to the utmost. Pretty soon the woman becomes reconciled. Whereupon the gypsy brings in a bucket about half full of splinters and coal, on which she sprinkles some kerosene. She starts a fire, and waits until it's burning good, and then she pours some kerosene on the phony knotted-up handkerchief. She saturates it with kerosene. Then she hands it to the woman, and tells her to throw it in the bucket. 'You have to do this part yourself,' the gypsy says. The woman throws it in, and it blazes up and starts burning. Then the gypsy tells the woman to kneel, and she kneels beside her. 'You pray your way,' she says, 'and I'll pray my way.' By and by the gypsy gets up and looks in the bucket. She makes sure the handkerchief and its contents have been destroyed, and then she pours some water on the fire. 'Now, dear,' she says, 'I want you to go straight home and lie down, and as it begins to grow dark the curse will begin to leave you. It'll leave you gradually, and at midnight it'll be gone entirely. Only I want to warn you, if you ever say anything to anybody about this matter the rest of your life, the split second the words are out of your mouth the curse will jump back on you and your bones will begin to rot.'

"Usually, at the conclusion of a *bajour,* whether it's been a sew-up or a burn-up, the woman is in a state of shock, she hardly knows where she is, and the gypsy has to take her by the arm and lead her to the door. The moment she leaves, the gypsies start packing. It doesn't take them long. In half an hour, or even less, they're out and gone."

(1955)

The Deaf-Mutes Club

*T*HE UNION LEAGUE OF THE DEAF, Inc., is a social club exclusively for deaf-mutes. It was founded in 1886 and has four hundred members. A man I know, a linotype operator for a morning newspaper, is a member. A couple of weeks ago he sent me a letter of introduction to Mr. Samuel Frankenheim, the club's historian. "Mr. Frankenheim is a retired Wall Street man and he kills a lot of time around the Union League," the linotype operator wrote in a note accompanying the letter. "If you'd be interested in writing an article about the club, he would be glad to see you. Drop in most any afternoon and he will be on hand. Take along a note pad, as you will have to write out your questions to him. He will reply the same way. In conversing with him, avoid the term 'deaf-mute' as much as possible. I don't mind it, and he probably doesn't, but many do. The club used to be called the Deaf-Mutes' Union League, but five years ago the name was changed because of this. Nearly all so-called deaf-mutes have normal vocal organs and can speak at least a few words if given a chance, and it provokes them to be considered 'mute' or 'dumb.' As a class, they prefer to be known as 'the deaf.' The people generally referred to as 'deaf' (the people you see with hearing aids attached to their heads) now insist on being called 'hard of hearing.' The two classes pretty much keep to themselves. As a rule, the hard of hearing do not belong to deaf organizations, and vice versa. The address of the Union League is 711 Eighth Avenue, just below Forty-fifth. Go to the top floor. You will see a door with two upraised hands painted on it. The hands represent 'U' and 'L' in the manual alphabet. Don't knock, as naturally no one will hear. Go right in, find Mr. Frankenheim, and hand him my letter."

I visited the Union League on a Saturday afternoon. Its address turned out to be a three-floor, walkup taxpayer. Near the landing on the third floor I found the door with the hands on it. Before opening it, I got out my note pad and wrote, "I am looking for Mr. Frankenheim." Then I went inside. The room was spacious and sunny. In one corner stood a big, soft-drink slot machine. On the walls were a number of framed group photographs, a bulletin board, an American flag, and a cloth banner on which was printed in red, white, and blue letters, "GOD BLESS AMERICA. WE ARE PROUD TO BE AMERICANS." Along one wall was a row of straight-backed chairs. In one of them sat a small, thin, grizzled man in a brown tweed suit. His hands were limp in his lap, his chin was on his chest, and he appeared to be sound asleep. In disarray at his feet lay a *Wall Street Journal*. There were three billiard tables in the room. A man with a derby on the back of his head was hunched over the middle table, deliberating on a shot. After he made it, I went over and handed him my pad. He read what I had written on it and a look of annoyance came on his face. He took a pencil out of his vest pocket and swiftly wrote on the pad, "What do you want to see Mr. F. in reference to? No salesmen allowed in here." I wrote, "I am not selling anything. I have a letter for him." The billiard player read this, shrugged his shoulders, and pointed at the sleeping man. Then he took the pad again and wrote. "That is Mr. F. asleep. O.K. to wake him up."

I went over and touched Mr. Frankenheim on the shoulder, and he opened his eyes and yawned. I gave him the letter. After reading it, he motioned to me to sit down. Then he got out a loose-leaf notebook, rested it on a knee, and began writing. When he reached the bottom of the leaf, he tore it out and gave it to me. His handwriting was small and meticulous. "Glad to meet you," he had written. "Nice day, isn't it? Paper said rain! Always glad to tell hearing people about the U.L. Great club. Best of its kind in the entire U.S. I am one of the founders. Our rooms have been located here eight years. Had rooms in a building on West 125th Street for 31 years. Burnt out there. A fire. Loss to club $7,000. Severe loss. Accommodations here are real nice, if I do say so. This is the billiard room. Equipped with the best tables money can buy. Many good players in the U.L. Adjoining this room is the cardroom and the officers' room. Will show them to you later."

While I was reading this, Mr. Frankenheim paid no attention to me but continued to write in his notebook. Presently he tore out another leaf and gave it to me. "Down the hall," this note read, "we have an assembly room. Seating capacity 500. Only use it for membership meetings and Lit. Nights. Name dates back to days when we began having debates in sign language. Debates were considered refined and literary in those days. On Lit. Nights we have lectures, silent movies, and sometimes a debate, and then push the chairs back, switch on the radio, and have dancing. The deaf are A-1 dancers. None better. We don't hear, but when we dance on a wooden floor most of us feel the vibrations of the music. To watch us dancing, you'd never guess we didn't hear anything at all. Even have a few jitterbug dancers. Can't say I think much of jitterbugs myself. A nuisance to one and all. The U.L. is exclusively for men, but we always invite the ladies to our affairs. We have many lectures on worthy topics, sometimes by hearing people. A hearing lecturer gets up on the platform and talks same as he would anywhere else. A hearing man who knows sign language stands beside him and interprets for us. We open all meetings by 'singing' the 'Star-Spangled Banner' in sign language. All stand erect and go through the entire song with our hands. Do you find these facts interesting?"

After reading this, I started to write a reply, but Mr. Frankenheim motioned to me to wait. He took back one of the leaves he had given me and wrote a sentence on the back of it: "I am 72 years old." I knew what was expected of me. On my pad I wrote, "You certainly don't look it, Mr. Frankenheim." I held this up, and he read it, smiled proudly, and began writing again. "Never worry!" he wrote this time. "That's the secret. Been a busy man all my life, but did not worry. Spent 23 years with Lee Higginson Corp. selling stocks and bonds to the deaf throughout U.S. and Canada. Travelled extensively. Retired three years ago. Taking it easy now. It's great fun! We will take a look at the cardroom. The U.L. has some of the sharpest pinochle players you ever saw. I myself prefer whist."

Mr. Frankenheim got up and I followed him to the door of an adjoining room. The door had been pegged open, and we stood at the threshold and looked in. In the room, sitting around big, circular, old-fashioned card tables, were about two dozen men, most of whom were middle-aged. A few were reading, one was writing a letter, one was working out a crossword puzzle, and one was repairing a cigarette lighter with a nail file, but the majority were intent on card games. It was not quiet in the room—pinochle players grunted angrily at each other, decks of cards were noisily riffled and cut, chairs were occasionally scraped back, and a couple of kibitzers were wandering around. At the table nearest us, two men were studying racing papers. One had a *Daily Racing Form* and the other had a past-performance page out of a *Morning Telegraph*. Suddenly they looked up and began talking to each other in sign language. They were obviously at odds about something; they closed and unclosed their hands in the air, wriggled their fingers, and made complicated gestures. I wrote on my pad, "What are they arguing about?" Mr. Frankenheim watched them for a few moments and wrote, "Their conversation is in reference to a horse."

A man came up behind us and we stood aside to let him in. He was a shoeshine man. He slid his shine box under a table, pulled off his cap, and sat down. Then he took out a handful of change and began counting it. Mr. Frankenheim sensed that I was curious about the man and he wrote, "Gentleman who just came in is a member. Shines shoes along Eighth Avenue. Well known in the neighborhood and has made many hearing friends. The pursuits of U.L. members are varied from common laborer right on up to one member who owns a big printing business and sells insurance to the deaf as a sideline. In the club all members are equal, no matter what line they are in, or race, or religion, etc. This is not a Park Avenue club. No man blackballed because of race or class. Political and religious matters taboo at our meetings. Most of the members now in the cardroom are night workers who take their leisure in the afternoon. Now let us step into the officers' room, and I will write you out a brief history of the club."

THE OFFICERS' ROOM was unpretentious. It was furnished with a roll-top desk, an iron safe, a long table, and half a dozen chairs. On the walls were framed souvenir programs of Union League balls, a bathing-girl calendar, a faded tintype of a brownstone house, and a row of photographs of the club's past presidents. Mr. Frankenheim's photograph was among them. Two men were sitting at one end of the table. One was a prematurely bald young man who wore spectacles with lenses so thick they made his eyes look protuberant. A Leica camera, slung from his neck, rested on his chest. The other man was middle-aged; he was stout and red-haired and had an unmistakably Irish face. They were examining some negatives. When we came in both men looked up, and Mr. Frankenheim conversed with them for several minutes in sign language. Then he and I sat down at the other end of the table. He sharpened his pencil with a pearl-handled knife and began scribbling in his notebook. After a while, I got out a cigarette. The prematurely bald young man looked up and watched me light it. Presently he said, "Could I bum a cigarette? I have a pipe, but I forgot my pouch this morning." I had not expected him to speak, of course, and I was startled. His voice was without inflection and not much louder than a whisper. He spoke haltingly and with obvious difficulty.

"Certainly," I said, sliding the pack down the table. He took one and slid the pack back. I offered the pack to the red-haired man, but he shook his head.

"Much obliged," he said, "but I don't smoke." His voice was normal. The bald young man lit the cigarette and then said, "You were surprised to hear me talk, weren't you?" I said that I had been, and asked him if he was a member of the Union League.

"I'm a member," he said, "but my friend here isn't. He's a hearing man, but he knows sign language. He drops in occasionally to shoot pool. I'm totally deaf myself, but I can talk a little and I'm a lip reader. I went deaf when I was around twelve. I had the measles and lost my hearing, but I retained the ability to talk."

"That's very interesting," I said. He frowned and looked at me fixedly for a few moments.

"It may be very interesting to you," he said finally, "but it isn't to me."

I was embarrassed and changed the subject. "Are you a photographer?" I asked.

He shook his head. "Just an amateur," he said. "I'm a bookbinder by trade."

I wanted to ask more questions, but at this moment Mr. Frankenheim tore a leaf out of his notebook and handed it to me. He had covered both sides of it with his precise handwriting.

"Will now tell you how the good old U.L. was founded," this message began. "It was founded in the parlor of my boyhood home at 531 Lexington Avenue. The old brownstone in the tintype picture on the wall is the house. It was later torn down to make way for the Hotel Shelton. I and three other young men met in the parlor one Saturday afternoon in January, 1886. All were grads of the Institution for the Improved Instruction of Deaf-Mutes, now known as the Lexington School for the Deaf, and all were great chums. Decided to form a social club exclusively for deaf-mutes. Each became an officer—I was the first president—and each chipped in to establish a treasury. Then we passed two resolutions. One required every member to learn how to dance and the other authorized a draft on the treasury for the purpose of having our photograph made. Went to Mrs. C. A. N. Smith's Tintype Gallery at Broadway and Thirteenth, which was famous in its day. Remember it as well as yesterday. How times flies! By the fall of 1888, the year of the blizzard, the club had grown to such an extent we decided to hold a ball. Hired old Lyric Hall on Sixth Avenue and every member was required to wear a full dress suit or pay a fine of $2. Ball was a gratifying success and won a name for the U.L. in deaf-mute circles all over. So we made it an annual affair. Now hold our balls in big hotels, such as the Astor.

"Club gradually got to be of great importance in the lives of the members. Like when the Grim Reaper stalked into the ranks and claimed a member, the club took full charge of the funeral arrangements. Still do that quite often. Always send a wreath to the funeral of a prominent deaf person, even when not a member. U.L. members have always been men of sterling character. Did have to expel one back in 1893 for deserting his young wife. Can't have that sort of thing. In the early days of the club we didn't have any regular headquarters, but we grew in strength like the green bay tree of yore and got tired of meeting here today and there tomorrow. So we began to rent clubrooms. First we had rooms in an Elks' lodge hall, then in Jacob Ruppert's old Central Opera House, then in a Broadway office building, then for years on West 125th Street, then here. Improved ourselves with each jump. At present we are in A-1 financial condition. Let us knock wood. We have 400 members. Have around three dozen out-of-town members, mostly from Jersey. They make the U.L. their headquarters when in town. A few who live in distant points go to great trouble and expense to come to Lit. Nights, just for the companionship, etc. Members good about helping each other find employment. Club gives freely to charities for the needy deaf. Has equipped many deaf athletic teams. I could sit here and write until far in the night, but have given you the main facts, and my fingers are tired, and you will have to excuse me. Pleased to have met you."

After I had finished reading this, I wrote a note to Mr. Frankenheim, thanking him, and then we shook hands. I got my hat and started to leave, but he grabbed my elbow and escorted me to the soft-drink machine in the billiard room. We had Coca-Colas and shook hands all over again. Then I left. The red-haired man followed me out of the room. In the hall he asked me, "Was Mr. Frankenheim telling you about the Union League?"

I said, "That's right."

"Are you interested in the deaf?" he asked.

I told him that I planned to write an article about the club.

"Well," he said, "the Union League is a wonderful organization, but it isn't the only deaf club in the city by any means. It's the biggest, but there are dozens of others. If you're interested, I could tell you about some of them." I suggested that we go somewhere and have a drink, and he said, "Downstairs in this building there's a place called Larry's Café. We could go there."

WE WENT DOWNSTAIRS to Larry's, which was a typical Eighth Avenue saloon, stood at the bar, and ordered Tom Collinses.

"My name is Jack Fitzsimmons," said the red-haired man. "I'm a proofreader. I work in a big job-printing plant in Brooklyn. I have a lot of deaf friends and I'm a sign-language interpreter. That's my hobby. My parents were deaf and I learned the signs from them. Practically all deaf clubs have honorary hearing members who know the signs and act as interpreters. I hold honorary membership in a small deaf club in Brooklyn, but I'll tell you about that later. If a deaf person has to go to court, or is called to the income-tax bureau, or wants to take out citizenship papers or a marriage license, or the like of that, he usually asks his organization's interpreter to go along and help him out. Like myself, most of these interpreters picked up the signs from their parents. The children of deaf parents are an interesting group in themselves. Helen Menken, the actress, is one. I don't know if she can sign, but I do know she does a lot of good propaganda work for the National Association of the Deaf, which has a chapter in the city. It isn't a social organization. It fights laws which interfere with the rights of the deaf to drive automobiles, and it has an impostor bureau, which investigates beggars who claim to be deaf and often aren't, and it has a nomenclature committee, which writes to newspapers when they use unpleasant phrases like 'deaf and dumb,' and it acquaints employers with the special capabilities of deaf workers, and it does a lot of things like that. By the way, how do you like this saloon?"

I said that I liked it all right.

"Nothing unusual about it," he said, "except that it's a hangout for the deaf. Gets more deaf trade than any other saloon in the city. On Union League meeting nights it's crowded. The owner is a fellow named Laurence Blau. He takes an interest in the deaf. He has a son named Sheldon, who tends bar at night. Sheldon knows finger spelling. I guess he's the only bartender in town who does. When you were upstairs in the club, did you happen to notice a shoeshine man?"

"Yes, I saw him," I said.

"Well, his name is Hughie Schmidt. To amuse himself, Hughie teaches hearing people how to converse with the deaf. He taught Sheldon. He also taught one of the cops on the beat, Henry O'Connor of the West Fifty-fourth Street station. When the Union League runs a big affair, the arrangements committee always gets in touch with the station house and asks that O'Connor be detailed to keep order. Not that they really need a cop. The deaf are very orderly and there aren't many drunks among them. It's just a custom. O'Connor is a patient man, and Hughie was able to teach him quite a little sign language, as well as finger spelling."

"What is the difference?" I asked.

"In the manual alphabet," Fitzsimmons said, "the letters are represented by the positions of the fingers of the hand, and talking with it is called finger spelling. It's tedious. The sign language is a great body of gestures which has been passed down from one generation to the next, each adding to it. If I put my right hand to my chin and pretend to pull an imaginary beard, which is a sign for 'old,' and then point my index finger at a deaf person a couple of times, he will understand that I'm asking 'How old are you?' Many deaf signs are used by the general public, and thousands of them are exactly like the signs used by the Plains Indians. An example is the sign for 'crazy.' You touch the forehead with the index finger and then move the finger in a circle over the forehead two or three times. In many conversations both signs and finger spelling are used. Unfamiliar names, for example, are always finger-spelled. Some signs require great skill in pantomime. No one person knows all the signs. Some are expert, others know just enough for simple conversations."

"How many deaf persons are there in the city?" I asked.

"In the five boroughs," Fitzsimmons said, "there are between five and six thousand so-called deaf-mutes. By and large, they live in a restricted world, a world of their own. They prefer their own company because most hearing people have a tendency to look upon them as peculiar, or mysterious, or unnatural. When they converse with each other in sign language out in public, they are stared at as if they had escaped from the zoo. On the street or in subways, no one takes them for granted; they are always stared at. Because of this, they like to go about in groups. Even the phrases used to describe them, particularly 'deaf and dumb,' show a lack of understanding. There is nothing wrong with the vocal organs or the intelligence of the average deaf person. One learns to speak by imitation, and the deaf child can't speak, simply because he can't hear. He doesn't know what speech is. It's like expecting a blind child to visualize a color.

"Only about thirty-five per cent of the deaf were born that way, and they are called the congenitally deaf. The bulk of the others lost their hearing during babyhood or childhood after having the measles, influenza, diphtheria, scarlet fever, meningitis, or some such disease, and they are called the adventitiously deaf. The vocal organs of practically all the people in both groups are normal, and it is possible to teach many of them to speak intelligibly, but it takes almost superhuman patience. This effort is made in most of the deaf schools in New York State. Finger spelling and the signs aren't permitted in classrooms in these schools. Instead, the pupils are taught to speak and lip-read. Some become proficient, particularly those who had talking experience before they went deaf, but others manage to learn only a few phrases. However, the speech of just about all deaf persons sounds queer to those unaccustomed to it. Hearing people complain that it is too guttural, or that it lacks modulations, or that it sounds animal-like. In any case, for one reason or another, it seems to make most of them ill at ease. If they don't understand a deaf person right off the bat, they motion to him to write out what he has to say. And they always stare. You see how it is. If the deaf use signs, they are stared at. If they speak, they are stared at. Upstairs a while ago you jumped when my friend asked you for a cigarette. Was his speech that unpleasant?"

"I'm very sorry. It wasn't that his speech was unpleasant," I said. "Mr. Frankenheim spoke to both of you in sign language when we came into the room, and I took it for granted all of you were deaf. When your friend suddenly spoke, I was startled."

Fitzsimmons shrugged his shoulders.

"The chief characteristic of the deaf is their clannishness," he said, abruptly changing the subject. "I don't mean to imply that they are embittered. Most of them are happy enough as humans go, but for understanding and companionship they have to depend almost entirely on each other. For this reason there is a slew of clubs, societies, leagues, lodges, federations, and associations exclusively for them. The majority are little informal groups or cliques. The club in which I hold honorary membership is one of these. It has fourteen members. They all come from Brooklyn. Our members are above the average in intelligence. They are great readers. One has an A.B. from Gallaudet College, the old National Deaf-Mute College, which is the only one of its kind in the world. It's in Washington. During the winter we meet above a cafeteria near Borough Hall. The cafeteria is owned by a relative of a member and he lets us use a vacant room on the second floor. We sit around and talk and smoke and drink beer until late at night. The deaf prefer cafeterias, by the way, particularly Automats. I know a deaf woman who has eaten in an Automat regularly for twelve years without ever uttering a single word. Every Sunday during the summer our club goes down to Coney. We always meet at the Brighton Beach Baths, which for some reason is popular with the deaf. Several clubs go there. On winter Sundays the club often goes in a body to the Metropolitan Museum, which has free lectures for lip readers. The deaf are great for museums. We have a couple of members who damned near live in the Metropolitan. We had a wedding in the club not long ago—a girl from our club and a fellow who belongs to the Union League. The deaf almost always marry the deaf. Look here, I'm tired of standing. Let's get a seat somewhere."

WE ORDERED ANOTHER ROUND of drinks and sat down in a booth in the back room.

"Our group is quite informal," Fitzsimmons continued. "We have officers and dues and we call ourselves the Borough Hall Ephphatha Society. 'Ephphatha' is a word that Jesus spoke when he healed a deaf man. You'll find it in St. Mark. It means 'Be opened.' It has been picked for a name by many Protestant and Catholic deaf clubs.

We seldom use it. Usually we just say 'the crowd' or 'the gang.' Once in a while we have a regular meeting with parliamentary order and everything, but mostly we just sit around and talk. That's the way it is with most of the small clubs. Then there are larger, better-organized groups who have religious affiliations and hold their meetings in churches. Four or five of these groups meet in the parish house of St. Ann's Church for Deaf-Mutes at 511 West 148th Street. This little church was the first of its kind in the world. The pastor is deaf, of course, and all services—sermons, weddings, funerals, christenings, everything—are conducted in sign language. During services the front of the chapel is flooded with light so the congregation won't have any trouble seeing the pastor's hands. It has a choir and the people in it sing hymns with their hands. St. Ann's is old. It was founded in 1852, and the building they're in now was put up in 1898.

"St. Ann's is Episcopal, but people of all religions go to it. The Catholics have many deaf organizations. The principal ones are the Knights and Ladies of De L'Epee Sick and Disability Association and the Ephphatha Society for the Catholic Deaf. Both are combined social and insurance organizations. They pay sick benefits, hold card parties and socials, and sponsor athletic teams. The De L'Epee Association meets in an office building in Brooklyn. It was named after an eighteenth-century French priest who founded what was probably the first deaf school. The Ephphatha Society meets at St. Francis Xavier's on West Sixteenth Street. Deaf athletic teams use the gym at this church for tournaments. Services in the sign language are held there the first Sunday of every month by an old Jesuit named Father Michael A. Purtell. He is a hearing man, now in his seventies, who has been working for the deaf since he was a young priest. He puts out a paper full of social notes about the deaf from all over the country, and it is widely read. It used to be called the *Catholic Deaf-Mute*, but not long ago he changed the name to *Ephphatha*. As a matter of fact, in the last ten or fifteen years almost every title with 'deaf and dumb' or 'deaf-mute' in it has been changed. Used to be that every school for the deaf had 'deaf and dumb' in its title."

"How do deaf Catholics confess?" I asked.

"There are a number of priests who know the signs, and they hear confession in sign language," Fitzsimmons said. "In Brooklyn, for example, you'll find them at St. Brigid's, St. Michael's, Transfiguration, St. Monica's, and Fourteen Holy Martyrs. Some of these priests had deaf parents. In membership, the Jewish organizations are next in size to the Catholic ones. The largest of these is the Society for the Welfare of Jewish Deaf, which rents space in a hall on West Eighty-fifth Street in Manhattan. It's a lively outfit. It gives classes in sign language. It has a dramatics group, which puts on plays and vaudeville in signs, a gym group, and several athletic teams. It has Friday-night religious services, in which an interpreter stands beside the rabbi and translates, and it has teas, lectures, movies, and Bingo parties. It even has a plot of its own in New Mount Carmel Cemetery in Brooklyn. Every so often, a delegation goes out and puts flowers on the graves of departed members. Also, this society has an employment service."

"I wanted to ask about that," I said. "How do the deaf go about finding jobs?"

"They have the devil of a time," Fitzsimmons said. "It is the thorniest problem they have to meet. There is one employment agency specifically for them. It is operated by an energetic young woman named Margarette Helmle, who used to be a personnel manager for General Motors, and it has office space in the New York State Employment Service building down on East Twenty-eighth Street. Miss Helmle is an expert signer. Her salary is paid by the three schools in which most of the deaf in the city are educated—the Lexington in Manhattan, St. Joseph's in the Bronx, and the New York School in White Plains. She tries to find jobs for all applicants, whether they come from these schools or not. She goes out and calls on the personnel managers of big corporations and talks up the deaf, and she averages twenty-two placements a month. The deaf are strongest in the printing trades. There are four in the job plant where I work, and you'll find two or three in most big newspaper plants. They can do any kind of work that doesn't absolutely require hearing. Employers usually write out orders to them. They make particularly good welders, power-machine operators, carpenters, and electricians."

WE HAD LONG SINCE FINISHED our drinks. Fitzsimmons appeared to be tired of talking and I suggested another round, but he refused. He said he thought he would go back upstairs to the Union League and play some pinochle. I left Larry's Café with him.

"This may interest you," he said, just before he started up the stairs. "The deaf, particularly lip readers, are suspicious of hearing people who begin sympathizing with them. They've learned that sooner or later these people will ask questions that are rather embarrassing. There is the type who right away wants to know exactly how it feels to live in a soundless world. One of the members of my club, the graduate of Gallaudet I told you about, has an answer. He got it out of some book or other, and all of our members have memorized it. It goes, 'The deaf live in a world of deadly silence. The singing of the birds, the inflections of the human voice, beautiful music, and the confusion of noises that proclaim life are lacking. Many things are in motion, but there is no sound.'

"Then there is a type of woman who has caused many a lip reader to think of murder. She will sigh and say, 'Sometimes I get so tired of the noise in the city, I think deafness would be a blessing.' All lip readers have had to put up with this remark scores of times. My friend upstairs, the fellow who asked you for a cigarette, is very meek and mild, but it always infuriates him. The last time a woman handed him this line, he gritted his teeth and said, 'Lady, please forgive me, but you sure are a god-damn fool.' "

(1941)

Santa Claus Smith

*A*RAGGED, WHITE-BEARDED OLD MAN who tells people
he is John S. Smith of Riga, Latvia, Europe, began hitchhiking
aimlessly on the highways of the United States early in 1934. He
has been seen as far north as Clinton, Connecticut, but he spends
most of his time in the South and Southwest. He wanders from
Louisiana to California and back again about twice a year. He is
approximately seventy years old. People who have had dealings with
him say he has a kind, honest face, speaks broken English, smokes
a pipe, wears an overcoat winter and summer, loves cats, and keeps
a supply of brown wrapping paper, cut into oblong slips, in a pack
he carries on his back. His behavior has puzzled waitresses, tourist-
camp proprietors, and housewives in at least twenty-three states,
and he is frequently a subject of conversation in highway lunchrooms
at which drivers of cross-country trucks pull up for hamburgers
and coffee.

On the night of October 23, 1936, for example, he strayed into
a lunchroom on a highway near Columbus, Texas, told the waitress
he had no money, and asked for a cup of coffee. She took him into
the kitchen and gave him a bowl of stew, a jelly roll, and coffee.
When he finished eating he took a grimy slip of brown paper out
of his pack and scribbled on it with an indelible pencil. He slid the
paper under his plate and hurried out into the night. When the
waitress picked it up she found that it was an improvised check for
$27,000, written on the Irving National Bank of New York and
signed "John S. Smith of Riga, Latvia, Europe." On the back of the
check was a note, "Fill your name in, send to bank." Four days

later he turned up at a diner on the outskirts of Yuma, Arizona, and asked the counterman for coffee. After Smith departed, a similar check, for $2,000, was found beside his cup. On October 30th he was wandering along a highway near Indianola, Mississippi. He asked a farmer's wife for something to eat and was so pleased with the flapjacks and molasses she gave him that he handed her two checks, one for $25,000 and the other for $1,000. On November 9th he asked the proprietor of a tourist camp near Denver if he could come in out of the cold for a few minutes. He sat beside the stove and filled his pipe with tobacco salvaged from a handful of cigarette stubs he took from his overcoat pocket. The proprietor made him a present of a dime can of tobacco. He wrote a check for $16,000, handed it to the proprietor, and went on his way. Five days later a housewife in Baldwin Park, California, gave him some scrambled eggs; he left a check for $12,000 beside the plate. Next day he gave checks aggregating $52,000 to waitresses in two cafés in Los Angeles. A month later he was back in Texas. On December 12th, on a street in Fort Worth, he asked a young woman sitting in a parked automobile for a nickel. She gave him a dime. Using a fender for a desk, he wrote her a check for $950. She laughed and thanked him. Then he took the check back, tore it up, and wrote another for $26,000. "That's for your sweet smile," he said.

All these checks, like the one he gave the waitress in Columbus, Texas, were written on the Irving National Bank of New York. This bank went out of existence on January 6, 1923, eleven years before John S. Smith of Riga, Latvia, Europe, began writing checks on it. Mail addressed to the Irving National Bank is eventually delivered to its successor, the Irving Trust Company, and in the last six years two hundred and forty letters, most of them enclosing checks, have turned up at the Irving Trust from beneficiaries of John S. Smith's generosity.

THE OLD MAN WROTE HIS FIRST CHECK on the Irving National on January 15, 1934. He handed it to a housewife in Dallas who had given him coffee. It was for $2,000. The housewife kept the check a few days, wondering if "it was just an old man's fancy."

Then she mailed it to the Irving National, and the Post Office delivered it to the Irving Trust. The teller who got the letter was startled. He went into a vault in which the Irving National's books are still kept and searched through them, finding no trace of a Latvian Smith. There had been John S. Smiths among the depositors, but it did not take long to ascertain that none of them could be this one. The perplexed teller wrote the woman in Dallas, asking for more information about the unusual transaction. While he waited for her answer, a letter arrived from a housewife in Los Angeles, inquiring if Mr. John S. Smith of Riga, Latvia, Europe, had an account in the Irving National Bank of New York, N.Y. She wrote that after she gave him something to eat he left her a check for $3,700. "This old man may not have good sense," she added.

Since then hardly a week has gone by that the Irving Trust has not received a hopeful letter from someone who has given food, tobacco, transportation, lodging, small change, or a sweet smile to Mr. John S. Smith, getting a check for a substantial amount in return. The checks contained in the letters have ranged from $90 to $600,000. He handed the biggest check to a waitress in New Iberia, Louisiana, who had given him a hamburger sandwich. The $90 check was received by a minister's wife in Terre Haute who gave him what she describes as "a good hot lunch"; evidently he did not think much of her cooking. The checks are always written on slips of brown wrapping paper and many are spotted with grease. Occasionally the old man writes the name of the recipient on a check. He gave a farmer's wife a check for $8,000 bearing her name, and when she asked him how he knew it, he pointed to the R.F.D. mailbox in front of her house. Most often, however, he leaves a space on the check in which the recipient may write his or her name. He always misspells "thousand," writing it "tousand." His handwriting is vaguely Gothic and is often difficult to read. He decorates many of his checks with a symbol. It is a crude face with a smile on it. There are two pencil dots for eyes, a dot for a nose, and a line turned up at both ends for a mouth. This symbol, evidently his trademark, appears in the upper right-hand corner of some checks; on others it follows directly after the signature.

Just why he picked the Irving National Bank always has been a mystery. At first it was thought that he might once have worked for the bank as a janitor or guard, but personnel lists have been vainly checked for a clue. Tellers and stenographers at the Irving Trust have been put to a lot of trouble by the old man's check-writing, but the trust company has never attempted to have him arrested, since no forgery is involved. So far as can be learned, he has never tried to cash a check or purchase anything with one. Irving Trust officials believe that John S. Smith is a simple-minded, goodhearted old man who feels that he should reward those treating him with kindness. The bank people call him Santa Claus Smith and wish that he had millions of dollars on deposit. Sometimes, for amusement, an official will get out the file of letters and, from postmarks, trace the old man's crazy progress back and forth across the continent. However, the relationship between the old man and the bank has long since become a routine matter. The bank used to send lengthy replies to people who wrote letters, enclosing checks; now, when such a letter comes in, it is handed to a stenographer who types out this unvarying reply: "We are sorry we have to disillusion you, but we have no record that John S. Smith of Riga, Latvia, Europe, has ever maintained an account with the Irving Trust Company, or its predecessor, the Irving National Bank of New York. From numerous inquiries we have received from various sections of the country, it appears that this individual, in return for gratuitous meals or lodging, has given what purport to be drafts for large amounts drawn on the Irving National Bank. Sincerely yours, Irving Trust Company."

ONE AFTERNOON NOT LONG AGO an official of the bank gave me permission to go through the file of letters written by John S. Smith's deluded beneficiaries. The file is kept in the company's main office at 1 Wall Street. First, however, I had to promise that I would not mention any of the names signed to the letters; the official feared that such mention might in some cases expose the writers to ridicule.

The first letter I read was from a waitress in a café at a tourist camp on U.S. Highway 11, near Gadsden, Alabama. It was written in pencil on two sheets of ruled tablet paper and dated March 27, 1936. She wrote that a few nights ago she had given a ham-and-egg sandwich to "a raggedy old man in his sixties or seventies with a pack on his back." Just before he left he handed her two slips of paper. One was a check for $25,000 and the other was a check for $1,000. This combination of checks turned up often. Possibly the check for $1,000 was Santa Claus Smith's idea of a tip.

"I naturally thought the old man was a nut going through the country," the waitress wrote, "but I studied the matter over, and it got my curiosity up, and I want to know has he got any money in your bank. As you know, strange things happen. If these checks are O.K., please send the money as I sure can use it to advantage. If not, please return same, as I desire to keep them for souvenirs."

The next letter I pulled out of the file was from a farmer's wife on Route 1, Metamora, Indiana. She also enclosed a check for $25,000 and one for $1,000.

"Just a word of information please," she wrote. "Is there a man by the name of John S. Smith of Riga, Latvia, Europe, that has dealings with your bank? I will explain to you. Late one evening last July about the 18th [1935] there was an old man with a long beard and a very kind face turned in our lawn. He seemed to be a tramp. It was almost dusk. He asked if there was a chance to get a piece of bread. It has always been my custom to give to tramps if I have anything I can handy give. He was carrying a pack on his back so I told him to set down on the lawn. I had a nice warm supper cooked so I served him on the lawn. He seemed to be very hungry. I gave him a second serving. When he finished he took from his pack two checks copied on brown paper looked like they were cut from paper bags. He came forward and handed these to me with his plate. His face was so kind it is hard to believe he meant anything false."

A similar confidence in the old man was displayed by a farmer of Silsbee, Texas, who wrote, "I received these checks from an old gentleman who ate breakfast at our home and I asked the bank here to handle same for me, and they seemed to think they were no good. I am different. This man had no reason to give us these checks knowing they were no good. So I still believe he wanted us to have this amount of money and we sure need it. Wishing you a merry Christmas and a happy New Year." The letter was dated December 20, 1937.

THE MAJORITY OF THE LETTER-WRITERS, however, are not so confident. They are suspicious but hopeful. Their letters follow a pattern. First the writers indicate that they are far too worldly-wise to believe that the checks are good; then in the next sentence they give the bank explicit instructions for forwarding the money. A waitress in San Antonio sent in a check for $7,000 and wrote, "I know this is just a joke, but a girl friend dared me to send it to you, so here it is. If he has an account with you, please send me the money by registered mail." A rather snippety waitress in a truck-drivers' café in Muncie, Indiana, wrote, "Enclosed you will find one cheque for $1,000 given me by an uncouth beggar on your bank. If it has any value to it, open an account for me in your bank and deposit amount of check." A waitress in a restaurant on South Halsted Street, Chicago, was blunter. To a check for $270,000 she attached a note: "I guess the old nut who gave me this is fresh out of the nut house, but send me the money if true." A woman in Alabama City, Alabama, sent in a check for $21,000 via air mail and special delivery. Her letter contained an interesting description of old John S. "He was baldheaded wearing an overcoat and whiskers all over his face and I could not understand anything much he said, and he also had a walking stick," she wrote.

Some of the correspondents were not only suspicious of John S. Smith; they also showed that they did not entirely trust the Irving National Bank of New York. I found seven letters from people who sent photostatic copies of checks and said they would deposit the originals in their local banks if John S. Smith was sufficiently solvent. Also in the file were letters from banks in which people had tried to cash or deposit his checks. A bank in Kansas City wrote, "A customer of ours has high hopes that the enclosed paper is an order on your bank for the payment of $15,000. We have looked it over and our foreign-exchange teller has examined it, but none of us have quite figured it out. If you can throw any light on the matter, we will appreciate it."

John S. Smith is far more generous to waitresses and housewives than he is to the motorists and truck-drivers with whom he hitches daylong rides. Evidently he places little value on transportation. He has never given a check exceeding $1,000 for an automobile ride; for a hamburger he has gone as high as $600,000.

The old straggler is a cat-lover. On July 6, 1934, he went into a café in Groton, South Dakota, and asked the wife of the proprietor to care for a cat he was carrying. She said she would. Then he wrote out two checks. One, for $4,000, was made payable "to person who upkeep the black and white cat name Smiles from John S. Smith of Riga, Latvia, Europe." On the other, which was for $1,000, he wrote, "Pay to anyone assisting care of cat."

THE LETTERS DO NOT THROW MUCH LIGHT on the mystery of John S. Smith's past. He told a woman in Tuscaloosa, Alabama, that he left home in 1934 and began to wander because the depression got on his mind. This woman expressed a belief that "there is something wrong with the old man's head." "I think he got loose from an institution and has been lost ever since," she wrote. He built up a romantic picture of himself for a young woman in San Antonio. She wrote, "I befriended a poorly dressed man who insisted upon writing me the attached order for $6,000. I put this paper away and attached no importance to it until recently when it occurred to me that so many strange things do happen that this might possibly be another instance. He stated that he purposely wore ragged clothes and rewarded those who helped him when he asked for help only through such an instrument as the attached as arrangements had been made with your bank to honor these and no others."

For a few minutes on the morning of July 19, 1936, it looked as if the mystery might be solved. On that day a letter from John S. Smith was delivered to the Irving Trust. The official on whose desk it was placed became excited. The envelope was postmarked Wabash, Indiana. Inside there was a letter scribbled wildly on the backs of seven lunchroom menus. It began, "Irv. Nat. Bank of N.Y. Dear Sir," and then became illegible. The official was exasperated. He glanced through page after page and none of the writing made sense. The letter had been written with an indelible pencil and had come in contact with water; most of the words had beome ugly purple blots. Also, it was evident that John S. Smith had carried the letter around in his pocket for days before mailing it. The sheets were mottled with grease and there were tobacco crumbs in the folds. The official got a magnifying glass and he and a colleague went to work. After a considerable amount of agonizing labor, they isolated the following phrases: "listen those three waitress," "put something in that bank," "in USA for 26 yrs 30 yrs 22," "mortgage and now," "to see about cats," "waitress girl in that place in Ohio," and "all over USA." To make matters worse, two of his ubiquitous checks were pinned to the letter. Both were made payable to the Irv. Nat. Bank and both were written on the Irv. Nat. Bank. One was for $6,000, the other was for $15,000.

WHEN I FINISHED READING the letters in the file I realized that I did not have a clear impression of John S. Smith. At first he reminded me vaguely of W. C. Fields, but that impression soon disappeared; for one thing, I found no letters indicating that he had ever given checks to bartenders. For a day or so after I read the letters I thought of him as a benevolent old screwball. Then I began to be troubled by the memory of those crude, grinning faces with which he decorated so many of the checks. I began to think of the vain hopes he raised in the breasts of the waitresses who had graciously given him hundreds of meals and the truck-drivers who had hauled him over a hundred highways, and to feel that about John S. Smith of Riga, Latvia, Europe, there is something a little sinister.

(1940)

The Don't-Swear Man

ONE DANK AFTERNOON I dropped into Shannon's, an Irish saloon on the southeast corner of Third Avenue and Seventy-sixth Street, and ordered a split of Guinness. "Fine pneumonia weather we're having," the bartender remarked. "Yes," I said, "it's one hell of a day." A portly old man standing a few feet up the bar gave a grunt, abruptly put down his beer glass, turned to me, and said, "My boy, a profane word never yet had any effect on the weather." The remark irritated me. I was in extremely low spirits; my shoes had been sopping wet all day and I felt certain that I was going to catch a cold and die. However, I nodded perfunctorily and said, "I guess that's right, Mister." "Oh, don't apologize," the old man said. Then he dug into a pocket of his coat and pulled out a small, pale-pink card. "Here," he said, "read this and think it over." The card said, "NEW HOPE FOR THE WORLD. GOD BLESS AMERICA AND OUR HOMES. HAVE NO SWEARING. BOYCOTT PROFANITY! PLEASE DO NOT SWEAR, NOR USE OBSCENE OR PROFANE LANGUAGE. THESE CARDS ARE FOR DISTRIBUTION. SEND FOR SOME—THEY ARE FREE. ANTI-PROFANITY LEAGUE. A. S. COLBORNE, PRES. 185 EAST SEVENTY-SIX STREET."

After reading this, I took a good look at the old man. He was over six feet tall and he had a double chin and a large paunch. His cheeks were ruddy and his eyes, behind steel-rimmed glasses, were clear and utterly honest. Instead of a vest, he wore a brown sweater. In the knot of his polka-dot tie there was a horseshoe stickpin. Three pencils and a fountain pen were clipped to his breast pocket.

He had placed his hat on the bar, upside down, to dry off. He had a white mustache and a fine head of white hair, several locks of which had been brushed down across his forehead, old bartender style. He looked, in fact, like a dignified, opinionated, old-fashioned bartender on his day off. I have always had a high regard for that kind of man, and I said, "If I offended you, sir, I'm sorry, only what makes you think 'hell' is a profane word?"

"Well, I tell you," he said gravely, "it might not be one-hundred-per-cent profanity, but it's a leader-on. You start out with 'hell,' 'devil take it,' 'Dad burn it,' 'Gee whizz,' and the like of that, and by and by you won't be able to open your trap without letting loose an awful, awful, blasphemous oath. It's like the cocaine dope habit. I know. I talked real rough myself when I was a young squirt, but I had the mother wit to quit. I haven't uttered a solitary profane word since a Sunday morning in the winter of 1886. I was running to catch a ferryboat and I got left, and let an oath out of me so awful I broke down and cried like a baby."

I was about to ask what the oath was, but thought better of it. Instead I said, "You remind me a lot of a man who used to work behind the bar at the Murray Hill Hotel. Are you a bartender?"

The old man did not answer me. He picked up his glass and finished his beer. Then, after a resounding smack of the lips, he said, "Profanity! Blasphemy! Evil tongues a-wagging and a-wagging! That's why the world is headed for wrack and ruin! Let me introduce myself. Name is Arthur Samuel Colborne. I'm the founder and head of the Anti-Profanity League. Founded 1901. An international organization. If the truth was known, I'm also the founder of the Safe and Sane Fourth of July movement. Founded 1908. On the Fourth I used to stand on the steps of City Hall and read the Declaration of Independence to all that would listen. People called me a crank, but I told them I wasn't crank enough to spend good money on firecrackers. Others took up the Safe and Sane, and I kept plugging away with the Anti-Profanity. I've spent the better part of forty years cleaning up profanity conditions. I and my members have passed out six million cards like the one I handed you. We call them profanity-exterminators. Six million. Think of it! I'm past seventy, but I'm a go-getter, fighting the evil on all fronts. Keeps me busy. I'm just after seeing a high official at City Hall. There's some Broadway plays so profane it's a wonder to me the tongues of the actors and the actresses don't wither up and come loose at the roots and drop to the ground, and I beseeched this high official to take action. Said he'd do what he could. Probably won't do a single, solitary thing. I wanted to have a chat with Mayor La Guardia, but they told me he'd just stepped out. That's what they always say. The Mayor's a pompish little fellow, as strutty as a duck. I've heard that he gets so profane when he loses his temper it's enough to make your head swim. You think that's true?"

"It wouldn't surprise me a bit," I said.

Mr. Colborne pursed his lips and sadly shook his head from side to side. "He ought to be ashamed of hisself," he said.

The bartender had poured my stout. I asked Mr. Colborne to have a drink with me. He drew out a thick gold watch, glanced at it, and said, "Much obliged, but I seldom take more than two, and I've had that. Nothing wrong in beer. Good for your nerves. I'd have another, but I want to get home in time for a radio program. Hillbilly singing. I'm a great believer in it. Very wholesome. I'm also a great believer in opera music, Hawaiian music, Kate Smith, and Charlie McCarthy. Here a while back, this Bergen feller had Charlie saying 'Doggone this' and 'Doggone that' on the radio, and I wrote him and attached an exterminator to the letter. 'Think it over, Mr. Bergen,' I said. Got a speedy reply. 'Won't happen again,' he said."

"Is 'doggone' a leader-on?" I asked.

"I'll say it is! One of the hardest to eradicate! Look here, my boy, I'd like to give you some exterminators to pass out to your friends, keep the ball rolling, but I'm cleaned out. Put a handful in my pocket this morning, but I gave some out on the subway, and I slipped a few into some cars that were parked in front of City Hall, including the Mayor's car, and I left a couple with the Mayor's secretary, and the one I handed you was the last of the lot. Drop into my headquarters sometime and I'll give you a supply. My address is printed on the exterminator."

"Thanks very much," I said.

He waved his hand deprecatingly. "Don't mention it," he said.

He put on his hat, paid for his beers, shook hands with me, and nodded to the bartender. Halfway to the door, he turned and came back to the bar. "Interesting case out in Chicago here a while back," he said to me. "Two big German butchers had been working at the same block in a slaughterhouse for eighteen years. One morning one butcher took up his cleaver and split the other butcher's head. Police asked him why he did it, and he said, 'I just couldn't stand his profanity any longer!' " I laughed, and Mr. Colborne gave an indignant snort. "Look here, my boy," he said, frowning at me, "first-degree murder's not a laughing matter. If you look at it the right way, there's a good lesson in that case. Think it over!" Then he left.

"Was the old gentleman kidding me?" I asked the bartender, who had been listening.

"Oh, no," the bartender said. "He's a big reformer. He's well known in the neighborhood. His headquarters are up the street half a block."

Mainly because he was the first beer-drinking reformer I had ever encountered, I resolved to visit Mr. Colborne. Several afternoons later I did. The address printed on the exterminator he had given me turned out to be an old, red-brick apartment house, on the front of which, just left of the stoop, was nailed a foot-square tin sign reading, "HEADQUARTERS ANTI-PROFANITY LEAGUE. CARDS THAT READ DO NOT SWEAR CAN BE HAD FREE." A woman with a poodle in her arms was standing on the stoop. She watched me read the sign, and when I walked up the steps she said, "If you're looking for the don't-swear man, he lives down in the basement." I rang the basement bell and Mr. Colborne let me in. Over his suit he had on a black, full-length apron, the kind printers wear. He held a frying pan in his left hand and a dish towel in this right. "Come in and make yourself at home," he said. "Take a seat, and I'll be with you soon as I finish washing up in the kitchen. This room here is the headquarters of the League. I sleep and eat in a couple of rooms in back. I'm a bachelor and I get my own meals. I'm a bit set in my ways, and I prefer the grub I cook for myself to the highest-class restaurant there is. Cleaner. While you're waiting, look at my scrapbook. You'll find it somewhere in that mess on my desk."

He went back to his kitchen and I took a look around the room. It was a long, narrow, low-ceilinged room. There were two windows, but not much light came through them. Both were shut, and there was a kitchen smell in the air. The floor was covered with linoleum. Running just below the ceiling were a couple of asbestos-sheathed steam-heat pipes. On the mantel stood a highly colored plaster statue of St. Michael trampling the Devil. The statue was wrapped in cellophane, doubtless to keep off dust. Along one wall were two tables and a small iron safe. There was a typewriter on one table, and on the other were a radio and a tall vase of artificial roses; dust was thick on the red petals of the roses. Two walls were hung with oil paintings from baseboard to ceiling. At least half were religious, many of them portraits of saints and of the Virgin; other subjects included a windmill in the moonlight, a mother sewing beside a cradle, a thatched cottage, and a Jersey cow standing belly-deep in a lush meadow. All were in gilded frames.

On Mr. Colborne's flat-topped desk were a coffee cup half filled with foreign stamps clipped from envelopes, a begonia plant and a geranium plant in little red pots, an alarm clock, and a great pile of correspondence, books, and religious magazines. There were also five neat stacks of exterminators. I found the scrapbook he had mentioned under some copies of a monthly magazine called the *Holy Name Journal*. Pasted in the scrapbook were scores of letters from publishers, politicians, actors, public officials, and moving-picture and radio-station executives, either replying to Mr. Colborne's complaints about "profanity conditions" or thanking him for sending them exterminators. Most of the letters were evasive, but all were extremely respectful. One, from William Randolph Hearst's secretary, said, "On behalf of Mr. Hearst, I want to thank you for the little cards you sent to him. It was very kind of you. Mr. Hearst is not in town, and therefore it is impossible to give them to him." I was about half through the book when Mr. Colborne returned, still wearing his black apron. He sat down, clasped his hands over his paunch, and yawned.

"I'm sort of sleepy," he said. "Sat up late last night studying over bar and grill profanity. Why, the women are worse than the men. And you can't talk to them! Why, they'll spit in your eye! I got a notion to revive the warnings I used to put up in saloons back before prohibition. In those days the liquor-dealing element cooperated with me. In 1916 I had posters tacked up in four thousand premises, bar and back room. I'll show you one." He ransacked a desk drawer and brought out a cardboard poster which said, "IN THE INTEREST OF CLEAN SPEECH AND COMMON DECENCY, PLEASE REFRAIN FROM THE OBJECTIONABLE USE OF PROFANE AND OBSCENE LANGUAGE AND EXPECTORATING IN PUBLIC PLACES. WOULD YOU USE SUCH LANGUAGE IN YOUR OWN HOME? RESPECT YOUR FELLOW MAN. ANTI-PROFANITY LEAGUE."

"Those warnings did a world of good," Mr. Colborne said. "They just about put a stop to saloon profanity, and then along came prohibition and tore down all my work. Looking at it from an anti-profanity standpoint, prohibition was an awful nuisance. Nowadays saloons don't even look like saloons, and I'm not sure they'll let me hang posters in them. In the old days saloonkeepers were generous friends of the League. They used to call me the Professor. Practically every place I put up posters, the boss would insist on making a contribution. I held them in high esteem. So much so that when Mayor Jimmy Walker, a fine man, was organizing his great beer parade up Fifth Avenue in May, 1932, I went to my most active members and I said, 'The liquor-dealing element was always nice to us, and now we should hit a lick for them. Let's have a delegation from the League in the beer parade.' The idea caught on, and during the morning of the parade we rounded up five hundred head of people and a brass band. That afternoon we marched right behind the Tammany Hall delegation. We carried tin growlers and shouted, 'We want beer!,' 'Down with profanity,' 'Beer for taxation,' 'Boycott profanity!,' and the like of that, and had a most enjoyable time. We wound up in a saloon and drank more beer than John saw."

Mr. Colborne was interrupted by the doorbell. He grunted and got up and opened the door. A thin, elderly woman came in. "I already passed out the exterminators you gave me last month," she said, with obvious pride. "You better let me have about two hundred this time." "Oh, my!" said Mr. Colborne. "That's good work. Keep at it, and one of these days you'll have the Bronx all cleaned up." He handed the woman a supply of cards held together with a rubber band and she dropped them in her handbag. "Mr. Colborne," she said, "do you think there's been an improvement over last year?" Mr. Colborne stood quite still for a few moments, deep in thought. "I've noticed a decline in street swearing," he said finally, "but there's an awful lot of work still to be done." "You never spoke a truer word," the woman said. "You know, it's disgusting to me the way the city's tearing down the elevated lines. There was always less swearing on the 'L' than on the dirty old subway. A lot less obscenity, too, if you ask me. It just means we'll have to redouble our efforts." "That's the spirit!" Mr. Colborne exclaimed. "We'll have to keep plugging away. Isn't that right?" The woman smacked her palms together. "That's right, Mr. Colborne!" she said emphatically. Then she left.

"She's a widow woman from the Bronx and one of our most active workers," Mr. Colborne said. "Look here, my boy, would you be interested in hearing how I came to start this work?"

I said that I would.

"Well, now," he said, "the history of the League and the story of my life are all wrapped up together, so I'll begin at the beginning, as the fellow said. I'm English-Irish by descent, born down on Avenue A and Fourteenth Street. I'm a Roman Catholic by religion, although some think I'm hooked up with the Salvation Army. Not that the Army isn't a fine thing. Some of those Salvation fellers are wonderful for passing out exterminators. By trade, I'm a picture-restorer, frame-maker, and gilder, the third generation in that line. I own a set of gilder's tools and a toolbox that was used by my grandfather and my father. I'm also a painter—not house but oil. I painted most of the pictures you see on the walls of this room. I went to work in the picture line when I was fresh out of knee britches and became a fine craftsman. Look at my hands, the hands of a man that knows his trade. In 1890, I took my savings and went over to Brooklyn and opened me up a store of my own, the Paris Art

Gallery, occupying an entire four-floor building at Broadway and Gates Avenue. Pictures, frames, gilding, and bric-a-brac. Did a big business.

"The Paris was the number-one thing in my life until on or about the middle of October, 1901, when I heard a sermon concerning the profanity evil that shook me up to such an extent I determined to go out in the highways and byways and do something about it. And I did, let me tell you! At first I would just step up to profane persons and reason with them, telling them that swearing was vile and vicious, out of place, uncalled for, and a snare and a delusion, signifying nothing. I would say, 'Your dear old mother never taught you to talk like that. Think it over!' Or I'd say, 'If you haven't got self-respect, please have some respect for the general public. Think it over!' Or I'd say, 'Now, aren't you ashamed of yourself, a grown man a-carrying on like that? Think it over!' But in those days I was a little bashful about talking to strangers, and one day the idea came to me: Why not let the printed word do the job? So I had a few thousand cards printed up requesting people to control their tongues. To make it look official, I had the printer put Anti-Profanity League down at the bottom.

"Then, when I had any spare time, I'd stuff my pockets full of cards and go out in search of profanity conditions. Like I would attend meetings in the union halls of the teamsters. They used to be bad for swearing, but not as bad as the truck-drivers of today. A teamster would just swear at his poor old nag, but a truck-driver will swear at anything, man or beast, quick or dead, going or coming. And when I saw a building in construction, I'd drop around at noon and ask the foreman for permission to address the bricklayers and hod-carriers. They would be squatting around eating their dinner out of buckets and I would give them a little oration. Some would laugh, but some would take heed. My, the fun we had! And I'd go to baseball parks and pass cards out right and left. Baseball is an incubator of profanity. And I'd go to prisons, to the Navy Yard district, to pool parlors, to saloons where longshoremen and the rowdy element hung out. Everywhere I went, subway, elevated, or streetcar, I passed out cards. Nobody rebuked me. In fact, in forty years of cleaning up profanity nobody has ever got their back up with me. Instead, they apologize. That's how I enrolled my first members. A man would say, 'You're dead right, Mister. What a fool a man is to swear!' Then I'd catch him up. I'd look him right in the eye and say, 'If you feel that way, my boy, take a few hundred cards and pass them out yourself.' Presently I had around three hundred and fifty card-passing members in the city. For some reason the city membership stays around that figure. Old ones drop out, new ones come in. Internationally, I just don't know how many members we have. It must run into thousands. I don't burden myself down with a lot of records."

I lit a cigarette, and Mr. Colborne sniffed the smoke wistfully.

"Used to be a great cigar-smoker, but the doctors made me cut it out," he said. "Nothing like a good cigar! Well, as I told you, my store in Brooklyn did a big business, but in 1905, after I had operated it for fifteen years, I lost interest. It was taking up too much of my time. I had saved up some money and I had no dependents. All my family is dead. Far's I know, I'm the last of the Colbornes. So I closed the store and retired from business. Friends tried to stop me, but I told them I didn't want to do anything but fight profanity. I became a world traveller. In fact, between 1905 and 1936, I crossed the ocean twenty-five times. Went to all the important cities of Europe, passing out exterminators and talking. On shipboard you can really talk to people. They can't get away. I had exterminators printed up in French, Italian, Spanish, and Hebrew. Here and there I'd meet a go-getter, and I'd prevail on him to establish a branch of the League in his home country. At present there's branches in Italy, Cuba, Australia, and Kingston, Jamaica. I always had great success in Rome. Pope Pius X and Pope Pius XI both wrote me letters, blessing my work. I wouldn't take a mint of money for those letters. I bought me an iron safe in a secondhand store just to keep them locked up in. In Rome, in 1926, I sent a note to King Victor Emmanuel on a League letterhead. I told him I represented a multitude of right-thinking Americans, and we had a chat that lasted all morning. I got him so stirred up he talked the matter over with old Mussolini, and next year the two of them passed drastic laws against profanity. They posted warnings everywhere, even in streetcars, and arrested hundreds. I figure I'm personally responsible for ridding Italy of the profanity evil."

"Did the money you saved between 1890 and 1905 keep you going all these years?" I asked.

"Oh, that money ran out a generation ago," Mr. Colborne said. "I live very economic, and I return to my trade when I run low. I restore paintings in big churches, including St. Patrick's Cathedral. Off and on, I do special frame-making and gilding jobs. Sometimes I'll keep a job for years. Between 1918 and 1926, I worked for the Hippodrome Theatre, repairing everything that got out of whack. Profanity conditions among those show people were past belief when I went to work for the Hippodrome, but I cleaned things up, let me tell you. When I was travelling all over the world, it didn't cost me much. I used to make most of my expenses guiding Americans. I know the big cities of Europe as well as I know this basement. I've guided many a party to the miraculous grotto in Lourdes, to Rome, and to the Holy Land. Anyhow, it doesn't take much to keep the League going. I can get a hundred thousand exterminators printed for fifty dollars. It's the postage that amounts up. The mail I get! It's a sight. I have to do a lot of pecking on my typewriter to answer all my mail."

Mr. Colborne suddenly chuckled and slapped his knee.

"I sure got upset here the other day," he said. "I had written a whole lot of letters and I went out to mail them. On the way I stopped at a grocery for a box of eggs, and I got to talking to the clerk about profanity. After a while I left the grocery, and I was crossing the street when I heard a cabdriver a-cussing at a truck-driver. I got out an exterminator and started over to the cabdriver, and just then the lights changed and he drove off, still a-cussing. He drove right past me and splashed some muddy water on my britches. It was very provoking! And when I got back to my door I found I had forgotten to mail my letters, and when I looked in my pocket for my keys I remembered I had left them on my desk. Well, I got so vexed I stomped my foot on the floor and the eggs fell down and broke all to pieces, and then I came right out and said it!"

Mr. Colborne slapped his knee again.

"What did you say?" I asked.

"I said, 'The dickens!' "

We both laughed. While we were laughing, the alarm clock on the desk began to ring.

"That's to remind me to turn on the radio," Mr. Colborne said. "There's a program due I don't want to miss. Hillbilly singing. Very wholesome."

I got up to go. Mr. Colborne counted out twenty-five exterminators and insisted that I take them and pass them out.

"I'm afraid that's too many," I said.

"Oh, you'll use them up in no time," he said.

At the door I asked him if he believed that there is less profanity now than in 1901, when he began his work.

"Oh, my goodness, yes!" he said. "Sooner or later we'll have it all eradicated. There was a story in the *Holy Name Journal* that has some bearing on your question. It seems that two big turtles and one little turtle went into a saloon and ordered beers. It began to rain and one big turtle said to the other big turtle, 'We should've brought our umbrellas. How about asking the little turtle to run home and get our umbrellas?' But the little turtle was listening and he said, 'I'll not go get your umbrellas, because when I'm gone you'll drink my beer.' The big turtles promised they wouldn't, so the little turtle started out. Two months later one of the big turtles said to the other, 'If that little turtle doesn't come back soon, I'm going to drink his beer.' And just then, at the end of the bar, a tiny voice said, 'If you do, I won't go get your umbrellas.' "

I laughed, but there must have been a puzzled expression on my face, because Mr. Colborne said, "You don't get the connection between those turtles and the total eradication of cussing, do you?"

"I'm afraid I don't," I said.

"Slow but sure!" Mr. Colborne said, laughing heartily and giving me a poke in the ribs with an index finger. "Slow but sure!"

(1941)

Obituary of a Gin Mill

*I*T MAKES ME LONESOME to walk past the old yellow-brick building, just south of Washington Market, once occupied by Dick's Bar and Grill. The windows are so dusty and rain-streaked and plastered with "For Rent" stickers that you can't see inside, and there is a padlock growing rusty on the door. Dick's prospered as a speakeasy throughout prohibition; after repeal, as a licensed establishment, it was just about as lawless as ever. A year or so ago, however, when Dick moved up the street, things changed. In his new place he commenced obeying the New York State Liquor Authority's regulations: he refused to let his customers shake Indian dice on the bar for rounds of drinks; he refused to put drinks on the tab; he refused to sell liquor by the bottle late at night after the liquor stores had closed. In the old days Dick was an independent man. He was delighted when he got an opportunity to tell a customer to go to hell. He and his bartenders, in fact, usually acted as if they loathed their customers and the customers liked this because it made them feel at home; most of them were men who were made ill at ease by solicitude or service. When Dick started abiding by the liquor laws, however, a hunted look appeared on his fat, sad-eyed, Neapolitan face. He began to cringe and bow and shake hands with the customers, and he would even help them on with their coats. When they finished eating, he would go over, smile with effort, and ask, "Was the pot roast O.K.?" In the old days he never acted that way. If someone complained about a gristly steak or a baked potato raw in the middle, he would grunt and say, "If you don't like my grub, you don't have to eat in here. I'd just as soon I never saw you again."

The change in Dick reflects the innovations in his new saloon, which is six blocks away from the old one—a big, classy place with a chromium and glass-brick front, a neon sign in four colors, a mahogany bar, a row of chromium bar stools with red-leather seats like those in the uptown cocktail lounges, a kitchen full of gleaming copper pots, a moody chef who once worked in Moneta's, a printed menu with French all over it, and seven new brands of Scotch. He told the bartenders they would have to shave every morning and made them put on starched white coats. For several days thereafter they looked clean and aloof, like people when they first get out of the hospital. The place was so stylish that Dick did not, for good luck, frame the first dollar bill passed across the bar; he framed the first five-dollar bill.

Dick's regular customers had always been clannish—hanging together two and three deep at the end of the bar near the greasy swinging door to the kitchen—and some of them began to congregate at the fancy bar in Dick's new place. Here they resented everything. They snickered at the French on the menu, they sneered at the bartenders in their starched white coats. One of them waved a menu in Dick's face. "What the hell does this mean," he demanded, "this here 'Country Sausage Gastronome'?" The question made Dick uncomfortable. "It means meat sauce," he said.

Before the night of the grand opening was half over, one of the customers, an amateur evangelist who used to deliver burlesque sermons regularly in the old place, climbed up on the shiny new bar and began to preach. He had given out his text for the evening and was shouting "Brothers and sisters! You full of sin! You full of gin! You and the Devil are real close kin! Are you ready for the Judgment Day? Where will you spend eternity? Ain't it awful?" when Dick came out of the kitchen and caught sight of him. "Oh, my God!" Dick screamed. "Do you want to ruin me? I can't have such monkey business in here. I got a big investment in here." There was so much genuine agony in his voice that the amateur evangelist jumped down from his pulpit and apologized. Thereupon the old customers felt sorry for Dick. Sitting behind his bar on a busy night in the old joint, Dick used to have the aplomb of a sow on her belly in a bog, but in the new place he soon became apprehensive and haggard. One night the kitchen door swung open and the old customers saw Dick bent over a big ledger, struggling with his cost accounting. From the look on his face they knew he was quite sick of the chromium stools and the French menu. "He don't like this joint, either," one of them said. From then on they would tone down anyone who started to holler and throw glasses when Dick insisted on obeying the letter and the spirit of one of the alcohol laws. "After all," they would say, "he's got a big investment in here. He don't want to lose his license." However, no matter how big the investment, I never felt the same about the new Dick's.

When he is asked why he moved, Dick grunts and mutters, "It was time to change the sheets," but I have learned that he opened the new place only because he wanted a bigger kitchen. Soon after he made up his mind to move, however, a salesman for a bar-fixtures concern got hold of him and sold him a bill of goods. I believe that bar-equipment salesmen have done more to destroy the independence and individuality of New York gin mills and their customers than prohibition or repeal; there is nothing that will make a gin mill look so cheap and spurious as a modernistic bar and a lot of chairs made of chromium tubing. Dick's old place was dirty and it smelled like the zoo, but it was genuine; his new place is as shiny and undistinguished as a two-dollar alarm clock. The bar-equipment salesman was so relentless that Dick, who merely wanted a bigger kitchen, ended up by keeping nothing from the old place but the big, greasy, iron safe and a framed and fly-specked photograph of Gallant Fox. He even threw away all the photographs of Lupe Velez, his favorite movie actress. He used to have about a dozen pictures of Miss Velez tacked up on the wall, and sometimes he would gaze at one of them, shake his head, and say, "I would crawl a mile over broken beer bottles just to get one look at her in the flesh."

Dick is proud of his new kitchen. Food always interested him more than alcohol. He used to say, "I keep an A-1 kitchen." Once I saw him stand at the bar and eat an eight-pound turkey the chef had cooked for the luncheon trade. Dick had intended to eat only a drumstick, but after he had satisfied himself there was nothing left but a plateful of bones. Maxie, the tub-bellied head bartender, watched admiringly as Dick dismantled the turkey. "The boss sure does have a passion for groceries," he said. Even in the old days Dick often put strange dishes on his mimeographed menu. He had a friend who worked in a soup cannery up the street and one day the friend gave him a bucket of turtle livers. Dick put them on the menu. A customer said, "Well, that's something I never et." He ordered them, and while he ate, Dick watched intently. When the man put down his fork Dick went over to his table.

"How were them turtle livers?" he asked.

The customer deliberated for a moment.

"Fact of the matter is," he said, "they were kind of unusual."

"Well," said Dick proudly, "I want you to know that you're the first man in New York to eat turtle livers, so far as I know."

The customer shuddered.

A few nights ago I saw turtle livers on the menu in the new place. They were listed as "Pâté de Foie de Tortue Verte." Until I saw those pretenious words I never fully realized how dead and gone were the days when Dick was the plain-spoken proprietor of a dirty, lawless, back-street gin mill. I am aware that it is childish, but sometimes, leaning against the spick-and-span new bar, I am overcome by nostalgia for the gutter; I long for a "cabaret night" in Dick's old place. Friday was pay day in many of the offices and factories in the neighborhood and Friday night was "cabaret night" in Dick's. A beery old saloon musician would show up with an accordion and a mob of maudlin rummies would surround him to sing hymns and Irish songs. The place would be full of hard-drinking, pretty stenographers from the financial district, and they would be dragged off the bar stools to dance on the tiled floor. The dancers would grind peanut hulls under their shoes, making a strange, scratchy noise.

Some of the drunks would try to push the bar over, putting their shoulders to it and heaving-to as they hummed the "Volga Boat-men." Dick often threatened to use a seltzer siphon on their heads. "I'll knock some sense in your heads someday, you goats!" he would yell at his straining customers. He once classified the nuts in his place as the barwalkers, the firebugs, the weepers, and the Carusos. The barwalker was a type of drunk who was not happy unless he was up on the sagging bar, arms akimbo, dancing a Cossack dance and kicking over glasses of beer. The most unusual barwalker was the ordinarily dignified city editor of an afternoon newspaper. He would crawl up and down the bar, making a peculiar, dreadful screech. Dick was always fascinated by him. One night he stared at him and said, "What in the hell is that noise you're making?" The city editor stopped screeching for a moment. "I'm a tree frog," he said, happily. The firebugs were those who found it impossible to spill whiskey on the bar without setting it afire. The bartenders would come running and slap out the fitful blue flames with bar towels. One drunk used to pour whole glasses of brandy on the bar and ignite it just to hear Dick yell. Once Dick hit this firebug over the head with a seltzer siphon. The blow would have fractured the firebug's skull if he hadn't been wearing a derby.

On those lovely, irretrievable nights a kind of mass hysteria would sweep through the establishment. The customers would tire of singing and dancing and shaking dice. There would be a lull. Then, all of a sudden, they would start bellowing and throwing their drinks on the floor. Arguments would commence. Someone would shout, "Take off your glasses!" One night an ambulance from Broad Street Hospital had to come and get two men who had differed over which had the more nourishment in it: buttermilk or beer. As in a comic strip, the air on these occasions would be full of missiles. Once a customer who had been standing moodily at the bar for hours suddenly let go with a little, heavy-bottomed whiskey glass and knocked a big, jagged hole in the mirror behind the bar. Maxie, the bartender, dodged out of the way. Then he remembered that the mirror cost fifty-five dollars. "Dick's going to dock me a week's pay because I ducked," said Maxie, groaning.

On cabaret nights one customer, an oyster shucker from Washington Market, would go off in a corner by himself, smiling happily, and lead an invisible jazz band, using a swizzle stick for a baton and sometimes yelling at an invisible trombone player, "Get hot, you bum!" Another customer, a tall, emaciated accountant, would hold up whatever object he got his hands on first and shout, "How much am I offered? Going, going, gone! Sold to that big dope over there with a cigar in his mouth." The accountant's name was Peterson, but Dick always called him Mr. St. Peter because he was so thin and old. Mr. St. Peter lived in a furnished room and spent whole days and nights in Dick's. Dick used to say that he had a bar-rail foot, that his right foot had become twisted by resting on the rail so much. Dick would point at him proudly and say, "Look at old Mr. St. Peter. When he goes home he walks on one heel." Mr. St. Peter's principal failing was an inability to make up his mind. For years he complained about the rolls in Dick's, wanting the poppy-seed variety. Dick finally ordered some and at lunch Mr. St. Peter said, "These sure are fine rolls." A moment later he added, "And then again, they ain't."

When he got tired of imitating an auctioneer, Mr. St. Peter would sidle over to the coat rack and slip such objects as beer pads and salt shakers into people's overcoat pockets. In Dick's, the customers wandered in and out of the kitchen at will, and once Mr. St. Peter got a mackerel out of the icebox and slipped it into someone's pocket. One cabaret night Dick got suspicious of Mr. St. Peter and found that the thin, undernourished rummy had slipped enough food into his own pockets to last him several days. In the old man's ragged overcoat Dick found eight cans of sardines and a big hunk of Swiss cheese. Dick was not angry. He was amused. "Mr. St. Peter reminds me," he said, "of a squirrel storing away nuts for a rainy day." In one stage of drunkenness Mr. St. Peter would spray people with a Flit gun; once he took the fire extinguisher off the kitchen wall and came out with it going full blast. Mr. St. Peter showed up for the grand opening night in Dick's new place, but I never saw him there again.

It was dangerous to pass out in Dick's old gin mill on a cabaret night. His customers thought there was nothing quite so funny as an unconscious man. They would strip him of his clothes and outfit him in a waiter's uniform or whatever garments, including raincoats, they could find in the lockers in the kitchen. Then they would stuff his pockets full of cryptic notes and drag him up the block, depositing him in a doorway and forgetting all about him. When the man woke up he would begin to scream and would never be the same again. I kept some of the slips one victim found in his pockets. They include the following: "The Shadow called. Said for you to call back." "Well, old boy, I guess your number is up this time." "Thursday afternoon at three. Make haste. The F.B.I. knows all about it." One man woke up with a rope around his neck.

There are never any good fist fights among the dried-up, mannerly men and women who hang out in Dick's new place. In the old saloon people were always slugging away at each other. The only rule of behavior Dick ever tried to enforce was "No fights outside on the street. It don't look nice. I don't want my store to get a bad name." (Like many old-fashioned saloonkeepers, Dick always referred to his place as "the store.") When a particularly violent cabaret-night seizure struck the gin mill, Dick usually locked the doors, knowing from experience that each newcomer would be infected with the hysteria and join right in. Dick would yell, "Lock the doors! We're having a nervous breakdown in here! Lock the doors!" Maxie was never unnerved. He would sometimes grin at the antics of a customer, shake his head, and say, "This place is a regular Bellevue Island." Once, in the middle of a furious Thanksgiving Eve, I saw him hunched over the bar reading a sports section and peacefully singing a song he learned in public school: "Glow, little glowworm, glisten, glisten."

In the new place, dressed like a drug clerk, Maxie is often called a sourpuss, but he laughed a lot in the old days. Nothing amused him so much as a customer with a hangover. "Did the Brooklyn boys get you?" he would ask. He would sing, "Shut the door, they're coming through the window. Shut the window, they're coming through the door." The suffering customer would shudder and beseech him to stop, but Maxie would keep on singing. "My God," he would wind up, triumphantly, "they're coming through the floor!"

Dick's old place was isolated; at night the streets surrounding it were deserted. Consequently there was always the fear of a holdup. When Maxie had the late trick and things were dull, he would take the money out of the cash register, hide it under the bar in a trash bucket, stretch out on the bar, and go to sleep, using his rolled-up overcoat for a pillow. "Let the robbers come," he would say, yawning. If more customers arrived, they would have to put pieces of ice in his ears to arouse him.

You never hear any conversation worth listening to in Dick's new place. In the old gin mill, when the customers got tired of whooping and sat down to talk to each other, they really had something to say. I remember a conversation I heard between two men in Dick's.

"So this friend of yours died, you mean?"

"Sure, she was murdered."

"How do you know she was murdered?"

"If you're murdered, you die, don't you, for God's sake?"

For a moment the two men were quiet, thinking.

"I'm preparing evidence," said the friend of the dead woman.

"What you got to do with it?"

"I'm afraid they might suspect me."

"Why should they suspect you?"

"Well, I'm getting everything ready in case they do."

Obeying the law spoiled Dick. Now he is just another gloomy small businessman, the same one day as the next. In the old days he was unpredictable. One night he would be as generous as a happy idiot, next night he would be stingy, setting up no drinks on the house at all.

Usually, when a customer came in, Dick would be expansive. He would call the customer by his first name and inquire about his health. However, if the customer got short of cash and began to put drinks on the tab, Dick would become distant in manner. His hearing would seem to fail. Soon he would begin using the customer's last name and putting an emphatic *"Mister"* in front of it. After a while the customer would be a total stranger to Dick. Then all Dick's civility would vanish and he would call the customer "You bum" or "You goat." If the customer got angry and said, "I'll never come into this place again," Dick's fat face would harden and he would lean forward and ask, "Will you put that in writing?"

One time Dick got drunk. Ordinarily he was able to withstand an enormous amount of liquor, but this time he got drunk. He had mixed up a big tub of May wine on a warm day and had sampled the brew as he mixed it. He developed fits of laughter, as though he were a schoolgirl with her first drink. The customers who came in looked funny to him. He pointed at them, slapped a thigh, and shook with laughter. Somebody suggested that he should buy drinks for everybody if he felt that good and he sobered up immediately. However, even on his stingy nights, Dick always gave a quarter to the grim Salvation Army women who came into the place, half-heartedly shaking tambourines. And I always liked the way he treated the scrubwomen from the skyscrapers in the financial district who would come in the place late at night for beer. Dick used to give them gin and say, "This is on the house. Drink hearty." He knew the old women really wanted gin but could not afford it.

You had to respect Dick, too, when you saw the way he behaved when one of his customers died. He would order a big, expensive wreath. Just before the funeral he and Maxie and the other bartenders would take off their aprons and shave themselves carefully at the sink in the kitchen. Then they would put on dark suits, and with solemn looks on their faces, they would get into Dick's automobile and go to the funeral, leaving the gin mill in the hands of the cook. Sometimes, particularly on dull, rainy nights, Dick would close up early and take all the customers left in the place to a burlesque show or to a basement chow-mein restaurant in Chinatown. He would take along a couple of bottles of Scotch and pay all the bills.

In the old days Dick often took part in the incessant dice game. He was an intense gambler. "This ain't ping-pong," he would yell when an unsteady player rolled the dice off the uneven bar. In the old gin mill they used to gamble for drinks and for money every night, but around Thanksgiving and Christmas they would have pig and turkey pools. For a quarter, a customer would get three throws of the dice. The dice would be thrown into a soup dish. After a certain number of games the customer with the highest score would get a live turkey or a suckling pig. One Christmas Dick kept the suckling pig in the window of the gin mill. The man who won the pig lifted it out of the window and named it Dick. He took off his necktie and tied it around the pig's belly. Then he lost interest in the pig and it ran around the saloon for hours, squealing and sniffing at the customers' shoes. Late that night the customer took the pig home with him in a taxicab. The customer lived in a hotel, and he put the pig in his bathroom. Next morning his wife found the pig and telephoned the A.S.P.C.A. to come and take it away.

The customers in the old place were always playing jokes on Dick. One night a man left the saloon, ostensibly to buy some aspirin. Instead, he went up the street to a telephone booth and called Dick, posing as a gangster. Warning Dick that he would have to pay for protection in the future, the customer said that two of the boys would be around to collect and for Dick to have fifty dollars in five-dollar bills ready to hand over. Otherwise it would be just too bad. Dick came out of the telephone booth with a frightened look on his face. After a while two strangers *did* happen to come in. They ordered beers. Trembling, Dick served them with the utmost courtesy. He had the money ready to hand over. When they finished their beers, the strangers went out, leaving two dimes on the bar. Dick sighed with relief. Presently one of the customers said, "Say, Dick, have you heard about the trick a lot of drunks have been playing on bartenders? They call them up and pose as gangsters. They tell them they have to pay protection or it'll be just too bad."

"Is that right?" said Dick, his face brightening.

"Yes," said the customer. "It's going on all over town. I'm surprised they haven't tried it on you."

"I'm surprised, too," said Dick, laughing heartily.

His worried look vanished. He even bought a round of drinks.

"Say, Dick," said the customer, after a while, "what would you do if some gangsters really tried to shake you down, God forbid?"

"What would I do?"

"Yes."

"Oh, hell," said Dick, "I just wouldn't stand for it. I'd reach across the bar and grab them and crack their heads together. I'd jar their back teeth loose."

(1939)

Houdini's Picnic

CALYPSO SONGS COME FROM TRINIDAD, a British West Indian island, six miles off the coast of Venezuela, which also provides the world with asphalt and Angostura Bitters. They are written and sung by a band of haughty, amoral, hard-drinking men who call themselves Calypsonians. The majority are Negroes. With guitars slung under their arms, they hang out in rumshops and Chinese cafés on Marine Square and Frederick Street in Port-of-Spain, the principal city of Trinidad, hunting for gossip around which they can construct a Calypso. Several brag truthfully that women fight to support them. Most of them are veterans of the island jails. To set themselves apart from lesser men, they do not use their legal names but live and sing under such adopted titles as the Growler, the Lord Executor, King Radio, Attila the Hun, the Lion, the Gorilla, the Caresser, the Senior Inventor, and Lord Ziegfeld. Some of their songs are based on sensational news stories—a bedroom murder, a switchblade fight between two prominent madams, the suicide of a concupiscent white Englishwoman. Other Calypso songs deal with abstract matters like love, honor, man's fall, the wisdom of marrying a woman uglier than you, or the question of which has the most ache in it, a rum hangover or a gin hangover. Others are character studies; one of these is called "They Talk about Nora's Badness." In it, Nora's frailty is defined in a recurring line: "She go to the old dance hall and drink alcohol with Peter and Paul."

Some Calypsonians sing in a patois which contains English, Spanish, French, and Hindu words and idioms, but the majority sing in

English with a peculiarly distorted British accent; in their mouths "parrot" becomes "pair-ott," "temperament" becomes "tem-pair-a-mint," and "hat" becomes "hot." They are fond of big words and their conversation is flamboyant. The Lion, for example, does not say "Hello"; he says, "I embrace the rotundity of conventionality and wish you good day." Many Calypso songs are considered obscene or subversive by the British colonial government; sometimes it bans a song and jails the singer. Just before the war, for what it said was a diplomatic reason, the government banned an arrogant Calypso called "Hitler Demands," in which the Growler sang, "Hitler, me lad, take things easily, otherwise we sure to run you out of Germany." By "we," the Growler meant the British Empire.

The most prolific of the Calypsonians is a Negro who calls himself Wilmoth Houdini. A few years ago he left Trinidad and worked his way to New York as a greaser on a freighter. Occasionally he goes back for a long visit, making expenses by singing in Port-of-Spain movie theatres under the billing of "The Calypso King of New York," but most of the time he lives in a furnished room on West 114th Street, in lower Harlem, where there is a large settlement of immigrants from Trinidad. His passport name is Edgar Leon Sinclair; in Harlem he is called Mr. Houdini. He took the name from a movie serial he saw in 1916 in which Houdini, the magician, was featured. He was the first Calypsonian to make recordings. He has turned out thousands of songs, and more than six hundred of them have been put on records. He is the author of many classics. They include "Old Man You Too Old, You Too Bold, in Fact You Too Cold," "I Like Bananas Because They Have No Bones," "Keep Your Money, Hot Daddy," and "Drunk and Disorderly." Houdini makes public appearances at "picnics" held in Harlem halls by an organization of convivial, homesick West Indians called the Trinidad Carnival Committee. He is the moving spirit of the Committee; other members are the manager of a beauty parlor, an ex-alderman, and a dentist. In Harlem there are two good hot West Indian bands, the Caribbean Serenaders and the Krazy Kats, and musicians selected from these bands are hired to supply the music at picnics. The Committee sends out folders bearing this proclamation: "Let us Dine and Dance!

People talk about Dance? Mister, look Dance! Madam, look Dance!"

One night I went to one of the Committee's picnics with Mr. Ralph Perez, a Puerto Rican of Spanish descent who works in the export department of Decca Records, Inc. He has been in the record business nearly twenty years, building up catalogues of Latin-American, Mexican, and West Indian music for several companies. Decca sends him to Port-of-Spain once each year. He arrives just before the pre-Lenten carnival, when Calypsonians set up palm-thatched "tents" in vacant lots and sing the pick of their newest songs. He rents a house, makes it soundproof, sobers up a few singers, and records a year's supply of Calypso.

The picnic Mr. Perez took me to was held in a long, narrow hall on the third floor of a seedy building on Lenox Avenue, just below 116th Street. When we arrived, at ten o'clock, only about fifty people were there. "Picnics are apt to start late and wind up at the break of day," Mr. Perez said. Against one wall there was a row of slat-backed chairs. A number of stout, middle-aged women were sitting on these chairs, smoking cigarettes and gossiping. A space had been roped off for the band. Beyond this space, in the far corner of the room, there was a short bar and five tables covered with white oilcloth. At these tables sat young Negro and Creole women in evening dresses, drinking. I saw one take a pint of whiskey out of her handbag. She poured some of the whiskey in a paper cup, drank it straight, and put the bottle back in her handbag. "They're waiting for their menfolks to arrive," Mr. Perez said. "The men in this neighborhood work late, most of them. The men you'll see here tonight will be elevator operators, barbers, hotel workers, musicians, and a few professional people." We went over and stood at the bar, which was tended by a buxom, smiling woman. Mr. Perez said she was Mrs. Lynch, a Committee member and manager of Isabel's Salon, a Harlem beauty parlor. Assisted by two solemn, pretty children, her daughters, Mrs. Lynch was transferring bottles of beer and pop to a washtub which was half full of cracked ice. Back of the bar was a sign: "PATTIES AND PAYLOU SERVED FREE AT THE BAR AT INTERMISSION. DRINKS WILL BE SOLD AT MODERATE PRICES." Mr. Perez said the favorite drink at a picnic is rye mixed with orange pop. "Most people bring their own whiskey," he said. When Mrs. Lynch finished putting the bottles on ice, she said, "I told Houdini to run out and get the whiskey we going to sell here tonight, and he's sure taking his time." Mrs. Lynch had white strings hanging from the lobes of her ears, and I asked her what they signified. "Just dental floss," she said. "I had my ears pierced for earrings, and the doc told me to keep the pierces open with floss. It may look unusual, but it don't hurt." I heard some noise on the stairs, and then the band arrived. It was made up of Gregory Felix and three members of his Krazy Kat band—a drummer, a violinist, and a piano-player. The piano-player was a girl named Wilhelmina Gale. "I'm the clarinet," said Mr. Felix, "and Houdini's going to play the shakers and the gin bottle. Consequently, we got a five-piece band." Miss Gale went to the upright piano and removed its front and top boards. Then, with no preliminaries at all, she and the others took their places and began playing a rumba. Almost immediately, as if by signal, people started coming up the stairs in droves. Soon there were more than two hundred Negroes in the little hall.

After the band had knocked off a couple of rumbas, a lean, gloomy-eyed man came up the stairs. There was a yellow rose in the lapel of his camel's-hair topcoat. Under one arm he had a bulky package, and under the other was a big roasting pan. The lid of the pan was tied on with a piece of heavy cord. "That's Houdini," Mr. Perez said. As Houdini walked jauntily past the band, he said, "I got whiskey and paylou, me lads." Mr. Perez said that paylou is joints of fowl cooked with rice and onions. (In Charleston it is spelled "pilau.") Houdini gave the pan of paylou to Mrs. Lynch. Mr. Perez introduced me to Houdini, and he said, "Please to make your acquaintance. Let's have a drink." He tore open his package and placed five quarts of whiskey on the bar. Then he went away for a moment and returned with a jug of a heavy, milky liquid. "Home-brewed ginger beer," he said. "This the drink that dominates alcohol. Whiskey can go to your feet when you got ginger beer inside you, but it can't go to your head because it's dominated." He poured some ginger beer into a paper cup and laced it heavily with rye. He drank it in one gulp. Then he said, "Where me shakers?"

Mrs. Lynch handed him a pair of maracas, which are gourds with shot inside. "First song's going to be 'Daddy, Turn on the Light,' " he said. He went inside the band enclosure, stood up on a chair, and yelled, "Now then, me lads!" The band livened up when he began shaking the maracas. Presently the hall was seething with Lindy-hop, Susy-Q, and shim-sham-shimmy dancers, and Houdini stuffed the maracas in the pockets of his jacket and picked up a megaphone. The dancers seemed to pay no attention as he sang, but the old women sitting stiffly on the slat-backs along the wall listened attentively with big smiles on their faces. The first verse was:

> *Please turn on the light, Dad-dee.*
> *Why you like to bite?*
> *Honey, don't squeeze me so tight.*
> *Act so you mean to kill me tonight.*

The song went on and on. It ended this way:

> *This is what I want you to know.*
> *It is indeed inescapably so.*
> *Daddy, don't treat me like that,*
> *You got to le' me go, le' me shake meself.*
> *By did de-dup, bick bick bickety buck,*
> *Le' me shake meself!*

When the song was finished, Houdini jumped off the chair and hurried to the bar. "Where me ginger beer?" he asked. Mrs. Lynch handed him the jug and he mixed drinks for the band. Men and women were standing three deep at the bar. Mrs. Lynch was kept busy measuring out rye at fifteen cents a jigger. Some held a bottle of orange pop in one hand and a jigger of rye in the other, following a gulp of rye with a long swallow of pop. A laughing, half-drunk girl got up on one of the tables opposite the bar and commenced to tap-dance. The table tilted and she screamed and leaped to the floor, ripping her dress in the rear. An older woman, evidently her mother, rushed to the girl and examined her dress. "Why don't you behave yourself, Miss Wriggle-Tail?" she said. "Now you've ruined your dress." "Oh, I don't care," the girl replied. "It was rump-sprung anyway." Houdini went behind the bar and got a spoon and a square green gin bottle. He showed the bottle to me. "I brought her from Trinidad," he said. "I beat out many a tune on her. I can make her palpitate. I call her Ol' Square Face." The bottle was a third full of water. The band struck up another rumba—whatever it played sounded like a rumba—and Houdini returned to the enclosure and got up on his chair. He began a rhythmic, tantalizing beat on the bottle with the spoon. Soon he was making more noise than all the other musicians. After a while, abruptly, he began to sing:

> *I look for miser-ee*
> *Wherever I meet Johnnie.*
> *People, people, be sorry to see*
> *The grave for Johnnie, the gallows for me.*

The old women along the wall began to smile again. "The name of this one is 'Johnnie Take My Wife,' " Mr. Perez said.

> *This Mr. Johnnie must be ver-ee nice,*
> *For me wife called Johnnie in her sleep last night.*
> *But from today I intend to go*
> *On a hunt for Mr. Johnnie, that gigolo.*
> *I went in the house to get me gun,*
> *Me wife seen me coming and she starts to run.*
> *But let me tell you where I lose me head:*
> *Mr. Johnnie was hiding underneath the bed.*
> *Johnnie, you should never do a t'ing like that,*
> *To stab Papa Houdini in the back.*
> *The judge and jury going to see me face,*
> *For the thing going to end in a murder case.*

Houdini's next number was also about unhappy love. It was excessively sentimental. At intervals he would quit singing and speak in an unknown tongue, "Bick bick bickety bong bong de dup." The chorus went, "But I'm sure you will pay for me love some good day, that is all what I have got to say." Only the old women along the wall listened to him. The men and women on the crowded dance floor minded their own business. Occasionally one of the expertly wanton dancers would shudder and let out a loud moan, and then all the others would laugh uproariously and scream, "Hold tight! Hold tight!" or "Peace, sister!" Mr. Perez looked at the sweating dancers and said, "There's a mixture of bloods in Trinidad. There's French, Spanish, Carib, Negro, Hindu, and Chinese. You can see it reflected in the faces here. You can see Hindu in the face of that big rumba-dancer. There are thousands of Hindus in Trinidad. The girl with him is a Creole." I looked at the Creole. Her face was lovely. She reminded me of Dolores Del Rio. Presently Houdini got tired and stepped off the chair. Mr. Perez asked him to sit with us and have a drink. He brought his jug of ginger beer to the table. I asked him how he became a Calypso singer, and he began to talk smoothly and rapidly, almost like a public speaker.

"I was inspired in 1916," he said. "Before that, I was just nobody. In the year 1916 a band were organized in Port-of-Spain by a distinguished girl named Maggie Otis. She was Queen of the band. I was King. It was called the African Millionaires. It had twenty-four men and girls. The men wore striped green silk shirts, flannel pants, and white shoes, and each had strung to him a camera, a stuffed crocodile, or a pair of field glasses. That was to ape the rich tourists who come to Trinidad. The girls dressed in a manner likewise. At Mardi Gras, which falls on the two days before Lent, the big stores and companies in Port-of-Spain give prizes of rum and money to the Calypsonian who improvises the best song about their merchandise. In 1916, with the African Millionaires in back of me, I entered the advertising competitions and won seven in one day, singing extemporaneously against men like the Senior Inventor and the Lord Executor. I collected the big prize from the Angostura Bitters people and the big prize from the Royal Extra Stout brewery people, and all like that. In those competitions you have to improvise a song on the spur of the moment, and it has to be in perfect time with the band. You must be inspired to do so.

"That night, in a tent, I had a war with some old Calypsonians. A tent is a bamboo shack with a palm roof. The Calypsonians sing in them during carnival and charge admission. A war is where three Calypsonians stand up on the platform in a tent and improvise in verse. One man begins in verse, telling about the ugly faces and impure morals of the other two. Then the next man picks up the song and proceeds with it. On and on it goes. If you falter when it comes your turn, you don't dare call yourself a Calypsonian. Most war songs are made up of insults. You give out your insults, and then the next man insults you. The man who gives out the biggest insults is the winner. I was so insulting in my first war the other men congratulated me. Since then I maintain my prestige and integrity as Houdini the Calypsonian. I got a brain that ticks like a clock. I can sing at any moment on any matter. If you say to me, 'Sing a song about that gentleman over there,' I swallow once and do so."

The lovely Creole came over to our table. She put a hand on Houdini's head and said, "Quit beating your gums together, Papa Houdini, and help me out with a drink." Houdini laughed and said, "The greatest pleasure, Madam!" He poured her a drink; she kissed him and walked away.

"Excuse the interruption," said Houdini, following the girl with his eyes. "As I say, I am a true Calypsonian, the only one in this country. Of course, I have to go back to Trinidad to renew me inspiration. It is like a door that has been shut a long time. The hinge get rusty. But the minute the rust fall off the hinge, the door come back supple again. I have to go back to Trinidad to drop off the rust on me. I have to go back and eat some calaloo. That's bluecrab soup. It's Sunday soup. I have to go back and drink some gin juleps. That's green-coconut water and gin. That builds up me vitamin and contributes to me inspiration. I tell you a most peculiar thing about me. I am born in Brooklyn. The year of 1902. Father was a steward, and the family were living in Brooklyn when I came. Of course, we return to Trinidad when I was two. I come from a wandering family.

"Houdini, come here!" Mrs. Lynch shouted.

"I be there in a minute," Houdini called. Then he took another drink and resumed the conversation. "I tell you," he said, "the thing I don't comprehend is why some big night club doesn't hire me to sing Calypso in it. It would be remarkable. It would be a rage. That will happen sooner or late. Whiskey don't murder me, Madison Square Garden is where I wind up.

"I am now in possession of a numerous amount of new compositions. They come to me at all hours, day and night. Last night I went to the Apollo Theatre and I ran home in the drizzling rain. So I decide to take a bath to keep off a cold. I was in the tub and a Calypso come to me. I beat on the side of the tub with me fingernails to get the tune. The name turned out to be 'From the Day of Birth I Been Told I Got Rhythm in My Soul.' Me trunk is so full of compositions I got no room for me suits. Pretty soon I think I make some new records. I used to get paid fifty dollars per record for me and the musicians, and a royalty of a penny per record. The royalties running thin, and I think I make some new ones. I am favorably known for suggestive Calypso, but I am a true Catholic and I have made many shouting Calypsos of a religious nature. One is a carol. It starts off like this: 'The Blessed Virgin had a baby boy. The baby came from the Kingdom and the name of the baby was Jesus.' "

He was interrupted again.

"You got to come help with the paylou!" Mrs. Lynch shouted. "It's intermission!"

"Everybody depend on me," Houdini said, getting up. "After a picnic I go to bed for a week."

He hurried to the bar and pulled the strands of cord off the roasting pan. He took off the lid and began dishing out the paylou, placing mounds of rice and joints of chicken on paper plates. Mrs. Lynch passed out the patties. They were small, herb-seasoned meat pies, wrapped in wax paper. Pretty soon Houdini sent a man to Mrs. Lynch's apartment for two more pans of paylou and patties. Each person who could show the stub of a fifty-cent admission ticket got a plate of paylou from Houdini and a patty from Mrs. Lynch. "I made those patties," Houdini said. "They got my signature on them." The people ate standing up. Presently the floor around the bar was strewn with paper plates and forks and empty pint bottles. An aged woman sat on a chair in a corner, peacefully sleeping with her mouth open, in the midst of the hubbub. "She sure did a good job of passing out," Houdini said. "If she don't wake up, she's going to miss out on the paylou." He went over and shook her awake and placed a plate of paylou on her lap. She blinked blearily and said, "I thank you. Now fetch me a fork." Intermission was over at two-thirty. Then the band went back to work. At three o'clock, Mr. Perez and I said goodbye to Mrs. Lynch and Houdini. After I turned to go downstairs, I looked back and saw Houdini climb up on his chair. He began beating out a tune on Ol' Square Face, the green gin bottle, and singing a Calypso called, Mr. Perez said, "Tiger Tom Kill Tiger Cat, Damblay Santapie and Rat." I asked him what the title meant. "I don't know," he said. "Something to do with a woman, I guess."

Downstairs Mr. Perez and I stopped in a fried-fish café for a cup of coffee. I asked him how Calypso originated, and he quoted a song written by the Lord Executor:

> Would you like to know what is Calypso?
> It was sung by the Creoles years ago.
> It was danced by the African drums in a bamboo tent
> And sung in patois for amusement.
> Now it is played in tone
> On a gramophone.

Mr. Perez said that Calypso is probably an old patois word meaning "work song." There seems to be no connection between Calypso songs and the Calypso of the "Odyssey." Historians on the island believe the institution had its origin when slaves, recently from Africa, would divide into competitive groups and sing ribald songs of derision at each other as they worked in the fields. In their huts at night, however, they directed the songs against their masters. A few Calypsonians still sing in this tradition. When Sir Alfred Claud

Hollis, once governor for the Crown in Trinidad, returned to England, a Calypsonian sang:

> *I must be very frank and say*
> *I was glad when Sir Hollis went away.*
> *He cared only for his own enjoyment*
> *And did nothing to help us find employment.*

The Growler and Attila the Hun have often been jailed for criticism of the colonial administration. The Crown officials evidently have mixed feelings about Calypso; at Mardi Gras they put up $500 in prizes for the best songs, yet they exercise a strict and sometimes stifling censorship over the singers. Mr. Perez must submit any song he wishes to record to the Colonial Secretary. Many of the most inspired songs are turned down because they are considered indecent, sacrilegious, or "detrimental to the Government." Some Calypsonians get in trouble with the administration by writing blackmail songs. Such a singer will learn an embarrassing fact about a prominent Trinidadian and write a song around it; then he will go to the man and offer to forget the song for a few dollars. Sometimes, after he has been paid off, he will sing it in the cafés and rumshops anyway, just for the hell of it.

The principal benefactor of the Calypsonians is a Portuguese businessman named Edward Sa Gomes, who operates a chain of music stores on Trinidad and Tobago, a nearby island. He lends them money, bails them out when they land in jail, and arbitrates their incessant disputes. He helps Mr. Perez round them up to make records. Mr. Perez pays the Calypsonians ten dollars a song and royalties. On one trip he recorded three hundred. When the singers get paid, they promptly spend their money for clothes and liquor. They are constantly fighting with each other, sometimes for a sly business reason. For example, Houdini once made an insulting record called "Executor, the Homeless Man." The Lord Executor answered with an equally insulting record, "My Reply to Houdini." People in Trinidad bought both records, just to see whose reputation was damaged more. The Lord Executor is dean of the Calypsonians. He is old and wizened and touchy. He walks the streets mumbling to himself. He says he is composing, but his colleagues say, "The Executor's got a mumbling jag on." His songs are all gloomy, such as "Seven Skeletons Found in the Yard" and "I Don't Know How the Young Men Living."

Few of the Calypsonians can read or write, but they are able to keep hundreds of songs in their heads. Even so, no Calypsonian ever sings a song the same way twice; that would bore him. They are contemptuous of each other. The hungrier they get the haughtier they get. It is characteristic of a Calypsonian to sing about his colleagues like this:

> Walking with a toothpick between their teeth,
> Making people understand they just done eat,
> Crediting beds from the stores in town,
> But the agents coming and unmount them down.

The Calypsonian is highly ethical in his own fashion. He will steal a bottle of rum from a colleague, or a pair of shoes, or a girl, but never a song. "The Executor would damn near cut his throat before he would sing one of Houdini's songs, and vice versa," Mr. Perez said. All Calypsonians believe that women are powerless to resist them. King Radio, a small, one-eyed man who wears dark glasses, boasts that he is supported by fifty women. Mr. Perez quoted one of Radio's songs:

> They can't find a lover like me again.
> I'm the only lover in Port-of-Spain.
> Fifty women now supporting me
> And all of them belong to high society.
> I even got a boy to tend the phone
> In case you should ring me up at home.

Many of Radio's songs contain advice about women. One song is "Man Smart, Woman Smarter." Another begins:

If you want to be happy and live a king's life,
Never make a pretty woman your wife.
That's from a logical point of view,
Always love a woman uglier than you.

The best-selling Calypso records in the United States are those based on the adventures of Nettie, Nora, Lizzie, and other loose girls. Those concerning the womanly qualities of Mrs. Simpson and the abdication of King Edward VIII also sell well. The abdication was the most popular subject in the history of Calypso; every singer had a go at it. It is generally conceded that the Caresser did the best job. He had an idea that "old Baldwin" kept the King imprisoned in England, preventing him from crossing the sea and marrying Mrs. Simpson in New York. This is the chorus of the Caresser's song:

It's love, it's love alone
That cause King Edward to leave the throne.

Some of the verses are:

Oh, what a sad disappointment
Was endured by the British Government.
On the tenth of December we heard the talk
That he gave the throne to the Duke of York.

Am sorry my mother is going to grieve,
But I cannot help, I am bound to leave.
I got the money, I got the talk,
And the fancy walk just to suit New York.

And if I can't get a boat to set me free
I'll walk to Miss Simpson across the sea.
He said my robes and crown is upon my mind,
But I cannot leave Miss Simpson behind.

If you see Miss Simpson walk down the street,
She could fall an angel with the body beat.
Let the organ roll, let the church bell ring,
Good luck to our second bachelor King.

The Gorilla, in his abdication song, was more defiant. He sang:

Believe me, friends, if I were King,
I'd marry any woman and give her a ring.
I wouldn't give a damn what the people say
So long as she can wash, cook, and dingo-lay.

(1939)

The Mohawks in High Steel

*T*HE MOST FOOTLOOSE INDIANS in North America are a band of mixed-blood Mohawks whose home, the Caughnawaga Reservation, is on the St. Lawrence River in Quebec. They are generally called the Caughnawagas. In times past, they were called the Christian Mohawks or the Praying Mohawks. There are three thousand of them, at least six hundred and fifty of whom spend more time in cities and towns all over the United States than they do on the reservation. Some are as restless as gypsies. It is not unusual for a family to lock up its house, leave the key with a neighbor, get into an automobile, and go away for years. There are colonies of Caughnawagas in Brooklyn, Buffalo, and Detroit. The biggest colony is in Brooklyn, out in the North Gowanus neighborhood. It was started in the late twenties, there are approximately four hundred men, women, and children in it, it is growing, and it shows signs of permanence. A few families have bought houses. The pastor of one of the churches in the neighborhood, the Cuyler Presbyterian, has learned the Mohawk dialect of the Iroquois language and holds a service in it once a month, and the church has elected a Caughnawaga to its board of deacons. There have been marriages between Caughnawagas and members of other groups in the neighborhood. The Caughnawaga women once had trouble in finding a brand of corn meal (Quaker White Enriched and Degerminated) that they like to use in making *ka-na-ta-rok,* or Indian boiled bread; all the grocery stores in North Gowanus, even the little Italian ones, now carry it. One saloon, the Nevins Bar & Grill, has become a Caughnawaga hangout and is referred to in the neighborhood as the Indian Bank; on weekend nights, two-thirds of its customers are Caughnawagas; to encourage their patronage, it stocks one Montreal ale and two Montreal beers. A saying in the band is that Brooklyn is the downtown of Caughnawaga.

Caughnawaga Reservation is on the south shore of the St. Lawrence, just above Lachine Rapids. It is nine miles upriver from Montreal, which is on the north shore. By bus, it is half an hour from Dominion Square, the center of Montreal. It is a small reservation. It is a tract of farmland, swamp, and scrub timber that is shaped like a half-moon; it parallels the river for eight miles and is four miles wide at its widest point. On the river side, about midway, there is a sprawled-out village, also named Caughnawaga. Only a few of the Caughnawagas are farmers. The majority live in the village and rent their farmland to French Canadians and speak of the rest of the reservation as "the bush." The Montreal-to-Malone, New York, highway goes through Caughnawaga village. It is the main street. On it are about fifty commonplace frame dwellings, the office of the Agent of the Indian Affairs Branch of the Canadian government, the Protestant church (it is of the United Church of Canada denomination), the Protestant school, and several Indian-owned grocery stores and filling stations. The stores are the gathering places of the old men of the village. In each store is a cluster of chairs, boxes, and nail kegs on which old men sit throughout the day, smoking and playing blackjack and eating candy bars and mumbling a few words now and then, usually in Mohawk. In the front yards of half a dozen of the dwellings are ramshackly booths displaying souvenirs—papoose dolls, moccasins, sweet-grass baskets, beadwork handbags, beadwork belts, beadwork wristwatch straps, and pincushions on which beads spell out "Mother Dear," "Home Sweet Home," "I Love U," and similar legends. In one yard, between two totem poles, is a huge, elm-bark tepee with a sign on it that reads, "Stop! & Pow Wow With Me. Chief White Eagle. Indian Medicine Man. *Herbages Indiens.*" Except on ceremonial occasions and for show purposes, when they put on fringed and beaded buckskins and feather headdresses of the Plains Indian type, Caughnawagas dress as other Canadians do, and if it were not for these front-yard establishments, most motorists would be unaware that they were passing through an Indian village. A scattering of Caughnawagas look as Indian as can be; they have high cheekbones and jut noses, their eyes are sad, shrewd, and dark brown, their hair is straight and coal black, their skin is smooth and coppery, and they have the same beautiful, erect, chin-lifted, haughty walk that gypsies have. White blood, however, has blurred the Indianness of the majority; some look dimly but unmistakably Indian, some look Indian only after one has searched their faces for Indian characteristics, and some do not look Indian at all. They run to two physical types; one type, the commoner, is thickset, fleshy, and broad-faced, and the other is tall, bony, and longheaded. Some of the younger Caughnawagas have studied a little of the Indian past in school and they disapprove of the front-yard establishments. They particularly disapprove of Chief White Eagle's establishment; they feel that it gives visitors a highly erroneous impression of Caughnawaga right off the bat. First of all, the old Mohawks did not live in tepees but in log-and-bark communal houses called longhouses, and they did not make totem poles. Also, there haven't been any chiefs in Caughnawaga, except self-appointed ones, since 1890. Furthermore, while all Caughnawagas have Indian names, some much fancier than White Eagle, few go under them outside their own circles, and those who do almost invariably run them together and preface them with a white given name; John Goodleaf, Tom Tworivers, and Dominick Twoax are examples. Caughnawagas discovered long ago that whites are inclined to look upon Indian names, translated or untranslated, as humorous. In dealing with whites, ninety-five per cent of them go under white names, and have for many generations. Most of these names are ordinary English, Scotch, Irish, or French ones, a number of which date back to intermarriages with early settlers. The names of the oldest and biggest Caughnawaga families are Jacobs, Williams, Rice, McComber, Tarbell, Stacey, Diabo (originally D'Ailleboust), Montour, De Lisle, Beauvais, and Lahache. The most frequent given names are Joe, John, and Angus, and Mary, Annie, and Josie.

On each side of the highway there is a labyrinth of lanes, some dirt, some gravel, and some paved. Some are straight and some are snaky. The dwellings on them are much older than those on the highway, and they range from log cabins to big field-stone houses with frame wings and lean-tos; members of three and even four generations of a family may live in one house. In the yards are gardens and apple trees and sugar-maple trees and piles of automobile junk and groups of outbuildings, usually a garage, a privy, a chicken coop, and a stable. Large families keep a cow or two and a plug horse; the French Canadians who rent the reservation farmland sell all their worn-out horses to the villagers. The dwellings in Caughnawaga are wired for electricity, just about every family has a radio and a few have telephones, but there is no waterworks system. Water for drinking and cooking is obtained from public pumps—the old-fashioned boxed-up, long-handled kind—situated here and there on the lanes. Water for washing clothes and for bathing is carted up from the river in barrels, and the horses are used for this. They are also used for carting firewood, and the children ride them. Most mornings, the cows and horses are driven to unfenced pastures on the skirts of the village. A few always mosey back during the day and wander at will.

The busiest of the lanes is one that runs beside the river. On it are the reservation post office, the Catholic church, the Catholic schools, a parish hall named Kateri Hall, and a small Catholic hospital. The post office occupies the parlor in the home of Frank McDonald Jacobs, the patriarch of the band. A daughter of his, Veronica Jacobs, is postmistress. The church, St. Francis Xavier's, is the biggest building in the village. It is a hundred years old, it is made of cut stone of a multiplicity of shades of silver and gray, and the cross on its steeple is surmounted by a gilded weathercock. It is a Jesuit mission church; at its altar, by an old privilege, masses are said in Mohawk. In the summer, sightseeing buses from Montreal stop regularly at St. Francis Xavier's and a Jesuit scholastic guides the sightseers through it and shows them its treasures, the most precious of which are some of the bones of Kateri Tekakwitha, an Indian virgin called the Lily of the Mohawks who died at Caughnawaga in 1680. The old bones lie on a watered-silk cushion in a glass-topped chest. Sick and afflicted people make pilgrimages to the church and pray before them. In a booklet put out by the church, it is claimed that sufferers from many diseases, including cancer, have been healed through Kateri's intercession. Kateri is venerated because of the bitter penances she imposed upon herself; according to the memoirs of missionaries who knew her, she wore iron chains, lay upon thorns, whipped herself until she bled, plunged into icy water, went about barefoot on the snow, and fasted almost continuously.

On a hill in the southern part of the village are two weedy graveyards. One is for Catholics, and it is by far the bigger. The other is for Protestants and pagans. At one time, all the Caughnawagas were Catholics. Since the early twenties, a few have gone over to other faiths every year. Now, according to a Canadian government census, 2,682 are Catholics, 251 belong to Protestant denominations, and 77 are pagans. The so-called pagans—they do not like the term and prefer to be known as the longhouse people—belong to an Indian religion called the Old Way or the Handsome Lake Revelation. Their prophet, Handsome Lake, was a Seneca who in 1799, after many years of drunkenness, had a vision in which the spirits up above spoke to him. He reformed and spent his last fifteen years as a roving preacher in Indian villages in upstate New York. In his sermons, he recited some stories and warnings and precepts that he said the spirits had revealed to him. Many of these have been handed down by word of mouth and they constitute the gospel of the religion; a few men in each generation—they are called "the good-message-keepers"—memorize them. The precepts are simply stated. An example is a brief one from a series concerning the sins of parents: "It often happens that parents hold angry disputes in the hearing of their infant child. The infant hears and comprehends their angry words. It feels lost and lonely. It can see for itself no happiness in prospect. This is a great sin." During the nineteenth century, Handsome Lake's religion spread to every Iroquois reservation in the United States and Canada except Caughnawaga. It reached Caughnawaga right after the First World War and, despite the opposition of Catholics and Protestants, began to be practiced openly in 1927. Handsome Lake's followers meet in ceremonial structures that they call longhouses. The Caughnawaga longhouse is on the graveyard hill. It resembles a country schoolhouse. It is a plain, one-room, frame building surrounded by a barbed-wire fence. Several times a year, on dates determined by the phases of the moon or the rising of sap in the sugar maples or the ripening of fruits and vegetables, the longhouse people get together and hold thanksgiving festivals, among which are a Midwinter Festival, a Thanks-to-the-Maple Festival, a Strawberry Festival, and a String Bean Festival. In the course of the festivals, they burn little heaps of sacred tobacco leaves, eat a dish called corn soup, make public confessions of their sins, and chant and dance to the music of rattles and drums. The smoke from the tobacco fires is supposed to ascend to the spirits. The sacred tobacco is not store-bought. It is a kind of tobacco known as Red Rose, an intensely acrid species that grows wild in parts of the United States and Canada. The longhouse people grow it in their gardens from wild seed and cure the leaves in the sun. The longhouse rattles are gourds or snapping-turtle shells with kernels of corn inside them, and the drums are wooden pails that barn paint came in with rawhide or old inner tubes stretched over their mouths. The Catholics and Protestants complain that for several days after a longhouse festival everyone on the reservation is moody.

The Caughnawagas are among the oldest reservation Indians. The band had its origin in the latter half of the seventeenth century, when French Jesuit missionaries converted somewhere between fifty and a hundred Iroquois families in a dozen longhouse villages in what is now western and northern New York and persuaded them to go up to Quebec and settle in a mission outpost. This outpost was on the St. Lawrence, down below Lachine Rapids. The converts began arriving there in 1668. Among them were members of all the tribes in the Iroquois Confederacy—Mohawks, Oneidas, Onondagas, Cayugas, and Senecas. There were also a few Hurons, Eries, and Ottawas who had been captured and adopted by the Iroquois and had been living with them in the longhouse villages. Mohawks greatly predominated, and Mohawk customs and the Mohawk dialect of

Iroquois eventually became the customs and speech of the whole group. In 1676, accompanied by two Jesuits, they left the outpost and went up the river to the foot of the rapids and staked out a village of their own, naming it Ka-na-wá-ke, which is Mohawk for "at the rapids"; Caughnawaga is a latter-day spelling. They moved the village three times, a few miles at a time and always upriver. With each move, they added to their lands. The final move, to the present site of Caughnawaga village, was made in 1719. Until 1830, the Caughnawaga lands were mission lands. In that year, the Canadian government took control of the bulk of them and turned them into a tax-free reservation, parcelling out a homestead to each family and setting aside other pieces, called the Commons, for the use of future generations. Through the years, grants of Commons land have grown smaller and smaller; there are only about five hundred acres of it left; according to present policy, a male member of the band, after reaching his eighteenth birthday, may be granted exactly one-fourth of an acre if he promises to build upon it. A Caughnawaga is allowed to rent his land to anybody, but he may sell or give it only to another member of the band. Unlike many reservation Indians, the Caughnawagas have always had considerable say-so in their own affairs, at first through chiefs, each representing several families, who would go to the Indian Agent with requests or grievances, and then through an annually elected tribal council. The council has twelve members, it meets once a month in the parish hall, and it considers such matters as the granting of Commons land, the relief of the needy, and the upkeep of lanes and pumps. Its decisions, when approved by the Indian Affairs Branch in Ottawa, are automatically carried out by the Agent.

IN THE EARLY YEARS at Caughnawaga, the men clung to their old, aboriginal Iroquois ways of making a living. The Jesuits tried to get them to become farmers, but they would not. In the summer, while the women farmed, they fished. In the fall and winter, they hunted in a body in woods all over Quebec, returning to the village now and then with canoeloads of smoked deer meat, moose meat, and bear meat. Then, around 1700, a few of the youths of the first generation born at Caughnawaga went down to Montreal and took jobs in the French fur trade. They became canoemen in the great fleets of canoes that carried trading goods to remote depots on the St. Lawrence and its tributaries and brought back bales of furs. They liked this work—it was hard but hazardous—and they recruited others. Thereafter, for almost a century and a half, practically every youth in the band took a job in a freight canoe as soon as he got his strength, usually around the age of seventeen. In the eighteen-thirties, forties, and fifties, as the fur trade declined in Lower Canada, the Caughnawaga men were forced to find other things to do. Some switched to the St. Lawrence timber-rafting industry and became famous on the river for their skill in running immense rafts of oak and pine over Lachine Rapids. Some broke down and became farm-ers. Some made moccasins and snowshoes and sold them to jobbers in Montreal. A few who were still good at the old Mohawk dances came down to the United States and travelled with circuses; Caugh-nawagas were among the first circus Indians. A few bought horses and buggies and went from farmhouse to farmhouse in New England in the summer, peddling medicines—tonics, purges, liniments, and remedies for female ills—that the old women brewed from herbs and roots and seeds. A good many became depressed and shiftless; these hung out in Montreal and did odd jobs and drank cheap brandy.

In 1886, the life at Caughnawaga changed abruptly. In the spring of that year, the Dominion Bridge Company began the construction of a cantilever railroad bridge across the St. Lawrence for the Ca-nadian Pacific Railroad, crossing from the French-Canadian village of Lachine on the north shore to a point just below Caughnawaga village on the south shore. The D.B.C. is the biggest erector of iron and steel structures in Canada; it corresponds to the Bethlehem Steel Company in the United States. In obtaining the right to use reservation land for the bridge abutment, the Canadian Pacific and the D.B.C. promised that Caughnawagas would be employed on the job wherever possible.

"The records of the company for this bridge show that it was our understanding that we would employ these Indians as ordinary day laborers unloading materials," an official of the D.B.C. wrote recently in a letter. "They were dissatisfied with this arrangement and would come out on the bridge itself every chance they got. It was quite impossible to keep them off. As the work progressed, it became apparent to all concerned that these Indians were very odd in that they did not have any fear of heights. If not watched, they would climb up into the spans and walk around up there as cool and collected as the toughest of our riveters, most of whom at that period were old sailing-ship men especially picked for their experience in working aloft. These Indians were as agile as goats. They would walk a narrow beam high up in the air with nothing below them but the river, which is rough there and ugly to look down on, and it wouldn't mean any more to them than walking on the solid ground. They seemed immune to the noise of the riveting, which goes right through you and is often enough in itself to make newcomers to construction feel sick and dizzy. They were inquisitive about the riveting and were continually bothering our foremen by requesting that they be allowed to take a crack at it. This happens to be the most dangerous work in all construction, and the highest-paid. Men who want to do it are rare and men who can do it are even rarer, and in good construction years there are sometimes not enough of them to go around. We decided it would be mutually advantageous to see what these Indians could do, so we picked out some and gave them a little training, and it turned out that putting riveting tools in their hands was like putting ham with eggs. In other words, they were natural-born bridgemen. Our records do not show how many we trained on this bridge. There is a tradition in the company that we trained twelve, or enough to form three riveting gangs."

In the erection of steel structures, whether bridge or building, there are three main divisions of workers—raising gangs, fitting-up gangs, and riveting gangs. The steel comes to a job already cut and built up into various kinds of columns and beams and girders; the columns are the perpendicular pieces and the beams and girders are the horizontal ones. Each piece has two or more groups of holes bored through it to receive bolts and rivets, and each piece has a code mark chalked or painted on it, indicating where it should go in the structure. Using a crane or a derrick, the men in the raising gang hoist the pieces up and set them in position and join them by running bolts through a few of the holes in them; these bolts are temporary. Then the men in the fitting-up gang come along; they are divided into plumbers and bolters. The plumbers tighten up the pieces with guy wires and turnbuckles and make sure that they are in plumb. The bolters put in some more temporary bolts. Then the riveting gangs come along; one raising gang and one fitting-up gang will keep several riveting gangs busy. There are four men in a riveting gang—a heater, a sticker-in, a bucker-up, and a riveter. The heater lays some wooden planks across a couple of beams, making a platform for the portable, coal-burning forge in which he heats the rivets. The three other men hang a plank scaffold by ropes from the steel on which they are going to work. There are usually six two-by-ten planks in a scaffold, three on each side of the steel, affording just room enough to work; one false step and it's goodbye Charlie. The three men climb down with their tools and take their positions on the scaffold; most often the sticker-in and the bucker-up stand on one side and the riveter stands or kneels on the other. The heater, on his platform, picks a red-hot rivet off the coals in his forge with tongs and tosses it to the sticker-in, who catches it in a metal can. At this stage, the rivet is shaped like a mushroom; it has a buttonhead and a stem. Meanwhile, the bucker-up has unscrewed and pulled out one of the temporary bolts joining two pieces of steel, leaving the hole empty. The sticker-in picks the rivet out of his can with tongs and sticks it in the hole and pushes it in until the buttonhead is flush with the steel on his side and the stem protrudes from the other side, the riveter's side. The sticker-in steps out of the way. The bucker-up fits a tool called a dolly bar over the buttonhead and holds it there, bracing the rivet. Then the riveter presses the cupped head of his pneumatic hammer against the protruding stem end of the rivet, which is still red-hot and malleable, and turns on the power and forms a buttonhead on it. This operation is repeated until every hole that can be got at from the scaffold is riveted up.

Then the scaffold is moved. The heater's platform stays in one place until all the work within a rivet-tossing radius of thirty to forty feet is completed. The men on the scaffold know each other's jobs and are interchangeable; the riveter's job is bone-shaking and nerve-racking, and every so often one of the others swaps with him for a while. In the days before pneumatic hammers, the riveter used two tools, a cupped die and an iron maul; he placed the die over the stem end of the red-hot rivet and beat on it with the maul until he squashed the stem end into a buttonhead.

After the D.B.C. completed the Canadian Pacific Bridge, it began work on a jackknife bridge now known as the Soo Bridge, which crosses two canals and a river and connects the twin cities of Sault Ste. Marie, Ontario, and Sault Ste. Marie, Michigan. This job took two years. Old Mr. Jacobs, the patriarch of the band, says that the Caughnawaga riveting gangs went straight from the Canadian Pacific job to the Soo job and that each gang took along an apprentice. Mr. Jacobs is in his eighties. In his youth, he was a member of a riveting gang; in his middle age, he was, successively, a commercial traveller for a wholesale grocer in Montreal, a schoolteacher on the reservation, and a campaigner for compulsory education for Indians. "The Indian boys turned the Soo Bridge into a college for themselves," he says. "The way they worked it, as soon as one apprentice was trained, they'd send back to the reservation for another one. By and by, there'd be enough men for a new Indian gang. When the new gang was organized, there'd be a shuffle-up—a couple of men from the old gangs would go into the new gang and a couple of the new men would go into the old gangs; the old would balance the new." This proliferation continued on subsequent jobs, and by 1907 there were over seventy skilled bridgemen in the Caughnawaga band. On August 29, 1907, during the erection of the Quebec Bridge, which crosses the St. Lawrence nine miles above Quebec City, a span collapsed, killing ninety-six men, of whom thirty-five were Caughnawagas. In the band, this is always spoken of as "the disaster."

"People thought the disaster would scare the Indians away from high steel for good," Mr. Jacobs says. "Instead of which, the general effect it had, it made high steel much more interesting to them. It

277

made them take pride in themselves that they could do such dangerous work. Up to then, the majority of them, they didn't consider it any more dangerous than timber-rafting. Also, it made them the most looked-up-to men on the reservation. The little boys in Caughnawaga used to look up to the men that went out with circuses in the summer and danced and war-whooped all over the States and came back to the reservation in the winter and holed up and sat by the stove and drank whiskey and bragged. That's what they wanted to do. Either that, or work on the timber rafts. After the disaster, they changed their minds—they all wanted to go into high steel. The disaster was a terrible blow to the women. The first thing they did, they got together a sum of money for a life-size crucifix to hang over the main altar in St. Francis Xavier's. They did that to show their Christian resignation. The next thing they did, they got in behind the men and made them split up and scatter out. That is, they wouldn't allow all the gangs to work together on one bridge any more, which, if something went wrong, it might widow half the young women on the reservation. A few gangs would go to this bridge and a few would go to that. Pretty soon, there weren't enough bridge jobs, and the gangs began working on all types of high steel—factories, office buildings, department stores, hospitals, hotels, apartment houses, schools, breweries, distilleries, powerhouses, piers, railroad stations, grain elevators, anything and everything. In a few years, every steel structure of any size that went up in Canada, there were Indians on it. Then Canada got too small and they began crossing the border. They began going down to Buffalo and Cleveland and Detroit."

Sometime in 1915 or 1916, a Caughnawaga bridgeman named John Diabo came down to New York City and got a job on Hell Gate Bridge. He was a curiosity and was called Indian Joe; two old foremen still remember him. After he had worked for some months as bucker-up in an Irish gang, three other Caughnawagas joined him and they formed a gang of their own. They had worked together only a few weeks when Diabo stepped off a scaffold and dropped into the river and was drowned. He was highly skilled and his misstep was freakish; recently, in trying to explain it, a Caughnawaga said, "It must've been one of those cases, he got in the way of himself." The other Caughnawagas went back to the reservation with his body and did not return. As well as the old men in the band can recollect, no other Caughnawagas worked here until the twenties. In 1926, attracted by the building boom, three or four Caughnawaga gangs came down. The old men say that these gangs worked first on the Fred F. French Building, the Graybar Building, and One Fifth Avenue. In 1928, three more gangs came down. They worked first on the George Washington Bridge. In the thirties, when Rockefeller Center was the biggest steel job in the country, at least seven additional Caughnawaga gangs came down. Upon arriving here, the men in all these gangs enrolled in the Brooklyn local of the high-steel union, the International Association of Bridge, Structural, and Ornamental Iron Workers, American Federation of Labor. Why they enrolled in the Brooklyn instead of the Manhattan local, no one now seems able to remember. The hall of the Brooklyn local is on Atlantic Avenue, in the block between Times Plaza and Third Avenue, and the Caughnawagas got lodgings in furnished-room houses and cheap hotels in the North Gowanus neighborhood, a couple of blocks up Atlantic from the hall. In the early thirties, they began sending for their families and moving into tenements and apartment houses in the same neighborhood. During the war, Caughnawagas continued to come down. Many of these enrolled in the Manhattan local, but all of them settled in North Gowanus.

At present, there are eighty-three Caughnawagas in the Brooklyn local and forty-two in the Manhattan local. Less than a third of them work steadily in the city. The others keep their families in North Gowanus and work here intermittently but spend much of their time in other cities. They roam from coast to coast, usually by automobile, seeking rush jobs that offer unlimited overtime work at double pay; in New York City, the steel-erecting companies use as little overtime as possible. A gang may work in half a dozen widely separated cities in a single year. Occasionally, between jobs, they return to Brooklyn to see their families. Now and then, after long jobs, they pick up their families and go up to the reservation for a vacation; some go up every summer. A few men sometimes take their families along on trips to jobs and send them back to Brooklyn by bus or train. Several foremen who have had years of experience with Caughnawagas believe that they roam because they can't help doing so, it is a passion, and that their search for overtime is only an excuse. A veteran foreman for the American Bridge Company says he has seen Caughnawagas leave jobs that offered all the overtime they could handle. When they are making up their minds to move on, he says, they become erratic. "Everything will be going along fine on a job," he says. "Good working conditions. Plenty of overtime. A nice city. Then the news will come over the grapevine about some big new job opening up somewhere; it might be a thousand miles away. That kind of news always causes a lot of talk, what we call water-bucket talk, but the Indians don't talk; they know what's in each other's mind. For a couple of days, they're tensed up and edgy. They look a little wild in the eyes. They've heard the call. Then, all of a sudden, they turn in their tools, and they're gone. Can't wait another minute. They'll quit at lunchtime, in the middle of the week. They won't even wait for their pay. Some other gang will collect their money and hold it until a postcard comes back telling where to send it." George C. Lane, manager of erections in the New York district for the Bethlehem Steel Company, once said that the movements of a Caughnawaga gang are as impossible to foresee as the movements of a flock of sparrows. "In the summer of 1936," Mr. Lane said, "we finished a job here in the city and the very next day we were starting in on a job exactly three blocks away. I heard one of our foremen trying his best to persuade an Indian gang to go on the new job. They had got word about a job in Hartford and wanted to go up there. The foreman told them the rate of pay was the same; there wouldn't be any more overtime up there than here; their families were here; they'd have travelling expenses; they'd have to root around Hartford for lodgings. Oh, no; it was Hartford or nothing. A year or so later I ran into this gang on a job in Newark, and I asked the heater how they made out in Hartford that time. He said they didn't go to Hartford. 'We went to San Francisco, California,' he said. 'We went out and worked on the Golden Gate Bridge.'"

In New York City, the Caughnawagas work mostly for the big companies—Bethlehem, American Bridge, the Lehigh Structural Steel Company, and the Harris Structural Steel Company. Among the structures in and around the city on which they worked in numbers are the R.C.A. Building, the Cities Service Building, the Empire State Building, the Daily News Building, the Chanin Building, the Bank of the Manhattan Company Building, the City Bank Farmers Trust Building, the George Washington Bridge, the Bayonne Bridge, the Passaic River Bridge, the Triborough Bridge, the Henry Hudson Bridge, the Little Hell Gate Bridge, the Bronx-Whitestone Bridge, the Marine Parkway Bridge, the Pulaski Skyway, the West Side Highway, the Waldorf-Astoria, London Terrace, and Knickerbocker Village.

NORTH GOWANUS IS AN OLD, sleepy, shabby neighborhood that lies between the head of the Gowanus Canal and the Borough Hall shopping district. There are factories in it, and coal tipples and junk yards, but it is primarily residential, and red-brick tenements and brownstone apartment houses are most numerous. The Caughnawagas all live within ten blocks of each other, in an area bounded by Court Street on the west, Schermerhorn Street on the north, Fourth Avenue on the east, and Warren Street on the south. They live in the best houses on the best blocks. As a rule, Caughnawaga women are good housekeepers and keep their apartments Dutch-clean. Most of them decorate a mantel or a wall with heirlooms brought down from the reservation—a drum, a set of rattles, a mask, a cradleboard. Otherwise, their apartments look much the same as those of their white neighbors. A typical family group consists of husband and wife and a couple of children and a female relative or two. After they get through school on the reservation, many Caughnawaga girls come down to North Gowanus and work in factories. Some work for the Fred Goat Company, a metal-stamping factory in the neighborhood, and some work for the Gem Safety Razor Corporation, whose factory is within walking distance. Quite a few of these girls have married whites; several have broken all ties with the band and the reservation. In the last ten years, Caughnawaga girls have married Filipinos, Germans, Italians, Jews, Norwegians, and Puerto Ricans. Many North Gowanus families often have relatives visiting them for long periods; when there is a new baby in a family, a grandmother or an aunt almost always comes down from the reservation and helps out. Caughnawagas are allowed to cross the border freely. However, each is required to carry a card, to which a photograph is attached, certifying that he or she is a member of the band. These cards are issued by the Indian Affairs Branch; the Caughnawagas refer to them as "passports." More than half of the North Gowanus housewives spend their spare time making souvenirs. They make a lot of them. They specialize in dolls, hand-bags, and belts, which they ornament with colored beads, using variations of ancient Iroquois designs such as the sky dome, the night sun, the day sun, the fern head, the ever-growing tree, the world turtle, and the council fire. Every fall, a few of the most Indian-looking of the men take vacations from structural steel for a month or so and go out with automobile loads of these souvenirs and sell them on the midways of state, county, and community fairs in New York, Connecticut, New Jersey, and Pennsylvania. The men wear buckskins and feathers on these trips and sleep in canvas tepees pitched on fairgrounds. Occasionally, on midways, to attract atten-tion, they let out self-conscious wahoos and do fragments of the Duel Dance, the Dove Dance, the Falseface Dance, and other old half-forgotten Mohawk dances. The women obtain the raw materials for souvenirs from the Plume Trading & Sales Company, at 155 Lexington Avenue, in Manhattan, a concern that sells beads, deer-skin, imitation eagle feathers, and similar merchandise to Indian handicraftsmen all over the United States and Canada. There are approximately fifty children of school age in the colony. Two-thirds go to Public School 47, on Pacific Street, and the others go to parochial schools—St. Paul's, St. Agnes's, and St. Charles Borro-meo's. Caughnawaga children read comic books, listen to the radio while doing their homework, sit twice through double features, and play stick ball in vacant lots the same as the other children in the neighborhood; teachers say that they differ from the others mainly in that they are more reserved and polite. They have unusual manual dexterity; by the age of three, most of them are able to tie their shoelaces. The adult Caughnawagas are multilingual; all speak Mohawk, all speak English, and all speak or understand at least a little French. In homes where both parents are Caughnawagas, Mohawk is spoken almost exclusively, and the children pick it up. In homes where the mother is non-Indian and the father is away a good deal, a situation that is becoming more and more frequent, the children sometimes fail to learn the language, and this causes much sadness.

The Caughnawagas are churchgoers. The majority of the Catholics go to St. Paul's Church, at Court and Congress streets, and the majority of the Protestants go to Cuyler Presbyterian Church, on Pacific Street. Dr. David Munroe Cory, the pastor at Cuyler, is a man of incongruous interests. He is an amateur wrestler; he is vice-president of the Iceberg Athletic Club, a group that swims in the ocean at Coney Island throughout the winter; he once ran for Borough President of Brooklyn on the Socialist ticket; he is an authority on Faustus Socinus, the sixteenth-century Italian religious thinker; he studies languages for pleasure and knows eight, among them Hebrew, Greek, and Gaelic. A few Caughnawagas started turning up at Cuyler Church in the middle thirties, and Dr. Cory decided to learn Mohawk and see if he could attract more of them. He has not achieved fluency in Mohawk, but Caughnawagas say that he speaks it better than other white men, mostly anthropologists and priests, who have studied it. He holds a complete service in Mohawk the first Sunday evening in each month, after the English service, and twenty or thirty Caughnawagas usually attend. Twenty-five have joined the church. Michael Diabo, a retired riveter, was recently elected a deacon. Steven M. Schmidt, an Austrian-American who is married to Mrs. Josephine Skye Schmidt, a Caughnawaga woman, is an elder. Mr. Schmidt works in the compensation-claim department of an insurance company. Under Dr. Cory's guidance, two Caughnawaga women, Mrs. Schmidt and Mrs. Margaret La-hache, translated a group of hymns into Mohawk and compiled a hymnal, *The Caughnawaga Hymnal,* which is used in Cuyler and in the Protestant church on the reservation. Dr. Cory himself translated the Gospel According to Luke into Mohawk. Dr. Cory is quiet and serious, his sermons are free of cant, he has an intuitive understanding of Indian conversational taboos, and he is the only white person who is liked and trusted by the whole colony. Caughnawagas who are not members of his congregation, even some Catholics and longhouse people, go to him for advice.

OCCASIONALLY, IN A SALOON or at a wedding or a wake, Caughnawagas become vivacious and talkative. Ordinarily, however, they are rather dour and don't talk much. There is only one person in the North Gowanus colony who has a reputation for garrulity. He is a man of fifty-four whose white name is Orvis Diabo and whose Indian name is O-ron-ia-ke-te, or He Carries the Sky. Mr. Diabo is squat and barrel-chested. He has small, sharp eyes and a round, swarthy, double-chinned, piratical face. Unlike most other Caughnawagas, he does not deny or even minimize his white blood. "My mother was half Scotch and half Indian," he says. "My grandmother on my father's side was Scotch-Irish. Somewhere along the line, I forget just where, some French immigrant and some full Irish crept in. If you were to take my blood and strain it, God only knows what you'd find." He was born a Catholic; in young manhood, he became a Presbyterian; he now thinks of himself as "a kind of a free-thinker." Mr. Diabo started working in riveting gangs when he was nineteen and quit a year and a half ago. He had to quit because of crippling attacks of arthritis. He was a heater and worked on bridges and buildings in seventeen states. "I heated a million rivets," he says. "When they talk about the men that built this country, one of the men they mean is me." Mr. Diabo owns a house and thirty-three acres of farmland on the reservation. He inherited the farmland and rents it to a French Canadian. Soon after he quit work, his wife, who had lived in North Gowanus off and on for almost twenty years but had never liked it, went back to the reservation. She tried to get him to go along, but he decided to stay on awhile and rented a room in the apartment of a cousin. "I enjoy New York," he says. "The people are as high-strung as rats and the air is too gritty, but I enjoy it." Mr. Diabo reads a lot. Some years ago, in a Western magazine, he came across an advertisement of the Haldeman-Julius Company, a mail-order publishing house in Girard, Kansas, that puts out over eighteen hundred paperbound books, most of them dealing with religion, health, sex, history, or popular science. They are called Little Blue Books and cost a dime apiece. "I sent away for a dollar's worth of Little Blue Books," Mr. Diabo says, "and they opened my eyes to what an ignorant man I was. Ignorant and superstitious. Didn't know beans from back up. Since then, I've become a great reader. I've read dozens upon dozens of Little Blue Books, and I've improved my mind to the extent that I'm far beyond most of the people I associate with. When you come right down to it, I'm an educated man." Mr. Diabo has five favorite Little Blue Books—*Absurdities of the Bible,* by Clarence Darrow; *Seven Infidel U.S. Presidents,* by Joseph McCabe; *Queer Facts about Lost Civilizations,* by Charles J. Finger; *Why I Do Not Fear Death,* by E. Haldeman-Julius; and *Is Our Civilization Over-Sexed?,* by Theodore Dreiser. He carries them around in his pockets and reads them over and over. Mr. Diabo stays in bed until noon. Then, using a cane, he hobbles over to a neighborhood saloon, the Nevins Bar & Grill, at 75 Nevins Street, and sits in a booth. If there is someone around who will sit still and listen, he talks. If not, he reads a Little Blue Book. The Nevins is the social center of the Caughnawaga colony. The men in the gangs that work in the city customarily stop there for an hour or so on the way home. On weekend nights, they go there with their wives and drink Montreal ale and look at the television. When gangs come in from out-of-town jobs, they go on sprees there. When a Caughnawaga high-steel man is killed on the job, a collection is taken up in the Nevins for the immediate expenses of his family; these collections rarely run less than two hundred dollars; pasted on the bar mirror are several notes of thanks from widows. The Nevins is small and snug and plain and old. It is one of the oldest saloons in Brooklyn. It was opened in 1888, when North Gowanus was an Irishtown, and it was originally called Connelly's Abbey. Irish customers still call it the Abbey. Its present owners are Artie Rose and Bunny Davis. Davis is married to a Caughnawaga girl, the former Mavis Rice.

One afternoon a while back, I sat down with Mr. Diabo in his booth in the Nevins. He almost always drinks ale. This day he was drinking gin.

"I feel very low in my mind," he said. "I've got to go back to the reservation. I've run out of excuses and I can't put it off much longer. I got a letter from my wife today and she's disgusted with me. 'I'm sick and tired of begging you to come home,' she said. 'You can sit in Brooklyn until your tail takes root.' The trouble is, I don't want to go. That is, I do and I don't. I'll try to explain what I mean. An Indian high-steel man, when he first leaves the reservation to work in the States, the homesickness just about kills him. The first few years, he goes back as often as he can. Every time he finishes a job, unless he's thousands of miles away, he goes back. If he's working in New York, he drives up weekends, and it's a twelve-hour drive. After a while, he gets married and brings his wife down and starts a family, and he doesn't go back so often. Oh, he most likely takes the wife and children up for the summer, but he doesn't stay with them. After three or four days, the reservation gets on his nerves and he highballs it back to the States. He gets used to the States. The years go by. He gets to be my age, maybe a little older, maybe a little younger, and one fine morning he comes to the conclusion he's a little too damned stiff in the joints to be walking a naked beam five hundred feet up in the air. Either that, or some foreman notices he hasn't got a sure step any longer and takes him aside and tells him a few home truths. He gives up high-steel work and he packs his belongings and he takes his money out of the bank or the postal savings, what little he's been able to squirrel away, and he goes on back to the reservation for good. And it's hard on him. He's used to danger, and reservation life is very slow; the biggest thing that ever happens is a funeral. He's used to jumping around from job to job, and reservation life boxes him in. He's used to having a drink, and it's against the law to traffic in liquor on the reservation; he has to buy a bottle in some French-Canadian town across the river and smuggle it in like a high-school boy, and that annoys the hell out of him.

"There's not much he can do to occupy the time. He can sit on the highway and watch the cars go by, or he can sit on the riverbank and fish for eels and watch the boats go by, or he can weed the garden, or he can go to church, or he can congregate in the grocery stores with the other old retired high-steel men and play cards and talk. That is, if he can stand it. You'd think those old men would talk about the cities they worked in, the sprees they went on, the girls that follow construction all over the country that they knew, the skyscrapers and bridges they put up—only they don't. After they been sitting around the reservation five years, six years, seven years, they seem to turn against their high-steel days. Some of them, they get to be as Indian as all hell; they won't even speak English any more; they make out they can't understand it. And some of them, they get to be soreheads, the kind of old men that can chew nails and spit rust. When they do talk, they talk gloomy. They like to talk about family fights. There's families on the reservation that got on the outs with each other generations ago and they're still on the outs; maybe it started with a land dispute, maybe it started with a mixed-marriage dispute, maybe it started when some woman accused another woman of meeting her husband in the bushes in the graveyard. Even down here in Brooklyn, there's certain Indians that won't work in gangs with certain other Indians because of bad blood between their families; their wives, when they meet on Atlantic Avenue, they look right through each other. The old men like to bring up such matters and refresh their recollections on some of the details. Also, they like to talk about religion. A miraculous cure they heard about, something the priest said—they'll harp on it for weeks. They're all amateur priests, or preachers. They've all got some religious notion lurking around in their minds.

"And they like to talk about reservation matters. The last time I was home, I sat down with the bunch in a store and I tried to tell them about something I'd been studying up on that interested me very much—Mongolian spots. They're dark-purple spots that occur on the skin on the backs of Japanese and other Mongolians. Every now and then, a full-blood American Indian is born with them. The old men didn't want to hear about Mongolian spots. They were too busy discussing the matter of street names for Caughnawaga village. The electric-light company that supplies the village had been trying and trying to get the Indians to name the streets and lanes. The meter-readers are always getting balled up, and the company had offered to put up street signs and house numbers free of charge. The old men didn't want street names; they were raising holy hell about it. It wouldn't be Indian. And they were discussing the pros and cons of a waterworks system. They're eternally discussing that. Some want a waterworks, but the majority don't. The majority of them, they'd a whole lot rather get behind a poor old horse that his next step might be his last and cart their water up from the river by the barrel. It's more Indian. Sometimes, the way an Indian reasons, there's no rhyme or reason to it. Electric lights are all right and the biggest second-hand car they can find, and radios that the only time they turn them off is when they're changing the tubes, and seventy-five-dollar baby carriages, and four-hundred-dollar coffins, but street names and tap water—oh, Jesus, no! That's going entirely too damned far.

"On the other hand, there's things I look forward to. I look forward to eating real Indian grub again. Such as *o-nen-sto,* or corn soup. That's the Mohawk national dish. Some of the women make it down here in Brooklyn, but they use Quaker corn meal. The good old women up on the reservation, they make it the hard way, the way the Mohawks were making it five hundred years ago. They shell some corn, and they put it in a pot with a handful of maple ashes and boil it. The lye in the ashes skins the hulls off the kernels, and the kernels swell up into big fat pearls. Then they wash off the lye. Then they put in some red kidney beans. Then they put in a pig's head; in the old days, it was a bear's head. Then they cook it until it's as thick as mud. And when it's cooking, it smells so good. If you were breathing your last, if you had the rattle in your throat, and the wind blew you a faint suggestion of a smell of it, you'd rise and walk. And I look forward to eating some Indian bread that's made with the same kind of corn. Down here, the women always use Quaker meal. Indian bread is boiled, and it's shaped like a hamburger, and it's got kidney beans sprinkled through it. On the reservation, according to an old-time custom, we have steak for breakfast every Sunday morning, whether we can afford it or not, and we pour the steak gravy on the Indian bread.

"And another thing I look forward to, if I can manage it—I want to attend a longhouse festival. If I have to join to do so, I'll join. One night, the last time I was home, the longhousers were having a festival. I decided I'd go up to the Catholic graveyard that's right below the longhouse and hide in the bushes and listen to the music. So I snuck up there and waded through the thistles and the twitch grass and the Queen Anne's lace, and I sat down on a flat stone on the grave of an uncle of mine, Miles Diabo, who was a warwhooper with the Miller Brothers 101 Ranch Wild West Show and died with the pneumonia in Wheeling, West Virginia, in 1916. Uncle Miles was one of the last of the Caughnawaga circus Indians. My mother is in that graveyard, and my father, old Nazareth Diabo that I hardly even knew. They called him Nazzry. He was a pioneer high-steel Indian. He was away from home the majority of the time, and he was killed in the disaster—when the Quebec Bridge went down. There's hundreds of high-steel men buried in there. The ones that were killed on the job, they don't have stones; their graves are marked with lengths of steel girders made into crosses. There's a forest of girder crosses in there. So I was sitting on Uncle Miles's stone, thinking of the way things go in life, and suddenly the people in the longhouse began to sing and dance and drum on their drums. They were singing Mohawk chants that came down from the old, old red-Indian times. I could hear men's voices and women's voices and children's voices. The Mohawk language, when it's sung, it's beautiful to hear. Oh, it takes your breath away. A feeling ran through me that made me tremble; I had to take a deep breath to quiet my heart, it was beating so fast. I felt very sad; at the same time, I felt very peaceful. I thought I was all alone in the graveyard, and then who loomed up out of the dark and sat down beside me but an old high-steel man I had been talking with in a store that afternoon, one of the soreheads, an old man that fights every improvement that's suggested on the reservation, whatever it is, on the grounds it isn't Indian—this isn't Indian, that isn't Indian. So he said to me, 'You're not alone up here. Look over there.' I looked where he pointed, and I saw a white shirt in among the bushes. And he said, 'Look over there,' and I saw a cigarette gleaming in the dark. 'The bushes are full of Catholics and Protestants,' he said.

'Every night there's a longhouse festival, they creep up here and listen to the singing. It draws them like flies.' So I said, 'The longhouse music is beautiful to hear, isn't it?' And he remarked it ought to be, it was the old Indian music. So I said the longhouse religion appealed to me. 'One of these days,' I said, 'I might possibly join.' I asked him how he felt about it. He said he was a Catholic and it was out of the question. 'If I was to join the longhouse,' he said, 'I'd be excommunicated, and I couldn't be buried in holy ground, and I'd burn in Hell.' I said to him, 'Hell isn't Indian.' It was the wrong thing to say. He didn't reply to me. He sat there awhile—I guess he was thinking it over—and then he got up and walked away."

(1949)

All You Can Hold for Five Bucks

*T*HE NEW YORK STEAK DINNER, or "beefsteak," is a form of gluttony as stylized and regional as the riverbank fish fry, the hot-rock clambake, or the Texas barbecue. Some old chefs believe it had its origin sixty or seventy years ago, when butchers from the slaughterhouses on the East River would sneak choice loin cuts into the kitchens of nearby saloons, grill them over charcoal, and feast on them during their Saturday-night sprees. In any case, the institution was essentially masculine until 1920, when it was debased by the Eighteenth and Nineteenth Amendments to the Constitution of the United States. The Eighteenth Amendment brought about mixed drinking; a year and a half after it went into effect, the salutation "We Greet Our Better Halves" began to appear on the souvenir menus of beefsteaks thrown by bowling, fishing, and chowder clubs and lodges and labor unions. The big, exuberant beefsteaks thrown by Tammany and Republican district clubs always had been strictly stag, but not long after the Nineteenth Amendment gave women the suffrage, politicians decided it would be nice to invite females over voting age to clubhouse beefsteaks. "Womenfolks didn't know what a beefsteak was until they got the right to vote," an old chef once said.

It didn't take women long to corrupt the beefsteak. They forced the addition of such things as Manhattan cocktails, fruit cups, and fancy salads to the traditional menu of slices of ripened steaks, double lamb chops, kidneys, and beer by the pitcher. They insisted on dance orchestras instead of brassy German bands. The life of the party at a beefsteak used to be the man who let out the most ecstatic grunts, drank the most beer, ate the most steak, and got the most grease on his ears, but women do not esteem a glutton, and at a contemporary beefsteak it is unusual for a man to do away with more than six pounds of meat and thirty glasses of beer. Until around 1920, beefsteak etiquette was rigid. Knives, forks, napkins, and tablecloths never had been permitted; a man was supposed to eat with his hands. When beefsteaks became bisexual, the etiquette changed. For generations men had worn their second-best suits because of the inevitability of grease spots; tuxedos and women appeared simultaneously. Most beefsteaks degenerated into polite banquets at which open-face sandwiches of grilled steak happened to be the principal dish. However, despite the frills introduced by women, two schools of traditional steak-dinner devotees still flourish. They may conveniently be called the East Side and West Side schools. They disagree over matters of menu and etiquette, and both claim that their beefsteaks are the more classical or old-fashioned.

The headquarters of the East Side school is the meat market of William Wertheimer & Son, at First Avenue and Nineteenth Street. It is situated in a tenement neighborhood, but that is misleading; scores of epicures regularly order steaks, chops, and capons from Wertheimer's. The moving spirit of the East Side school is Sidney Wertheimer, the "Son" of the firm. A dozen old, slow-moving, temperamental Germans, each of whom customarily carries his own collection of knives in an oilcloth kit, are the chefs. Mr. Wertheimer is not a chef. He selects, cuts, and sells the meat used at the majority of the old-fashioned beefsteaks thrown in East Side halls, like the Central Opera House, the Grand Street Boys' clubhouse, the Manhattan Odd Fellows' Hall, and Webster Hall. The caterers for these halls get an unusual amount of service when they order meat from Mr. Wertheimer. If the caterer wishes, Mr. Wertheimer will engage a couple of the old Germans to go to the hall and broil the meat. He will also engage a crew of experienced beefsteak waiters. He owns a collection of beefsteak-cooking utensils and does not mind lending it out. The chefs and waiters telephone or stop in at Wertheimer's about once a week and are given assignments. Most of them work in breakfast and luncheon places in the financial district, taking on beefsteaks at night as a sideline. For engaging them, Mr. Wertheimer collects no fee; he just does it to be obliging. In addition, for no charge, he will go to the hall and supervise the kitchen. He is extremely proud of the meat he cuts and likes to make sure it is cooked properly. He succeeded old "Beefsteak Tom" McGowan as the East Side's most important beefsteak functionary. Mr. McGowan was a foreman in the Department of Water Supply who arranged beefsteaks as a hobby. He was an obscure person, but in 1924 his hearse was followed by more than a thousand sorrowful members of Tammany clubs.

Mr. Wertheimer had almost finished cutting the meat for a beefsteak the last time I went to see him. Approximately three hundred and fifty men and women were expected that night, and he had carved steaks off thirty-five steer shells and had cut up four hundred and fifty double-rib lamb chops. In his icebox, four hundred and fifty lamb kidneys were soaking in a wooden tub. The steaks and chops were piled up in baskets, ready to be delivered to the uptown hall in which the beefsteak was to be thrown. (Technically, a beefsteak is never "given" or "held"; it is "thrown" or "run.") Mr. Wertheimer, a pink-cheeked, well-nourished man, looked proudly at the abundantly loaded baskets and said, "The foundation of a good beefsteak is an overflowing amount of meat and beer. The tickets usually cost five bucks, and the rule is 'All you can hold for five bucks.' If you're able to hold a little more when you start home, you haven't been to a beefsteak, you've been to a banquet that they called a beefsteak."

Classical beefsteak meat is carved off the shell, a section of the hindquarter of a steer; it is called "short loin without the fillet." To order a cut of it, a housewife would ask for a thick Delmonico. "You don't always get it at a beefsteak," Mr. Wertheimer said. "Sometimes they give you bull fillets. They're no good. Not enough juice in them, and they cook out black." While I watched, Mr. Wertheimer took a shell off a hook in his icebox and laid it on a big, maple block. It had been hung for eight weeks and was blanketed with blue mold. The mold was an inch thick. He cut off the mold.

Then he boned the shell and cut it into six chunks. Then he sliced off all the fat. Little strips of lean ran through the discarded fat, and he deftly carved them out and made a mound of them on the block. "These trimmings, along with the tails of the steaks, will be ground up and served as appetizers," he said. "We'll use four hundred tonight. People call them hamburgers, and that's an insult. Sometimes they're laid on top of a slice of Bermuda onion and served on bread." When he finished with the shell, six huge steaks, boneless and fatless, averaging three inches thick and ten inches long, lay on the block. They made a beautiful still life. "After they've been broiled, the steaks are sliced up, and each steak makes about ten slices," he said. "The slices are what you get at a beefsteak." Mr. Wertheimer said the baskets of meat he had prepared would be used that night at a beefsteak in the Odd Fellows' Hall on East 106th Street; the Republican Club of the Twentieth Assembly District was running it. He invited me to go along.

"How's your appetite?" he asked.

I said there was nothing wrong with it.

"I hope not," he said. "When you go to a beefsteak, you got to figure on eating until it comes out of your ears. Otherwise it would be bad manners."

That night I rode up to Odd Fellows' Hall with Mr. Wertheimer, and on the way I asked him to describe a pre-prohibition stag beefsteak.

"Oh, they were amazing functions," he said. "The men wore butcher aprons and chef hats. They used the skirt of the apron to wipe the grease off their faces. Napkins were not allowed. The name of the organization that was running the beefsteak would be printed across the bib, and the men took the aprons home for souvenirs. We still wear aprons, but now they're rented from linen-supply houses. They're numbered, and you turn them in at the hat-check table when you get your hat and coat. Drunks, of course, always refuse to turn theirs in.

"In the old days they didn't even use tables and chairs. They sat on beer crates and ate off the tops of beer barrels. You'd be surprised how much fun that was. Somehow it made old men feel young again. And they'd drink beer out of cans, or growlers. Those beef-steaks were run in halls or the cellars or back rooms of big saloons. There was always sawdust on the floor. Sometimes they had one in a bowling alley. They would cover the alleys with tarpaulin and set the boxes and barrels in the aisles. The men ate with their fingers. They never served potatoes in those days. Too filling. They take up room that rightfully belongs to meat and beer. A lot of those beefsteaks were testimonials. A politician would get elected to some-thing and his friends would throw him a beefsteak. Cops ran a lot of them, too. Like when a cop became captain or inspector, he got a beefsteak. Theatrical people were always fond of throwing beef-steaks. Sophie Tucker got a great big one at Mecca Temple in 1934, and Bill Robinson got a great big one at the Grand Street Boys' clubhouse in 1938. Both of those were knockouts. The political clubs always gave the finest, but when Tammany Hall gets a setback, beefsteaks get a setback. For example, the Anawanda Club, over in my neighborhood, used to give a famous beefsteak every Thanks-giving Eve. Since La Guardia got in the Anawanda's beefsteaks have been so skimpy it makes me sad.

"At the old beefsteaks they almost always had storytellers, men who would entertain with stories in Irish and German dialect. And when the people got tired of eating and drinking, they would harmonize. You could hear them harmonizing blocks away. They would harmonize 'My Wild Irish Rose' until they got their appetite back. It was the custom to hold beefsteaks on Saturday nights or the eve of holidays, so the men would have time to recover before going to work. They used to give some fine ones in Coney Island restaurants. Webster Hall has always been a good place. Local 638 of the Steamfitters holds its beefsteaks there. They're good ones. A lot of private beefsteaks are thrown in homes. A man will invite some friends to his cellar and cook the steaks himself. I have a number of good amateur beefsteak chefs among my customers. Once, during the racing season, a big bookmaker telephoned us he wanted to throw a beefsteak, so we sent a chef and all the makings to Saratoga. The chef had a wonderful time. They made a hero out of him."

When we reached the hall, we went directly to the kitchen. Two of Mr. Wertheimer's chefs were working at a row of tremendous gas ranges. One had a pipe in his mouth; the other was smoking a cigar. There was a pitcher of beer on a nearby table and at intervals the chefs would back away from the ranges and have some beer. They were cooking the four hundred high-class hamburgers. The air was heavy with the fragrance of the meat. The steaks, chops, and kidneys were racked up, ready for the broilers. A strip of bacon had been pinned to each kidney with a toothpick. I asked a chef how many minutes the steaks were kept on the fire. "It's all according," he said. "Twelve on one side, ten on the other is about the average. Before they go in, we roll them in salt which has been mixed with pepper. The salt creates a crust that holds the juice in." In a corner, waiters were stacking up cardboard platters on each of which a dozen half-slices of trimmed bread had been placed. "This is day-old bread," one of them said. "The steak slices are laid on it just before we take them out to the tables. Day-old bread is neutral. When you lay steak on toast, you taste the toast as much as the steak."

In a little while I went out to the ballroom. The Republicans were arriving. Most of them were substantial, middle-aged people. They all seemed to know each other. At the hat-check booth, everybody, men and women, put on cloth butcher's aprons and paper chef's hats. This made them look a lot like members of the Ku Klux Klan. The hats had mottoes on them, such as "It's Hell When Your Wife Is a Widow" and "Prohibition Was Good for Some. Others It Put on the Bum." Before sitting down, most couples went from table to table, shaking hands and gossiping. After shaking hands, they would say, "Let's see what it says on your hat." After they read the mottoes on each other's hats, they would laugh heartily. On each table there were plates of celery and radishes, beer glasses, salt shakers, and some balloons and noisemakers. Later, a spavined old waiter told me that liquor companies send balloons and noisemakers to many beefsteaks as an advertisement. "In the old days they didn't need noisemakers," he said contemptuously. "If a man wanted some noise, he would just open his trap and howl."

While couples were still moving from table to table, a banquet photographer got up on the bandstand and asked everybody to keep still. I went over and watched him work. When he was through we talked for a while, and he said, "In an hour or so I'll bring back a sample photograph and take orders. At a beefsteak I usually take the picture at the start of the party. If I took it later on, when they get full of beer, the picture would show a lot of people with goggle eyes and their mouths gapped open."

As the photographer was lugging his equipment out, waiters streamed into the ballroom with pitchers of beer. When they caught sight of the sloshing beer, the people took seats. I joined Mr. Wertheimer, who was standing at the kitchen door surveying the scene. As soon as there was a pitcher of beer in the middle of every table, the waiters brought in platters of hamburgers. A moment later, a stout, frowning woman walked up to Mr. Wertheimer and said, "Say, listen. Who the hell ever heard of hamburgers at a beefsteak?" Mr. Wertheimer smiled. "Just be patient, lady," he said. "In a minute you'll get all the steak you can hold." "O.K.," she said, "but what about the ketchup? There's no ketchup at our table." Mr. Wertheimer said he would tell a waiter to get some. When she left, he said, "Ketchup! I bet she'd put ketchup on chocolate cake." After they had finished with their hamburgers some of the diners began inflating and exploding balloons.

I heard one of the chefs back in the kitchen yell out "Steaks ready to go!" and I went inside. One chef was slicing the big steaks with a knife that resembled a cavalry sabre and the other was dipping the slices into a pan of rich, hot sauce. "That's the best beefsteak sauce in the world," Mr. Wertheimer said. "It's melted butter, juice and drippings from the steak, and a little Worcestershire." The waiters lined up beside the slicing table. Each waiter had a couple of the cardboard platters on which bread had been arranged. As he went by the table, he held out the platters and the chef dropped a slice of the rare, dripping steak on each piece of bread. Then the waiter hurried off.

I went to the kitchen door and looked out. A waiter would go to a table and lay a loaded platter in the middle of it. Hands would reach out and the platter would be emptied. A few minutes later another platter would arrive and eager, greasy hands would reach out again. At beefsteaks, waiters are required to keep on bringing platters until every gullet is satisfied; on some beefsteak menus there is a notice: "2nd, 3rd, 4th, etc., portions permitted and invited." Every three trips or so the waiter would bring a pitcher of beer. And every time they finished a platter, the people would rub their hands on their aprons. Sometimes a man would pour a little beer in one palm and rub his hands together briskly. At a table near the kitchen door I heard a woman say to another, "Here, don't be bashful. Have a steak." "I just et six," her friend replied. The first woman said, "Wasn't you hungry? Why, you eat like a bird." Then they threw their heads back and laughed. It was pleasant to watch the happy, unrestrained beefsteak-eaters. While the platters kept coming they did little talking except to urge each other to eat more.

"Geez," said a man. "These steaks are like peanuts. Eat one, and you can't stop. Have another." Presently the waiters began to tote out platters of thick lamb chops.

Then a man stepped up to the microphone and introduced a number of politicians. Each time he said, "I'm about to introduce a man that is known and loved by each and every one of you," a beaming politician would stand and bow and the constituents would bang the tables with their noisemakers. There were no speeches. A politician would have to be extraordinarily courageous to make a speech at a beefsteak. When all the Republican statesmen of the Twentieth A.D. had been introduced, a band went into action and two singers stepped out on the dance floor and began singing numbers from "Show Boat." By the time they got to "Ol' Man River," the four hundred and fifty double lamb chops were gone and the waiters were bringing out the kidneys. "I'm so full I'm about to pop," a man said. "Push those kidneys a little nearer, if you don't mind." Then the lights were dimmed. Here and there a couple got up, grunting, and went out on the dance floor. The band played waltzes. Done by aproned, middle-aged people, ponderous with beefsteak and beer, the waltz is an appalling spectacle. The waiters continued to bring out kidneys and steak to many tables. There was no dessert and no coffee. Such things are not orthodox. "Black coffee is sometimes served to straighten people out," Mr. Wertheimer said, "but I don't believe in it."

When the Republicans began dancing in earnest, the activity in the kitchen slackened, and some of the waiters gathered around the slicing table and commenced eating. While they ate, they talked shop. "You know," said one, "a fat woman don't eat so much. It's those little skinny things; you wonder where they put it." Another said, "It's the Cat'lics who can eat. I was to a beefsteak in Brooklyn last Thursday night. All good Cat'lics. So it got to be eleven-fifty, and they stopped the clock. Cat'lics can't eat meat on Friday." The two weary chefs sat down together at the other side of the room from the waiters and had a breathing spell. They had not finished a glass of beer apiece, however, before a waiter hurried in and said, "My table wants some more steak," and the chefs had to get up and put their weight on their feet again. Just before I left, at midnight, I took a last look at the ballroom. The dance floor was packed and clouds of cigar smoke floated above the paper hats of the dancers, but at nine tables people were still stowing away meat and beer. On the stairs to the balcony, five men were harmonizing. Their faces were shiny with grease. One held a pitcher of beer in his hands and occasionally he would drink from it, spilling as much as he drank. The song was, of course, "Sweet Adeline."

The West Side school of beefsteak devotees frequents the Terminal Hotel, a for-gentlemen-only establishment at Eleventh Avenue and Twenty-third Street. Its chef is Bob Ellis, an aged, truculent Negro, whose opinion of all other beefsteak chefs is low. Of them he says, "What they call a beefsteak ain't no beefsteak; it's just a goddamn mess." Mr. Ellis is also a talented clambake and green-turtle chef and used to make trips as far west as Chicago to supervise one meal. His most unusual accomplishment, however, is the ability to speak Japanese. He once worked on freighters that went to the Orient, and he sometimes reminds people who hang out around the belly-shaped Terminal bar that he has a wonderful command of the Japanese language. When someone is skeptical and says, "Well, let's hear some," he always says haughtily, "What in hell would be the use of talking Jap to you? You wouldn't comprehend a word I was saying."

Among the groups of rough-and-ready gourmands for whom Mr. Ellis is official chef are the I.D.K. ("I Don't Know") Bowling Club, a hoary outfit from Chelsea, and the Old Hoboken Turtle Club. This club was founded in 1796, and Alexander Hamilton and Aaron Burr were charter members; now it is an exclusive association of West Side and Jersey butchers, brewers, saloonkeepers, boss steve-dores, and businessmen. Most of the members are elderly. Mr. Ellis has cooked for them since 1879. In 1929 they gave him a badge with a green turtle and a diamond on it and made him a Brother Turtle. The Turtles and the I.D.K.'s and many similar West Side organizations always hold their beefsteaks in the Terminal cellar, which is called the Hollings Beefsteak Keller after John Hollings, a former owner of the hotel, who sold out in disgust and moved to Weehawken when prohibition was voted in. He used to store his coal in the cellar. Mr. Ellis refuses to call it a *Keller*; he calls it "my dungeon."

"In the old days all steak cellars were called dungeons," he told me. "To me they're still dungeons."

The dungeon has a steel door on which is printed the initials "O.I.C.U.R.M.T." That is a good sample of beefsteak humor. Also on the door is a sign: "WHEN YOU ENTER THIS KELLER YOU FIND A GOOD FELLER." The dungeon has a cement floor, over which sawdust has been scattered. The ceiling is low. On the trellised walls are yellowed beefsteak photographs ranging from an 1898 view of the M. E. Blankmeyer Clam Bake Club to a picture of a beefsteak thrown in 1932 by the New York Post Office Holy Name Society. Over the light switch is a warning: "HANDS OFF THE THIRD RAIL." In one corner is a piano and a platform for a German band. The dungeon will hold a hundred and twenty-five persons. "When a hundred and twenty-five big, heavy men get full of beer, it does seem a little crowded in here," Mr. Ellis said. Beer crates and barrels were once used, but now people sit on slat-backed chairs and eat off small, individual tables. Down a subterranean hall from the dungeon is the ancient brick oven, over which Mr. Ellis presides with great dignity.

"I'm not one of these hit-or-miss beefsteak chefs," he said. "I grill my steaks on hickory embers. The efflorescence of seasoned hardwood is in the steak when you eat it. My beefsteaks are genuine old-fashioned. I'll give you the official lineup. First we lay out celery, radishes, olives, and scallions. Then we lay out crabmeat cocktails. Some people say that's not old-fashioned. I'm getting close to ninety years old, and I ought to know what's old-fashioned. Then we lay out some skewered kidney shells. Lamb or pig—what's the difference?

"Then comes the resistance—cuts of seasoned loin of beef on hot toast with butter gravy. Sure, I use toast. None of this day-old-bread stuff for me. I know what I'm doing. Then we lay out some baked Idahoes. I let them have paper forks for the crabmeat and the Idahoes; everything else should be attended to with fingers. A man who don't like to eat with his fingers hasn't got any business at a beefsteak. Then we lay out the broiled duplex lamb chops. All during the beefsteak we are laying out pitchers of refreshment. By that I mean beer."

Old Mr. Ellis lives in the Bronx. He spends most of his time at home in a rocking chair with his shoes off, reading the Bible or a weekly trade paper called "The Butcher's Advocate." Whenever Herman Von Twistern, the proprietor of the Terminal, books a beefsteak, he gets Mr. Ellis on the telephone and gives him the date. Usually he also telephones Charles V. Havican, a portly ex–vaudeville actor, who calls himself "the Senator from Hoboken." He took the title during prohibition, when everything connected with Hoboken was considered funny. Mr. Havican is a celebrated beefsteak entertainer. Most often he sits down with the guests and impersonates a windy, drunken senator. He also tells dialect stories and gives recitations. In his repertoire are "The Kid's Last Fight," "Christmas Day in the Workhouse," "The Gambler's Wife," and "Please Don't Sell My Father Rum."

"If I am not previously known to people at a beefsteak, I sometimes impersonate a dumb waiter," Mr. Havican told me, listing his accomplishments. "I spill beer on people, bump into them, step on their feet, and hit them in the face with my elbows. All the time I look dumb. It is a very funny act to people with a keen sense of humor. Of course, some people just don't have a keen sense of humor."

"What do they think of your act?" I asked.

"Well, I tell you," said Mr. Havican, "look at this scar on my forehead. And I guess you noticed that I walk with a limp."

(1939)

A Mess of Clams

PRACTICALLY ALL THE LITTLENECK and cherrystone clams served on the half shell in New York restaurants come out of the black mud of the Long Island bays. They are the saltiest, cleanest, and biggest-bellied clams in the world. The most abundant beds are in Great South Bay and are owned by the towns of Islip and Babylon. Right after dawn every weekday about seventy licensed clammers from these towns go out on the Bay in a fleet of dilapidated sloops and catboats and spread out over the beds. They work over the sides of their anchored boats, using long-handled tongs and rakes; the clams are bedded in bottoms which lie under eight to ten feet of water. At noon the buy-boats of two clam-shipping firms—Still & Clock of Bay Shore, and G. Vander Borgh & Son of West Sayville—go out and anchor near the fleet, and from then until 4 P.M. the clammers bring their catches to the buy-boats in bushel bags and sell them over the rail for cash.

One muggy June day I made a trip to the South Bay beds with Captain Archie M. Clock, who commands the Still & Clock buy-boat. This boat is the *Jennie Tucker,* a battered, stripped-down, 38-foot sloop powered with a motor the Captain took out of an old Chrysler. Captain Clock and his partner, Louis Still, are members of families which have fished, oyster-farmed, and clammed on the South Shore since the middle of the eighteenth century. I arrived at their weather-beaten clam shed on Homan Avenue Creek in Bay Shore at ten in the morning and found Captain Clock on the narrow wharf at the rear. He was sitting on an overturned clam bucket, smoking his pipe. A man I know who runs a wholesale shellfish business in Fulton Fish Market had written me a note of introduction to the Captain, and I handed it to him. He read it, grunted, and said, "You picked a good day to see the beds. We're going out a little early." He motioned toward a bucket with the stem of his pipe. "Have a seat and make yourself at home," he said. "Do you care much for clams?"

I sat down on the bucket and told him that one Sunday afternoon in August, 1937, I placed third in a clam-eating tournament at a Block Island clambake, eating eighty-four cherries. I told him that I regard this as one of the few worth-while achievements of my life.

"Well, you can eat yourself a bellyful today," he said. "I feel like having a few myself. They tell me brewers sometimes get so they hate beer, and sometimes I get so I can't stand the sight of a clam, but I'm real hungry this morning."

The *Jennie Tucker* was lying alongside the wharf, and the mate, a muscular young man named Charlie Bollinger, was sloshing down her decks with buckets of water. "Give her plenty of water, Charlie," the Captain told him. He turned to me and said, "You have to be extra clean when you're handling clams. Let a few dead clams lie around and you'll breed up a smell that'll make a strong man weak, a smell that'll knock your hat off, unravel the knot in your necktie, and tear holes in your shirt." He stood up, yawned, spat, and went into a little office in the shed. When he returned he carried an armful of gear which included a lunch bucket, a tattered old ledger, and a green metal box. Later I learned that this box contained the cash with which he would buy the day's load.

"Everything O.K., Charlie?" he asked.

"She's clean as a whistle, Archie," said the mate.

"Let's get going then," he said. We went aboard and the Captain stowed his gear in the sloop's tiny cabin. The Captain was stocky, slow-moving, and sleepy-eyed. He was deeply tanned, but he had smeared some white salve on his nose and ears to guard against sunburn. He was roughly dressed; he wore patched pants, a blue work shirt, and a long-visored swordfisherman's cap. He took the tiller, which he handled expertly, until we were well out in the Bay. Then he turned it over to Bollinger, got his ledger, and sat down beside me on the hatch. "The beds they're clamming lie about four miles down the Bay," he said, motioning with his head in the direction of Babylon. He opened the ledger and got a new page ready, writing down the names of the clammers. The wind from the ocean ruffled the pages as he worked. Most of the names he wrote down were old Long Island ones like Doxsee, Ricketts, Baldwin, Crowell, and Tooker.

"Most of the clammers come from families that have been around this bay so many generations they long since lost track," he said. "The bulk of them are of English descent or Holland Dutch, and there's quite a few squareheads. They know the bottom of the Bay like they know their wife's face. Clamming is back-breaking, but a man can get a living if his muscle holds out. I looked through this ledger last night and figured I paid one clammer eighty-some-odd dollars last week, but that's unusual. Most of them average between five and ten bucks a day. It's all according to how good a man can handle the tongs."

He laid his ledger on the hatch, stretched his arms, and yawned. The morning had been cloudy, but the sun came out soon after we left the wharf and now it was burning off the haze on the Bay. After it had been shining fifteen minutes, we could see the striped Fire Island lighthouse and the long, glistening dunes on Oak and Captree islands. I asked the Captain if any bayman can go out to the beds and clam.

"He cannot," the Captain said. "He has to get a Conservation Department license that costs two and a half, and he has to be a resident of the town that owns the beds he works. A Babylon man can't clam in Islip water, and vice versa. In fact, they're always fussing among themselves about the division line. That's a fuss that'll go on as long as there's a clam left in the mud."

"How much do you pay for a bushel?" I asked.

"The price is based on the size of the clam and the demand in Fulton Market," the Captain said. "Prices may fluctuate as much as a dollar in a single season, but right now I'm paying the boys two dollars a bushel for littlenecks and a dollar and a half for cherrystones. That's for the half-shell trade. For the big ones—what we call chowders—I pay a dollar a bushel.

"The bulk of the clams in South Bay are hard-shells—they're called quahogs in New England. There's a few soft-shells, or steamers, around the shores of the Bay, but we don't bother with them. Most of the steam clams you see in the city come from New England. The hard-shell is the king of the clams. He can be baked, fried, steamed, put into chowder, or served on the half shell. I *will* say that the best chowder is made with a mixture of softs and hards. Out here we believe in Manhattan-style chowder, a couple of tomatoes to every quart of shucked clams. Our chowder clams are around four years old, a couple of years older than littlenecks. We truck our necks and cherries to dealers in Fulton Market and to restaurants in Manhattan and Brooklyn, and we truck the chowders to the Campbell's soup factory in Camden, New Jersey. They take around fifteen hundred bushels of chowders off us every week." He turned to the mate. "I'll take her now, Charlie," he said.

Soon after Captain Clock took the tiller, we approached the fleet. The little boats were laying with the wind and the tide about two miles southeast of Babylon. Captain Clock said the majority of the boats were anchored near the imaginary line dividing the beds, and that some were hugging it. "Human nature," he said. "The boys from Islip just itch to work the Babylon water, and the Babylon boys think they could tong up twice as many if they could get over on the Islip territory." A few of the boats carried two clammers, one for each side, but one man to a boat seemed to be the rule. When we were about fifty yards from the nearest clammer, the Captain ducked into the cabin and cut off the motor. Bollinger hurried to the bow and threw out the anchor.

"Now I'll show you how to clam," said Captain Clock. "We'll tong up a few pecks for us to eat."

He rolled up his shirtsleeves and picked up a pair of tongs, an implement with two sets of teeth fixed to the ends of two fourteen-foot handles. He lowered the tongs into the water, which was nine feet deep, and pushed the opened teeth into the mud; then he brought the handles together scissors-fashion, closing the teeth. Just before hauling the tongs over the rail, he doused the closed teeth in the water several times, washing out the mud. He opened the teeth on the deck and out dropped a dazed spider crab, two bunches of scarlet oyster sponge, a handful of empty shells, and twelve beautiful clams. The shells of the clams were steel blue, the color of the Bay water.

"A good haul," he said. "I got four cherries, two necks, two chowders and four peanuts." He said that a state law forbids the sale of clams less than an inch thick and that such undersized clams are called peanuts. He tossed the peanuts and the crab back into the water. Then he put the tongs overboard again. He sent the teeth into the mud seven times and brought up forty-three clams. Then he laid aside the tongs and got two clam knives off a shelf in the cabin. He gave me one and we squatted on the deck and went to work opening the cherries. When the valves were pried apart, the rich clam liquor dribbled out. The flesh of the cherries was a delicate pink. On the cups of some of the shells were splotches of deep purple; Indians used to hack such splotches out of clamshells for wampum. Fresh from the coal black mud and uncontaminated by ketchup or sauce, they were the best clams I had ever eaten. The mate sat on the hatch and watched us.

"Aren't you going to have any?" I asked.

"I wouldn't put one of them goddamn things in my mouth if I was perishing to death," he said. "I'm working on this buy-boat ten years and I'm yet to eat a clam."

He scornfully watched us eat for a few moments; then he went into the cabin and came out with a portable radio, which he placed on the cabin roof, and tuned in on a news broadcast. While the Captain and I opened and ate clams we looked out at the fleet and watched the clammers. The Captain said that a clammer works both sides of his boat until the tongs start coming up empty; then he lets out slack in his anchor cable and drifts into unworked territory. "Most of them are patient," he said, "but some will be lifting and dropping their anchors all day long. When a man does that we say he's got the runs." The fleet was made up largely of catboats stripped of their rigs and powered with old automobile motors. The majority of the men were tonging, but here and there a man worked with a rake. The Captain said that rakes are used only on stretches of soft bottom. "The handle of a rake is twenty-two feet long," he said, "and it takes a Joe Louis to pull it." Some of the clammers were stripped to their belts, but most of them worked in their undershirts. Occasionally a man would lay aside his tongs or rake and squat in the bottom of the boat and bag up his clams. Captain Clock said it is customary for the clammers to sell their catches in the early-afternoon hours, so the shippers will have time to cull and barrel the clams for trucking in the evening.

The Captain and I were finishing the last of the forty-three clams when a whistle in Babylon blew for noon. "We better eat dinner, Archie," Bollinger said. "They'll start bringing their loads over pretty soon now." Intent on his last clam, the Captain nodded. Bollinger brought out their lunch buckets and a thermos jug of iced tea. I had bought a couple of sandwiches in Bay Shore and I got them out of my raincoat. Bollinger tuned in on a program of waltzes broadcast from a Manhattan hotel. We sat on peck baskets in the hot sun and ate and listened to the waltzes. We were drinking tea out of tin cups when the first of the clammers came alongside. Bollinger jumped up, tossed the clammer a rope, and helped him make fast to the *Jennie Tucker*. The clammer was a small, spry old man in hip boots.

"What you got?" Captain Clock asked him.

"Nothing to speak of," he said. "Just a mess of clams. I been scratch-raking off Grass Island. I got two bushels of cherries, a bushel of necks, and two bushels of chowders." Gripping the bags by their ears, he passed them to Bollinger. Captain Clock took a five and two ones out of his cashbox and handed them to the clammer, who carefully placed them in an old-fashioned snap purse. Then he picked up two conches from the bottom of his boat and tossed them to Bollinger.

"I was about to forget your konks," he said. He threw aside the ropes, pushed off, and started his engine.

"Be good," yelled Captain Clock.

"I'm getting so old," the clammer said, "I can't be anything else."

Bollinger deposited the conches in a rusty wire basket. "Konks are my racket," he said. "They get caught in the tongs and the boys save them for me instead of throwing them back. One of the truckdrivers takes them in and sells them to Italian clam stands in downtown New York and we divvy up. It's just cigarette money. The Italians boil the konks and make something called *scungili*."

We drank some more tea, and then another clammer, a gloomy-eyed, sunburned young man, pulled alongside. He was in a catboat that had been patched with tin in a dozen places.

"Hello, Tarzan," said Bollinger. "Didn't that old eelpot sink yet? How many clams you got?"

"I been croshaying the mud for six hours and I barely took enough to bait a hook," the young man said. "They was thin where I was tonging."

"Quit bellyaching," said Bollinger. "If it was to rain clams, you wouldn't be satisfied." The young man passed over a bushel of necks, two bushels of cherries, a scanty peck of chowders, and three conches. Captain Clock handed him five ones and twenty cents. He folded the bills into a wad and stuffed it in his watch pocket. "Another day, another dollar," he said. "My back feels like it was run over by a load of bricks." He cranked his engine and moved off, heading for Babylon. "He'll get drunk tonight," Captain Clock said. "I can tell by the way he was talking." The Captain bent over a bag of cherries. He scooped a double handful out of the mouth of the bag and spread them on the deck. "Beauties," he said. "Uniform as peas in a pod. The shells are blue now, but they'll turn gray or white before we get them to town." He opened a cherry and balanced it on his palm. He looked at it admiringly. "A spawner," he said. "Now, that's the beauty of a clam. He doesn't make a bit of fuss about spawning. An oyster's just the opposite. He spawns from May through August—the months without an 'r' in them— and he gets so milky you can't eat him on the half shell. You can fry him, but you can't eat him raw. A clam is better behaved. He never gets milky enough to notice and he's just as good in the midsummer months, when he's spawning, as he is on the coldest day of the winter."

Captain Clock said that once a year the town of Islip buys a couple of truckloads of hardshells from Massachusetts or New Jersey to scatter on its beds. "Foreign clams put new life in the natives," he said. "They improve the breed. The spawn mixes and we get a better set. Hey, Charlie, hand me a knife. I'm going to try some of these chowders." The Captain opened a dozen chowders and arranged them in a semicircle on the hatch. We were eating them when Bollinger suddenly shouted, "Here come the cops!" He pointed in the direction of Babylon, and I saw a launch flying a green flag. In a minute it cut the water just off our bow, heading for the fleet. The clammers stopped work and commenced yelling. "They're warning each other," Bollinger said. "That's the police boat from Babylon. The cops go through the beds every day or so. You never know when they'll show up. If they spy an Islip man in Babylon water, they give him a ticket and he has to go to court and get fined." The clammers leaned on their tong and rake handles while the police boat slowly picked its way through the fleet. It did not halt; evidently the clammers were behaving themselves.

Presently another clammer called it a day and came alongside. He was a gaunt, stooped man, who silently handed over four bushels of necks, three bushels of cherries, and a bushel and a peck of chowders. He collected thirteen dollars and seventy-five cents, bit a chew of tobacco off a plug he took from his hip pocket, mumbled "Good night, Cap," and pushed off. "He's one of the best clammers on Long Island," said Captain Clock. "I bet he's got ten thousand dollars in the bank, and he's so saving he gets his wife to cut his hair." The gaunt clammer's departure from the beds appeared to be a signal to the others. Soon after he left, they began moving toward the buy-boat in twos and threes. In twenty minutes the *Jennie Tucker* was surrounded by loaded boats, waiting their turns to come alongside. "They all have to come at once," Bollinger said indignantly. Captain Clock stood at the stern, hunched over his ledger, which he had placed on the cabin roof. Bollinger helped the clammers heft their bags over the rail. He piled the chowders aft, the cherries on the hatch, and the necks forward. When a boat finished unloading he would call out the number of bushels, and the Captain would make a notation in his ledger and then pay off the clammer.

To get out of Bollinger's way, I went to the bow and sat on a bale of empty bags. Standing in their boats, the waiting clammers smoked cigarettes and shouted insults at each other. I couldn't tell if the insults were good-natured or genuine. "If I was you, I'd take that old cement-mixer home and set fire to it," one yelled at his neighbor. "I wouldn't be caught dead in that dirty old boat." "Well, it's paid for," said the master of the cement-mixer, "and that's more'n you can say." "Paid for!" screamed the first man. "You mean you stole it off the beach. Nothing's safe when you're around. Why, by God, you'd steal a tick off a widow's belly!" Most of the clammers seemed to be irritable. "Hello, Pop," a young clammer said to the man in an adjoining boat, a sullen old man in wet overalls, "how's your hammer hanging?" "Shut up!" said the old man. The young clammer snickered and said, "Didn't get your share of clams today, did you, Pop?" "Shut up!" said the old man. "Why, hell," said the young clammer, "I was just passing the time of day." "Shut up!" said the old man.

At a quarter after four the last clammer finished unloading, cast off, and made for home. The Captain snapped his cashbox shut and we sat down and drained the iced tea in the thermos jug. Then Bollinger hoisted the anchor, started the motor, and pointed the *Jennie Tucker* for her wharf. The decks were piled high. "A regular floating clam mountain," said Bollinger. The Captain rearranged some bags on the hatch, clearing away a space to sit. He lit his pipe and added up the row of figures in his ledger.

"We took a hundred and forty-five bushels," he said. "One day I took two hundred bushels. I emptied my cashbox for that load. The stern was awash on the trip in." He pointed toward Oak Island. "See those boats over there? Some of the boys are still out, but they don't sell over the rail like the others. They have bigger boats and they stay out until late in the afternoon and bring their loads right to our shed. We buy every clam that's offered, no matter if there's a glut in New York or a big demand. Some days we buy more clams than we can get rid of, and we take the surplus out to some lots of water we lease from the town of Islip and shovel them overboard. In the last five weeks we've planted thirteen hundred bushels of cherries and five hundred bushels of necks in those lots.

When we need them, we go out and tong them up. No waste that way. In the old days, when clams were very dear, we used to have clam pirates. They would steal up at night and tong our lots, but not any more. We keep a watchman, just in case."

At five o'clock, the *Jennie Tucker* puttered up to her wharf. Mr. Still, the senior partner of the firm, was standing in the back doorway of the shed, waiting. He looks after the office end of the business. He is a shellfish expert and belongs to the family which once ran Still's, a renowned sea-food restaurant and hangout for Tammany gluttons on Third Avenue, and which still runs a thriving oyster business in a scow anchored in Pike Slip, beneath Manhattan Bridge. When the *Jennie Tucker* scraped against the wharf, Mr. Still shouted, "Here she is," and four men came out of the shed. The moment the buy-boat was tied up, two of these men leaped aboard and began lifting the bags to the wharf. The others placed them on handtrucks and wheeled them into the culling room. This was a long, cool room, which smelled like a clean cellar. There the clams were poured in great heaps on tables built against the walls. The tables and the cement floor had recently been hosed down and they were wet and immaculate. Captain Clock, Mr. Still, and Bollinger took places at the tables and culled the clams, tossing aside those with broken shells or gapped-open lips.

After they had been culled, the clams were poured into woven-wire baskets and dipped in a tank of tap water in which an antiseptic solution had been poured. Then some were emptied into great, three-bushel barrels and others into tubs holding three pecks. Soon the room was crowded with loaded barrels, and Mr. Still got a hammer out of the roll-top desk in the little office adjoining the culling room. He tacked tags on the heads of the barrels, addressing them to various restaurants and Fulton Market dealers. Then they were wheeled into one of the company's three trucks. At seven o'clock, this truck contained sixty-five barrels and twenty-two tubs. "She's ready to roll," said Mr. Still. "If you're a mind to, you can ride into the city with this load." He introduced me to Paul Boice, the driver, and I climbed into the cab of the truck. It was one of those massive, aluminum-painted trucks.

We took the Sunrise Highway. At Valley Stream, we stopped at a diner for hamburgers and coffee. The counterman knew Boice. "Care for some clams tonight, Paul?" he asked, grinning. "How about a dozen nice clams for supper?" The driver laughed perfunctorily. Evidently it was an old joke. "When I want clams for supper," he said, "I'll notify you. Fix me a hamburger." We did not tarry long in the diner. In Brooklyn the driver deftly guided the heavy truck through a maze of side streets. "I've been hauling clams over this route eight years and I know every short cut there is," he said. "Clams are nowhere near as perishable as oysters, but I don't like to dawdle." When we rolled off Manhattan Bridge he glanced at his watch. "Took less than two hours," he said. "That's good time."

He made his first delivery at Vincent's Clam Bar, at Mott and Hester streets, unloading three clam tubs and the basket of *scungili* conches Bollinger had gathered during the day. The proprietor brought Boice a goblet of red wine. "I get a drink on the house every time I hit this place," he said. He drove down Mott Street, passing slowly through Chinatown. Entering South Street, he had to climb out of the cab and drag a sleeping drunk out of the road. "Truck-drivers have to slow-poke through here just because of drunks," he said. "I drag one out of my way at least once a week." The Fulton Market sheds were dark, deserted, and locked up when we arrived. "I make four deliveries in the Market," Boice said, "and then I head uptown and make stops at big restaurants in the theatrical district." He backed the truck up to the door of a shellfish wholesaler and we climbed out of the cab. We looked up and down the street and did not see a soul. "There's a night watchman down here who helps me unload," Boice said, "and I always have to wait for him to show up." We sat down on the steps of the wholesale house and lit cigarettes. Across the street, on top of a pile of broken lobster barrels, three overfed fishhouse cats were screeching at each other. We sat for fifteen minutes, watching the cats screech and fight, and then I said goodbye. "If you order clams or chowder tomorrow," Boice said, peering up the dark street for the night watchman, "like as not you'll eat some of the ones we hauled in tonight."

(1939)

The Same as Monkey Glands

ETURNING FROM A LATE VACATION, I stopped off in Savannah, Georgia, and made a pilgrimage to Mr. Will Barbee's diamondback-terrapin farm on the Isle of Hope, a small, lush island nine miles below Savannah. I was there on the first day of autumn, when he starts shipping live terrapin to Northern hotels, clubs, seafood dealers, and luxury restaurants, and was in time to see his Negro foreman barrel up three dozen nine-year-old cows, or females; this, the first shipment of the season, was dispatched to a dealer in Fulton Fish Market. The diamondback is a handsome reptile, whose meat, when properly stewed, is tender and gelatinous. Gastronomically, it is by far the finest of the North American turtles, and terrapin stew is our costliest native delicacy. Three styles of stew— Philadelphia, Maryland, and Southern—are made in bulk by a man in Fulton Market and sold to families and clubs; what he calls Maryland style, in which dry sherry and thick cream are used, costs $10 a quart. In Manhattan hotels the price is never less than $3.50 a plate. A live terrapin in New York City brings from $3.50 to $7 retail, according to the length of its belly shell. For the last decade, under the protection of conservation laws, the diamondback has been slowly increasing in numbers in brackish sloughs all along the Eastern seaboard, but it still is scarce enough to make the fecundity of Mr. Barbee's farm of the utmost importance to chefs in New York, Baltimore, Philadelphia, Washington, and New Orleans, the cities in which the stew is most respected. Mr. Barbee is the country's largest shipper; in one year he shipped three hundred dozen live terrapin at an average price of $30 a dozen. He also put up four thousand cans of stew meat. In addition, on the porch of a rustic dance pavilion which he operates as a sideline, he sold terrapin dinners to hundreds of Yankee yachtsmen who stopped at the farm on their way to Florida through the Inland Waterway, which skirts the Isle of Hope. His wife, Rose, who looks after the cooking, is revered by yachtsmen, and her terrapin stew, Southern style, is famous from Cape Cod to Key West.

My train arrived at Union Station in Savannah at 9:30 the morning of the day I visited the farm, and an unselfish cab-driver I consulted advised me to check my bag and take a streetcar to the Isle of Hope. "I could drive you there," he said, "but if you want to see some old-fashioned yellow-fever country, you better take the street-car." I am thankful I followed his advice. The Isle of Hope line is a single-track interurban railroad; in its steam-engine days it bore the stirring title Savannah, Thunderbolt & Isle of Hope Railroad. I recommend a trip on it to lovers of Americana. There were only three passengers on the car I boarded. We rattled through Savannah and its suburbs and plunged into a swampy forest of live oaks whose great limbs dripped with a parasite plant called gray moss. Occasionally we crossed tracks over marshes in which rice was once grown with slave labor, and we passed through a number of small farms whose door-yard bushes were heavy with ripe, crimson pomegranates, the autumn fruit of the South. About five miles out of Savannah, the streetcar rounded a curve and the motorman suddenly put on his brake. A fat milk cow was on the track, grazing on nut grass that grew between the ties. The motorman pulled his whistle cord, but the cow did not budge. Some Gullah Negroes were digging yams in a patch beside the track; one hurried over and kicked the cow and she ambled off. The motorman, who was laughing, stuck his head out and said, "I give you fair warning. Next time she gets on my right of way I'm going to climb out and milk her." The Negro, also laughing, said, "Help yourself, Captain. She's got enough for the both of us."

A short while later we crossed a bridge spanning one of the rice marshes and reached the Isle of Hope. The streetcar line came to an end directly in front of several weatherbeaten frame buildings, on one of which there was a sign: "ALEXANDER M. BARBEE'S SON. DANCE PAVILION. OPERATING THE ONLY DIAMONDBACK TERRAPIN FARM IN THE WORLD. OYSTERS, SHRIMP, FANCY CRABMEAT. YOU ARE WELCOME." This building extended out over the water on piles, and two battered shrimp sloops were tied to the wharf abutting it; later I learned that this water was the Skidaway, a tidal river. I entered the building and found Mr. Barbee behind a counter, opening bottles of Coca-Cola for some shrimp fishermen. I recognized him from a description given by a Northern yachtsman who told me about the farm just before I went on vacation; he said Mr. Barbee looked "like an easygoing country storekeeper." I introduced myself and told him I was from New York and wanted to see his terrapin farm.

"Well, sir," he said, "I'm glad to see you. I'll show you the whole works, and I'll see that you get all the terrapin stew you can hold. We're going to barrel up a few terrapin for the New York trade today. The season opens up North around the second week of October, and we commence shipping on the first day of autumn. I've got forty-five hundred in my fattening pen ready to go and I want you to see them, but first we'll go up to the breeding farm. It's up the road a ways." He took off his apron and called to his wife, who was upstairs. "We keep house on the second floor of the pavilion," he told me. His wife came downstairs and he introduced us, saying, "Rose, I've invited this gentleman to have dinner with us. Make sure he gets a bait of terrapin." Mrs. Barbee, a pretty, red-cheeked young woman, smiled and said, "Mighty glad to have you."

I followed Mr. Barbee out on the front porch of the pavilion. "Right off the bat," he said, "I better tell you that the most important thing about terrapin meat is its tonic quality. It fills you full of fuss, fight, and gumption. Eat enough of it, it'll make an old rooster out of you. Why do you think so many rich old men eat terrapin? Well, sir, I'll tell you why. A terrapin is loaded down with a rich, nourishing jelly, and this jelly makes you feel young again. To be frank, it's the same as monkey glands. If you were to take and feed terrapin stew to all the people of this country, the birth rate would jump like a flash of lightning. There was a time when the coastal marshes were so full of terrapin they fed the meat to plantation slaves. It was cheaper than sowbelly. Well, I was up to City Hall in Savannah one day and a man there showed me some old papers he had dug out that said the plantation owners of Chatham County were forced to quit feeding terrapin to slaves because it made them breed too much. They wanted them to breed, of course, but they didn't want them to breed that much. Why, they spent all their time breeding. After all, there's a limit to everything."

We started up an oyster-shell lane that ran beside the river, and I said, "It must be convenient to have the streetcar line end right in front of your pavilion."

"To tell you the truth," Mr. Barbee said, "that's no accident. In a way, that's how the terrapin farm began. My daddy, Alexander Barbee, was a conductor on that road back in steam-engine days. He was French descent, and he liked to eat. He used to buy terrapin the colored people along the railroad would capture in the marshes. At first he just bought a mess now and then for his own table, but in time he took to trading in them, shipping them up to Maryland by the barrel.

"Well, around 1895, diamondbacks got so scarce the price shot up. They had been fished-out. When an old millionaire up North got ready to throw a banquet, he sometimes had to send men up and down the coast to get a supply. So in 1898 it came to pass that my daddy decided to make a stab at raising terrapin in captivity during his off hours from the railroad. Some Yankee scientists he wrote to said it was a foolish idea, absolutely impossible, but he went out at night with the colored people and bogged around in the salt marshes and got so he understood terrapin better than any man in history. When he got ready to buy land for his terrapin farm, he naturally thought of the end of the railroad line. The land there had always looked good to him. It was the most beautiful scene in the world; when he reached it he could knock off and have a cigar. So he bought a few swampy acres, built a shed, and stocked it with terrapin. Every time he got to the end of the run he would jump out and tend to them. He got them in a breeding mood, and by 1912 they were breeding to such an extent he quit his job on the railroad. From time to time he bought more land down here. He was an unusual man. He played the cornet in a band up in Savannah and he had a high opinion of fun, so he built a dance pavilion down here. The pavilion isn't any gold mine, but we still keep it going. I sort of like it. People come out from Savannah on hot nights to smell the ocean and cool themselves off, and you know how it is—you like to see them."

We reached the end of the oyster-shell lane and came upon a long, rather dilapidated shed in an oak grove. Green moss was growing on the shingled roof and the whitewash on the clapboards was peeling. There was a big padlock on the door. "This shed is the breeding farm," Mr. Barbee said. "They're born in here, and they stay here until they're around nine summers old. At the beginning of the ninth summer they're put in the fattening pen and allowed to eat their heads off. In the autumn, after they've been fattened for four or five months, they're sent to market. You can eat a terrapin when it's five years old, but I think they taste better around nine. Also, it's wasteful to eat young terrapin, when you consider it takes two nine-year-olds to produce a good pint of clear meat." He unlocked the door but did not open it. Instead, as if he had suddenly changed his mind, he turned around on the steps of the shed and resumed the story of his father.

"Daddy passed away ten years ago and I took charge," he said. "He was quite a man, if I do say so. That white house we passed up there at the bend in the lane was his home. His room is just the way he left it. It's called the Barbee Musical Room, because everything in it plays a tune. Touch the bed, and a music box in the mattress plays a tune. Hang your hat on the rack, and the same thing happens. Pick up anything on the table from a dice cup to a hair-brush, and you get a tune. Why, there's one hundred and fifty objects in that room that'll play a tune if you just touch them. There's a rubberneck wagon up in Savannah that brings tourists down here to the island just to see it, and we employ a colored girl to stay in the room and answer questions. I bet half the yachtsmen that go to Florida in the winter have visited it.

"Three things Daddy truly admired were diamondbacks, music boxes, and William Jennings Bryan. In 1911, just before he quit the railroad, he put a clutch of terrapin eggs in his grip and went up to Washington and called on Mr. Bryan at his hotel. He had one egg that needed only a few minutes to hatch, and he said to Mr. Bryan, 'Sir, I have long been an admirer of yours and I want to ask you a slight favor. I want you to hold this here terrapin egg in your hand until it hatches out.' Mr. Bryan leaped out of his chair and said, 'I never heard of such a fool idea. Get away from me with that nasty thing.' But Daddy was known for having his own way. People said he could argue his way through a brick wall. They said he could argue the tail off a dog. So he argued Mr. Bryan into holding the egg, and in about twenty minutes a little bull terrapin hatched out right in Mr. Bryan's fist. Daddy thanked him and said he was going to name the little fellow William Jennings Bryan, but Mr. Bryan begged him to have mercy on him and call it something else. So Daddy named it Toby. He kept that Toby terrapin for years and years. He would carry it in his coat pocket everywhere he went. He had it trained so it would wink its right eye whenever he said, 'See here, Toby, ain't it about time for a drink?' "

Mr. Barbee laughed. "Yes, siree," he said, "Daddy was a sight." He swung the shed door open. A rickety catwalk extended the length of the shed, and on each side of it were nine stalls whose floors swarmed with thousands of terrapin of all ages. Some were the size of a thumbnail and some were as big as a man's hand. There was a musky but not unpleasant smell in the shed. The diamondback is a lovely creature. On both sides of its protruding, distinctly snakelike head are pretty, multi-colored lines and splotches. The hard shell in which it is boxed glints like worn leather. On the top shell, or carapace, are thirteen diamond-shaped designs, which may be pale gold, silvery, or almost black. Sometimes a terrapin shows up with fourteen diamonds on its shell; Mr. Barbee said that people on the Isle of Hope save these rare shells for good luck. The belly shell, or plastron, is the color of the keys of an old piano. "We measure them by placing a steel ruler on the belly shell," Mr. Barbee said, bending over and lifting a terrapin out of a stall. The creature opened its sinister little jaws, darted its head from left to right, and fought with its claws. "This cow will measure six and a half inches, which means she's around eight years of age. Next year she'll be ready for the stewpot. The price a terrapin brings at retail is largely based on shell length. In New York you'd pay between three and a half and five dollars for a seven-inch cow. An eight-inch one might bring seven dollars." Mr. Barbee noticed that I was watching the terrapin's jaws. "Oh, they never bite," he said.

"Are bull terrapin used in stews?" I asked.

"A bull's meat is tougher but just as palatable," he said. "A bull doesn't grow as big as a cow. You seldom see one longer than five inches. Also, from eggs hatched in captivity we get eighteen cows to every bull. That's a fact I can't explain. The bulls have a tendency to get a little overexcited at breeding time, and to keep them from working themselves to death we always put some wild bulls in the pens to help them out. This strengthens the herd. We employ hunters to go out and capture wild terrapin in the winter, when they hibernate. Wild terrapin don't eat a thing from frost until around March. They burrow in the marsh mud and sleep through the winter. They always leave an air hole in the mud, and that's what hunters look for. Some hunters use dogs called terrapin hounds, which are trained to recognize these holes. When a hound finds a hole he bays, and the hunter digs the terrapin out. We buy wild terrapin and ship them right along with our home-grown stock. My terrapin are raised so naturally they taste exactly like wild ones just pulled out of the mud. The difference is impossible to detect."

Mr. Barbee returned the terrapin he had been holding to its stall, and she crawled off. He said that, just as in the wild state, captive cows begin laying eggs in the late spring, nesting in shallow holes which they dig with their hind claws in sand on the stall floors. A cow may lay twice in a season, depositing a total of twenty eggs. The eggs are about the size of pecans and are elastic; they do not crack under pressure. In the tidal marshes the eggs hatch in from two to three months; on the farm they are stolen from the nests and incubated. Just how this is done, Mr. Barbee flatly declined to tell. "That's the Barbee family secret," he said.

An old Negro came into the shed. "Looky, looky, here comes Cooky," he said. He was carrying a bucket. "Jesse Beach, my foreman," Mr. Barbee said. "His bucket is full of crab legs and chopped-up oysters." The old man went down the catwalk, tossing a handful of food into each stall. I had noticed that the moment he entered the shed, the terrapin commenced crawling toward the front of their stalls. "They know Jesse," Mr. Barbee said. The terrapin converged on the food, shouldering each other out of the way, just as puppies do. They ate greedily. "Diamondbacks make wonderful pets," Mr. Barbee said. "I sell a lot of babies for that purpose. They are much more interesting than the dumb little turtles they sell in pet shops."

We followed the old Negro out of the shed and Mr. Barbee locked the door. "We'll take a look at the fattening pen now," he said. We went to one of the shacks alongside the pavilion. It housed a crabmeat cannery, another of the thrifty Mr. Barbee's enterprises. Between the shack and the riverbank, half in the water and half in the shore mud, was a board corral. The shallow, muddy water in it seethed with forty-five hundred full-grown terrapin. "This is a terrapin heaven," Mr. Barbee said. On one side of the corral was a cement walk, and when we stepped on it our shadows fell athwart the water and the terrapin sunning themselves on the surface promptly dived to the bottom. The tips of their inquisitive heads reappeared immediately and I could see hundreds of pairs of beady eyes staring up. "They're fat and sassy," Mr. Barbee said. "There's a pipe leading from the shucking table in the crab cannery right into the pen, and the legs and discarded flesh from the shucked crabs drop right into the water. The terrapin hang around the spout of the pipe and gobble up everything that comes along. Sooner or later those terrapin down there will appear on the finest tables in the country. God knows they're expensive, but that can't be helped. I feed a terrapin nine years before I sell it, and when you think of all the crabmeat and good Georgia oysters those fellows have put away, you can understand why a little-bitty bowl of terrapin stew costs three dollars and a half." While we stood there gazing down into a muddy pool containing more than $11,000 worth of sleek reptiles, the Negro foreman walked up toting an empty barrel and a basket of tree moss. After dousing some of the moss in the river, he made a bed with it on the bottom of the barrel. The barrel had air holes cut in it. Then he reached in the pool and grabbed six terrapin. He scrubbed them off with a stiff brush and placed them on the wet moss. Then he covered them with moss and placed six more on this layer, continuing the sandwiching process until the barrel contained three dozen. While he was putting the head on the barrel, Mrs. Barbee came to a window of the pavilion and called, "Come to dinner."

The table was laid on the back porch of the pavilion, overlooking the Skidaway, and there was a bottle of amontillado on it. Mr. Barbee and I had a glass of it, and then Mrs. Barbee brought out three bowls of terrapin stew, Southern style, so hot it was bubbling. The three of us sat down, and while we ate, Mrs. Barbee gave me a list of the things in the stew. She said it contained the meat, hearts, and livers of two diamondbacks killed early that day, eight yolks of hard-boiled eggs that had been pounded up and passed through a sieve, a half pound of yellow country butter, two pints of thick cream, a little flour, a pinch of salt, a dash of nutmeg, and a glass and a half of amontillado. The meat came off the terrapins' tiny bones with a touch of the spoon, and it tasted like delicate baby mushrooms. I had a second and a third helping. The day was clear and cool, and sitting there, drinking dry sherry and eating terrapin, I looked at the scarlet leaves on the sweet gums and swamp maples on the riverbank, and at the sandpipers running stiff-legged on the sand, and at the people sitting in the sun on the decks of the yachts anchored in the Skidaway, and I decided that I was about as happy as a human can be in this day and time. After the stew we had croquettes made of crabmeat and a salad of little Georgia shrimp. Then we had some Carolina whiting that had been pulled out of the Atlantic at the mouth of the Skidaway early that morning. With the sweet, tender whiting, we had butter beans and ears of late corn that were jerked off the stalk only a few minutes before they were dropped in the pot. We began eating at one o'clock; at four we had coffee.

Three afternoons later, back in Manhattan, I visited the terrapin market of New York, which is located in three ancient buildings near the corner of Beekman and Front streets, in Fulton Market. The largest of these is occupied by Moore & Co., an old black-bean, turtle-soup, and terrapin-stew firm now owned by a gourmet named Francesco Castelli. Each winter it sells around two thousand quarts of diamondback stew. In Mr. Castelli's establishment I saw the barrel of terrapin I had watched Mr. Barbee's foreman pack on the Isle of Hope. "I order a lot of Barbee's stuff and I ordered it from his father before him," Mr. Castelli said. "I also use terrapin from the Chesapeake Bay area, from the Cape Hatteras area of North Carolina, from New Jersey, and Long Island." Mr. Castelli believes that turtle and terrapin meat is the most healthful in the world and likes to tell about a fox terrier which lived in his factory and ate nothing but turtle meat until he died in 1921, aged twenty-five. He uses all his terrapin in his stewpots and sells no live ones.

Live ones are sold by a rather sharp-spoken old Irishman on Front Street named D. R. Quinn, who has been in the business most of his life and has not developed a taste for the meat, and by Walter T. Smith, Inc., also on Front Street. Smith's is sixty-two years old and is one of the largest turtle firms in the world; its cable address, Turtling, is known to many European chefs. It sells all kinds of edible turtles, including treacherous snappers and great 150-pound green turtles out of the Caribbean, from which most turtle soup is made. Snappers, prized for soup in Philadelphia, are not popular here. They can knock a man off his feet with their alligatorlike tails and have been known to snap off the fingers of fishermen; few New York chefs are hardy enough to handle them. I had a talk with Mr. Kurt W. Freund, manager of the firm, and he took me up the sagging stairs to the room in which his tanks are kept and showed me diamondbacks from every state on the Eastern seaboard except Maine. A few were from sloughs on Long Island. He said that in the local trade all terrapin caught from Maryland north are called Long Islands. He said that in the North, terrapin hunting is a fisherman's sideline and that few hunters north of Maryland catch more than a couple of dozen a year.

"I imagine you're under the impression that millionaires buy most of our terrapin," Mr. Freund said. "If so, you're mistaken. The terrapin business was hard hit by prohibition, and it never has got on its feet again, and for years the poor Chinese laundryman has been the backbone of our trade. I'd say that seventy per cent of the sixteen thousand live diamondbacks sold on this street last year were bought by old Chinese. Come look out this window and see my sign." Hanging from the second-floor window was a red-and-white wooden signboard smeared with Chinese characters. Mr. Freund said the characters were pronounced "gim ten guoy" and meant "diamondback terrapin." He said that each autumn he hires a Chinese to write form letters quoting terrapin prices, which are distributed by the hundred in Chinatown.

"An old Chinese doesn't run to the doctor or the drugstore when he feels bad," Mr. Freund said. "He saves his pennies and buys himself a terrapin. He cooks it with medicinal herbs and rice whiskey. Usually he puts so much whiskey in it he has himself a spree as well as a tonic. In the autumn and in the spring crowds of old Chinese come in and bargain with me. They balance terrapin on their palms and stare at them and deliberate an hour sometimes before making a selection. They tell me that the turtle has been worshipped in China for centuries. It's supposed to be a kind of holy reptile. Most of my steady Chinese customers are old laundrymen, and I know that some of them are practically penniless, but they think terrapin meat will do them more good than a month in the hospital, and they're willing to pay the price."

I told Mr. Freund that Mr. Barbee professed to believe that the consumption of terrapin meat is better than monkey glands for regaining youthfulness.

"Seriously," I said, "do you think there's anything to it?"

"I've been around terrapin for years and years, and I eat the meat myself, and I've talked the matter over with dozens of old Chinese fellows," Mr. Freund said, "and I wouldn't be the least bit surprised."

(1939)

Goodbye, Shirley Temple

I'VE BEEN GOING TO MADAME VISAGGI'S Third Avenue spaghetti house off and on since speakeasy days, and I know all the old customers. Madame Visaggi calls them "the regulars." Peggy is one. She is an Irish girl, around thirty-five, who works in the office of a wholesale butcher on First Avenue. She is in Madame Visaggi's practically every night. Most often she is full of brandy when she leaves, but her apartment is only a few blocks away, in Tudor City, and she always gets home all right. The butcher is her uncle and doesn't say anything if she shows up late for work. Peggy is an attractive girl despite a large birthmark on her left cheek, which makes her self-conscious. When she comes in, usually between five-thirty and six, she is always tense. She says, "I got the inside shakes." Then she sits in one of the booths across from the bar, orders a brandy, and opens an afternoon newspaper. By the time she has finished with the newspaper, she has had two or three drinks and has conquered her self-consciousness. Then she doesn't mind if one of the other regulars comes over and sits in the booth with her. She knows many bitter Irish stories, she uses profanity that is fierce and imaginative, and people like to listen to her. All the regulars are familiar with the fact that Eddie, the bartender, has been in love with her for several years. Eddie has an interest in the restaurant. He is big, cheerful, and dumb. He is always begging Peggy not to drink so much and asking her to go out with him. Once Madame Visaggi sat down with Peggy and said, "Say, Peggy, sweetheart, what's the matter you don't like Eddie? He's such a nice boy."

Peggy snorted and said, "The back of my hand to Eddie." Then she laughed and said, "Oh, Eddie's O.K."

Another one of the regulars is Mike Hill. He works in an office around the corner, on Lexington, and usually drops in for a couple of drinks before going down to Grand Central to get his train. Each Wednesday night his wife comes into town, and they have dinner in Madame Visaggi's and go to the theatre. One Wednesday night they brought their little girl in to show her to Madame Visaggi. Mrs. Hill said she had been shopping most of the afternoon, and she looked tired, but the little girl was full of life. She appeared to be about five and she had curls. Madame Visaggi lifted her up, kissed her on both cheeks, and sat her on the bar. "Hello, Shirley Temple," she said. Eddie took a little white horse off the neck of a whiskey bottle and gave it to the child. Then Madame Visaggi told Eddie to take a bottle of champagne out of the refrigerator. "On the house," she said. She turned to Mrs. Hill and said, "We'll have dinner together tonight. Special. On the house." They had Martinis at the bar and then they went into the dining room in the rear. At the door, Madame Visaggi turned and said, "Send in a bottle of ginger ale for Shirley Temple, Eddie."

In a little while the child came back into the bar. "Hello, young lady," said an old man standing at the bar. "Hello," said the child. The old man said, "How do you like this place?" The child said, "I like it," and the people along the bar laughed. This pleased the child. She said, "I have a riddle. Do you know Boo?" The old man thought a moment, and then asked. "Boo who?" "Please don't cry," the child said. Then she laughed and ran back into the dining room. In a minute or two she was back again. This time she walked along the row of booths, looking into each. I was sitting in one of the middle booths with Peggy and a girl named Estelle, a friend of Peggy's. The child looked at us and smiled. Peggy said, "Hello there." "Hello," said the child. She started to leave, and then Peggy asked, "What's your name?" The child said, "My name is Margaret." "Why, that's my name, too," Peggy said. Estelle lifted the child into the booth and put an arm around her. The child stared across the table at Peggy and said, "What's that on your face?"

Peggy hesitated a moment. Then she said, "It's something God put there, Margaret."

"Won't it come off?" the child asked.

Estelle interrupted. "Do you go to school?" she asked.

"No," said the child. She looked at Peggy again and said, "Why did God put it there?"

"Because I was a bad girl," Peggy said.

"What did you do?"

Peggy asked Estelle for a cigarette. While Peggy was lighting it, the child gazed at her.

"What did you do?" she asked again.

"I shot off my father's head and cut out his heart and ate it," Peggy said.

"When?"

Estelle interrupted again.

"How old are you, sweetheart?" she asked.

"Five and a half," said the child.

She looked at Peggy and said, "Can I touch it?"

Peggy said, "Sure." She bent over and the child touched her left cheek. Then Madame Visaggi came out of the dining room, looking for the child. She picked her up. "You've got to come eat your soup, so you'll be a big girl," she said.

"Goodbye," the child said to Peggy.

"Goodbye, Shirley Temple," Peggy said.

Everything was quiet in the booth for a few minutes. I was afraid to say anything. Then Estelle asked Peggy to go with her to a movie at Loew's Lexington.

"It'll do you good," Estelle said.

"The hell with it," Peggy said.

A game of Indian dice started at the bar, and Estelle and I went over and got in it. Peggy said she wasn't interested. There were six in the game, playing for drinks. The second time the dice went down the bar, I glanced at Peggy, thinking I would ask her if she wanted a drink; Mike Hill's little girl was back again. She was standing just outside Peggy's booth. I saw Peggy lean over and speak to her. The child stared at Peggy, fascinated. When Peggy stopped talking, the child walked backward a few steps, retreating. Then she turned and ran headlong into the dining room. It was a long dice game with two ties, and we played one-tie-all-tie. I got stuck. I paid for the round, and Estelle and I went back and sat down with Peggy.

"I see the kid came back to see you," I said.

Peggy laughed.

"I sent Shirley Temple back to her mamma," she said.

Every twenty minutes or so, Estelle and I would go over to the bar and shake for drinks with the others. Every time we came back to the booth, we brought Peggy a brandy. We tried to get her to talk, but she wouldn't pay any attention to us. She was morose and silent.

At ten o'clock, Mrs. Hill came out of the dining room with Madame Visaggi. "Thanks for everything," Mrs. Hill said. "It was a wonderful dinner, and thank you so much for the champagne." "No, no, no," said Madame Visaggi. "It was nothing." Then Mike came out. He had the little girl in his arms. She looked sleepy now. They said good night to Eddie and started for the door. When they approached the booth in which we were sitting, the little girl began to kick and scream hysterically. Mike sat her down on a bar stool and said, "What in the world is the matter, baby doll?" The child continued to scream. "She's all tired out and nervous," Mrs. Hill said. "The day was too much for her. Here, let me take her." Suddenly Peggy said, "Damn it to hell." She got up abruptly and hurried toward the door. We thought she was going out of the restaurant and I got up to follow her, but at the front end of the bar she turned left and went into the ladies' room. As soon as Peggy was out of sight, the child calmed down. "She should've been in bed hours ago," Mrs. Hill said. Then they said thanks and goodbye to Madame Visaggi all over again, and left.

After a while another dice game began. While we were shaking, Peggy returned. She didn't go back to the booth. She came and stood next to me and put her elbows on the bar. I could see that she had been crying. Eddie automatically poured her a brandy.

"How's it, Peggy?" he asked.

Peggy didn't answer. She drank the brandy. Then she said, "You want to take me home, Eddie?"

"You kidding?" Eddie asked.

"No," Peggy said.

"You drunk?"

"I certainly am not," Peggy said.

"Look," Eddie said, "I'm not supposed to knock off until midnight, but I'll ask Madame to put one of the waiters behind the bar."

"O.K., Eddie," Peggy said.

(1939)

On the Wagon

*I*T HAD BEEN SIX WEEKS, but Mike couldn't get used to it. "A month and a half," he said, "and I've just got started. Sooner or later I'll get used to it. I got to get used to it."

Half past five was quitting time in the office, and that was the hardest part of the day. He would walk it off. He would leave as if in a hurry to get home, and then walk eighteen blocks to his furnished room. He would wash up and go over to a diner on Third Avenue. While he ate, he would try to look preoccupied. Mike was embarrassed by his loneliness; he didn't want anybody, not even a counterman in a diner, to guess that he was lonesome. Like many lonesome people, he felt there was something shameful about it. Some nights after dinner he couldn't force himself to go back to his furnished room, and he would go for a ride on the Third Avenue "L." It would please him to see the four enormous, beautifully polished copper kettles in the windows of Ruppert's brewery, and it would please him to smell the wet hops, a lovely smell that blew into the car as it rattled past. He would get off the "L" at the Hanover Square station, light a cigarette, and walk back and forth on the cement plaza in front of the Cotton Exchange. He found it comforting to walk there in the dark and listen to the whistles of the tugs in the East River. The best job he ever had had been in a coffee warehouse a block from Hanover Square. That had been four years ago, and since then he had lost three other jobs, all because of drinking. After a while he would leave the plaza and get back on the "L." And all the way uptown he would stare down into the street, watching for the cheerful, flickering neons over the entrances of barrooms. "Six weeks on the wagon," he would say. "Six weeks and not even a beer!" Whenever the "L" got on his nerves, he would get out and walk until he was so tired he could sleep. Sometimes, walking at night, he saw things that made him feel better because they took his mind off himself—a street fight, an automobile wreck, a boat unloading dripping bushels of mackerel at a Fulton Market pier. He seldom stopped to look at such things, however; his purpose in walking was to tire himself out.

The hardest part of the day for Mike, certainly, was the moment he put on his coat and hat and left the wholesale drug company where, for three weeks, he had been assistant bookkeeper. But lunchtime was almost as bad. The others in the office, even Miss O'Brien, the fussy file clerk, ate across the street in the bar and grill, but he always went up the street to the coffeepot. After work, Mr. Schmidt, the bookkeeper, and Clancy, the head shipping clerk, would go across the street for beers. Once Mr. Schmidt, getting into his coat, turned to Mike and said, "I never see you across the street, Thompson. Why don't you drop in and have a beer with me and Clancy?" Mike said, "My liver isn't all it should be," and Mr. Schmidt had said, "That's tough. Take care of yourself." There was nothing wrong with Mike's liver. Mike loathed the coffeepot, but he was afraid to go across the street. He would make up his mind to have lunch in the bar and grill with the others and then he would get to thinking, and he would say to himself, "I better go up to the coffeepot. Like Betty said, unless I stay on the wagon I'll never be able to hold down a job. I'm thirty-nine and I'm not getting any younger. I had an awful time getting this job and I got to hold on to it."

He dreaded Sunday. The Sunday which marked the beginning of his seventh week on the wagon was cold and clear. He spent the afternoon in his furnished room, reading a newspaper. Late in the day he pulled his chair to the window and sat there. Acres of tenement roofs stretched out beneath his window; on one roof a pigeon-keeper was waving a bamboo pole and frightening his birds aloft. Each time they were driven off their coop the birds flew into the air, wheeled around, and settled immediately a couple of roofs away on chimneys decorated with the yellow-paint signs of the New York Frame & Picture Co. They perched on the chimneys a few tentative moments and then flew back to their coop and were driven aloft again. Mike was amused by the game. After a while the pigeon-keeper locked the birds in their coop, took a paper bag out of his pocket, and tossed some corn into each pen. Then he left the roof, and Mike felt deserted. While he sat at the window, leaning forward, with his elbows on the sill, it became dark and he began to feel bad. He had slept little the night before. A hot bath had done no good and aspirin had made him even more shaky. He had been too jittery and too lonesome to sleep. Staring out over the dark roofs, he tried to get control of himself, but it was no use. He began to cry. He took off his glasses and rubbed his eyes. His eyes were strained by sleeplessness and the tears made them smart. Mike had got so he talked to himself. "I cry as easy as an old maid in the dark at a movie," he said. "I got to hold on to myself somehow." He walked up and down in the shabby room. When he could bear it no longer he stretched out on the bed, face downward. After a while he sat up. He reached into a pocket of his coat, which hung on the back of a chair, and got his cigarettes. He sat on the edge of the bed, smoking in the dark. When he had finished the cigarette he put on his coat, got his hat, and felt in the dark for the doorknob. He didn't want to turn on the light and see, on the bureau, the photograph of Betty. As he walked downstairs, Mike thought, "I can't blame her much for leaving me. I can't blame anybody but myself." On the street he felt that people looked away when they saw his strained face.

He walked down the street, hunting for a new place to eat. For six weeks he had eaten in places that did not sell liquor—diners, coffeepots, cafeterias, and chow-mein joints. He was hungry. After he had sent the weekly money order to Betty Saturday afternoon and paid the rent on the furnished room, he had fourteen dollars left. In the old days he had spent twice that on a Saturday night, making a round of barrooms, and had thought nothing of it. "I'm sick of the junky grub in those cafeterias," he said. "I'm going someplace and get a decent meal." He stared into the neon-lit window of a bar and grill. There was a row of booths parallel with the bar. The place was not crowded. He could eat in peace. Mike went in. He ordered a steak. An old man and a young man were standing at the bar, hunched over beers. The old man was quiet, but the young man hummed a song. He would hum a few moments, absent-mindedly, and then he would break out into a verse.

" 'Oh,' " he sang, " 'the wheel flew off the hearse, and the coffin rolled out in the road. The widow got out of her carriage and she said—' "

The bartender came out of the kitchen and gave the young man a stern look; he quit singing in the middle of the verse.

"Don't look at me like that," the young man said, frowning at the bartender. "I know I'm a nuisance. I know I'm a no-good bum. No good to myself, no good to nobody. Day I was born, I wish they'd dropped me in a tub, like I was a cat. Let me have a beer. 'Oh, the wheel flew off the hearse, and the coffin rolled out in the road.' What's the matter with you? Did you have a stroke? Let's have that beer."

"Keep your pants on," said the bartender.

"None of your lip," said the young man. "Let's have that beer."

"I think he wants a beer," said the old man, not looking up.

The bartender took the empty glass and went reluctantly to the spigot.

"I never saw a man could drink so much beer," he said angrily. "It ain't human."

"I drink so much beer," said the young man, winking at his companion, "because I'm afraid if I was to drink whiskey, it would make me drunk. They say whiskey makes you drunk. I sure wouldn't want that to happen to me."

The old man snickered.

Eating his steak and potatoes, Mike felt at ease. The atmosphere of the barroom, the bickering of the men at the bar, the beer smell comforted him. It was a small barroom, a neighborhood joint. Over the bar was a poster advertising a Monster Bingo Party at the Catholic church around the corner. When he had finished his coffee,

Mike got up and walked over to the bar and stood there. The bartender was out in the kitchen. Mike stood at the bar, one foot on the rail, with his right hand in a pocket of his trousers. He rubbed coins together in his pocket and his palm was sweating. Suddenly he realized he hadn't left a tip for the waitress. He went back to the table and put fifteen cents beside his coffee cup. Then the bartender came out and Mike handed him his check and a dollar bill. "Eighty-fi' cents," said the bartender, ringing up Mike's bill. He gave Mike his change and Mike put on his overcoat and started for the door. He glanced at the clock on the wall; it was eight-thirty. He remembered the furnished room with the unshaded electric light hanging from the middle of the splotched ceiling and his heart sank, and he thought, "I just can't stand it any longer." At the door he paused. He turned and walked over to the cigarette machine. "Six weeks," Mike thought, "and not even a beer." Opening the package of cigarettes, he walked back to the bar. The bartender came and stood in front of him.

"What'll it be?" he asked.

Mike stared nervously at the bottles behind the bar and noticed a blue Bromo-Seltzer bottle, upended in its rack.

"Fix me a Bromo," Mike sid.

The bartender mixed the Bromo in two beer glasses. Mike drank the violently bubbly mixture.

"Good for what ails you," the bartender said, smiling.

The young man looked at Mike.

"You got a hangover, too?" he asked.

"Well, not exactly," Mike said.

"I got a hangover would kill a horse, damn near," said the young man.

"Hell," said the old man, "you don't know what a hangover is."

The young man grunted.

"Once I had a job in a liquor store," said the old man. "Some mornings I'd come in with a hangover and I'd have to stand there all day with thousands of bottles of the stuff staring me in the face. I'd have to say, 'Yes, sir, that's an A-1 grade of Scotch. Best we have in stock,' when just to look at it made me rock back on my heels. It was worse than a bartender with a hangover, because he can sneak a drink to brace himself, but I worked in that store six months and I never saw a cork pulled out of a bottle."

"Geez," said the young man.

"Talk about a hangover," said the old man, hunched over his beer. "You don't know what a hangover is."

Mike laughed. He thought, "A beer or two won't hurt me. A couple of beers, and I'll go home. I'll have a couple of beers and maybe I can get some sleep. I got to get some sleep. A man can't live without sleep." The bartender saw Mike looking at the rack of bottles behind the bar.

"You want something?" he asked.

Mike heard himself say, "A beer."

The bartender spanked the foam off the beer with his black paddle. Then he held the glass under the spigot an instant longer. He set the glass in front of Mike and Mike put a dime on the wet bar.

"First in six weeks," said Mike. "I been on the wagon six weeks now."

The bartender did not seem impressed.

"It don't hurt nobody to leave the stuff alone for a while," he said. "Once I was on the wagon eight months."

"Yeah?" said Mike.

"Yeah," said the bartender. "I was in a hospital."

They both laughed.

"St. Vincent's," said the bartender. "Auto accident."

Mike took a deep drink of the beer. In a little while the old man and the young man finished their beers and walked toward the door. "Pleasant dreams," the bartender called out, and took their glasses away. Left alone, Mike suddenly felt desolate. He finished his beer and lit a cigarette. He had made up his mind to leave when two women came in and sat down on bar stools at the end of the bar, next to the cigarette machine. They knew the bartender. "How's it, Tommy?" said one. "Never better," said the bartender. "What'll it be, two Manhattans?" "How'd you guess?" asked the woman, smiling. Mike felt cheerful again. When he had finished with the women, the bartender looked at Mike's empty glass.

"Fill her up?" he asked.

"Fill her up," said Mike.

A man came in with a *Daily News*. He stood at the bar and looked through a comic strip in the back of the paper. He did not order, but the bartender automatically placed a bottle of rye, a whiskey glass, and a glass of water on the bar in front of him. When he finished the comic strip, the man laughed.

"Hey, Tommy," he called to the bartender, "don't miss Moon Mullins. Kayo certainly pulled a fast one on Lord Plushbottom."

Mike smiled. On his way home he would pick up the *News* and see what had happened to Lord Plushbottom. He would get a *News* and a *Mirror* and read himself to sleep. His glass was empty again.

"I tell you," he said to the bartender, "let's have a rye this time. Beer chaser."

"O.K.," said the bartender. "Rye and a small beer."

He placed the bottle of rye in front of Mike.

"It looks the same," said Mike, filling his glass.

(1939)

The Kind Old Blonde

I WAS IN SHINE'S, an Irish restaurant near the Pennsylvania Station, eating bluefish. A man and a woman came in and took the table opposite mine. While they were getting settled at the table, the man told the waiter they had just come in from the Belmont track. The waiter seemed pleased to see them. The man was bald and red-faced and substantial. He looked like a contractor, or maybe he had something to do with the horses. The woman was a big, sound, well-dressed blonde. She might have been the co-leader of a Tammany club, or an old vaudeville actress who had saved her money or perhaps married well. The waiter passed out menus and the man began to study his at once, but the woman ordered an Old-Fashioned before she opened hers. The man kept running a finger under his stiff blue collar and twisting his head from side to side. When the waiter placed the cocktail in front of the woman, the man looked at it sullenly.

"That's the only way I know to get ten cents for a little piece of orange peel," he said, staring at the cocktail. "Same amount of whiskey you get in a quarter drink. They stick in a strip of orange peel and charge you thirty-fi' cents."

"I like it," said the blonde.

"Rather take mine straight," he said.

She was considering clams and planked shad. He said he thought he would have some spaghetti. He spoke without enthusiasm.

"I'm going to have another cocktail before I order," she said.

"Go right ahead," said the man.

The way he said it made her look up from her menu. She closed it and looked at him.

"You not drinking, Jim?"

"No."

"That why you been so gloomy all day?"

"I guess so. I'm sorry."

"Is there something wrong, Jim?"

"I don't know. I haven't had a drink for three days. I went up to see my doctor, Doctor Phillips. I got orders to lay off the stuff. He told me I been digging my grave with cigars and booze. I been worried. It worried me."

The waiter came and the woman told him she wanted another cocktail and a dozen clams. She reached in her handbag and took out her cigarettes. The man held a match for her. She took a deep breath; then she let the smoke out through her nostrils.

"Had a friend used to like spaghetti," said the blonde, settling her fat elbows on the tablecloth. "I bet he weighed three hundred pounds. Big as a horse. He was a handicapper. Used to kill a quart a day, and in the summer he'd take ten, fifteen beers at one sitting."

The man grunted.

"He was an Eyetalian fellow, name of Al," said the blonde, "but he never drank wine. One fall he got shooting pains. Doctor told him he better lay off the booze. He wasn't no good after that; had to quit operating. He was up to my place for dinner one night and I told him, 'Al,' I said, 'your system's like a machine. It's got to have erl to operate. You taking the erl away and it's killing you.' I was right. Year and a half later I was to his funeral. Been here now if he'd a gone ahead and drank with some moderation. In my humble opinion he was murdered by the doctor."

"I guess it was a shock to his heart," said the man.

"What I told him," said the blonde. "I said to him, 'Al, it's a strain on your heart. Your heart can't stand it.'"

"How old a man was he?"

"He was fifty-some-odd, Jim. He was about your age, Jim. He thought he'd live to be ninety if he gave up the booze. He said all the men in his family lived to hit ninety. Poor old Al. In a year and a half he was dead and gone. Died broke. Left hardly enough to take care of the funeral."

They were silent for a little while, and then the man sat up in his chair.

"Well, it just goes to show," he said.

The waiter brought the woman's second cocktail and the plate of clams. She looked at them critically.

"If you don't mind," she said to the waiter, "these clams are mighty small. I'd like to have the cherrystones. If you don't mind."

The waiter picked up the plate of littlenecks.

"Jim, please," she said to the man. "If I was you, I'd have a drink."

When the waiter was about six steps from the kitchen the man called him back.

"I want a drink of rye," he said. "Let me have a drink of rye."

"You want soda or ginger ale?"

"Rye and plain water," said the man.

WHEN THE WAITER brought the cherrystones, the blonde looked at them and said, "Now, that's more like it." She picked up the little fork and went to work on the clams. The man poured the rye into the plain water and stirred it. Drinking it, he took his time.

"Tell you what," he said to the blonde, "I think I'll change my mind. Think I'll have some shad roe and bacon. Before you know it the season for shad roe will be over and gone."

She had a cherrystone halfway to her mouth.

"Personally, Jim, I always liked the shad better than the roe," she said, smiling at him. "You feel better now, don't you, darling?"

(1938)

I Couldn't Dope It Out

*T*HERE IS AN EATING PLACE on River Street in Hoboken, across from the piers and a couple of blocks from the Lackawanna ferry shed, called the My Blue Heaven Italian Restaurant. One summer I came back from Copenhagen on a Hog Island freighter and the food was bad, and when the freighter finally docked in Hoboken the first place to eat that I saw was the My Blue Heaven, and I went directly to it with my suitcase in my hand. I sat down and the waiter handed me a menu, but before I started looking at it he said that the combination that day was risotto and calamari and that he recommended it. "It's rice," he said, "and squid." At that time I had never eaten risotto, let alone calamari, but I ordered the combination, impulsively, and I found it to be extraordinarily appetizing. Since then I have gone back to the My Blue Heaven really quite often, considering that I live in Greenwich Village and have to cross the river on the ferry to get to it, which, of course, is part of the fun. I have got to know the people who run the place and some of the regular customers. (I have never asked about the name, and I guess it is because I sense that there is something sentimental or even cute about it, and I have such a good opinion of the place and the people who run it that I would just as soon not know.)

One Sunday not long ago I woke up in the middle of the morning. It was a beautiful day and I decided to take a ferry over to Hoboken and have lunch in the My Blue Heaven.

When I arrived at the place around noon, Paulie, the bartender, was sleepily polishing glasses. A grouchy dock superintendent named Chris, who hangs out there, was sitting at a front table drinking Dutch beer and reading a Newark Sunday paper. Udo, the cook, and a waiter named Vinnie were at a table in the rear, opposite the door to the kitchen. Udo was drinking coffee and Vinnie was feeding free-lunch liverwurst to the kitchen cat. I sat down with Chris. While I had lunch, he scornfully read aloud a story in the Newark paper speculating on a fight between Joe Louis and "Two Ton" Tony Galento, the fat, eccentric New Jersey heavyweight. Paulie stopped polishing glasses and came over to our table and we got into a discussion about Galento.

While we were talking, a man and a woman came in. I would say they were in their late forties. She was small and red-haired and quite good-looking in a scrawny, slapdash way. I remember that she had on a green dress that was very becoming. The man was heavyset and his face was double-chinned and gloomy. The main thing I remember about him is that he was wearing a blue serge suit that seemed to be too tight, as if he had been putting on weight. In the front of the My Blue Heaven are two small tables pushed close together so the sun coming in through the window will strike them. Chris, Paulie, and I were sitting at one of them. The newcomers sat down right across from us at the other sunny table.

Vinnie came out of the kitchen, bringing them menus and glasses of water. Without looking at the menu or at Vinnie, the man ordered a hot roast-beef sandwich. He had a *Herald Tribune* and he slipped out the news and sports and tossed the other sections on a stand back of his chair, on which stacks of napkins are kept. He didn't pay any attention to the woman, but let her order for herself. She studied the menu quite a while before she made up her mind.

"Charlie," she said when the waiter had gone, "I want to see the magazine section, please."

He was reading the sports. He didn't look up when she spoke, but motioned with his head in the direction of the napkin stand behind him. She stared at him, waiting to see if he would get the paper for her. Then she stood up, walked around to the stand, and got it herself. At our table we resumed the discussion about Galento.

"Galento won't take things serious," Paulie said. "He thinks it's funny to train on beer and hot dogs. If he'd quit boozing around and really train, he could take Joe Louis."

"Nuts!" said Chris. "It would be like dropping a safe on his head. It would be murder."

There were two big photographs of Louis and Galento in the Newark paper. Chris had the page spread out on the table. Paulie bent over and studied the photograph of Galento.

"He looks like a tough man to shave," he said.

"He just *looks* tough," said Chris. "There wouldn't be any sense to a fight like that. It would be first-degree murder. Tony couldn't take Joe if Joe was tied up hands and feet and Tony was fighting with a baseball bat."

The man with the woman stopped reading. He turned around in his chair and looked at Chris. He appeared to be annoyed.

"What makes you so sure about everything?" he asked Chris.

"Beg your pardon?" said Chris, surprised.

"What makes you so sure it would be murder?" he asked. "Are you a big fight expert or something?"

The woman grabbed him by the wrist.

"Charlie," she said. "Please, for my sake."

"Shut up, stupid," he said.

He pulled his hand away and turned again to Chris. "You think you're an expert?" he asked.

"My friend," said Chris, "I think Galento is a bum. If it's anything to you."

"An expert," said the man.

"My friend," said Chris, "do you happen to know what Tommy Loughran said to the referee? What he said when Sharkey got through with him that time?"

"What?"

"He said, 'Could I please sit down some place?' "

"So what?"

"So I'm just making a prediction."

At that moment Vinnie came up, bringing the woman some

tomato juice. The man turned around in his chair. "Another one of those Jersey experts," he said, returning to his sports section. Chris shrugged his shoulders. He told Paulie he wanted a beer and Paulie hurried off to draw it. There was no more conversation at our table. I drank my coffee and Chris turned back to his paper and his beer. Presently the man at the other table stopped reading, stretched his arms, and yawned.

"I'm tired," he said to the woman.

"Tired?" said the woman. Her face was strained.

"Yeah," he said. "Tired. Ever hear of it?"

VINNIE BROUGHT THEIR ORDERS. The woman had an omelet and Udo had fixed the man a big roast-beef sandwich. When they finished eating, the woman said, "How was the sandwich, Charlie?"

"Worst roast-beef sandwich I ever had," he said. "I think it'll stunt me for life."

"My omelet was very good," she said.

"What about a drink?" the man said. "Maybe it would improve your disposition."

"*My* disposition!" she said, opening her eyes in amazement. "What's the matter with my disposition?"

"Nothing," he said, "except you haven't cracked a smile since Christ left Cleveland."

The woman laughed nervously.

"No," she said, "I don't care for a drink."

The tables were so close together Chris and I could hear everything they said, and it made us ill at ease. I tried to reopen the prizefighting discussion, but Chris had become sullen. He wouldn't answer me.

"It's a lovely day, isn't it, Charlie?" the woman said.

He didn't answer her. A moment later he said, "Didn't I tell you you should go see the dentist?" The woman nodded.

"I know, Charlie," she said hastily. "I know."

"I never saw such crooked teeth," he said. "You got to have some work done on your teeth. You look like you been in a wreck.

Didn't you promise me a dozen times you'd go see the dentist?"

Her lips trembled. Vinnie came up to clear the dishes away, and while he was at the table she was smiling. It was a strained, painful smile. When Vinnie left, she got a handkerchief out of her purse, not looking down at the purse in her lap but searching in it blindly. Her eyes were full of tears. Chris and I stared out of the window.

We could hear the man angrily rattling his paper. Then he got up and went to the washroom. A minute later the woman walked over to the slot-machine phonograph at the end of the bar. She selected a record and slipped a nickel in the slot. It was "Night and Day," a Frances Langford record. The music sounded a little hysterical. While she stood there, bent over the titles in the glass front of the phonograph, he came out of the washroom and sat down. She did not return to the table until the record was finished.

"What did you put that on for?" he asked when she sat down.

"I don't know," she said nervously. "I just did."

" 'In the silence of my lonely room,' " he sang, nasally mocking the song, " 'I think of you.' "

"Let's go, Charlie," she said.

"It was your idea," he said scornfully, "a ferryboat ride."

"I thought it would be fun, like a fool," she said. "Let's go, Charlie."

Vinnie put a check on their table. The man paid Paulie and they walked out.

"Gee," said Paulie, as soon as they reached the street, "what a nasty guy!"

"I shoulda bopped him one," said Chris. "He wasn't even drunk."

"The way he treated that woman!" said Paulie indignantly. "Gee, that's no way to treat a woman."

I STAYED IN THE MY BLUE HEAVEN until about two. Then I walked up River Street. At the head of the street I went down the hill and walked out on the Gdynia American pier. I killed most of the afternoon on the pier, sitting on a stringpiece in the sun and watching the traffic out in the river. Late in the afternoon I climbed the hill, turned back into River Street, and headed for the Lacka-wanna ferry shed. On the cement plaza in front of the shed a crowd was watching a man feed the flock of pigeons that haunts the Hoboken piers. It was the man I had seen in the My Blue Heaven, the nasty guy. He was tossing peanuts to the pigeons. The woman was standing beside him, holding a bag of peanuts. They were having a good time. The man was kneeling. He would reach up and get some peanuts out of the bag, shell them, and fling them out. The arrogant pigeons would hurry across the cement, shouldering each other out of the way and walking across the shoes of the onlookers, and the woman would laugh. When she laughed she was very attractive. I remember I thought, "I bet he's poisoning the pigeons."

I went into the ferry shed and got a cup of coffee at the lunch stand. After a while the gates to the ferry slid back and I went aboard. I walked to the front of the ferry and stood at the rail. While the ferry was moving out of the slip the man and woman walked out on the deck, arm in arm. They walked up and put their elbows on the rail. The woman stood right beside me. They were talking. He said something to the woman that I didn't hear, and she laughed and said, "You wouldn't kid me, would you?" I didn't hear his answer. Then the woman, laughing happily, said, "I bet you tell that to all the girls." They were talking that way, laughing and talking, all the way across the river. I couldn't dope it out.

(1938)

The Downfall of Fascism in Black Ankle County

*E*VERY TIME I SEE MUSSOLINI shooting off his mouth in a newsreel or Göring goose-stepping in a rotogravure, I am reminded of Mr. Catfish Giddy and my first encounter with Fascism. In 1923, when I was in the ninth grade in Stonewall, North Carolina, Mr. Giddy and Mr. Spuddy Ransom organized a branch of the Knights of the Ku Klux Klan, or the Invisible Empire, which spread terror through Black Ankle County for several months. All the kids in town had seen "The Birth of a Nation," and they were fascinated by the white robes and hoods worn by the local Klansmen, and by the fiery crosses they burned at midnight on Saturdays in the vacant lot beside the Charleston, Pee Dee & Northern depot. On Tuesday and Friday, the Klan's meeting nights, the kids would hide in the patch of Jerusalem-oak weeds in the rear of the Planters Bank & Trust Company and watch the Klansmen go up the back stairs to their meeting hall above the bank. Sometimes they reappeared in a few minutes, dressed in flowing white robes, and drove off mysteriously. I spent so many nights hiding in the weed patch that I failed my final examinations in algebra, the history of North Carolina, English composition, and French, and was not promoted, which I did not mind, as I had already spent two years in the ninth grade and felt at home there.

Now, when I look back on that period and reflect on the qualities of Mr. Giddy, Mr. Ransom, and their followers, I wonder why the people of Black Ankle County, particularly the people of Stonewall, stood for the Ku Klux Klan as long as they did. Traditionally, the people of Stonewall are sturdy and self-reliant. In fact, the town was named General Stonewall Jackson, North Carolina, when it was founded right after the Civil War; later the name was shortened to Stonewall. There was certainly nothing frightening about Mr. Giddy, the Führer of the local Klan. His full name was J. Raymond Giddy, but he had a mustache on his plump face which he treated with beeswax and which stuck out sharply on both sides, and consequently he was almost always referred to as Mr. Catfish Giddy, even in the columns of the weekly *Stonewall News*. He was rather proud of the nickname. He used to say, "I may not be the richest man in Black Ankle County, but I sure am the ugliest; you can't take that away from me." Mr. Giddy was a frustrated big businessman. Before he got interested in the Klan, he had organized the Stonewall Boosters and a Stonewall Chamber of Commerce, both of which died after a few meetings. He was always making speeches about big business, but he was never much of a big businessman himself. At the time he and Mr. Ransom organized the Klan he was a travelling salesman for a chewing-tobacco concern. When he returned from a trip he would never brag about how many boxes of cut plug he had sold. Instead, he would brag that the cut plug manufactured in North Carolina in one year, if laid end to end, would damn near reach to Egypt, or Australia, or the moon, or some other distant place.

"In the manufacture of chewing tobacco, my friends," he would boast, "the Tarheel State leads the whole civilized world."

He was the town orator and the town drunk. In his cups, he would walk up and down Main Street, singing. He had a bass voice and his favorite songs were "Old Uncle Bud," new verses for which he would make up as he went along, and a song about Lydia Pinkham's vegetable compound and its effect on the human race, a song he had learned when he was a young man attending a business college in Atlanta. The high-school boys and girls, drinking Coca-Colas in the Stonewall Drug Company, would run to the door and stare and giggle when Mr. Giddy got drunk and marched up Main Street. "Old Uncle Bud," he would sing, "is the jelly-roll king. Got a hump on his back from shaking that thing."

Mr. Ransom was far more frightening than Mr. Giddy. He was

a gaunt, wild-eyed farmer. He was a religious fanatic, always screaming about wickedness. Even when he was dressed in his Ku Klux
Klan outfit, he could easily be identified because he walked with a
peculiar, hobbledehoy gait. He was a deacon in the Stonewall Jackson
Baptist Church, the church I went to, and he used to ring the bell
before services until he got a little too impassioned one Sunday
morning and pulled the rope so hard the bell came unscrewed and
fell out of the loft, giving a glancing blow to his left shoulder as it
fell. After that accident he always walked as if his next step would
be his last. Like Mr. Giddy, he had a nickname. He was christened
John Knox Ransom, but he was called Mr. Spuddy because he
habitually argued that the Southern farmer should quit planting
cotton and tobacco and plant Irish potatoes. "Something you can
eat," he would argue, smacking his palms together for emphasis.
"Goodness gracious, my friends, if you can't sell your crop, you can
put it on the table and eat it." One winter he tried to live on Irish
potatoes and got so thin his belt wouldn't hold his pants up. His
worried wife would urge him to eat some meat to get his strength
back, and he would shout, "Is a mule strong? Does a mule eat
meat?" His wife, who was a sensible woman, would ask meekly,
"Does a mule eat Irish potatoes?"

I don't think Mr. Giddy, the drunken drummer, and Mr. Ransom,
the fanatical deacon, thought very highly of each other until Mr.
Giddy returned from a selling trip in the winter of 1923 with some
booklets about the Klan he had picked up in Atlanta. Mr. Giddy
discreetly distributed the booklets among some of the loafers in
Stonewall, and Mr. Ransom got one. After reading it, he came to
the conclusion that the best way to fight wickedness, the best way
to drive corn-whiskey distillers, loose women, gypsy mule traders
and fortune tellers, chautauquas, and Holy Roller preachers out of
Black Ankle County was to organize the Klan there.

He and Mr. Giddy got together, hired the hall over the bank,
painted the windows black for the sake of secrecy, and enrolled
seventeen men in the Klan. They included a tobacco auctioneer, an
undertaker, a grocery clerk, an indolent house painter, and a number
of farmers. The farmers were all like Mr. Ransom in that they spent

less time in their fields than they did around the pot-bellied stove of the Stonewall Hardware & General Merchandise Company, arguing about religion and politics. Most of the men joined the Klan because it gave them an excuse to get away from their wives at night and because it seemed to them to have even more mystery and ceremony than the Masons or the Woodmen of the World. The undertaker and Mr. Ransom were the only "respectable" men in it; most of the others, according to the standards of Stonewall, were either "common" or "sorry." Some were both—the house painter, for example. I once heard him summed up by an old woman in Stonewall, who said, "He's common. Fishes in the summer and hunts in the winter, and when it rains he sits by the stove and plays checkers. He sure is one sorry man."

The fathers of some of my friends joined the Klan and gradually I learned many of the Klan secrets. I learned that the initiation fee was ten dollars and that the robe and hood cost six-fifty. A friend of mine swiped his father's Klan books. One was called "The Platform of the Invisible Empire." I persuaded him to let me have it in exchange for Zane Grey's "Riders of the Purple Sage." I still have it. On the cover is this declaration: "The Ku Klux Klan stands on a platform of 100-per-cent Americanism, white supremacy in the South, deportation of aliens, purity of womanhood, and eradication of the chain store." In the book are a number of denunciations of Catholics, Jews, Negroes, and labor unions. The kids in Stonewall spied on the Klan much as kids now play G-men and gangsters; it was a game. We were frightened by the Klansmen, but not too frightened to hide in the weed patch and watch them come and go. I remember one kid, lying beside me in the weeds, pointing to a robed figure and hoarsely whispering, "There goes Pa."

Mules are used almost exclusively instead of horses in the tobacco and cotton fields of Black Ankle County, and during the first weeks of the Klan's existence in Stonewall the members rode plough mules on their night rides about the countryside. They preferred to ride cross-country, probably because that made them feel invincible, and they couldn't use automobiles because they would quickly bog down in the sticky mud of the bottom fields and the sloblands, the black mud which gives the county its name. The mules were supplied by Mr. Ransom and by other members who were farmers. That lasted until Mr. Giddy and Mr. Ransom, as the leaders, sent to Klan headquarters in Atlanta for some white horse-robes. They draped the robes over their mules one dark night and rode out to a sawmill in a swamp to keep a rendezvous with their followers. When they galloped up on their shrouded steeds the mules of the other Klansmen got frightened; they let out angry neighs, reared back on their heels, and stampeded into the swamp with their riders. One Klansman was thrown from his mule and suffered a broken leg and three fractured ribs. After that the Klansmen gave up cross-country riding. They stuck to the highways and used automobiles. Fat Mr. Giddy undoubtedly felt out of place on the sharp back of a plough mule, anyway.

The Klansmen began their terrorism by burning fiery crosses, huge crosses made of fence rails sprinkled with kerosene, in the yards of all the Negro churches in the lower part of the county. Then they kidnapped an aged, irritable blacksmith who was celebrated for his profanity. They covered him with tar. They sprinkled chicken feathers over the tar. Then they tossed him into Bearcat Millpond. I have heard that the old blacksmith crawled out of the millpond with ten brand-new oaths. A few nights later the Klansmen went after a mentally defective woman who used to wander about the county with her fatherless children, sleeping in tobacco barns and haylofts. They flogged her, clipped her hair close to her scalp, and branded a "K" on her head. Next day a rural policeman found the bleeding, frantic woman on a ditch bank beside a country road and took her to a hospital. Later she was sent to an asylum. One night, a few weeks later, they broke into a chain grocery in Stonewall, the A. & P., and wrecked it. The same night they went to a Negro café in the Back Alley, the Negro section of Stonewall, and smashed a big, loud Edison phonograph, which the proprietor of the café had mortgaged her home to buy. Then they began threatening a quiet, lonesome Jew who lived above his dry-goods store on Main Street. Some of the members of the Klan had charge accounts, long unpaid, at his store. At the post office one night, waiting around for the evening mail to be sorted, I heard Mr. Giddy talking about him. He said, "He sits up there all night long, reading books. No telling what he's plotting." The dry-goods merchant went to the hardware store one morning at a time when some of the Klan members were sitting around the stove and bought a double-barrelled shotgun and three boxes of twelve-gauge shells. He was not threatened any more.

Late that spring it was rumored in Stonewall that the Klan had decided to do something about the corn-whiskey-distilling situation. The biggest distiller was Mr. Sledge MacKellar; he employed four men at his copper still in Pocahontas Swamp. We knew he was immune from the Klan because he was Mr. Giddy's personal bootlegger, because he was fabulously expert with a shotgun, and because he had publicly served notice on the Klan. Mr. MacKellar came out of the swamp one afternoon and said he was prepared for "the Bed-Sheets." By that time Klansmen were called "the Bed-Sheets." He said, "I'm a Democrat and I got my rights. The first time one of them Bed-Sheets sticks his head in my front gate, I'm going to take his head right off. I got a shotgun and I got it loaded and I'm just aching to pull the trigger."

We knew the distillers the Klan had in mind were the Kidney boys, and we were not surprised when we heard that a date had been set on which they were to be tarred and feathered. The Kidney boys were three drunken Irish brothers who lived in a house about two and a half miles out from Stonewall and operated a still in Big Cherokee Swamp, behind their house. Their names were Patrick, Pinky, and Francis. They drank about half the whiskey they manufactured. When they came to town that week for supplies, the clerks in the stores kidded them. "I hear the Bed-Sheets are going to call on you boys for a pot of tea Friday night," one clerk said.

The Kidney boys had a hired man, an aged Negro named Uncle Bowleg, who later worked for a relative of mine. One time Uncle Bowleg told me how the Kidney boys brought about the downfall of the Invisible Empire in Black Ankle County. There were three entrances to the Kidney house—a front door, a back door, and a side door. When they heard the Klan was planning a call on Friday

351

night, the brothers rented three dynamite outfits from a man who made his living blasting out tree stumps. They swapped him a gallon of charcoal-cured corn whiskey for the use of the outfits. They buried three great charges of dynamite in the yard, under the three paths leading to the entrances of the house. Wires led from the buried dynamite to batteries, to which switches were attached. The Kidney boys placed the batteries in the house, beneath three windows where they could sit and watch for approaching Klansmen. They planned to throw a switch the moment the Klansmen walked up one of the paths.

That night the Kidney boys turned off all the lights and took places at the windows with the dynamite batteries and switches in their laps. Uncle Bowleg was in the house with them. The Kidneys soon got tired of staring out into the yard, waiting for Klansmen, and ordered Uncle Bowleg to fetch them a jug of whiskey and a pitcher of water. Uncle Bowleg said he was kept busy running from one Kidney to another with the whiskey. The whiskey made them happy and they began to talk, speculating on how much noise their blasts would make. "We'll blow those Bed-Sheets to Kingdom Come," said Pinky.

About ten o'clock, when the moon was high, Francis Kidney, who was guarding the side door, decided he could wait no longer. The whiskey had given him an irresistible desire to throw the switch on his battery.

"Get ready!" he shouted suddenly. "I just can't wait no longer. I'm going to test this dynamite. The Bed-Sheets won't come in by the side door, anyway."

He threw the switch and there was a blast that shook the entire lower half of Black Ankle County. It caused people to leap out of their beds. We heard the blast in my home, and I remember that my grandmother said she thought that Judgment Day or the Second Coming was at hand.

Uncle Bowleg said the blast tore up a massive longleaf pine tree in the yard of the Kidney house and threw it into the highway. Uncle Bowleg was so frightened he jumped under a bed and hid. The Kidneys ran to the front porch and looked at the great tree lying in the highway. It pleased them. They laughed and slapped each other's shoulders. They came in and poured themselves some drinks. Then Patrick and Pinky took their places again, but Francis had thrown his switch, so he lost interest and went to sleep in his chair. In about half an hour, Patrick Kidney, who was guarding the rear door, heard a rustle out in back of the house. He knew it was the wind rustling the leaves on the chinquapin bushes, but all he wanted was an excuse to throw his switch.

"I think I hear them coming!" he shouted to Pinky, who was sitting at the front door with his hand on his switch. "Get ready. I'm going to let go."

Pinky needed some excitement, too. "Throw the switch!" he yelled.

Patrick threw his switch. The blast rattled Pinky and he threw his switch, too. The blasts were almost simultaneous. The slats fell out of the bed under which Uncle Bowleg was hiding and bruised him all over. A big framed picture of the mother of the Kidney brothers fell off the wall and hit Francis on the head. The legs dropped off the kitchen range and it fell apart. The entire back porch was torn loose from the house. The blast blew up the chicken house and a barrel in which the two hounds slept. All the chickens were killed, except an old rooster, and he never crowed again. Next morning there were six dead hens on the roof of the house and dead hens and ducks were scattered all over the yard. The South Carolina line runs near the rear of the Kidney house, and Uncle Bowleg swears that the hounds landed in South Carolina and were so shocked and outraged they never crossed back into North Carolina again. The mule's stall fell in.

"The roof fell down on that old plug," Uncle Bowleg told me, "and he bolted out into the road with the roof on his back like a saddle and galloped two miles before he felt safe enough to slow down and look around. And there was a rocking chair on the back porch and the dynamite set it to rocking. Next morning it was still rocking."

When the noise died down that night, and when things stopped falling apart, the Kidney brothers looked at each other. They were shamefaced. Suddenly they felt frightened. Without their dynamite, they felt naked and defenseless. "If the Bed-Sheets come now, we're sure done for," Francis said. His mother's picture was raising a bump on his head. All of a sudden the Kidney boys ran out of the house and made a dash for Big Cherokee Swamp, with Uncle Bowleg following. Early next morning Uncle Bowleg got hungry and went back to the house for something to eat but the Kidney boys stayed in the swamp until noon.

As a matter of fact, they would have been just as safe in their wrecked house as they were in the swamp, because the Ku Klux Klan never did show up. The Klan had postponed its scheduled call because Mr. Giddy had arrived at the hall over the bank too drunk to take any interest in Klan matters. However, while the Kidneys were still snoring in the swamp, Mr. Ransom, who hadn't been able to get any sleep because of the three strange blasts, drove into Stonewall in his Ford and picked up Mr. Giddy. Mr. Ransom was sleepy and irritable and Mr. Giddy had a bad hangover, and they were not a happy pair. They drove out to the Kidney house to see what had happened during the night. When they arrived, Uncle Bowleg was sitting in the rocking chair on the front porch, eating a plate of corn bread and molasses. Mr. Giddy and Mr. Ransom walked into the yard and looked into the three gaping holes. Uncle Bowleg watched them like a hawk.

"Spuddy," said Mr. Giddy as he peered into the hole out of which the longleaf pine had come, "that sure is a damned big hole. I sure am glad I wasn't around when those holes were dug."

"Catfish," said Mr. Ransom in a frightened voice, "somebody might of got murdered last night. It's a good thing the Klan didn't ride last night."

Uncle Bowleg said they both stared into the holes and shuddered. Then they got into the Ford and drove away rapidly. During the day all the members of the Invisible Empire took occasion to drive by the Kidney house. They also shuddered when they saw the dynamite pits.

Late that afternoon Mr. Giddy showed up on Main Street. He was drunk again. He walked down Main Street, but he didn't sing.

He stopped each person he met and said, "Friend, I have resigned." "Resigned from what, Mr. Catfish?" people asked. "Don't make no difference what I resigned from," he answered. "I just want you to know I resigned." The Ku Klux Klan never held another meeting in Stonewall. In a week or two the black paint was scraped off the windows in the hall above the bank and a "For Rent" sign was hung out. One woman ripped up her husband's Klan robe and made a pillowcase out of the cloth. Others heard about it and did the same. Mrs. Catfish Giddy ripped up her husband's robe and told her friends he was so fat she found enough material in it for two pillowcases, an apron, and a tablecloth.

(1939)

I Blame It All on Mamma

MRS. COPENHAGEN CALHOUN, who lives on a riverbank watermelon farm in Black Ankle County, about a mile from the town of Stonewall, is the only termagant I have ever admired. She has no fondness for authority and is opposed to all public officials, elected or appointed. Once a distinguished senator came to Stonewall and spoke in the high-school auditorium; just after he finished telling how he made it a practice to walk in the footsteps of Thomas Jefferson, she stood up and said, "Senator, you sure are getting too big for your britches." A mayor of Stonewall once tried to get her fired from her job as cook in the station restaurant of the Charleston, Pee Dee & Northern Railroad. A woman who got drunk in public, he said, was a disgrace to the town. She kept her mouth shut until he came up for reelection; then she went up and down Main Street making speeches which helped defeat him. "Why, the stuck-up old hypocrite!" she said in one of her speeches. "He goes to the country club on Saturday night and gets as drunk as a goose on ice, and Sunday morning he stands up in the Methodist choir and sings so loud the whole church echoes for a week." She believes that public officials are inclined to overlook the fact that Americans are free, and when she is brought into court for disturbing the peace she invariably begins her address to the judge by stating, "This is a free country, by God, and I got my rights." She has a long tongue, and Judge Elisha Mullet once said she could argue the legs off an iron pot. She has many bad qualities, in fact, and her husband often complains that she has made his life a hell on earth, but when I go back to Stonewall for a visit and find that she is still insisting on her rights, I always feel better about the vigor of democracy.

I was in the tenth grade when I became one of her admirers. At that time, in 1924, she was unmarried and had just come up from Charleston to cook in the station restaurant. It was the only restaurant in Stonewall; railroad men ate there, and so did people from the sawmill, the cotton gin, and the chewing-tobacco factory. After school I used to hang around the station. I would sit on a bench beside the track and watch the Negro freight hands load boxcars with bales of cotton. Some afternoons she would come out of the kitchen and sit on the bench beside me. She was a handsome, big-hipped woman with coal-black hair and a nice grin, and the station agent must have liked her, because he let her behave pretty much as she pleased. She cooked in her bare feet and did not bother to put shoes on when she came out for a breath of fresh air. "I had an aunt," she told me, "who got the dropsy from wearing shoes in a hot kitchen." Once I asked her how she came to be named Copenhagen. "Mamma named all her babies after big towns," she said. "It was one of her fancy habits. Her first was a boy and she named him New Orleans. Then my sister came along and she named her Chattanooga. Mamma was real fond of snuff, and every payday Pa would buy her a big brown bladder of Copenhagen snuff. That's where she got my name."

One Friday night, after Miss Copey had been working at the restaurant a couple of months, the station agent wrote her a pass and she went down to Charleston to see her family. When she returned Monday on the 3:30, she was so drunk the conductor had to grab her elbows and help her down the train steps. She paid no attention to him but sang "Work, for the Night Is Coming." She bustled into the kitchen, kicked off her shoes, and began throwing things. She would pick up a pot and beat time with it while she sang a verse of the hymn, and then she would throw it. "Work till the last beam fad-eth, fad-eth to shine no more," she would sing, and then a stewpot would go sailing across the room. I stood at a window and stared. She was the first drunken woman I had ever seen and the spectacle did not disappoint me; I thought she was wonderful. Finally the chief of police, who was called Old Blunderbuss by the kids in town, came and put her under arrest. Next day she was back at work. In the afternoon she came out to sit in the sun for a few minutes, and I asked her how it felt to get drunk. She gave me a slap that almost knocked me off the bench. "Why, you little shirttail boy," she said, "What do you mean asking me such a question?" I rubbed my jaw and said, "I'm sorry, Miss Copey. I didn't mean any harm."

She leaned forward and held her head in her hands like a mourner and sat that way a few minutes. Then she straightened up and said, "I'm sorry I slapped you, son, but that was a hell of a question to ask a lady. Drinking is a sad, sad thing, and I hate to talk about it. I was a liquor-head sot before I got past the third grade, and I blame it all on Mamma. I had the colic real often when I was a little girl, and to ease the pain Mamma would take Pa's jug and measure out half a cup of liquor and sweeten it with molasses and dose me with it, and I got an everlasting taste for the awful stuff. If I knew then what I know now, I would've got up from my sickbed and knocked that liquor outa my mamma's hand." She sighed and stood up. "Still and all," she said, and a broad smile came on her face, "I got to admit that it sure cured my colic."

Miss Copey had not worked at the restaurant long before she got acquainted with Mr. Thunderbolt Calhoun. He has a watermelon farm on the bank of Shad Roe River in a section of the county called Egypt. He is so sleepy and slow he has been known as Thunderbolt ever since he was a boy; his true name is Rutherford Calhoun. He is shiftless and most of his farm work is done by a Negro hired boy named Mister. (When this boy was born his mother said, "White people claim they won't mister a Negro. Well, by God, son, they'll mister you!") Mr. Thunderbolt's fifteen-acre farm is fertile and it grows the finest Cuban Queen, Black Gipsy, and Irish Gray watermelons I have ever seen. The farm is just a sideline, however; his principal interest in life is a copper still hidden on the bank of a bay in the river swamp. In this still he produces a vehement kind of whiskey known as tanglefoot. "I depend on watermelons to pay the taxes and feed me and my mule," he says. "The whiskey is pure profit." Experts say that his tanglefoot is as good as good Kentucky bourbon, and he claims that laziness makes it so. "You have to be patient to make good whiskey," he says, yawning, "and I'm an uncommonly patient man."

After Miss Copey began buying her whiskey from him, she went on sprees more often; his whiskey did not give her hangovers or what she called "the dismals." At least once a month, usually on a Saturday afternoon, she would leave her kitchen and walk barefooted down Main Street, singing a hymn at the top of her voice, and she seldom got below Main and Jefferson before she was under arrest. Most of the town drunks meekly paid the usual fine of seven dollars and costs or went to jail, but Miss Copey always took advantage of the question "What have you got to say for yourself?" First she would claim that the right to get drunk is guaranteed by the Constitution, and then she would accuse the judge of being a hypocrite.

"I got a right to let loose a hymn when I feel like it," she would say. "That don't harm nobody. Suppose I do make a little noise? Do they put 'em in jail for blowing the whistle at the sawmill? And anyhow, I don't drink in secret. There's nothing so low-down sorry as a man that drinks in secret. You're a secret sot, Judge Mullet, and don't try to deny it."

"I like a drop now and then, to be sure," the Judge would reply, "but that don't give me the right to run up and down the highways and byways in my bare feet."

"Now you're trying to tell me there's one law for a judge and another for a railroad cook," Miss Copey would say triumphantly. "That's a hell of a way for a judge to talk."

Miss Copey had been cooking in the station restaurant about two years when a stovepipe crumpled up and fell down on her head, stunning her. It made her so angry she quit her job and threatened to sue the railroad for a thousand dollars. She settled out of court, however, when a claim agent offered her a check for seventy-five. "I haven't got the patience to fight a railroad," she said. She cashed the check, insisting on having the sum in one-dollar bills, and hurried out to Mr. Thunderbolt's to buy a Mason jar of tanglefoot. When he saw her roll of bills he said he felt they ought to celebrate. He drew some whiskey out of a charred-oak keg that had been buried in the swamp for five years, and they sat in rocking chairs on the front porch and began to drink to each other. After an hour or so, Mr. Thunderbolt told her he was a lonesome man and that he had grown mighty damned tired of Mister's cooking. He wound up by asking her to be his wife. Miss Copey broke down and sobbed. Then she said, "I'll make you a good wife, Thunderbolt. We better hurry to town before the courthouse closes. If we wait until you're sober, I'm afraid you'll change your mind." Mister drove them to Stonewall in Mr. Thunderbolt's old Ford truck. They stopped at Miss Copey's rooming house and picked up her trunk; then they went over to the courthouse and were married. Judge Mullet was surprised by the marriage but said he guessed Mr. Thunderbolt's star customer wanted to get closer to the source of supply. For a week the bride and groom went fishing in Shad Roe River in the morning, got drunk in the afternoon, and rode about the country in the Ford truck at night. Then, Saturday morning, Miss Copey woke up, looked out a window, and saw that the figs were ripe on the door-yard bushes; she shook her husband awake and said, "The honeymoon's over, Thunderbolt. I got to get busy and can them figs before they drop on the ground."

For a couple of months, Miss Copey was a model wife. That autumn I hunted squirrels practically every afternoon in the swamp that runs alongside Mr. Thunderbolt's farm, and I used to stop by and see her. She showed me scores of jars of watermelon-rind pickles and fig preserves she had canned and arranged on the cellar shelves. She had spaded a pit in the back yard for barbecues, and in the corncrib she had a big barrel of scuppernong grapes in ferment. She had bought four Rhode Island Red hens and four settings of eggs, and she had a yardful of biddies. She proudly told me that every night when Mr. Thunderbolt came home from the swamp, worn out after a day of squatting beside his still, he found a plate of fried chicken and a sweet-potato pie on the kitchen table waiting for him.

After a while, however, she began to get bored. "It's too damned still around here," she told me one evening. "I need some human company. Sometimes a whole day goes past and I don't get a single word out of Thunderbolt. He lived by himself so long he almost lost the use of his tongue." There is a Baptist church a half mile up the river, and one lonesome Sunday she attended a service there. She picked an unfortunate time, because there was a fight in progress in the congregation. In fact, at that period, which was the autumn of 1926, there was dissension in many rural Baptist churches in the South over the ceremony of immersion. One group believed a convert should be immersed three times face forward in the still water of a pond and the other favored a single immersion in the running water of a river. The opposing groups were called the Trine Forwardites and the Running Riverites. Miss Copey became a churchgoer merely because she wanted to sing some hymns, but she soon got mixed up in this theological wrangle. The second Sunday she attended services she was sitting in a back pew when a man got up and advocated changing the name of the church from Egypt Baptist to Still Water Trine Forward Baptist. He said any sensible person knew that a calm pond was more spiritual than the troubled waters of a river. This did not seem right to Miss Copey; she arose and interrupted him. "Jordan wa'n't no pond," she said. "It was a running river. On that rock I stand." "That's right, sister!" exclaimed a man up front. "You hit the nail on the head." He went back and asked Miss Copey to come forward and sit with the Running River faction. "Why, I'll gladly do so," Miss Copey said. "What's this all about, anyhow?"

Presently the argument between the factions grew bitter, and Miss Copey arose again and suggested singing "On Jordan's Stormy Banks," a revival hymn. The leader of her faction said, "Let's march out of this church as we sing that hymn." Thereupon seven men and women marched up the aisle. Miss Copey got up and followed them. In the yard outside, they held a meeting and decided to organize a new church and call it the Running River One Immersion Baptist. "You can meet at my house until you locate a more suitable place," Miss Copey suggested. "Let's go there now and sit on the porch and do some singing. I feel like letting loose a few hymns." The Running Riverites were pleased by this suggestion. With Miss

Copey leading, they marched down the road singing "There Is a Green Hill Far Away." When Mr. Thunderbolt saw them heading up the lane, he was sitting on the porch, playing his harmonica. He leaped off the porch and fled to the swamp. Miss Copey arranged chairs on the porch and announced that her favorite hymns were "There Is a Fountain Filled with Blood" and "The Old Time Religion Is Good Enough for Me." All afternoon they sang these hymns over and over. At sundown Miss Copey said, "If you're a mind to, we'll meet here again next Sunday. We'll show those Trine Forwardite heathens!" Then the meeting ended. Late that night Mr. Thunderbolt came in, raging drunk. "Listen, you old hoot owl!" he shouted. "If you bring them hymn-singers to this house again, I'll leave you and never come back!" "Don't threaten me, you drunk old sinner," Miss Copey said. "You start threatening me, I'll pull a slat out of the bed and fracture your skull."

Next Sunday afternoon the hymn-singers held another meeting on Miss Copey's porch, and that night Mr. Thunderbolt did not come home at all. Monday night he was still missing. Early Tuesday morning, Miss Copey went down to Mister's cabin and found that he was missing too. She looked in the barn and found that the Ford truck was gone. On my way home from the swamp that afternoon I stopped by to see her, and she was sitting on the front steps, moaning. There was a carving knife in her lap. "I'll cut his black heart out," she said. "I'll put my trademark on him. The wife-deserter!" I sat down and tried to comfort her. Presently two of the hymn-singers came up the lane. "How are you this fine fall day, sister?" one called out. Miss Copey ran out to meet them. "You come another step closer, you old hymn-singers," she said, "and I'll throw you in the river! You've turned a man against his wife! You've broke up a happy home!" After a while we went in the house and she made some coffee. We were sitting on the back porch drinking it when Mister drove up in the Ford truck. "Hey there, Miss Copey!" he yelled. "They got Mr. Thunderbolt in jail down in Charleston." "Why, bless his heart," said Miss Copey. She ran in the house and got her hat and her purse. "Get back in that truck," she said to Mister, "and take me to him." The three of us climbed in the seat.

In Charleston, the jailer let us go in and see Mr. Thunderbolt. He was lying in his cell playing his harmonica. He was in fine spirits. He told us the hymn-singing had made him so angry he had ordered Mister to drive him to Charleston. There was a moving-picture theatre near the place they parked the truck, and Monday night he decided to go in and see a show; he had never seen a moving picture. Mary Pickford was in it, he said, and he became so absorbed in her troubles that he crouched way forward in his seat and got a cramp in his left leg. At first he tried not to notice it, but when he could bear it no longer he decided to try the old-fashioned remedy of kicking the cramp out. He got out in the aisle, held on to an end seat, and began kicking backward, like a mule that is being shod. All the time he kept his eyes on the picture. "I didn't want to miss a thing," he said. People began to yell for him to sit down, he said, and an usher hurried up and told him to stop kicking. "Please go away and don't bother me," he told the usher. The usher got the manager and together they grabbed him. "I couldn't properly defend myself," Mr. Thunderbolt told us. "I couldn't fight them two busy-bodies and keep up with what was happening to Miss Mary Pickford and kick the cramp out of my foot all at the same time. It was more than any one human could do." The usher and the manager hustled him to the lobby, and when he realized he wouldn't be able to see the rest of the picture, he put all his attention on self-defense and knocked the two men flat. Then a policeman came and arrested him for disorderly conduct.

"Why, it's a damned outrage, honey," Miss Copey said. "I'm going right down and bail you out."

"Just a minute," Mr. Thunderbolt said. "You're not going to bail me out until I get your solemn promise to leave them hymn-singers alone. It's real quiet in this jail."

"Oh, hell, Thunderbolt!" said Miss Copey. "I threw them hymn-singers in the river before I left home."

(1940)

363

Uncle Dockery and the
Independent Bull

I OFTEN FIND IT COMFORTING to think of Uncle Dockery Fitzsimmons, a serene old bright-leaf tobacco farmer who lives in Black Ankle County, about six miles from Stonewall. He is the only man I have ever known who has absolutely no respect for the mechanical genius of Western civilization. One day, when I was about fifteen, we were fishing Little Rump River for blue bream and a motorboat chugged by, scaring all the fish to the bed of the river, and Uncle Dockery said, "Son, the only inventions that make sense to me are the shotgun, the two-horse wagon, the butter churn, and the frying pan. Sooner or later such contraptions as the motorboat will drive the whole human race into Dix Hill." Dix Hill is a suburb of Raleigh, where the North Carolina State Asylum for the Insane is located.

Uncle Dockery is still opposed to the automobile. "I don't want to go nowhere," he used to say, "that a mule can't take me." His hatred of automobiles embraces people who ride in them. One summer afternoon we were sitting on his veranda, eating a watermelon, when a neighbor ran up the road and said, "There's been a terrible auto accident up on the highway, Mr. Fitzsimmons." The news pleased Uncle Dockery. He placed his rasher of watermelon on the rail of the veranda, smiled broadly, and asked, "How many killed?" "Four," said the neighbor. "Well, that's just fine," said Uncle Dockery. "Where were they going in such a rush?" "They were going to the beach for a swim," said the neighbor. Uncle Dockery nodded with satisfaction and said, "I guess they figured the Atlantic Ocean wouldn't wait."

Uncle Dockery did not often leave his farm, but once, during a series of revival meetings at the General Stonewall Jackson Baptist Church, he spent the night in Stonewall at the home of his married daughter. In the middle of the night there was a frightful uproar in his room, and his daughter and her husband ran in to rescue him. They thought someone was trying to murder him. They found he had got out of bed to get a drink of water and had pulled the electric-light cord loose from the ceiling. He said, "I tried to turn the damned thing on, but I couldn't somehow seem to make it work. I thought maybe if I grabbed hold of it and gave it a jerk, the light would come on." He was so maddened by his mistake that he wouldn't spend the balance of the night in the room. He asked his daughter to take some blankets and spread a pallet for him outside on the porch. In the morning he denounced her for having electric lights installed in her house. "A fat-pine knot or a kerosene lamp was good enough for Grandpa, and it was good enough for Pa, and it was good enough for Ma, and by God, Miss Priss, it's good enough for me," Uncle Dockery told her.

Although I always called him Uncle Dockery, we are not related. Most of the families in Black Ankle County have been there since the time of the Lords Proprietors, most of them are Scotch-Irish, and most of them *are* related. (There are, however, no aristocrats in the county; in fact, the first mint julep I ever saw was in Lundy's seafood restaurant in Sheepshead Bay in the summer of 1934.) Because almost everybody in the county is at least a cousin by marriage of everybody else, it is natural for young people to use the word "Uncle" for old men they like. People in the county seem to take it for granted that everybody is kin to them.

I remember an incident which illustrates this. There is a ragged, epileptic old Cherokee Indian in Stonewall. He wears a rooster feather in the band of his hat and his beard comes down level with his belt buckle and he looks like Henry Wadsworth Longfellow. People call him Uncle John. He goes from house to house saying, "Have you please got something for poor old Uncle John?" and housewives customarily give him a nickel. One time an aunt from South Carolina was visiting us and she went to the door when Uncle John knocked. She was rather frightened by him. The old Indian bowed and said, "I don't think you know me. I'm Uncle John." My aunt said, "Goodness gracious! Which side of the family are you on?"

I spent a lot of time at Uncle Dockery's when I was a boy. I liked him, and I liked Aunt Dolly, his wife. When I was fourteen, I was given a horse and I used to ride out in the country after school and I often stopped at his farm. Most people in Stonewall disliked him. They used to say, "That old man would just as soon shoot you as tell you howdy-do." He always went out of his way to be sarcastic, and they considered him a public nuisance. On his rare trips to Stonewall he would walk down Main Street grinning to himself, as if he had a private joke on the human race. Once he saw a display of electric fans in the show window of the Stonewall Hardware & General Merchandise Co. and commenced to laugh. He went in and said, "Sell many of them things?" The clerk said, "Selling quite a few." Uncle Dockery said, "Be damned if the whole town don't belong in Dix Hill. A man that'd pay out good money for a breeze shouldn't be allowed to run loose." One time he visited the Black Ankle County Fair and stood around in front of a game-of-skill tent until the barker yelled at him, "Why don't you try your luck, old man?" Then Uncle Dockery pointed to the shabby merchandise offered as prizes and said, "Hell, Mister, I'm afraid I might win something." Uncle Dockery was particularly disliked by Senator C. B. McAdoo, the wealthiest man in Stonewall. Uncle Dockery knew a disgraceful story about him, and told it every time he got a chance. "C.B. hasn't spoken to me in Lord knows when," Uncle Dockery used to say, "but I knew him real well when we were boys. He was raised on a farm right down the road a piece from me, and we grew up together. He was every bit as stingy then as he is now. One summer when we were boys there was a big celebration in Stonewall. They had just finished laying the tracks for the Charleston, Pee Dee & Northern Railroad, and the first train was due to come through, and the whole town was going to take a holiday and celebrate. All the country people for miles around drove in, and the streets were crowded. A peddler came up from Charleston and set up a lemonade tent right near the depot. He brought some ice packed in sawdust in a barrel. Ice in summer was a highly unusual sight in those days, and the people stood around and watched him crack it up. And lemons were unusual, too. The peddler squeezed out his lemons and made a big tubful of lemonade, and then he hollered out, 'Made in the shade, stirred with a spade, come buy my lemonade.' Well, C.B. walked up with his girl, Sarah Ann Barnes. C.B. was a big, overgrown country boy, and he was all dressed up. He had garters around his shirtsleeves and his hair was slicked back with tallow. He and his girl went up to the lemonade tent. C.B. reached away down in his britches and drew out a nickel, and he put the nickel on the table, got a glass of lemonade, took a swallow, and smacked his lips. Then he turned to his girl and he said, 'Mighty good stuff, Sarah Ann. Better buy yourself some.' "

I learned a lot from Uncle Dockery. He taught me how to bait a hook for blue and red-breast bream, how to use a shotgun, how to tell the age of a mule by examining his teeth, how to set a hen, how to dress partridges for the skillet, how to thump a watermelon to tell if it is green or ripe, and how to chew tobacco. He was what is called a "target chewer." He would light a candle and stick it up on a stump; then he would take up a stance five yards away and extinguish the flame without upsetting the candle. I admired this trick and he tried his best to teach it to me. He advised me to practice on pigeons, saying, "It's always best to practice on a moving target." There were pigeons all over the front yard and he would point to one and make me aim at it. He told me I might get a job with a circus when I grew up if I became a good shot. If I had been blessed with perseverance, I might be travelling about the country right now with Ringling Brothers and Barnum & Bailey.

Sometimes when I rode out, Uncle Dockery would be busy, and I would turn my horse loose in the mule lot and go fishing in Briar Berry Swamp with Little Dock. When Uncle Dockery was almost sixty, he and Aunt Dolly had a son. Aunt Dolly always referred to her husband as Old Man Dock, and their son came to be known as Little Dock. Their other children had grown up, married, and left home, and the old people were extremely fond of Little Dock; Aunt Dolly used to say, "He was mighty slow getting here, but he's the best of the lot." He was a wild, strange boy. When people in the village wanted to be polite about him, they said, "The poor boy isn't quite bright." Otherwise they said, "He's crazy as a bedbug. Takes after his Pa." I was three years older, but I liked to fish with him. He was a wonderful fisherman, except that he talked all the time. He would strike up a conversation with anything, animate or inanimate. He would talk to a fence post. He would catch a fish and say, "Hello, little sun perch, quit flopping around. You're going to make a nice supper for Little Dock."

He took a great interest in religion, but Uncle Dockery wouldn't let him go to Sunday school in Stonewall because he was afraid the town boys would make fun of him. Little Dock was always asking his father about Jesus. One day the three of us were sitting under the shed of the tobacco barn, and Little Dock said, "Pa, where is Jesus located, anyhow? Is he located up in Raleigh, or in Washington, or where?" Uncle Dockery, who was, in his own way, a deeply religious man, told him Jesus was everywhere—in the air, in the sky, in the water. Little Dock smiled, as if he didn't altogether believe the explanation. Later that afternoon, however, he pointed excitedly toward the top of a wild plum tree and said, "There goes Jesus! Lord God, how he can fly!" Uncle Dockery said, "Son, you musta got Jesus confused with a jay bird. I don't see nothing up there but some old blue jays." Little Dock said, "Oh, I saw him all right. He waved to me when he flew over the plum tree." I have always admired Uncle Dockery's behavior on that occasion. He patted the boy on the shoulder and said, "Son, I'm proud of you. It ain't everybody that's got such good eyesight." Anyone who joked about Little Dock's peculiarities in Uncle Dockery's presence made an enemy for life.

Little Dock aped his father. They talked alike. Uncle Dockery often spoke of himself in the third person. He would say, "Dockery went fishing this morning and brought back a trout big as a ham." Little Dock often spoke in the same manner. Once he told me, "Little Dock tried to harness the mule and got the hell kicked out of him. Little Dock sure does hate that mule." Uncle Dockery and Little Dock got a lot of pleasure out of talking to each other. And sometimes, on autumn afternoons, they would sit on kegs in the corncrib and drink sour persimmon beer and sing together. They sang "By and By We're Going Up to See the King," "The Hell Bound Train," and "If You Don't Like My Peaches, Please Quit Shaking My Tree." Their favorite, however, was a minstrel-show song called "Just the Same." I remember two verses of it:

> *"White girl wears a high-heel shoe.*
> *Yellow girl does the same.*
> *Black girl wears no shoe at all,*
> *But she gets there just the same.*
>
> *"White girl lives in a big brick house.*
> *Yellow girl does the same.*
> *Black girl lives in the county jail,*
> *But it's a brick house just the same."*

Uncle Dockery had his bad points. He was too stubborn and contrary for his own good. One bleak January his two mules got sick and died of something the veterinarian called vesicular stomatitis, or horsepox. Uncle Dockery was so indignant he refused to buy new mules. He owned a big bull and he decided he would force it to take the place of both mules. "I'll make a work bull out of him if it kills me," he said. A few mornings later, a bitter-cold morning with snow all over the ground, he woke up and found there was no firewood in the house. It was so cold the water in the pigpen trough had frozen solid. Aunt Dolly had no stovewood with which to cook breakfast. Uncle Dockery had some firewood cut and piled in the swamp but nothing he could use to haul it up to the house except a two-horse wagon, and he didn't think the bull could pull it without help. He called Aunt Dolly out of her cold kitchen and said, "Dockery is going to harness himself and the bull to that two-horse wagon and haul some wood." Alarmed, Aunt Dolly begged him to go borrow a mule from a neighbor to work beside the bull, but he said, "I ain't the borrowing kind." He took the heavy mule collar off a harness, tightened it up, and put it around his neck; then he strung some leather traces from the collar to the whiffletree of the wagon. Then he hitched himself securely to one side of the wagon tongue. When that was done, he ordered Aunt Dolly to harness the bull to the other side of the tongue. He said, "Dockery and the bull make a fine team, better than any two mules I ever saw." When everything was ready, he reached over and gave the bull a kick and said, "Let's go, bull." The bull, made frisky by the cold day and the unaccustomed snow, hurtled forward, pulling the wagon and Uncle Dockery with him. The driverless wagon rattled and bounced. The bull kept circling the house with a head-long lope and it was all Uncle Dockery could do to keep up with him. Although the harness restricted him, Uncle Dockery took high, nimble steps, because he knew if he stumbled once, he would fall down and the bull would drag him across the frozen ground. Aunt Dolly stood in the front yard, moaning. Every time the bull and Uncle Dockery clattered past, she waved her apron, which frightened the bull and made matters worse. Finally the bull got tired and he and Uncle Dockery slowed down simultaneously to a walk. Aunt Dolly ran to her husband's aid. She rushed up and started to take his harness off. Uncle Dockery was frantic; he was afraid the bull would start away again. He caught his breath and said, "Dolly, don't bother with me." He pushed her away and said, "Take out the bull. Dockery will stand." That afternoon he limped into Stonewall and bought a span of mules. When he got home, he and Little Dock butchered the bull for winter meat. Uncle Dockery said, "On a farm, it's teamwork that counts, and I can't stand a bull that won't cooperate."

(1939)

ABOUT THE AUTHOR

JOSEPH MITCHELL came to New York City on October 25, 1929 (the day after the stock-market crash), from a small farming town called Fairmont, in the swamp country of southeastern North Carolina. He was twenty-one years old and looking for a job as a newspaper reporter. He eventually managed to find work as an apprentice crime reporter at Police Headquarters for *The World*. He was as a reporter and feature writer—for *The World, The Herald Tribune*, and *The World-Telegram*—for eight years, and then went to *The New Yorker*, where he remained until his death, on May 24, 1996, at the age of eighty-seven.

Aside from writing, Mr. Mitchell's interests included the waterfront of New York City, commercial fishing, Gypsies, Southern agriculture, Irish literature, and the architecture of New York City. He served several terms on the board of directors of the Gypsy Lore Society, an international organization of students of Gypsy life and the Gypsy language, which was founded in England in 1888. *Bajour*, a musical comedy based on stories about Gypsies by Mitchell, ran for 232 performances on Broadway in 1964-65. He was one of the founders of the South Street Seaport Museum and one of the original members of the Friends of Cast-Iron Architecture. For five years he was also one of the Commissioners of the New York City Landmarks Preservation Commission.

Mr. Mitchell was married to the photographer Therese Mitchell, who died in 1980; they had two daughters, Nora Sanborn and Elizabeth Mitchell.